Wreading

MODERN AND CONTEMPORARY POETICS

Series Editors

CHARLES BERNSTEIN

HANK LAZER

Series Advisory Board

MARIA DAMON

RACHEL BLAU DUPLESSIS

ALAN GOLDING

SUSAN HOWE

NATHANIEL MACKEY

JEROME MCGANN

HARRYETTE MULLEN

ALDON NIELSEN

MARJORIE PERLOFF

JOAN RETALLACK

RON SILLIMAN

JERRY WARD

Wreading

A Poetics of Awareness, or How Do We Know What We Know?

Jed Rasula

with Joel Bettridge, Nathan Brown, Mike Chasar,
Ming-Qian Ma, Evelyn Reilly, Leonard Schwartz, and Tony Tost

The University of Alabama Press   Tuscaloosa

The University of Alabama Press
Tuscaloosa, Alabama 35487–0380
uapress.ua.edu

Typeface: Minion

Cover caption: Illustration from Agostino Ramelli's *Le diverse et artificiose
machine del Capitano Agostino Ramelli*, 1588; courtesy Library of Congress
Cover design: David Nees

Cataloging-in-Publication data is available from the Library of Congress.
ISBN: 978-0-8173-6030-6
E-ISBN: 978-0-8173-9391-5

Contents

Illustrations

Preface

THERE'S A PASSAGE in *Walden* in which Thoreau suggests that hunters and fishermen and woodchoppers, through constant proximity, are better situated to observe nature than poets and philosophers, "who approach her with expectation," as he puts it (1992, 141). *Expectation* is the word. Poets are encumbered by expectation. One way to get a sense of what he means is to dip into any anthology of nineteenth-century verse, where you'll quickly be immersed in references to sylvan glades and leafy bowers, where frolicsome dryads cavort with satyrs wielding panpipes. The primary expectation revealed by such neoclassical versifying is that nature is a rhetorical topos—that is, something presumed to be already known, and known *through poetry*. This bucolic tradition in the West goes back to Hesiod and Theocritus and Virgil, in whose poetry "nature" is far from the wildness Thoreau celebrates. Instead, it consists of barnyard rhapsodies, odes to domestication in which the human sensibility learns to domesticate itself. Grow wild according to your nature, Thoreau recommends in the face of this legacy.

From my perspective as a teacher, handling expectations is a primary concern, especially in a university environment now governed almost exclusively with reference to accountability, tasks and goals, measurable results, and value-for-dollar. In the prevalent corporate model, teaching is expected to contribute to "learning outcomes" that can be specified. So, after a French class at a certain level the student might be expected to carry on a conversation; a business major can handle a double-entry account book; a forestry student will take soil samples. It gets more complicated when the subject is poetry, or literature more broadly. Accounting for what a student *can* do after a literature class is really a shot in the dark; the most you can say is that the student *has* done such and such. It's impossible to maintain that having read *Walden*, a student will have a special outlook on the natural world, a renewed respect for wildlife, or be a confirmed vegetarian. *Walden* contains inducements to these ends but brings no guarantees.

Walden is not a "product," of course; it doesn't traffic in goods and services. Its steady cascade of pithy aphorisms and moral exhortations are unlikely to be received as messages with bullet points. Why? Because *Walden* has too many other words, other ways of *being in language* that do not declare themselves. Call it occult. Shadowed. Heavily wooded. It's a book in which you take a walk. It's not a consumer product. It *has* been used like the brickbat in *Krazy Kat* cartoons, but it's neither a weapon, tool, toolkit, passport, internet browser, nor a cell phone app. Most importantly, *Walden* is a book that confounds expectations. Confounding expectations seems to be its purpose.

In order to confound expectations, you have to know what's expected. You also have to know that the very enterprise of confounding expectations feeds into the expectations, so it's easy for an audience to build up an appetite for being shocked and confounded. That is the way of the entertainment industry. As the educational system adapts itself to the business model, it also adopts tactics from successful businesses like Hollywood, an industry that thrives on expectations. Concessions to expectation are so thoroughly integrated into the system that the mass audience no longer sees movies but consumes products that have been prescreened to sample audiences whose sanction is prerequisite to a broader release. Characters in a drama disappear, or their screen time is enlarged; subplots expand or dissolve; endings are changed. In the old studio system, moguls were often accused of meddling with the product. Now the audience (demographically speaking) is the mogul, and the meddling is called marketability.

If I seem to have gotten off topic, it's because the entire enterprise of education has gotten off topic, as it were. The great etymologist Joseph Shipley writes about its cluster of Indo-European roots: "Note that *education* means 'leading out' not 'pouring in'" (62). The entertainment industry has consumerism as its aim, and *to consume* means "pouring in." Education is the opposite. You don't fill a student like an empty jug, you *animate* a sentient creature to get it moving, to go on the prowl. "We need to witness our own limits transgressed, and some life pasturing freely where we never wander." This is Thoreau's observation (1992, 212) about his experience at Walden Pond. Everyone has a Walden Pond, but it's not as if you can order up the land survey coordinates or use GPS to find it. But it is possible to coax a transgression of limits. And the first limit to be overcome is the aura of expertise. Education is purportedly in the hands of professionals, accredited experts, which of course reinforces the sense that a teacher holds in reserve some precious distillation of knowledge that can be transmitted to the student like balm from an eyedropper. That can happen, but it may be the most negligible aspect of teaching. Arousing and nurturing curiosity, in my view, is more important. And it's hard for people to be curious about a foregone conclusion. If, as a teacher, I think of my mission as delivering content, I've obliged myself to stick to the task, and at the same time obliged students to identify a target. There may be things to be learned, but there are no limits to be transgressed, no glimpse of anything outside what's expected.

Fundamental to pedagogy is promoting skills in pattern recognition, something I think is almost the sole content of education. Patterns are signals that can be hard to distinguish from noise. So I find myself engaged in a kind of cross-eyed pedagogy: while you look at *this*, think about *that*. My inclination derives in part from my own mental deficiencies: in school I was rarely able to understand something by concentrating on it, bringing it into focus, parsing its features. As a child I seem to have been an inept phenomenologist: I never knew what to bracket out. Every mental effort was accompanied by a whole environment. How could I separate molecular activity in a test tube from a pigeon strutting outside the classroom windowsill, and the rumbling in my belly? To this day I find that my understanding and my perceptions tend to be oblique, advancing by way of some mental equivalent of peripheral vision. I realize now that I touched on this in the interview Evelyn Reilly conducted with me for *Eco Language Reader*, when I said that my experience as a poet was "that point of engagement I have with dysfunction where I am otherwise most functional: in language." As a pedagogic strategy, the point sustains my conviction that one learns most effectively in moments of peril or risk—that is, when your confident advance along a familiar route is shadowed by the grim awareness that you're losing your grip, that this isn't quite what you expected, that the attention you "pay" is no longer secured by the gold reserve of your intellectual capital.

"I'm going to help you lose your way, then help you find you never lost it." That's a sentence I wrote a long time ago thinking about Ralph Waldo Emerson (I suppose I was summarizing the strategy of his prose style). Bear that in mind when reading the pages that follow, augmented by this proviso by the Concord sage: "In the transmission of the heavenly waters, every hose fits every hydrant" (1983, 676).

Acknowledgments

FIRST AND FOREMOST, a lion's share of this book is collaborative, involving exchanges that span fifteen years. The interview with Tony Tost appeared online in *Fascicle* (2006); the interview with Leonard Schwartz was broadcast on his *Cross Cultural Poetics* program on KAOS in 2007 and published in *Golden Handcuffs Review* (2010); the interview with Evelyn Reilly was included in *Eco Language Reader*, edited by Brenda Iijima (2010); and the exchange with Mike Chasar appeared in *Boston Review* online (2012). The interview with Ming-Qian Ma was undertaken from 2016 to 2018 and appeared in *CounterText* 7.3 (2021). Previously unpublished are the exchanges with Joel Bettridge (2014–2018) and, conducted for this book, the discussion with Nathan Brown (2020). I owe a thumping "thanks" to these inquisitive and welcoming people, who have enabled me to actively participate in dialogical exchanges continually since 2005.

The "Deep Image" chapter previously appeared in *Don't Ever Get Famous: Essays on New York Writing after the New York School* (2006), whose editor, Daniel Kane, solicited it. "From Corset to Podcast: Or, the Condition of Poetry When Everybody Is a Poet" draws from articles published in *American Literary History* (2009) and the Chinese journal *Foreign Literature Studies* (2012). "A Potential Intelligence: The Case of the Disappearing Poets" is the fruit of an invitation by Paul Bové to contribute to a special issue of *Boundary 2* (2017). "Flesh Dream Books" was solicited by Pierre Joris and Peter Cockelbergh for the festschrift *A City Full of Voices: Essays on the Work of Robert Kelly* (2019).

Three keynote addresses factored into these essays. "The Condition of Poetry When Everybody Is a Poet" was delivered at the first convention of the Chinese/American Association for Poetry and Poetics in Wuhan, China (2011). "Panorama, Sentence by Sentence" was given at the Silliman Symposium at the University of Windsor in Canada (2011), and "Bringing in the Trash: The Cultural Ecology of Dada" for the biennial conference of the Association for the Study of Literature and Environment at the University of Worcester, England (2012). Many thanks for the invitations, the venues, and the stimulating responses.

The incentive to gather this material into a book was provoked by a symposium in 2018 at my alma mater, the University of California at Santa Cruz, on the life and work of Norman O. Brown, who was a true mentor to me. "Anarchy in an Environment That Works" was my contribution to that occasion.

In the fall of 2014 I taught a graduate seminar on modern American poetry, with a syllabus of more than five hundred books. Here's the prospectus:

> This course will be an experiment in time travel. Participants will commit to a total immersion in the poetry and discourse about poetry in America during the first half of the twentieth century. Books will be read largely in first edition issues as were available at the time. Collectively, the class will function as a weekly interest group, moving consecutively through the years, discussing the changing scene of poetry as new books are published. Working chronologically from a list of eligible titles (1913–1949), each participant will be charged with assessing his or her readings, conveying these perspectives through conversations in and out of class, and writing book reviews in the idiom of the period. The point of this approach is to depose the post-facto reception history and its inherited assumptions, to confront an unfolding adventure in poetry as it was initially encountered in all its local power and peculiarity. Scrutiny of periodicals and anthologies will also contribute to this immersive historical experience. The reading load is considerable, but it is also discretionary. The experience will be immersive, but the depth of the water is yours to calibrate.

While I'm indebted to all the students who participated in this adventure, three in particular (all formidable poets in their own right) continued to work with me and, in doing so, enhanced the perspectives developed in the essays and interviews gathered here: Jackie Kari, Jake Syersak, and Connor Fisher.

ESSAYS

A Potential Intelligence

The Case of the Disappearing Poets

IN AN APPENDIX to his *Anthology of American Poetry* (1930), Alfred Kreymborg listed two hundred recommended titles, later adding seventy more to the 1941 edition of his book. Most are from the twentieth century, and with few exceptions (twenty titles by Eliot, Frost, and a few others) the list would confound most readers conversant with modern poetry.[1] His list raises the question: What do we actually know of the history of American poetry in the first half of the twentieth century? In *Our Singing Strength: An Outline of American Poetry (1620–1930)* (1929), Kreymborg produced discerning commentary on nearly two hundred poets active in the first three decades of the century. About 120 poets make the grade in Horace Gregory and Marya Zaturenska's *A History of American Poetry 1900–1940* (1946). But by the time Donald Stauffer published *A Short History of American Poetry* (1974), the numbers had declined to sixty-five, slightly more than the fifty in Hyatt Waggoner's *American Poets, from the Puritans to the Present* (1984).

The case of this vanishing population is even more starkly apparent in anthologies. The 1930 edition of Louis Untermeyer's *Modern American Poetry* put 121 poets in play. In the same year, Kreymborg packed 149 from the first three decades of the century into *An Anthology of American Poetry*. In 1932 Harriet Monroe and Alice Corbin Henderson stocked *The New Poetry* with 116 authors. But by the end of the century, only twenty-nine poets from *The New Poetry* appeared with any regularity in anthologies, with thirty-two each from Kreymborg and Untermeyer. The numbers are chastening, although the attrition rate could be considered normal. Yet these anthologies end twenty years before midcentury, two decades during which there was no letup in annual publications of poetry. By 1950, with the appearance of a revised edition of *The Oxford Book of American Verse*, a template was established that persists today. Of this anthology's thirty-two poets, all but a few (personal friends of editor F. O. Matthiessen) constitute the lion's share of those poets still being anthologized.[2]

So where did they go, the hundreds of American poets deemed worthy of critical commentary and a place in anthologies up to the end of World War II, but unceremoniously dismissed thereafter? The casual assumption is that they must have been minor, "second rate." Even if true of anthologists' judgments, that's no excuse for expunging them altogether from the *historical* record. And the historical account would appear to be thriving. The scholarly market offers up a glut of competing compendia: *The Oxford Handbook of Modern and Contemporary American Poetry* edited by Cary Nelson (2012), *A Companion to Modernist Poetry* edited by David Chinitz and Gail McDonald (2014), *The Cambridge Companion to Modern American Poetry* edited by Walter Kalaidjian (2015), *The Cambridge Companion to American Poets* edited by Mark Richardson (2015), *The Cambridge History of American Poetry* edited by Alfred Bendixen and Stephen Burt (2015), *A History of Modernist Poetry* edited by Alex Davis and Lee M. Jenkins (2015), and *A History of Twentieth-Century American Women's Poetry* edited by Linda Kinnahan (2016). Totaling 4,312 pages and 209 chapters by nearly as many authors (some contribute to more than one anthology), the trend suggests that a history of modern American poetry is necessarily collective. After all, it's been more than forty years since a single author attempted such a thing. Thoughtful and informative as much of this material is, these pages reveal more about the preoccupations of midcareer scholars than about the full range of modern American poetry.

In his introduction to *The Cambridge Companion to Modern American Poetry*, Walter Kalaidjian suggests that the volume "gathers together major critical voices that represent the best practices of contemporary critical approach and method" (2015, 2). This is refreshingly honest about curatorial priorities, though it awkwardly implies that the subject itself is merely a way of showcasing "best practices." Chinitz and McDonald are equally explicit. Their *Companion to Modernist Poetry* "brings recent scholarship to bear on the subject of modernist poetry while also providing guidance on poets who are historically important and who are likely to appear on syllabi and to attract critical interest for many years to come" (2014, 2). Acknowledging the market priority of the syllabus is truth in advertising, but extending this into an indefinite future forecloses the prospect of recovering the past. The most responsible editorial statement from any of these compilations comes from Cary Nelson, who cautions that "true expertise means accepting and accounting for the necessarily limited and partial nature of your knowledge. It means realizing you cannot even entirely name what you do not know" (5). But even if you can't name what you don't know, you might surely be expected to know the names of those you've chosen to overlook—unless you've lacked the initiative to search them out in the first place.

Contributors to these volumes are well versed in the professional norms of literary scholarship, applying due diligence to race, gender, class, disability, globalism, and cultural studies—and, ostensibly, poetry. Two of them are not restricted to American poetry, and others devote considerable space to poetry before the twentieth century and after World War II, so the applicable page count boils down to roughly eighteen hundred pages on the poetry of 1910–1950. Nonetheless, between these volumes some sixty pages are devoted to Eliot, nearly the same to Pound, Williams, and Moore; slightly less to Loy and Hughes; forty to Stein and Stevens, thirty to Frost and almost as much to H. D. After that, individual poets come and go like commuters in Grand Central Station, barely glimpsed in the throng—though it doesn't amount to much of a throng in the end. It's pointless to carp about particular omissions—even Hart Crane barely makes a dent in these volumes, and Edwin Arlington Robinson is omitted from two of them—but collectively they convey a starkly delimited profile in which a dozen poets comprise a procession of Titans, while most of the rest are avoided altogether or dispatched in a police blotter profile. These compendia confirm, along with current anthologies, that the repertoire has shrunk so dramatically as to qualify as an auto-da-fé of American poetry before midcentury.

After completing his two-volume *History of Modern Poetry* (1976, 1989), David Perkins embarked on a reconsideration of his endeavor, asking in the title of his 1992 book, *Is Literary History Possible?* "The question," he writes, "of whether literary history is possible is really whether any construction of a literary past can meet our present criteria of plausibility" (17). Such criteria can have the unanticipated effect of rendering aspects of the past invisible, or beneath notice. "A function of literary history," Perkins therefore avows, "is to set the literature of the past at a distance, to make its otherness felt." "If we ask why this is desirable," he adds, "one answer is that we do not want to be prisoners of the present" (185). Judging from current evidence, it would seem that *being professional* is tantamount to being *imprisoned in the present*. The cost to historical perspective is acute.

Another pressure point is the twentieth century as a totality, whereby the (premature) winnowing of the first half of the century has been finalized by the need to accommodate the population bulge of the second half. The contemporary scholar, heeding the clamor at the gates of an army of living poets born between the 1920s and the 1990s, understandably has little incentive to probe library stacks in hopes of turning up some unheralded gem from before midcentury. Yet continued references to *history* make it clear that the word means something different to English professors than to historians.

A key reference largely missing from these compendia is the work of Joan Shelley Rubin, author of the most informative study of modern American poetry published in the past decade or more; but she is a historian, and the dearth of citations suggests her revelatory research is of negligible interest to literary critics. Referring to "the literary history told here," Linda Kinnahan prefaces *History of Twentieth-Century American Women's Poetry* by suggesting that "fundamental questions of who, when, why and how—questions of visibility and record are inseparable from questions of analysis and interpretation" (2016, 3). I agree, but these recent compendia convince me that the priority given to analysis and interpretation far outweighs visibility. What's more, the analytic drive works like a magic wand to reduce whole populations to convenient exempla, in lists smarting of the desultory "et cetera."[3]

In 1920 Maxwell Bodenheim wrote that "the poet is not a being separated from his fellow-men in his fundamental substances. He is merely a being in whom the unbroken fundamentals of other men break into myriads of elastic, expanding branches" (96). Here, Bodenheim is noticing a potentiality unique to poetry. Where others use words in an executive and transitive manner, poets linger with the words, watching the way they splice and multiply. Some forty years later, Bodenheim's old friend William Carlos Williams was asked whether he was writing for a particular audience. "No, I don't think of myself as writing for any definite audience," he responded. "I write for a potential intelligence" (1976, 62). A potential intelligence has been precisely what's reaped such benefits from the apertures opened by claims of feminism, political urgency, race, class. Cary Nelson's American Poetry Recovery Series (University of Illinois Press) resurrected a roster of leftist poets, augmented by some reprints from the National Poetry Foundation (University of Maine). And even an enterprising small press can play a role, as in Gregory Wolfe's edition of queer poet Dunstan Thompson, *Here at Last Is Love: Selected Poems* (2015). Indispensable as such recovery efforts are, they unintentionally reinforce the claims of the present, delimiting "potential intelligence" by mandating particularities of intelligence that, however deserving of attention, can't help but elbow out other perspectives. The claims of the present thereby obscure the otherness of the past by forwarding current concerns.

"Literary works," suggested John Guillory in *Cultural Capital*, "must be seen as the vector of ideological notions which do not inhere in the works themselves but in the context of their institutional presentation, or more simply, in the way in which they are taught" (1993, ix). The institutional matrix of literary studies is now dominated by what he identified as "the professional-managerial class" (45). But what are the objectives of this class? Matthew Hofer wonders: "What, exactly, are twenty-first-century critics of modernist poetry searching for?" Such a question, he suggests, "demands that we reconsider seriously not only how we read but also what and why and to which ends" (2014, 566). Do we want better interpretations, or simply more of them? Do we want to arrive at a broadly informed background, a thicker context? Or are we on the lookout for personal strategies of professional development? If the first two questions can be answered affirmatively, the third reveals a more troublesome orientation. Careerism weighs heavily on its focal plane, compromising the putatively valued enterprise of recovering the past.

Historical perspective is inflected by prevailing trends, and the dismal academic job market has accelerated the impact of these trends. A job candidate is more likely to succeed by being up on the latest paradigms, not by uncovering forgotten texts. To be sure, such trends often entail overdue conceptual readjustments, and as such the sanguine canon of white men has been under siege for decades now. Yet the historical record of American poetry in the first half of the twentieth century has shrunk to a slim profile at odds with the rhetoric of inclusiveness, diversity, and cultural specificity. We now face a curious discrepancy, with historicist protocols affirmed routinely even as the actual breadth of historical detail shrinks. By "detail" I mean the most basic integer in literary studies: the names of the authors.

"Transport *by* is transformation *of*," as media theorist Régis Debray's formula has it. "That which is transported is remodeled, refigured, and metabolized by its transit. The receiver finds a different letter from the one its sender placed in the mailbox" (2000, 27). This is demonstrably what happened with the history of modern American poetry as it was channeled through the curatorial lens of New Criticism. "When the New Critics professionalized literary criticism," observes Melissa Girard, "they simultaneously deprofessionalized a rich critical and aesthetic discourse produced by women poets in the modernist era" (2012, 116). Four authors—Louise Bogan, Edna St. Vincent Millay, Genevieve Taggard, and Elinor Wylie—provide Girard with an intelligible matrix for demonstrating the pertinence of an orientation in the twenties that embraced neither the masculine bravado of emerging modernism nor the persistent siren call of genteel sentiment. Wylie's faith in "a small clean technique" (1923, 14) might then be as worthy of respect as William Carlos Williams's "machine made of words" (1944, 8).

Girard's essay enhances available perspectives on familiar names, while passing up an opportunity to put less-familiar ones into play, like Léonie Adams, Helen Hoyt, Evelyn Scott, Leonora Speyer, Winifred Welles, or Audrey Wurdemann—all figures who would illuminate other aspects of twenties' poetry.[4] Nevertheless, it's a notable effort along the lines spelled out by John Timberman Newcomb. "We need not only to surround the old titans with fresh contexts, but also to situate a much wider variety of poets into those contexts," he urges. "The success of this kind of recovery work requires that we stop condescending to such poets as curiosities or 'interesting' failures, and instead treat them as potentially formative to our evolving sense of what modern American poetry was" (2012, 251). Scholars today would concur, although actual practice suggests that the keyword "recovery" is just lip service. Nearly two decades ago, Joseph Harrington diagnosed a situation that still prevails. Citing the familiar roster of Pound, Eliot, Williams, Stevens, Frost, H. D., and Moore, he suggested that "not only does this picture continue to marginalize other interesting poets, it presents a reified, inaccurate picture of poetry, including 'modernist' poetry, of the period" (2002, 2).

Why, then, despite such cautionary reminders, has an underinformed picture persisted? To reiterate Debray's formulation, "transport *by* is transformation *of*," and a primary medium of transport, where poetry is concerned, is the anthology. We are now long past the inclusive commercial compendia of Untermeyer and Kreymborg cited earlier. The most recent offering in the omnibus vein was Hayden Carruth's *The Voice That Is Great Within Us* (1970)— possibly the last time the likes of Winfield Townley Scott and Thomas Hornsby Ferril were included in a commercial anthology. The market now preselects contents, minimizing actual editorial control, so as to ensure access to the textbook trade.

Postwar histories of American poetry may be classified as primers beholden to the canonical anthologies servicing the classroom. Roy Harvey Pearce's *The Continuity of American Poetry* (1961), Waggoner's *American Poets* (1968), Stauffer's *Short History* (1974), and Perkins's *History of Modern Poetry* (1976, 1989) conform to an unvarying organization and format. This is not to suggest they're unhelpful, but the help they offer is plainly at the dictates of the syllabus. None can be taken seriously as a *history*. Instead, they could plausibly be given the subtitle: *Commentaries on a Delimited Roster of American Poets for the Inquisitive Undergraduate*. Only Perkins (having more space in a two-volume work) bothers to cite poets outside the charmed canonical circle, albeit in a chapter on "Conservative and Regional Poets," in which Edwin Ford Piper, H. L. Davis, Roy Helton, and DuBose Heyward are dispatched in short paragraphs.

It's not as if these critics were heedless of the greater scope of the subject they were addressing. Symptomatic is the heartfelt lament of Waggoner: "Having to leave out of account such more recent poets, several of them favorites of mine, as John Wheelwright, S. Foster Damon, John Peale Bishop, Richard Eberhart, Jeremy Ingalls, and Delmore Schwartz was really distressing" (xvii). The distress of forty years ago no longer registers, because the task of history has been delegated to the flourishing academic market in the ubiquitous "companion" or "guide." The trend is for editors to solicit or assign topics that resonate with prevailing critical preoccupations. In this way, the mission is given over to a species of literary history diagnosed by Perkins. "Critical literary history," he calls it, "deliberately rejects a historical point of view. It does not perceive the literature of the past in relation to the time and place that produced it, but selects, interprets, and evaluates this literature only from the standpoint of the present and its needs" (1992, 179).

What are the needs of the present? The system currently in place tacitly sanctions as a need the opportunity for scholars to build resumés, and scholarly publishers compliantly provide such opportunities. But the need to develop a career has no intrinsic correlation with historical research, especially given that the default setting in literary studies remains the interpretive "reading." The combined pressures of the syllabus and following current trends in academic discourse set the parameters not only of research but even of basic awareness. Perennial underfunding of research in the humanities doesn't help either, making the massive warehousing of poets' archives in special collection libraries a tantalizing resource out of fiscal reach for many.

If scholars didn't habitually pledge faith in historicism, it might be less alarming to see the past deployed as a building supply depot for today's projects. The situation is not new. In 1960 Roman Jakobson diagnosed the quandary of literary scholarship. "Unfortunately," he observed, "the terminological confusion of 'literary studies' with 'criticism' tempts the student of literature to replace the description of the intrinsic value of a literary work with a subjective, censorious verdict" (364). By *intrinsic value* he means the structural vocation of any work in the medium of its moment. That moment is forfeited whenever a casual assumption is made that divides the domain into the handful of poets about whom we ceaselessly strive to know more, and the multitude thereby consigned to oblivion.

Consequently, a kind of institutional obscurantism prevails, proving Rubin's point that "the practice of writing literary history only as a succession of attempts to 'make it new' has obscured the ways in which innovation, instead of completely displacing older forms, coexisted alongside them" (2000, 129).[5] The crucial term is *coexistence*: for the majority of poets at any given moment do not identify programmatically with a given cause, group, or practice. Especially in the American milieu, in which the rhetoric of the avant-garde has been marginal, the coexistence of seemingly incommensurable varieties of poetry has been the norm. Yet the triumphalist tale of modernism continues unchecked, leaving behind a vast body of poetry that merits attention on both historical and literary grounds—some of which might plausibly earn a place in the canon. So how might we become familiar with the considerable number of poets, circa 1910–1950, not eligible for recovery under the profession's prevailing search engines?

One clue may be gleaned from the response of Louis Untermeyer to *The*

Waste Land in *American Poetry since 1900*, a 1923 revision of his 1919 survey, *The New Era in American Poetry* (1919b). He regarded Eliot's recently published poem as "not so much a creative thing as a piece of literary carpentry, scholarly joiner's work" (Untermeyer 1923, 358). Although technical skill is implied by the analogy, Untermeyer was unwilling to credit Eliot with mastering the profusion of components in this "pompous parade of erudition," with its "jumble of narratives, nursery-rhymes, criticism, jazz-rhythms, Dictionary of Favorite Phrases and a few lyrical moments." Most revealing now, however, is his disclosure that the publication of Eliot's poem "was the occasion for a controversy as bitter as that which signaled the appearance of *Spoon River Anthology*" (359, 360, 356). The hegemony of Eliot and company has prevailed for so long now that it's shocking to find *The Waste Land* and *Spoon River Anthology* in the same sentence.

Eliot unquestionably reigns supreme as *the* unavoidable modern poet, making for a presumptive and unhelpful overexposure. There are in fact ways to defamiliarize Eliot: the meteoric impact of *The Waste Land*, for instance, was not confined to the Anglo-American sphere. Suspected of being a hoax in Eliot's native land, the poem went viral on the international stage. It was translated into Greek by future Nobel laureate George Seferis, into Japanese by a major poet (Junzaburo Nishiwaki), and into German and Italian by eminent humanist scholars (Ernst Robert Curtius, Mario Praz). It had Spanish translations in Mexico and Catalonia, and readers of French, Russian, Czech, Hebrew, and even Urdu soon had access to *The Waste Land*. Its collage aesthetic, it seems, was far more amenable to translation than the more normative verses of Eliot's American peers, like Edgar Lee Masters, whose sepulchral effluvia in *Spoon River Anthology* still bears a reproachful point today:

> At first you will not know what they mean,
> And you may never know,
> And we may never tell you:— (1915, 214)

I can't help but hear in these lines a warning to those in search of carrion for the textbook trade.

The role of Louis Untermeyer in setting the agenda for modern American poetry via his critical studies and anthologies cannot be overestimated. *The New Era in American Poetry* set an emphatic agenda. Poets now, he proclaimed, were emancipated from "a vague elegance, from a preoccupation with a poetic past, from the repeating of echoes and glib superficials." The poet was henceforth free "to look at the world he lives in; to study and synthesize the startling fusion of races and ideas, the limitless miracles of science and its limitless curiosity, the growth of liberal thought, the groping and stumbling toward a genuine social democracy—the whole welter and struggle and beauty of the modern world" (1919b, 13). This was a pledge straight out of the pages of *The Seven Arts* magazine, and like his fellow members on its editorial board, Untermeyer was wary of modernism.[6] He was dubious about Alfred Kreymborg's circle, deeming "capitalized emotions and lower case letters" a bit much, judging the enterprise of *Others* little more than "the careful probing of a soap-bubble" (324, 328). Still, he thought the venture sufficiently noteworthy to devote a chapter to it in *New Era*, retained in the revised version of 1923.

Untermeyer's orientation was signaled by the plaster bust of Robert Frost serving as frontispiece for *American Poetry since 1900*, as if the poet's gravitas were sanctioned by antiquity. Nevertheless, his penchant for documentation prevailed over personal taste. This was especially notable in the anthologies. Beginning with *Modern American Poetry* in 1919, and reprised in numerous editions over subsequent decades, Untermeyer's selections were invariably copious. Restricting selections to two or three poems per poet enabled him to marshal legions. But despite their comprehensive purview, new editions could only accommodate new poets by ejecting some from the older versions. So his anthologies constituted a revolving door, in which many poets entered for one or two editions only to find themselves outside again. In Robert Hillyer's sardonic verse:

> Taste changes. Candid Louis Untermeyer
> Consigns his past editions to the fire;
> His new anthology, refined and thrifty,
> Builds up some poets and dismisses fifty.
> And every poet spared, as is but human,
> Remarks upon his critical acumen. (1937, 4)

Only two dozen poets from Untermeyer's 1921 edition persisted to 1950, by which point they were much the same as those found in Matthiessen's anthology. (I cite 1921 because Untermeyer had not yet included Stephen Crane, Eliot, or Stevens in 1919.) This might be taken as evidence of editorial unanimity about the canon, but by 1950 Untermeyer was clearly catering to the textbook market, a market created in part by his demonstrated willingness to supply periodically revised editions—an initiative originally suggested by his publisher.[7]

The twentieth century underwent a surgical split in 1950. Before then, a large retinue of poets filled anthologies and critical/historical accounts of the period. But the rising hegemony of the New Criticism was the cleaver. Its formalist orientation offered no incentive to sociological curiosity: which is to say, the prewar poetry world had no status, in part because the new pedagogic protocols disavowed literary history. By that point, the length, population displacements, and traumas of World War II had consigned much of the previous decades to oblivion. Postwar programs of recovery, combined with the sudden escalation into a geopolitical Cold War, left generations of poets behind. Nonetheless, many prewar poets had career-culminating publications in the Cold War era.[8] But these publications, by and large, had little or no impact on the emerging consensus as to what counted as American poetry, in part because of the postwar urgency to start fresh, unencumbered by past legacies.

What happened, is a matter of generational succession, favoring those whose careers began shortly before or during the war. They were marked as the up-and-coming generation by John Ciardi's 1950 anthology, *Mid-Century American Poets*, the most successful launch site of new careers in the history of American poetry. At the same time, the high modernists were of an age to garner career appraisal by a new generation of scholars like Hugh Kenner and Donald Davie. Pound, Eliot, Williams, Stevens, and Frost cast an obliterating shadow over the next generation(s), whose profiles languished in the dubious aura of "prewar"—or, more accurately, the interregnum between world wars. In that context, the midcentury transfiguration of poetic profusion to canonical tidiness was handled with industrial efficiency, consolidating a canon in which genealogical continuity, rather than historical breadth, was the overriding rationale.[9] It's important to stress that this was an academic mission: prewar poetry had been handled, promoted, and scrutinized by poets doubling as critics and editors. Postwar, the boom in higher education transformed John Crowe Ransom, Allen Tate, and Robert Penn Warren into managers of the syllabus, editors of textbooks, and contributors to a rising managerial class of professors, for whom the messy business of cultural striving was left at the door. The well-wrought urn, like the military buzz cut, was the order of the day.

No greater contrast to the New Criticism could be imagined than the infusion of cultural studies into the study of poetry, notably Joan Shelley Rubin's *Songs of Ourselves: The Uses of Poetry in America* (2007) and Mike Chasar's *Everyday Reading: Poetry and Popular Culture in Modern America* (2012). From this vantage, a veritable Niagara of poetry has been coursing through every conceivable public venue throughout the twentieth century, "in school, at civic gatherings, in women's clubs, as parlor entertainment and bedtime routine, within religious ceremonies, at celebrity performances, and around Girl Scout campfires," in Rubin's enumeration (2007, 4); a phenomenon that continues apace today in "television programs, talk shows, movies, novels, advertisements, Web sites, blogs, new video formats, and interactive social media, including chat rooms, Facebook, and Twitter," in Chasar's update (2012, 6). The prehistory explored by Chasar ranges from Burma Shave roadside jingles and Hallmark greeting cards to private scrapbooks, revealing that poetry has never lacked a mass audience. Critical discourse about poetry (not to mention lamentations about its purported decline) is thus all too parochial in its outlook. This panoramic revelation of poetry at work in the world at large, provocative and necessary as it is, can't help but disclose an overlooked issue: namely, the concurrent existence of a poetry world.

The expression *poetry world* is less familiar than *art world*, which refers not only to creative activity but to a robust financial realm. Still, "poetry world" is commonly used now to indicate a professional milieu, the way a bond trader might refer to Wall Street, or a BP stoker to an oil tanker. A world unto itself: if you're not *in it* and *of it* you wouldn't understand. French discographer Charles Delaunay, asked about his youthful immersion in jazz, put it well: "It was our world. We lived among our citizens" (Wellburn 1983, 196). Where poetry is concerned, at least, it's the factor that never makes it into Hollywood movies, which tend to focus on the poet as a preening cockatoo while omitting the "world." Every world is a closed shop in its way. You're either in or out, but if you're *in* it provides you with subsoil and starry constellations, its elements roiling with flux and pockets of stability.

Edward Said had something like that in mind when, forty years ago, he cautioned against the tendency to conceive cultural change in terms of Titanic combat. But, he asked, "what is it that maintains texts inside reality? What keeps some of them current, while others disappear? How does an author imagine for himself the 'archive' of his time, into which he proposes to put his text? What are the centers of diffusion by which texts circulate?" (1976, 342). These sensible questions too often fade into casual assumptions, and the circumambient context of filiation and repudiation within which all artists operate dissolves, leaving the misleading spectacle of major figures silhouetted against a vacant space.

The practice of aligning conspicuous writers in a consecutive timeline in order to simulate "history" misleadingly implies that each of the personae in question was primarily cognizant of the others we now deem salient, as if they'd been cohabiting a textbook all along. Yet such awareness is patently unavailable in situ. Overinflated reputations subside with time, but it's not as if such reputations seem bogus in the moment, not least because the chatter (ranging from sycophantic to dismissive) about a given figure adds contextual weight to the reputation, and a context cannot be casually shrugged off. It's also the case that agitators can adopt an aggressively exclusive tactic, as did Ezra Pound, issuing proclamations, conscripting personnel like a military commander, and pointedly turning a deaf ear to much of the ambient buzz emanating from other centers of interest. Pound and his "men of 1914" have long been understood as a power bloc, but what's been left unattended are the other blocs.

One might consider, for instance, the reign of Stephen Vincent Benét and his older brother William Rose Benét—who, not incidentally, was married to Elinor Wylie. Stephen's tenure as steward of the Yale Younger Poets has been unjustly overshadowed by that of a successor in that role, W. H. Auden. Other poet couples prominent on the literary scene were Joseph Auslander and Audrey Wurdemann (great-great-granddaughter of Percy Bysshe Shelley), Horace Gregory and Marya Zaturenska, and on the West coast Yvor Winters and Janet Lewis.[10] But power blocs of the moment can sputter over time. Reflecting on the way Oscar Williams cultivated Zaturenska and her husband as if they were movers and shakers, Zaturenska ruefully reflected that the ones with real influence were Archibald MacLeish and Mark Van Doren, operatives in a milieu rife with "frightful advertising slogan conversation" and "unconscious cynicism" (2002, 145). Genealogy is indifferent to such acutely human factors.

A striking example of the liability—or in this case the gain—of the genealogical paradigm is the status of Objectivism in current surveys and anthologies. Yet in the thirties the names Zukofsky, Reznikoff, Rakosi, and Oppen, if known at all, were buried among scores of others in little magazines. The asymmetrical development of a "potential intelligence" in poetry means that Objectivism was not validated until substantial reprints and other publications were made available thirty years later. Also consequential was the critical advocacy of Hugh Kenner, Rachel Blau DuPlessis, Charles Bernstein, and others. The salutary rise of Mina Loy and H. D. are comparable instances of successful special interest campaigns. Deserving of attention as all these poets are, their prominence reflects the influence of Kenner's "Pound Era."

A daunting challenge in recovering the full spectrum of American poetry from the first half of the twentieth century is identifying basic resources. The notable initiative of the Modernist Journals Project and Suzanne Churchill's online database Index of Modernist Magazines offer orientation to periodicals, some of which are now digitized. Unfortunately, because of changes to the law governing copyright expiration, digital access to journals and books is compressed into the first two decades of the century, leaving the subsequent decades in the odd position of being a terra incognita, relatively speaking. And as I've been indicating here, it's all too easy for scholars to assume that the historical coverage has been adequate, while remaining unaware that a multitude of poets await notice on the dark side of the historical moon.

In some sense, we're lucky that so considerable a body of poetry has been overlooked, for this is work untainted by canonical deliberations and school-room exercises. To peruse hundreds of forgotten titles is like stepping into the Trocadero before it was organized as an ethnographic collection, a time when Picasso was spooked by the hoard. Plunging into this motley assortment, what would it mean to arrive at a more comprehensive profile of American poetry in the first half of the twentieth century? There are predictable consequences. Catholicity reveals variety while also disclosing the tics of a period that tend to flatten apparent variety into undifferentiated authorship—a phenomenon I first noticed regarding the sixties thirty years later. But variable aspirations become evident; it can even be a relief to read journeyman's work by unpretentious poets in which, nonetheless, singularities gleam out. It's the unpredictable encounters that are most gratifying, in part because the historical sense is enriched but also because the spectrum of poetry is itself extended, like discovering a new bandwidth on a radio.

From a cultural studies perspective—with its emphasis on the consumption and circulation of poems across a broad social spectrum—the parameters of the "poetry world" are relegated to the background, the focal plane instead being a world at large into which poetry is variously injected. In principle, it makes little difference if the poem is by a legislative figure like Eliot or by a postal worker whose sole output may be a single poem. In the poetry world, bestsellers like Walter Benton or Rod McKuen are inadmissible, but it would be hazardous to ignore them from a cultural studies outlook. It's easy for scholars to dismiss the reading habits of the untutored masses—untold hordes beyond the ministrations of their classrooms—but the broader readership disclosed by Chasar and Rubin, among others, needs to be factored into the historical record. And surveying trends revealed by published books discloses unsuspected points of contact between poets and readers.

Submersion in the books of a given period—augmented by perusal of periodicals and book reviews—provides a compass hardly imaginable within the torrent of recent scholarship. The scholarship resembles a video game, in which predictable obstacles arise to challenge the player, who has to toggle around the specters of Eliot and Loy, Lowell and Bishop, the pace of the game inhibiting any sidelong glance. The prospect Williams envisaged of poetry soliciting a "potential intelligence" founders in the gymnastics of such administered routines. The radical challenge I'm proposing is total immersion, submitting to the siren calls that emerge when personal tastes are depersonalized by the historical distance traversed. There's a distinct difference between spot-checking the anthologies and turning the pages of a dated volume of poetry, giving it a chance to have its way with you.

In the poetry world, authorship is in constant interplay with a series of factors. These include peer and aspirant networks traditionally associated with literary journals, reading series, group hangouts, and publication venues. These venues include small presses, often rich with local associations or with a particular aesthetic, and trade publishers, whose lists can also suggest a kind of name brand or credential. Most poetry titles before midcentury were commercially published. Small presses were restricted to a few expatriate publishers in the 1920s and Four Seas Company in Boston, followed in subsequent decades by a small orbit of domestic outfits like New Directions, Alan Swallow, James Decker, Kaleidoscope, Wagon & Star, Dynamo, Colt Press, Black Cat, Centaur, Cummington, Ward Ritchie, Bruce Humphries, Bern Porter, Brentano's, Arrow Editions, International Publishers, and the Contemporary Poetry Series. Unlike the postwar scene with its raw/cooked dichotomy, though, there's little evident distinction between small press and trade publications in prewar poetry. Some, like Cummington, specialized in limited editions of authors like Wallace Stevens and Allen Tate, whose works were routinely published by trade presses. Others, like Swallow and Decker, cultivated authors who tended to stay with them rather than moving on to the New York trade outfits.

One benefit in scrutinizing original publications is the historical specificity of the book as object. It makes a difference to experience the variety of formats, especially in works known largely through reprints. E. E. Cummings's *No Thanks* (1935), for instance, prints the poems outward from the spine, not from top to bottom of the pages; and his *W* (1931, also known as *ViVa*) is in a large format, 12" x 7". Larger still is *Prelude to Man* by Chard Powers Smith (1936), part of a planned trilogy of book-length poems on evolution, large enough at 16" x 11" to handle double columns. By contrast, William Carlos Williams's seminal title *The Wedge* (1944) was literally pocket size, reportedly because the poet favored a diminutive format for the convenience of soldiers. Muriel Rukeyser's first book was in a substantially larger format than other Yale Younger Poets titles, and the sans-serif font used for the text made *Theory of Flight* (1935) seem emphatically modern. Merrill Moore's gargantuan *M: One Thousand Autobiographical Sonnets* (1938) did not stint in page count, reserving a single page for each sonnet, printed in larger type with expanded leading. By contrast, Rolfe Humphries's first collection, *Europa* (1928), used a font so small (no larger than six point) that the poems resemble footnotes.

In collected editions everything is averaged out, neutralizing the singularity of prior presentations. It's also commonly the case that poets revise or expunge earlier work in subsequent or collected editions, so it can be challenging to know what actually made an initial impact on readers. Symptomatic is Edwin Arlington Robinson's biographer, Scott Donaldson, who misleadingly treats *Avon's Harvest* as the "title poem" of a collection, when in fact it was the only poem in the book (Donaldson 2007, 364). Donaldson's

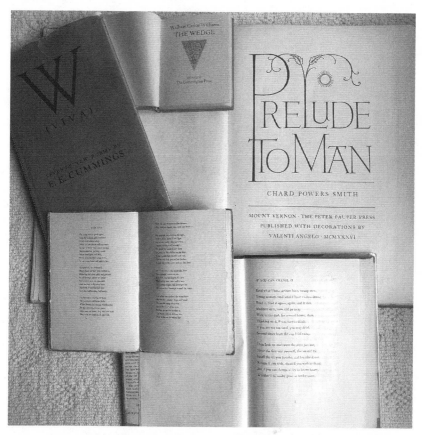

Figure 1.1. E. E. Cummings, *ViVa* (1936); Chard Powers Smith, *Prelude to Man* (1936); William Carlos Williams, *The Wedge* (1944); Merrill Moore, *M* (1938); Rolfe Humphries, *Europa* (1928)

reference to the poem being thirty pages suggests he's following the text of the *Collected Poems* (1937), where it is indeed thirty pages of a section titled "Avon's Harvest, Etc.," followed by a dozen or so shorter poems, including the much anthologized "Mr. Flood's Party." Rare is the case of Wallace Stevens, who preserved the contents of his volumes largely unrevised for the "whole Harmonium" of his *Collected Poems* (1955) (which omitted "Owl's Clover" altogether, the poem having undergone notable revision from its first appearance as an Alcestis Press book to its inclusion in *The Man with the Blue Guitar*). Arrangements of contents can also be instructive. Frost was an inveterate organizer, titling six sections of poems in *West-Running Brook* (1928), three in *New Hampshire* (1923a), six in *A Further Range* (1936), and five in *Steeple Bush* (1947). He sorted the contents of his 1923 *Selected Poems* into no less

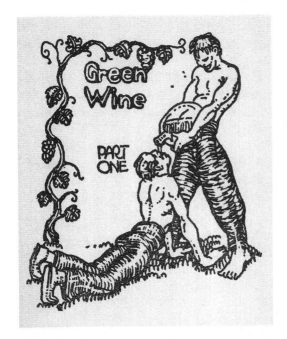

Figure 1.2. H. Phelps
Putnam, *Trinc* (1927),
uncredited illustration

NEW HAMPSHIRE
A POEM WITH NOTES
AND GRACE NOTES BY
ROBERT FROST
WITH WOODCUTS
BY J. J. LANKES
PUBLISHED BY
HENRY HOLT
& COMPANY : NEW
YORK : MCMXXIII

Figure 1.3. Robert Frost, *New Hampshire* (1923a), frontispiece by J. J. Lankes

than eight untitled sections (1923b). But the various collected editions dispensed with such organizing templates. Williams interspersed untitled poems with the prose throughout *Spring and All* (2011), adding titles when they were extracted for the Objectivist Press *Collected Poems 1921–1931* (1934). But a few years later, when New Directions issued *The Complete Collected Poems of William Carlos Williams 1906–1938* (1938), the titles were dropped and the poems restored to their former numerical sequence.

Collected editions tend to omit ancillary material from original editions, like illustrations. It was quite common for poetry collections to include visual images, though it was rare to find anything as saucy as the uncredited illustrations in *Trinc* by H. Phelps Putnam (1927) (see figure 1.2). Frost's *New Hampshire* (1923a) included several full-page wood engravings by J. J. Lankes (see figure 1.3). *West-Running Brook* (1928) has two that appear to be by Lankes, though there's no credit given. Lankes also illustrated titles by New England poets Charles Malam, Robert P. T. Coffin, and Genevieve Taggard. His contributions to Frost's books set a precedent for the illustrations by John O'Hara Cosgrave II in *Come In* (1943), much expanded as *The Road Not Taken* (1951), Louis Untermeyer's substantial selection of Frost's poems with running commentary. A precedent for this copiously illustrated selection of a poet's work was *The Dream Keeper* by Langston Hughes (1932), which had been reprinted eight times before Frost's book appeared, with Helen Sewell's illustrations appearing on nearly every page. The illustrations signal African American for *Dream Keeper* as consistently as those in Frost's book signify rural life, and in both cases the presentation is designed to entice readers unlikely to keep up with contemporary poetry. Vachel Lindsay was an inveterate doodler, prancing on the margins throughout *Going-to-the-Sun* (1923), *Going-to-the-Stars* (1926)—both presented as "Pictures and Verses"—*The Candle in the Cabin* (1926), and *Every Soul Is a Circus* (1929), which also includes illustrations by George M. Richards, who provided the flamboyant dust jacket (see figure 1.4). Don Blanding's many books are heavily illustrated by him, emphasizing their exotic settings. Few poetry titles were as profusely illustrated as his, and in cases where a plurality of images appeared they tended to be diminutive insignia, commonly cited on the title page as "decorations." Yet some of the most vivid and plentiful "decorations" are in Countee Cullen's books, all by Charles Cullen (white, and unrelated to the poet), who also illustrated an edition of *Leaves of Grass* in 1933 (see figure 1.5).

Cullen's stylizations are close to art deco, which was at its heyday in the twenties when *Color, Copper Sun,* and *The Black Christ* were published, with roots in the arts and crafts idiom of the turn of the century, when *Songs of Vagabondia* and *More Songs of Vagabondia* appeared (fondly remembered by Ezra Pound decades later). It created a template for early titles by William

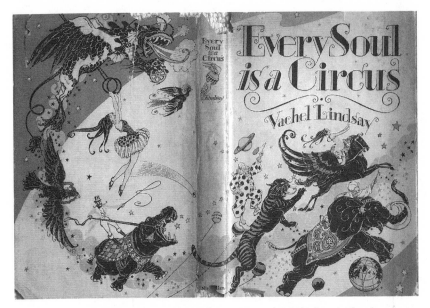

Figure 1.4. Vachel Lindsay, *Every Soul Is a Circus* (1929), dust jacket by George M. Richards

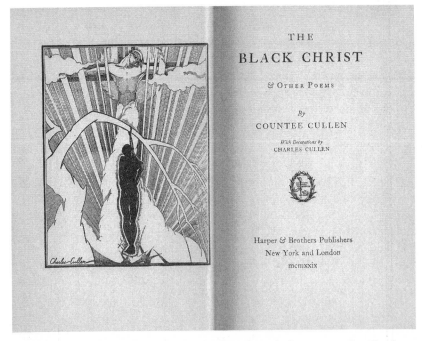

Figure 1.5. Countee Cullen, *The Black Christ* (1929), frontispiece by Charles Cullen

Figure 1.6. John Peale Bishop and Edmund Wilson Jr., *The Undertaker's Garland* (1922), dust jacket illustration by Boris Artizibasheff

Rose Benét, Robert Hillyer, Herbert S. Gorman, and Hildegarde Flanner. Its decadent apotheosis is evident in *The Undertaker's Garland* by John Peale Bishop and Edmund Wilson (1922) (see figure 1.6). Of the fifty-plus illustrated poetry titles in my library, published from 1902 to midcentury, half of them date from the twenties, with another twenty from the next decade, then a swift decline in the forties. Woodcuts and pen and ink drawings prevailed, though sometimes photography played a role, and in rare instances like Wilbert Snow's *Before the Wind* (1938) a lavish multicolored production was involved. Apart from Vachel Lindsay and Don Blanding, the only other book illustrated by the poet is Roy Helton's *Lonesome Water* (1930). E. E. Cummings was a deft illustrator, and while his line drawings regularly appeared in *The Dial* he never contributed visual material to his poetry collections. In many respects a pinnacle of illustrated poetry can be found in the limited editions of Pound's early *Cantos*, with fabulous black and red initial capitals by Henry Strater and Gladys Hines (see figure 1.7). Pound's wife

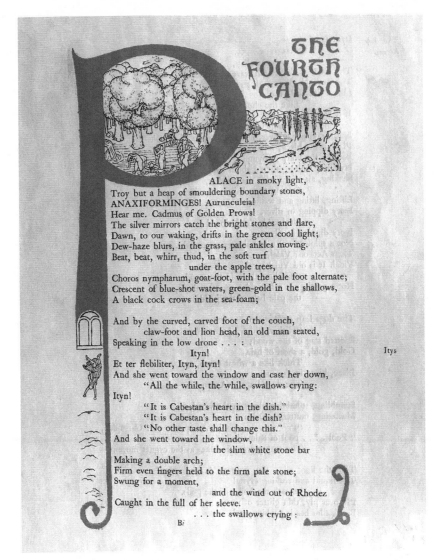

Figure 1.7. Ezra Pound, *A Draft of XVI Cantos* (1925), illustrated initial by Henry Strater

Dorothy provided capitals in the Vorticist style for the Hours Press limited edition of *A Draft of XXX Cantos* in 1930. Illustrators were generally credited in poetry titles, but few were important artists, exceptions being Stuart Davis's frontispiece for William Carlos Williams's *Kora in Hell* (1920), Aaron Douglas's contributions to *God's Trombones* by James Weldon Johnson (1927), the Walker Evans photographs in the Black Sun Press edition of *The Bridge* by Hart Crane (1930—Evans's photo of Brooklyn Bridge was retained for the frontispiece and dust jacket cover of the Liveright commercial edition), and Pavel Tchelitchew's cover and frontispiece for *The Garden of Disorder* by Charles Henri Ford (1938). Many poetry books had cover designs with visual material, of course, but being restricted to dust jackets they have largely disappeared from ready access, and in any case the illustrators were rarely credited.

In conducting historical research, much can be gleaned from dust jackets, although access is limited since libraries routinely discard them. During World War II, many jackets had appeals for war bonds—in one instance pitched by the poet, Frederick Mortimer Clapp, in *Against a Background on Fire* (1943). "No one can make too great a sacrifice to buy them and keep on buying them until the future of our freedom is bonded into our lives," he wrote on the back jacket. It was routine for publishers to advertise titles from their poetry lists on dust jackets, but a more genealogical prompt appeared on the rear flyleaf of Hart Crane's *White Buildings*, plugging Ezra Pound (see figure 1.8). Author photos can also make a statement. Headshots of square-jawed Paul Engle on his books suggest solid midwestern stock, almost a certificate of authenticity for his regional verse. Thomas Hornsby Ferrill at his typewriter reminds prospective readers of his prominence as a Denver newsman. It's rare to see photos of women on their books, but in the case of Jeremy Ingalls an image reveals her to be a woman despite the first name. The most arresting author photo I've come across is that of Hargis Westerfield, on the jacket of *Words of Steel* (1949). He's identified as having been "a rifleman in G Company, 163 Infantry Regiment, 41st Infantry Division," albeit presently "an Instructor at C.C.N.Y." But words can't do justice to the visage of him in helmet and combat fatigues (see figure 1.9).

The myth of the poet as an avatar of untrammeled expression has skewed literary history, overshadowing contributions to poetry by those known better for other things. That Willa Cather and William Faulkner published volumes of verse tends to be regarded as a vocational inconvenience best overlooked, just as the plays of Henry James and D. H. Lawrence are dispassionately set aside. But there *are* novelists who made intriguing forays into poetry; and it's worth remembering that in a pre-AWP era the literary zones were more fluid and aspiring writers tried various genres with equal avidity. John Dos Passos, Sherwood Anderson, and Theodore Dreiser published worthy collections of poetry, as did James Agee and Kay Boyle. The enormous success of *All the King's Men* somewhat compromised the view of Robert Penn Warren as a poet first and foremost. Thomas Wolfe became a poet posthumously when John S. Barnes extracted segments from his novels into poetic vignettes, with titles invented to focus attention on his lyrical flights, in *A Stone, a Leaf, a Door* (1945).

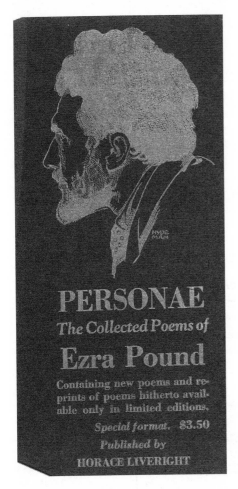

Figure 1.8. Hart Crane, *White Buildings* (1926), rear dust cover flap, illustration for *Personae* by Ezra Pound

That Edmund Wilson could be lauded (by Allen Tate, no less) as having written "some of the most accomplished poetry of our time" would be news even to Wilson's keenest admirers (1983, 86). There were other accomplished poet-critics. R. P. Blackmur published three solid poetry titles; S. Foster Damon was an original poet before his impact as a Blake scholar; and Yvor Winters's profile as a poet preceded his eminence as critic. From the art world, painters Marsden Hartley and Louis Grudin, Frick curator Frederick Mortimer Clapp, and dance critic Edwin Denby were all accomplished poets. Film scholar Parker Tyler started out as a poet. After his initial success in poetry, Mark Turbyfill immersed himself in the dance world. And although the dispiriting experiences of Fitzgerald and Faulkner have consistently linked Hollywood with fiction, there is a considerable retinue of poets (most un-

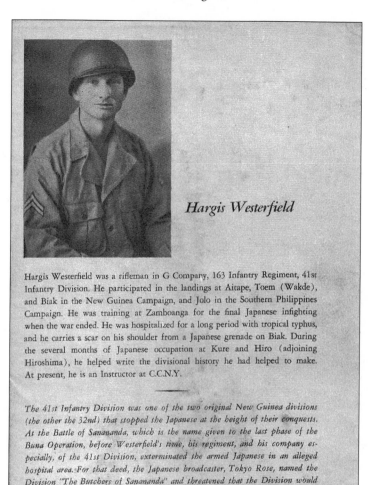

Hargis Westerfield

Hargis Westerfield was a rifleman in G Company, 163 Infantry Regiment, 41st Infantry Division. He participated in the landings at Aitape, Toem (Wakde), and Biak in the New Guinea Campaign, and Jolo in the Southern Philippines Campaign. He was training at Zamboanga for the final Japanese infighting when the war ended. He was hospitalized for a long period with tropical typhus, and he carries a scar on his shoulder from a Japanese grenade on Biak. During the several months of Japanese occupation at Kure and Hiro (adjoining Hiroshima), he helped write the divisional history he had helped to make. At present, he is an Instructor at C.C.N.Y.

The 41st Infantry Division was one of the two original New Guinea divisions (the other the 32nd) that stopped the Japanese at the height of their conquests. At the Battle of Sanananda, which is the name given to the last phase of the Buna Operation, before Westerfield's time, his regiment, and his company especially, of the 41st Division, exterminated the armed Japanese in an alleged hospital area. For that deed, the Japanese broadcaster, Tokyo Rose, named the Division "The Butchers of Sanananda" and threatened that the Division would never leave New Guinea. The Division did leave New Guinea to refit in Australia, and then returned to complete the conquest of New Guinea and then leave it for the Philippines and later Japan — and it proudly bore the name "Butchers" all the way with it.

Figure 1.9. Hargis Westerfield, *Words of Steel* (1949), dust jacket rear

justly forgotten) connected with the film industry, including Henry Bellamann, Harry Brown, Vincent G. Burns, Kenneth Fearing, James Norman Hall, Alfred Hayes, DuBose Heyward, Joseph Moncure March, Lionel Wiggam, and John V. A. Weaver.

A phenomenon completely overlooked by scholars is the preponderance of book-length poems published between the wars. This is all the more surprising given that four of the Pulitzer prizes for poetry in its first decade were for narratives: *The Man Who Died Twice* and *Tristram* by Edwin Arlington Robinson (the very first Pulitzer in 1922 was for his *Collected Poems*), *Conquistador* by Archibald MacLeish, and the best-selling *John Brown's Body* by Stephen Vincent Benét. In 1944 Benét was posthumously awarded a Pulitzer for his unfinished epic, *Western Star*, two years after his brother's massive autobiographical narrative *The Dust Which Is God* took the same prize (see figure 1.10). Robinson Jeffers's stratospheric rise to prominence rested largely on the narratives that constituted the bulk of his collections. Conrad Aiken's career was launched with the publication of six book-length poems from 1916 to 1923, presaging the consistency with which this was a normative practice, albeit one rarely sampled in anthologies and thus relatively hidden from later scrutiny. Frost didn't write at such length, but *North of Boston* consists almost entirely of lengthy conversational narratives.

Because much of the attention to long poems has been fixated on Pound's *Cantos*, Williams's *Paterson,* and Zukofsky's *"A,"* the narrative legacy in poetry has been overshadowed. But verse novels, as they were often called, were hardly an anomaly. In fact, I suspect that their success in awards and in the marketplace encouraged publishers to overinvest in the genre. I know of a hundred published from 1915 to midcentury. One of the few to have been resurrected is Joseph Moncure March's *The Wild Party*, illustrated for a 1994 edition by Art Spiegelman (author of the Pulitzer winning graphic novel *Maus*). March's other verse novel, *The Set-Up* (1928b), was made into a movie starring Robert Ryan in 1949. Another title making the transfer to silver screen was *Glory for Me* by MacKinlay Kantor, becoming the Academy Award winning Best Picture *The Best Years of Our Lives*. Although it wasn't adapted from the poem, John G. Neihardt's *The Song of Hugh Glass* (1915) features an historical figure depicted in a more recent Best Picture recipient, *The Revenant.*

Beyond the sphere of the verse novel, the profusion of longer poems in the interwar period is considerable, with over 150 I'm aware of. These include sequences like H. D.'s war trilogy, architectonic arrangements like Eliot's *Four Quartets*, thematic compilations like *Spoon River Anthology*, book-length meditations, and poems long enough to fill much of the volume in which they appeared. (I cite familiar examples because the reader would likely draw a blank if I were to substitute for the titles above *Phases of the Moon* by Charlotte Wilder, *Journey to the Coastal Marsh* by James Feibleman, and *Man with a Bull-Tongue Plow* by Jesse Stuart.) Apart from the modernist canon, these works are rarely mentioned, reflecting the impact of anthologies with their restrictive focus on lyric and other diminutive forms. But to overlook long poems is to ignore a vast amount of material integral to what constituted poetry at the time, not least because an audience responded favorably to verse novels.

Figure 1.10. William Rose Benét, *The Dust Which Is God* (1942)

Another area favored by readers is light verse. When compiling his *New Anthology of American Poetry* (1938), Selden Rodman cited Untermeyer and Aiken as "the two outstanding anthologists of recent years," while faulting them for "an excess of high seriousness" (27). For his part, Rodman adopted a different approach. "Poetry is the greatest of the arts because everyone can—and does—practice it. The ad-man and the gag-man, the housewife and the corner-grocer are latent poets" (45). While he refrained from including popular magazine and newspaper verse of his day, Rodman made a point of including humorous verse, blues lyrics and spirituals, and even inspirational slogans, pressing the issue of genre by including Bartolomeo Vanzetti's closing address at his trial as a kind of folk poetry—following the precedent of Yeats's setting of Walter Pater's prose in poetic lines for the 1936 *Oxford Book of English Verse* (1).

Rodman's inclusion of humorous verse is rare among anthologists, though the idiom was not spurned by serious poets, Eliot's practical cats being a familiar instance. Untermeyer's parodies of his contemporaries are his most durable verse (e.g., "*—and Other Poets*" [1916], the quotation marks being part of his title). Leonard Bacon's diverse output was respected by his contemporaries—*Sunderland Capture* garnered a Pulitzer in 1940—but he had a gift for humor, reflected in titles like *Guinea-Fowl and Other Poultry* (1927) and *Rhyme and Punishment* (1936) (see figure 1.11). His mock-epic *The Furioso* (1932) is a rare late entry in the idiom perfected by Byron. The names Ogden Nash, Dorothy Parker, Phyllis McGinley, Robert Morley, Stoddard King, Arthur Guiterman, and Marjorie Fishback, in their day, would have been recognized by the general public more readily than Stevens or Moore; and E. E. Cummings's characteristic typography would have been less familiar than the strictly lower-case ingenuities of Don Marquis's fabled Archy and Mehitabel in a series of titles that overshadowed his other books like *Love Sonnets of a Cave Man* (1928). Nor should we overlook parody, a sterling example being "The Moist Land," published by Samuel Hoffenstein in his deftly titled *Year In, You're Out* (1930).

Although regionalism holds a notable place in American literary history, examples tend to favor fiction. The practice of anointing poets as state laureates has probably contributed to the sense that local identity is the mark of poetry best left unread (by which I mean simply that "serious" readers of poetry will rarely be familiar with these regional laureates). Yet in the early twentieth century, regionalism could be a point of pride for poets. Robert Frost is the most famous instance, with his careful cultivation of a New England persona, but his eminence has overshadowed Vermont nativists Walter Hard and Charles Malam, Maine coastal poet Wilbert Snow, and Robert P.

Figure 1.11.
Leonard Bacon,
*Rhyme and Pun-
ishment* (1936),
illustrated cover by
Charles Child

Tristram Coffin, who celebrated the "pine tree state" in his poems and fiction through a long career. It would be revealing to place Frost in this company, not because it would affect his reputation but because it would clarify the stakes (and liabilities) of regionalism.

Chicago and the Midwest took pride of place in regional profiles almost as soon as *Poetry* commenced publication in 1912 in the city that then epitomized ultramodernity. Carl Sandburg, Edgar Lee Masters, and Vachel Lindsay personified both the new poetry and the Janus-faced stance of the nation's middle. Some verse by Jay G. Sigmund has been reprinted under the rubric "America's Forgotten Regionalist" (Jack 2008). Sherwood Anderson's *Mid-American Chants* (1918) reveal his eagerness to seize the moment not only in his fiction. Paul Engle, now remembered as the director of the Iowa Writers Workshop from 1941 to 1965, gained notoriety as a distinctly Midwest-

Figure 1.12. Carl
Carmer, *Deep
South* (1930)

ern poet with *Worn Earth* (1932), *American Song* (1934), and *Corn* (1939).
Gwendolen Haste and Robert Nathan are among numerous others who sounded
the theme of the Midwest.

The South has primarily been associated with the poetry of the Fugitives,
and while it's evident enough in the work of Ransom, Tate, Warren, and
Donald Davidson, nobody would link Laura Riding or Merrill Moore with
the South (or any other) region, though they too were Fugitives. Hervey Allen
and DuBose Heyward cultivated a regional perspective in their collaborative *Carolina Chansons* and their individual titles, much as farmer and novelist Jesse Stuart put Kentucky on the poetic map. Carl Carmer's *Deep South*
(1930) (see figure 1.12), like Lawrence Lee's *Monticello* (1937) and *The Tomb
of Thomas Jefferson* (1940), make the region explicit in their titles, but one has
to peruse the contents of Anderson Scruggs's *Glory of Earth* (1933) and James
Still's *Hounds on the Mountain* (1937) to verify locality. Although he was ini-

tially associated with the London of the Imagists, John Gould Fletcher's Arkansas background was increasingly evident in his later poetry.

Robinson Jeffers's name was synonymous with the California coast during the decades when he was one of the most famous poets in America, and the Hellenistic roots he drew upon made that locale seem vivid in a way not quite compatible with regionalism. When Kenneth Rexroth and William Everson extolled the Golden State in the 1940s, it still retained this sense of a place beyond regional configuration, setting the stage for later phenomena like the Berkeley Renaissance followed by the arrival of the Beats and the Sierra watershed of Gary Snyder. But California never took on the distinctive character of the Old West that provided such a fetching locale for poetry from early in the century.

Most people would associate the phenomenon of cowboy poetry with the National Cowboy Poetry Gathering in Elko, Nevada, an annual event since 1984. But there were widely published, prominent cowboy poets of Harriet Monroe's generation, such as Badger Clark Jr., Henry Herbert Knibbs, Arthur Chapman, William Haskell Simpson, and others like Glenn Ward Dresbach who were not trail hands but enthusiasts and chroniclers of western life in the long wake of Frederick Jackson Turner's Frontier Thesis of 1893. John G. Neihardt's cultivation of Native American themes informed five verse narratives, and Carl Sandburg acclaimed Lew Sarett as one who "says Yes to life" in his adaptation of Native American lore and chants (on the dust jacket of Sarett's *Many Moons* [1920]). Titles by these poets often make the regional identity emphatic: *Out Where the West Begins*, *The Enchanted Mesa*, *Along Old Trails*, and *Wood Smoke*. During the vogue for verse narratives, the West provided a reliable backdrop for *The Westward Star* by Frank Ernest Hill (1934), *Snow Covered Wagons* by Julia Altrocchi (1936), and *Westward under Vega* by Thomas Wood Stevens (1938), contemporaneous with the rise of the Hollywood western from *The Virginian* and *Cimarron* to *Stagecoach* (see figure 1.13) By that point the memory may have dimmed of the five poems John G. Neihardt gathered under the collective title *A Cycle of the West* in 1949, which had established a durable template for frontier narratives early in the century.

Santa Fe and Taos, like Carmel on the Big Sur coast, have long had a reputation as arts colonies, not least because of legendary sojourners like Georgia O'Keeffe and D. H. Lawrence. In his early free verse collections, Yvor Winters soaked up the enchantment of the Southwest during his residence in New Mexico for health reasons, writing the modernist poems of *The Magpie's Shadow* and *The Bare Hills* he later renounced. The region drew numerous poets, including Alice Corbin, Witter Bynner, Phillips Kloss, and Haniel Long—undeservedly demoted, if known at all, because of their remove from metropolitan literary politics. Lincoln Fitzell and Thomas Hornsby Ferril extended

Figure 1.13.
Frank Ernest
Hill, *The West-
ward Star* (1934)

this regional torque north into the Colorado Rockies. While "local color" can
be commercially viable, scholars of poetry have kept their distance, too quick
to assume that the hula-hula tropics of Don Blanding and Clifford Gessler
typify the trend (see figure 1.14). Much remains to be done to document a
continuum from kitsch to classic where regionalism is concerned. Taken nationally, the varieties of local color can disclose the invariability of certain
themes and prototypes not contingent on place at all, revealing ways in which
an era's voice-over permeated poetry at large.

It may seem I've evoked a parallel universe here, with little bearing on canonical poets. But scholarship has already provided significant bridges, particularly in the case of Robert Frost. What Frost's career reveals is precisely
that dimension I've called the poetry world, for in many respects he was the

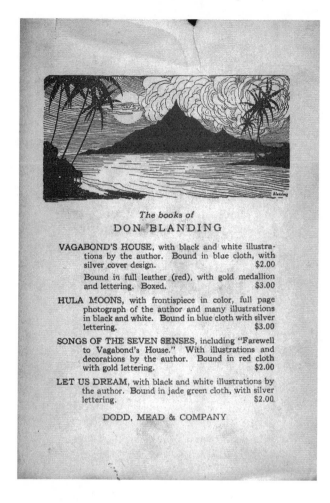

The books of
DON BLANDING

VAGABOND'S HOUSE, with black and white illustrations by the author. Bound in blue cloth, with silver cover design. $2.00
Bound in full leather (red), with gold medallion and lettering. Boxed. $3.00

HULA MOONS, with frontispiece in color, full page photograph of the author and many illustrations in black and white. Bound in blue cloth with silver lettering. $3.00

SONGS OF THE SEVEN SENSES, including "Farewell to Vagabond's House." With illustrations and decorations by the author. Bound in red cloth with gold lettering. $2.00

LET US DREAM, with black and white illustrations by the author. Bound in jade green cloth, with silver lettering. $2.00

DODD, MEAD & COMPANY

Figure 1.14. Don Blanding, *Let Us Dream* (1933), dust jacket rear advertisement, illustrated by Don Blanding

figure through whom its contours were revealed to his contemporaries. He was an inveterate careerist, even while retaining (and playing up) the posture of intransigent outsider. His irascible temperament became the model for other poets of how to fashion a poetic persona on the model of a locomotive's cow guard—and it remains to be considered how Frost prefigured the aw-shucks demeanor of Hollywood stars like Gary Cooper and John Wayne. It's now known that he was a canny poseur of folk wisdom, but less remembered is how intent he was on the *wisdom*. He was, above all, not the local sage of anthology chestnuts with which he's been identified. The publication of Frost's *Notebooks* (2006) in the ongoing Harvard University Press edition of his works is revelatory, plentifully stocked with the sensible attitudes for which he's best known ("I should hate to spend the only life I was going to have here in being annoyed with the time I happened to live in" [405]), scores of sentence fragments in vernacular formulations suggesting they're tryouts for poems, alternating with probing yet whimsical deliberations on issues of the day.

Frost also had concerns about modern poetry. He distinguishes between the adventurous and the experimental:

> Experimental belongs to the laboratory, Adventure with life. Much of recent art has been merely experimental. It tries poetry with first one element then another omitted. It leaves out the head Then it is too emotional. It leaves out the heart Then it is too intellectual It leaves out the feet Then it is free verse. Adventure ends up in the poorhouse Experiment in the madhouse Water spout theory of learning from above down from below up till it meets (2006, 213)

The text simply breaks off midsentence, as is often the case in his *Notebooks*. Frost's ruminations here reflect the perplexity felt by his contemporaries, whether those on the side of adventure or on the side of experiment; though the majority, like Frost, struggled to find a middle ground.

To survey the full breadth of early twentieth-century poetry is to encounter up close the terms of the struggle. Nearly anyone who started publishing in the teens had internalized the rhythms and postures of the genteel verse of their childhood, which got leached out in volumes of verse like an expired medication circling the drain. In some cases it was retained with a vengeance, against prevailing trends, in the desperate conviction that there was one true faith to which only a blessed few had access. John Hall Wheelock, Harvard classmate and friend of Van Wyck Brooks, epitomizes that strain, and is one among many likely to strike readers now as simply wearisome. Mark Van Doren may superficially seem more approachable, but as Allen Tate realized, his "chief defect as a poet seems to be his ease of expression," a liability hardly unique to their generation (1983, 171). Tate shrewdly proposed the issue of defects as a defining characteristic of his peers: "One of the most valuable kinds of poetry may be deficient in imagination, and yet be valuable for the manner in which it meets its own defect" (122).[11] A potential intelligence can hardly do without the clues dropped along the way by such defects.

To read through the abundance of published poetry from the interwar period is to see how adventure and experiment offered practical ways of meeting the defect, and how that engagement led some to "write for a potential intelligence" in Williams's terms, while others sought the consolation of some local intelligence, despite its seeming lack of potentiality. Yet one comes to respect such modesty, particularly as it reveals the beneficent side of influence. For, unlike the "strong poets" celebrated by Harold Bloom, whose appropriations take such Byzantine turns, others are content to fashion a voice compliant with a prevailing idiom, dwelling in its overtone like a sanctuary. Yeats provided the template for many even after his death, succeeded for the wartime generation by Auden—in both instances reminders that a trans-Atlantic precedent often prevailed over native models. But, to quote the byline of Kreymborg's little magazine, "there are always others."

It is precisely those others who are at risk of disappearing altogether, apparently no longer even serviceable as footnotes. Clearly, a canonical profile casts an obliterating shadow on the past. So it's instructive to recognize that some of those who addressed contemporary poetry before midcentury still have merit, not least of which is the disclosure of quaint but serviceable perspectives. In *The American Way of Poetry* (1943), for instance, Henry Wells traced a legacy of regionalism becoming a "new nationalism" followed by a "new internationalism"; but rather than offer profiles of accomplishment, he focused on certain poets for how they illuminated the topic (4).[12] In *This Modern Poetry* (1935), Babette Deutsch covered realism, imagism, traditionalism, symbolism, "Filiations with the Metaphysicals," and vitalism and provides a survey of the postwar scene. Her fluid account settles on select poets for substantive but not prolonged deliberation, so at least twenty (including British) poets rise to the surface for five or ten pages until being submerged back into the general flow.[13] These approaches—more expansively undertaken by Kreymborg and Gregory/Zaturenska in their larger volumes—are in striking contrast to the monumentalizing tendency of postwar criticism. Before midcentury, the question of American poetry was current, fresh, and unsettled: not yet pickled.

I've advocated here for recovering a range of poets who may still be of interest to a potential intelligence.[14] A *potential* intelligence is contingent on the ecological variety of the poetry world and its emergent rather than foreclosed possibilities. The danger of any canonical configuration is the reduction of the field to a parade of show ponies. But Pound and Stevens and clan were never show ponies in the first place, and to cast them in the light of some "coherent splendor" (to cite the title of a book by Albert Gelpi [1987]) does a disservice to all poets, both canonical and forgotten. It's imperative to retain some working sense that the past is not over. It's understandable that the primary medium for negotiating the past is through prominent figures—representative men, Emerson called them. The lengthening bookshelf of published correspondence by Eliot, Pound, Frost, and others, along with new editions of primary works, continues to disclose new dimensions of familiar figures. But this enlargement *within* the canonical core also places a heavy lid over the portals through which a variable past might yet be encountered.

Recently puzzled by a resurgence of interest in John Berryman—a poet who had slipped into obscurity for decades—I discovered his centenary had prompted publishers to reissue his work. This sort of resuscitation has nothing to do with historical interest; instead, it consigns literary history to the roulette wheel of market forces. Material circumstances now impinge upon potential recovery in other ways, as librarians face shrinking shelf space. It's possible that most of the poets I've mentioned here are housed in off-site repositories, no longer available for interested browsing. The past is losing its visibility while the present is unmanageably enlarged, and the exponential expansion of twenty-first-century poetry threatens to obliterate the memory of so recent a past as the end of the twentieth. The first half of the twentieth century is further compressed by the weight of the canon convened in mid-century, the cost of which I've outlined here. Should we, then, resign ourselves to the inevitable and unintended obliteration of significant chunks of the past? Literary study in other historical periods has been revitalized by lost figures, whose recovery enhances the "thick description" endorsed long ago by Clifford Geertz (1973).[15] Comparatively speaking, the early twentieth century now risks being *more* obscure than the centuries that preceded it, in terms of any substantive record concerning the range of published poetry.

Why bother making the effort to retrieve these figures dusted over by time, these faintly human outlines resembling bodies covered by volcanic lava? First, as I've reiterated throughout, if "history" is really part of what we profess, we should exercise historical responsibility, which means examining primary materials. And that starts with a modicum of awareness of what those materials are. The recent spate of compendia purporting historical coverage fall far short of living up to that obligation. To fault the editors and the authors would be misguided, however, since they're clearly conforming to disciplinary norms. But norms breed habits, and bad habits sustained by disciplines tend to pass unnoticed as the acceptable decorum of professional behavior. So who's to gain by changing our ways? You'd no doubt be disappointed if I didn't say that there are riches to be unearthed, and there are. Will any of these forgotten titles dislodge *Harmonium* or *Observations*? No, but the whole enterprise isn't about canonical bullion. Shouldn't we sanction a basic human *interest* in the efforts of those we've never heard of who invested so much of their creative imagination in books we might actually read?

The layering of decade upon decade in modern times begins to resemble laminate wood pulp. The lesson from its application: structure is rendered invisible in the finishing stages. Plasterboard façades trump interior scaffolding. So the old (Heideggerian) question recurs: how do we propose to acknowledge this space as dwelling? Shall we consign the vanished legions of poets to a layer of duff on the forest floor? If so, how do we acknowledge their human sapience? Is it too much to accredit those whose labors filtrated poetry into the environment as *creators*? And, if we relegate them to a communal registry in which individuation is disallowed, who then are they? And, pertinently: Who are we? Shortly before she died, Gwendolyn Brooks insisted, "The first thing that any critic writing about the history of Black poetry should do is read the poetry" (Ford 2012, 369). The same now applies all around: *read the poetry*.

From Corset to Podcast

Or, the Condition of Poetry When Everybody Is a Poet

As a way of conserving message and insight, tradition is a model of utility. But it's also invested in repetition, shutting out noise, deviation, excess. Any system needs to be revitalized periodically, but a fresh input of energy harbors the risk of alterity. Put simply, innovation always looks like distortion, viewed from inside the communicative norms of a tradition, because a tradition conserves itself by means of performative criteria, whereas innovation is propositional, and primary among its propositions is a critique of first principles. This critique can pose simple but pointed questions: Does a poem have to rhyme? Must a novel tell a story? Should a picture replicate what we can see? From within the tradition, such impertinent questions have pestilential consequences—that is, until the consequences become the tradition. American poetry over the past forty years has finally caught up with early twentieth-century modernism, accepting dissonance as an intrinsic source of aesthetic energy. Does that mean disruption is "traditional"? Or does it suggest, instead, that innovation is part of a tradition?

American literary politics has been periodically haunted by the shadow of an easily revived anti-intellectualism. Resentful accusations of "difficulty" usually mean that the reader (or critic) doesn't want poetry to think. This attitude consigns the poem to a kind of hotel bar cocktail hour pianism, a strictly decorative role. It doesn't proscribe thoughts from the poem but asks that the thoughts be familiar enough so as not to disturb the atmosphere—that is, the idle chatter, the drinks, the flirting. Difficulty was embraced with a vengeance in the context of Black Mountain, but not always in the obvious terms of intellectualism. Robert Creeley's work, for instance, is as accessible as that of Carl Sandburg on the level of diction and vocabulary; but it renders even the simplest declarations instances of a moral challenge. Creeley's is a poetry difficult in its claims, and foremost among its claims is the thought of simplicity.

Difficulty challenges attention, and the New Criticism arose in part as a response to modernism, advocating close reading over historical and biographical approaches. But there's a different challenge in the case of work that's unresponsive to the protocols of that model of close reading, namely Language poetry. If not quite as sectarian in practice as Surrealism under André Breton's fearsome gaze, Language writing was still sufficiently integrated in its New York and Bay Area centers to exert pressure on the vast middle, at that time (the late seventies) dominated by the postconfessional idiom of the writing programs (several of the Language poets were in fact disaffected refugees from such programs). It was a time when the reigning ideology of self-expression maligned formalism as an impediment to authenticity, and free verse was embraced as the golden road to well-being. Apart from carving out a place for actual experimentation in poetry and launching the careers of Charles Bernstein, Lyn Hejinian, Ron Silliman, and others (including Susan Howe and Michael Palmer, commonly cited as Language poets even though they were not affiliated), the real impact of Language writing was on the next generation whose plunge into poetry coincided with the rise of the internet. Charles Olson's 1950 essay "Projective Verse" famously urged the use of the typewriter as a poet's prerogative; but his was a belated manifesto for what the modernists had long been doing, as documented by Hugh Kenner in *The Mechanic Muse*. Just as the typewriter began impinging on poetry a century ago, the internet has inaugurated a new poetic domain. Generally speaking, Language poetry primed the first internet generation of readers with a considerable tolerance for indeterminacy and respect for stochastic operations, while also exposing them to language pulverized by converging ideological tectonic plates.

Robert Bly once published an anthology of poems affirming the ecstatic immediacy of the cosmos and the everyday, calling it *News of the Universe.* Poetry now has to suffer the diffusion of the matrix, the network, the database, the code; it has to endure in the very temper of language a rapid modulation of signal to noise and noise to signal in order to keep pace with infusions of freshness and novelty that periodically replenish art and artifice with the vernacular. Now, in the wake of Ashbery and the Language poets, a certain toleration for cognitive dissonance has inflected American poetry; readers find it less objectionable when the sign not only fails to achieve union with what it signifies but is openly set adrift amid a swarm of other signifiers. We've passed from news of the universe to noise of the universe. And *noise*, it's worth recalling, is a technical term in information theory, denoting the antithesis of *signal*. Information theory is the developmental impetus behind computational technologies. And contemporaneous with Language poetry was the attempt by certain programmers to consign poetry to a realm of bytes and pixels.

Reviewing *The Waste Land* in 1923, John Crowe Ransom noted Eliot's indulgence in free verse, "the medium of a half-hearted and disillusioned art" (2001, 168). Ransom implied that those who forego metrics were laggards, social misfits lacking the "Can Do" attitude. The advent of digital poetry resurrected the preoccupation with form from another angle altogether: if poetry is to be identified with sheer hard work, the laurel should go to programmers rather than to adherents of the sonnet or the alexandrine. Verse formalists, of course, may dismiss digital encoding as beside the point. For them, poetry is hard work with words, not codes. But this debate goes back to the dawn of modernism. Edmund Wilson's famous 1931 book *Axel's Castle* (featuring *The Waste Land* as exhibit "A") is named after Villiers de l'Isle-Adam's play, in which a character famously remarks, "As for living, our servants can do that for us." Now it might be said of poetry, our computers can write it for us.

As Christopher Funkhouser has chronicled in *Prehistoric Digital Poetry*, its history can't be understood without a sense of its laborious, exasperating, and sometimes lunatic "prehistory." In 1973 Richard Bailey sounded a note from modernist avant-garde manifesto rhetoric: "Computer poetry is warfare carried out by other means, a warfare against conventionality and language that has become automatized" (2007, 79): Marx, Pound, and Shklovsky in one cluster grenade. A quarter century later, Eduardo Kac insisted that "a new poetry for the next century must be developed in new media" (2007, 255)—virtually repeating a chorus of proclamations from the modernist avant-garde ("Once there is a new form, a new content follows," in Alexei Kruchenykh's formulation [1988, 77]; "For a new world, a new art," declared Blaise Cendrars [1992, 91]). My point is not that Bailey and Kac are invalidated by their perhaps unwitting repetition of older vanguard slogans, but that the afterlife of those slogans has a parasitical relation to evolving technological media. It seems impossible to acclaim the new without repeating bygone acclamations. And this very tendency to valorize the future in the jargon of the past suggests what digital poetry is up against. No matter how vigorous and populous the domain of web-based poetry becomes, it will be segregated from the anthologies, the prizes, the routine scuttle of literary reputation—just as the avant-garde has often been.

The potential of digital poetry is succinctly indicated by Michael Joyce's observation: "Print text stays itself, electronic text replaces itself" (2007, 112). With this, the legacy of print fixity as a requisite of literacy is dissolved. Furthermore, the distinction between reader and writer is significantly blurred. In

Funkhouser's criteria, "'cyberpoetry' does not necessarily qualify as a cybertext if the reader's input makes little impact on the poem's construction" (241). For partisans of the print canon, this menacing prospect means that "readers" are mutating into something more like technicians, able to apply filters to their aesthetic input channels. Certainly, the animation and interactivity of digital poetry may be a compensatory sop to a "readership" disinclined to *read* in the first place. Some digital poetry has a greater affinity with video games and cartoons than with anything generally understood to be poetry. Still, the challenges to the conventions of poetry are inescapable when the digital environment reallocates the reader's share of the compositional process to a degree previously unimaginable. In a telling distinction, Funkhouser says "digital poems not only have a surface but an interface, often with transparent depths to explore" (148). These depths are reflected in the way the online Electronic Literature Directory organizes materials into eight categories: Hypertext, Reader Collaboration, Other Interaction, Recorded Reading/Performance, Animated Text, Other Audio/Video/Animation, Prominent Graphics, and Generated Text. Pondering these categories, one senses entire domains of critical vocabulary collapsing into irrelevance.[1] How does one begin to address texts about which it can be said, "There is no convenient way to reproduce the poetry; the only ways to document the program are by video or by screen capture" (231)?

Reading Funkhouser's chronicle, one can't help but admire the pluck and fortitude of pioneers who spent years to get a computer to produce faint simulacra of what a stoned undergraduate could produce circa 1969—but 1969 was also a year when computers helped put a man on the moon. Funkhouser's title is sagely chosen. Consider his account of Charles O. Hartman's experiments with his "meter checker" programs, AleaPoem and Scansion Machine:

> Hartman discovered that the complexities of combining human language and computer programming into a provocative yet understandable text is handled more capably in the creation of prose, which could be shaped into a poem. Thus, the AutoPoet's metrical filtering was removed and a writing tool called Prose was invented, which generated a series of syntactically correct sentences that were then edited into poetry. (68)

This could serve as an allegory of modern poetry in general. Throughout much of the twentieth century, various constituencies of verse culture launched fireballs of innovation, countered by strategic "returns" to the sestina, the sonnet, the heroic couplet, and the ballad—vehicles of proportional human value, reaffirming thoughts and feelings in a framework of reiterations. Now out of the computer a swarm of new terms emerges: cin(e)poetry, electronic po-

etry, holopoetry, hypermedia poetry, hypertextual poetry, infopoetry, net po-
etry, new media poetry, poetechnics, transpoetics, virtual poetry, web poetry,
polymedia, or in a phrase with unfortunate geriatric implications, "computer-
assisted literature" (Funkhouser 102).

Consider the assistance provided by a hypercard program by Jim Rosenberg called *Intergrams*. "A single stanzalike form emerges from a mass of unreadable text," writes Funkhouser. "Passing the cursor beneath the center of
the bottom box brings up the following:

> connection child seeing first flying helm spokes
> as madness feather floe knives
> owing us a smoother stunt haphazard other world
> safe enough without the stacked
> dimness peddler tether flight totem scrapings
> blown together for starting a memory fire." (166)

Language poetry acclimated readers to the diminished ratio of signal to noise
in passages like this, albeit before hypertext or digital programming methods
were widely available. If Language poetry now appears to be a bit passé for
younger readers, it's because there's something archaic about turning page
after page of printed books and encountering word salad that *plays* much better on a screen, in live action. One virtue of digital poetry is that the reader
is spared the subliminal expectation that a printed poem might end up in
the canon. How a canon of digital poetry will emerge and be handled I don't
know, but the term "monument" will surely seem an inept way of characterizing it. The future in pixels will not be monumental.

What, then, of the well-wrought urn? Will it yield the field to the well-
designed program? A workaround that generated much notoriety in the first
decade of the twenty-first century was conceptual poetry, its tenets amassed
in the robust anthology *Against Expression* edited by Craig Dworkin and
Kenneth Goldsmith (a rare instance in which the editorial apparatus invites
a closer reading than the works themselves). These tenets thrived on the
fact that the internet revitalized the lived experience of open-source culture
through file sharing and the fugitive if enlivening circulation of materials beyond the pale of copyright, which is a legal mechanism for endowing cultural
products with monumentality. With conceptualism, monumentality could
be alleviated from preexisting aesthetic burdens. "In conceptual writing the
idea or concept is the most important aspect of the work," according to Goldsmith. "When an author uses a conceptual form of writing, it means that all
of the planning and decisions are made beforehand and the execution is a
perfunctory affair. The idea becomes a machine that makes the text" (2005,

98). Christian Bök suggests such work is "a genre of word processing or data management, in which our tedium is the message," disclosing the reservoir of boredom latent whenever the medium is itself the message (2005, 66). Considering the excess or waste product of Goldsmith's books—which he serenely avows are unreadable—Bök reflects, "Words become disposable pollutants in a milieu of urban ennui, and language is sublime, not for its quality, but for its quantity—which in turn has an uncanny quality all its own" (65). The sheer bulk of Goldsmith's books makes a tacit mockery of the monumental impulse; and their putative unreadability draws attention to the constraints and opportunities for the act of reading in the different venues of print and screen. Goldsmith's megabooks in the archaic medium of print stand judiciously poised against the fleeting slipstream of the Twitter feed.

Rae Armantrout, affiliated with the Language group, won the Pulitzer Prize for poetry in 2010, a few years after she began publishing poems in the *New Yorker*, around the same time Dan Chiasson became the staff poetry reviewer for the magazine. As he said of her work at the time, "I just can't read it."[2] Chiasson's remark is an expression of personal taste, but it raises the issue of the unreadable. Since that time, there have been several challenges to American poetry, each of which is a variant of the unreadable. This is distinct from the category of the inadmissible, which is a canonical matter. At the most rudimentary level, "unreadable" is strictly a byproduct of time. That is, poetry now is mass produced by a statistically enormous number of poets, and keeping up with it all can only be achieved by sampling, watching trends, listening in on the latest chatter. It's a process in which actually *reading* poetry can be set aside, having the status of a bucket list destination you might not be able to afford, though you keep the link on your favorites tab just in case. The value of Goldsmith's avowedly unreadable books is that they force the issue of what one reads for. His is the genius of disavowal: "Faced with the unprecedented amount of available text," he says, "the problem is not needing to write more of it; instead, we must learn to negotiate the vast quantity that exists" (2011, 1).

Another domain of the unreadable has been theorized as "micropoetry" by Maria Damon—which, she says, "refers positively to the rawness of fragmentary, ephemeral, nonliterary, unintentional, or otherwise considered unviable poetry: doggerel, occasional verse by amateurs, and other paraliterary detritus," including "the banal that raises its spectrally perverse dread-head in the field of the 'poetic': the clunker, the cringe-worthy line, the obstinate appearance of the groaner in the field of niceness" (2011; 5, 194). Damon's advocacy of micropoetries makes her book, *Postliterary America*, more readable than the writing she studies. In a utopian vision, she imagines that "in postliterary studies, we'll be listening to the cries of infants with fetal alcohol syndrome and drug addictions…we'll be going to slams in bars and community centers, writing on housing project walls" (116). Damon is clearly determined to resituate poetry in a "postliterary" zone of the abject in which there's no overlap with anything that might end up in the canon. Still, she is venturing out into a public world that has a great appetite for poetry, an appetite indifferent to taste, expertise, or any criterion but use value. Damon quotes a woman who found solace in poetry while grieving for her daughter: "I don't know about words, but for poetry, it's the new love in my life since Ariel's death. I think there's something about poetry that says it without wearing you out by saying too much; especially for a grieving person to be given words that are really dense and full is really helpful. . . . It's like medicine, concentrated" (196).

This attitude toward poetry as medicinal tonic typifies another challenge to poetry today. If the conceptual is unreadable, and postliterary micropoetries are unheeded or unread, popular poetry is *over*-read, filtered through a web of enticements that have little to do with poetry and more to do with marketability. To approach this domain, it's convenient that Marjorie Perloff's book on conceptualist poetics, *Unoriginal Genius*, is echoed in the title *Ordinary Genius* by poet Kim Addonizio. Despite their titles they diverge in their audiences. This is reflected by the sales figures on Amazon, which soon after publication had *Unoriginal Genius* hovering around seventy-two thousand (meaning there were more than seventy thousand other titles ahead of it), while *Ordinary Genius* did very well at eighteen thousand (putting it in the vicinity of Beckett's *Endgame* and various books by Maxine Hong Kingston, Don DeLillo, and W. G. Sebald).[3] Why the difference? Well, it's possible that the University of Chicago Press didn't have the market reach of W. W. Norton, publisher of Addonizio's book, which also had the advantage of being in paperback. But there's another hook, reflected in Addonizio's subtitle: *Ordinary Genius: A Guide for the Poet Within*. Norton is in publishing as a business, and guidebooks are lucrative, especially guidebooks for aspiring poets. Another steady seller is *The Poetry Home Repair Manual* by former poet laureate Ted Kooser, who proudly confesses he's never been to Europe while offering advice about penning a successful Paris poem. But for sheer sales strength, these titles are left in the dust by Mary Oliver's *Poetry Handbook*, which regularly places in the two-to-four thousand range on Amazon, where it jostles with *The Poet's Companion: A Guide to the Pleasures of Writing Poetry* by Dorianne Laux and Kim Addonizio. The striking thing about the sales figures is that these and other how-to guides to poetry tend to be more commercially viable than actual books of poetry. Only Ginsberg's *Howl* can compete with *Poetry Handbook* and *The Poet's Companion*. A cynical appraisal of this data is that, in the United States, commerce always prevails; and while it's a truism that poetry doesn't sell, the truism is misleading. Poetry may not sell as much as John Grisham and the other idols of the bestseller list, but it certainly sells—and tutoring aspirational poets is profitable.

Poetry and commercial success were not incompatible terms in the nineteenth century, when Longfellow and Bryant were paid exorbitant sums for their poems. In 1874 Longfellow received a three-thousand-dollar advance from the *New York Ledger* for a single poem, a figure that in relative wages would be nearly four hundred thousand dollars today, a sum no living poet now could imagine (for annual salary, let alone a single publication), though it makes more sense to compare the author of *Hiawatha* with today's best-selling novelists. The familiar model of a poetry tradition in which modernism was the decisive seismic event obscures the persistence and continuity of the populist legacy typified by Longfellow. The traditional role of poetry in American public life has been largely extracanonical, located in the classroom, in civic affairs and ceremonies, in women's clubs, performances on the celebrity circuit, at bedtime, in church, in the domestic sphere, eventually on radio, and in Girl Scout camps—a scenario that gave rise to a popular anthology called *Magic Ring* based on young girls sharing memorized poems around the campfire. A 1927 collection edited by Edwin Osgood Grover, *The Nature Lover's Knapsack: An Anthology of Poems for Lovers of the Open Road*, suggests the Whitmanian expedience of this characteristically American outlook on poetry as practical aid to a robust life.

As a register of all this activity, consider an observation in 1911 by lawyer, poet (and future collaborator with Witter Bynner of the Spectra hoax in 1916, that endearing spoof of Imagism), Arthur Davison Ficke: "Just now there appear to be more writers of verse than there have been at any time in the history of literature." Ficke noted that the public service provided by all these poets was to create a sanctuary in which "the tired or baffled mind may resort for consolation and forgetfulness" (429, 432). A social measure of this service is reflected in the exemption of poets from the military draft during World War I because poetry was deemed an essential industry. In an article titled "The Poetry Cure: A Novel Remedy for Weary Hearts," readers of *Good Housekeeping* were told in 1925 that "poetry affords us a respite in which we may gather renewed strength for the old struggle to adapt ourselves to reality" (Schauffler 37).[4] Still, the mild-mannered world of poetic consolation was being eroded by modern life, and even *Good Housekeeping* couldn't ignore it. At the same time, Gene Stratton-Porter complained: "In the short cuts to conveniences, nothing has cost us as a nation such mental and spiritual poverty as the banishing of poetry and home-made music from our homes. It has left the door wide open for insidious moving pictures, for machine-made jazz music and cubist painting, all tending toward moral laxity" (200).

Stratton-Porter contrasts the youth of 1925—"motoring, dancing, and attending over-sexed picture shows" (35)—to the halcyon days of her own youth, with its classroom and fireside memorization of poems. "We were so full of poetry that we transposed it to fit the exigencies of life," she recalls. But now the "revolutionists are being given a hearing," she informs her readers (195).[5]

Remarkably, these bromides from the lingering parlors of Gilded Age America persisted to the end of the twentieth century. "Poetry is the highest expression in language of our deepest longings, and it represents our most concentrated efforts to find a language adequate to our experience," Jay Parini ponderously intoned in 1995 (18). The grandiosity of this posture—highest! deepest!—doesn't so much anthologize poems as recruit them as sanitary captions, inviting readers to bask in the reflected glory of surplus cultural capital, as one thing (the poem) stands in for another (a hierarchy of taste and privilege). It's a meritocracy of initiates, paved with seemingly egalitarian gestures of inclusion by the rhetoric of "we" and "ours," accompanied by the paternalistic vocabulary of "letting the poems speak for themselves." But letting the poems speak for themselves discloses a subterfuge, as poets don't generally write for anthologies, so we have to face the conundrum that anthologists surreptitiously repatriate poems to a promised land, a land to which the poems, said to be speaking "for themselves," are coerced into pledging allegiance to something else entirely. To get around the discrepancy between poetic practice and editorial needs, the editorial voice-over implies that the anthology is perennially preexistent, a golden land to which all poems aspire to return. This is the primary labor of the canonical anthology in particular: to *await the exemplary* so that, when it is certified, it appears to be fulfilling a prophecy, while filling a prescription. The tacit goal of these protocols is the formation and validation not of poems, but of canonical subjects. In another turn of the screw, the presumptive role of "representation" has been floridly enhanced by claims of multiculturalism and pluralism. As a result, anthologies prioritizing representation are driven by quantitative criteria, subject to social welfare and actuarial considerations masquerading as aesthetic decisions. The anthology is thereby repurposed from aesthetic clinic to public utility, servicing the needs of rehabilitation and resocialization for underserved populations. It is, of course, a fitting retort to all those anthologies filled with white men.

The genteel faith in the restorative power of poetry continues unabated today, thanks to the efforts of numerous poet laureates, the outreach programs devised by Dana Gioia in his tenure heading the National Endowment for the Arts, and that pandering phenomenon National Poetry Month (the corporate cynicism of which roused Charles Bernstein to propose an International Anti-Poetry Month [2011, 30]). Poetry advocacy in high quarters has been relentless in its pursuit (or recovery) of an audience at all costs. Billy Collins, poet laureate from 2001 to 2004, inaugurated a program called "Poetry 180: A Poem a Day for American High Schools," spawning several anthologies and a website designed to coax students into an unpressured appreciation of the art. "I am convinced," he said, "that for every nonreader of poetry there is a poem waiting to reconnect them to poetry" (2003, xxii). Extolling the virtues of reading poetry aloud as elocutionary training, and memorizing poems as mental gymnastics, Collins was resurrecting widespread practices from a century ago when poetry was a chastening yet inspiring voice in a public sphere in which anthologies played a crucial role—but not the canonical varieties that organize works by author. The consequential popular anthologies, instead, arrange poems thematically. The work of such anthologies is genuinely noncanonical: that is, their purpose is not to elevate the reputation of particular authors, though that might be a byproduct. Still, it's worth reflecting on the role played by such works in promoting a generalized public notion of poetry, since these anthologies are, in some real demographic sense, the only ones that count.

It's easy to dismiss these anthologies because they often seem so narrow in focus. But they often have fetching titles: *Never Before: Poems About First Experiences* (2005); *Varied Rhymes for Leisure Times* (1976); *We Are All Lesbians* (1973); *Deaf American Poetry* (2009); *Visit Teepee Town: Native Writings after the Detours* (1999); *Blood and Bone: Poems by Physicians* (1998); *Working Classics: Poems on Industrial Life* (1990); *Counting Caterpillars and Other Math Poems* (1998); *Sweeping Beauty: Contemporary Women Poets Do Housework* (2005); *My Pious Friends and Drunken Companions: Songs and Ballads of Conviviality* (1927); *Beyond Forgetting: Poetry and Prose about Alzheimer's Disease* (2009); *Congressional Anthology: Poems Selected by Senators and Representatives* (1958); *Hummers, Knucklers, and Slow Curves: Contemporary Baseball Poems* (1991); *Cowboy Poetry from Utah* (1985); *Unleashed: Poems by Writers' Dogs* (1995); *Homespun: An Anthology of Poetry by the General Federation of Women's Clubs* (1936); and *Death in the Dark: A Collection of Factual Ballads of American Mine Disasters* (1974). For the general reader, this list would a straightforward menu, inviting access to poetry on the basis of a designated topic. It's easy to sort these anthologies in terms of identity politics, moral aspiration, or sheer novelty—and that's the point. Very few people want to read poetry just because it's poetry. If they want it at all, it's because of what poems are thought to deliver.

There is a sizeable audience for books offering the seemingly straight up, tell-it-like-it-is approach of radio personality Garrison Keillor, who produced three bestselling anthologies: *Good Poems* (2003), *Good Poems for Hard Times* (2005), and *Good Poems, American Places* (2011). Each volume offers a dozen or more thematic clusters, with titles like "The Place Where We Were Naked," "A Comforting Immensity," and "A Sort of Rapture." "Poetry is church," Keillor assures readers of *Good Poems for Hard Times*, and "American poetry is the truest journalism we have" (xix)—has the pulpit ever been nudged so close to the press? "The meaning of poetry is to give courage," he insists (xviii). "A poem is not a puzzle that you the dutiful reader is obliged to solve. It is meant to poke you, get you to buck up, pay attention, rise and shine, look alive, get a grip, get the picture, pull up your socks, wake up and die right" (xvii). Keillor is drawing on an old legacy of poetry as moral uplift, typified by *Silver Linings: Poems of Hope and Cheer* (1927). "To all lovers of the helpful, the practical, the inspiring in poetry, is this volume cordially dedicated," writes one editor, "with the hope that its contents may encourage many to press on in the overcoming of obstacles, the conquering of discouragement, the inspiring to greater service in behalf of our great, throbbing, common humanity." To aid the reader, the editor of *Poems of Pep and Point for Public Speakers* (1918) organizes the contents in ninety-six categories, ranging from Ambition and Contentment to Pessimism, Restlessness and Zeal.[6] So pervasive was this kind of topical orientation that even *The Poet's Tongue*, edited by W. H. Auden with John Garrett in 1935, provided a handy index, although given Auden's formalist penchant most of the entries itemize types of poems and meters. It's worth reflecting that Auden's public eminence in his lifetime was due more to his trafficking in this legacy of populism than his coterie apparition as a modernist.

The market for such books has been constant. The celebrated rivalry between Donald Allen's *New American Poetry* and Donald Hall's *New Poets of England and America* obscures that fact that neither could complete in the marketplace with *The Family Album of Favorite Poems* (1959), its sixteen sections running the homespun gamut from "Just Folks" and "Sound the Trumpets!" to "The Faith Within Us" and "The Children's Hour." The poetry of uplift consistently trumped anything called "new." Another specimen from 1960 is *The Healing Power of Poetry* by Smiley Blanton (wonderful name), with a foreword by self-help guru Norman Vincent Peale. Blanton prints so many poems in their entirety that it might as well be an anthology, but the running commentary makes the book pass for a guide to the consolations of poetry—or "What Poetry Can Do For You," the title of the opening chapter. Each chapter specifies a circumstance: "When You Need Courage," "When You Are Lying Awake at Night," "When You Are in Love," and so on. There is no more telling emblem of the persistence of this legacy—its devout hope in the power of the word—than Edward Hirsch's *How to Read a Poem and Fall in Love with Poetry* (1999).

The bracing stimulus of the conceptual, the ethnographic challenge of postliterary micropoetries, and the vast tide of populist consolations, taken together, constitute an indelible mug shot of the art of poetry. But where are the poets in all this?—by which I mean the authors of roughly two thousand new books of poetry published annually for the American market.[7] It's not implausible that some diehard could read all these books, at a pace of five and a half daily. But when does this hypothetically stalwart trooper manage to absorb anything published last year, the year before last, and the preceding train of years (and centuries)? The answer is *never*. Not possible. Like Charlie Chaplin's tramp in *Modern Times*, the incessant interlocking gears of the dynamo permit no idle moments, no time to play catch-up. It's all or nothing, and the instant is all. Presumably, nobody tries to keep up to this extent and, judging by the readers I've consulted, the most avid may absorb no more than a couple hundred titles a year: in other words, 10 percent maximum—a figure that should chasten any pretense to speak with authority on the state of poetry today.

Anthologies fitfully persist, of course, but it seems unlikely that anything resembling the "anthology wars" of sixty years ago will erupt again. One reason is demographic. In 1960, when two anthologies famously duked it out—the American population was 178 million.[8] With the figure now approaching 330 million, it would take at least four anthologies (with no overlap of contents) to begin to replicate that distant moment when the Beats and other outsiders clamored at the gates of official verse culture. But such a simple numerical calculation is misleading: one would also have to factor in the vast increase in percentage of the college educated population, and within that educated portion, take into account the graduates of creative writing programs (of which there are now nearly five hundred in the United States, most established in the past forty years—a fact that presages some future revolt like the Romantics' distrust of art academies in Europe, which had grown from nineteen in 1720 to more than a hundred by 1800 [Blanning 2011, 13]). There are other reasons that make a return of the anthology wars unlikely. Demographic proliferation of poets has been accompanied by a corresponding proliferation of constituencies. The old paradigm of insiders and outsiders, establishment figures and renegades, makes little sense now.

Purveyors of populism would be dismayed to learn that dedicated readers of new poetry are generally poets themselves, but there's another catch. Most poets now teach. The colleges and universities that offer graduate degrees in poetry employ around two thousand faculty members to support the cause. But the institutions granting higher degrees are more than doubled when we factor in the number of undergraduate programs. All these folks must comply with the norms for faculty in academic institutions, filing annual reports of their activities, in which the most important component is publication.

With that in mind, I don't need to spell out the truly exorbitant numbers involved. In a positive light, this has sanctioned a surfeit of small presses—the hundreds represented by Small Press Distribution—to say nothing of all the Webzines (the distinction between paper and pixels is quickly evaporating). From another perspective, it has remade poetry on the model of scholarship. In academia, the syndrome of specialization has long prevailed, and scholars customarily publish in specialist journals and speak at specialist conferences to a modest constituency. It's rare for scholarly books to sell more than a few hundred copies. Coincidentally, this was about the norm for poetry books even before poets were absorbed into the universities. So you could say it's a natural fit. Poets and scholars alike are specialists, speaking to the converted.[9]

Poets in the academy tend to behave as scholars do, attentive to the work of their peers, responding to paradigm shifts, research protocols, and so forth. With poets, though, there's rarely a research agenda to speak of, so attention tends to settle on who's doing what in the poetry world. The "poetry world" is a big place, too big, so how do poets know what to read? Pragmatically speaking, the younger grad-student poet or junior poet-professor is now plugged into social media sites, navigational tools for keeping abreast of a manageable domain *within* the poetry world. Since you can't read everything, you read what friends and colleagues are reading; or you find a conversation that feels agreeable. These conversations, though, unfolding under the pressure cooker of careerism, legislate a style of reading once, quickly and opportunistically, for the purposes of the conversation itself. It's hard to imagine what might have become of T. S. Eliot's *Love Song of J. Alfred Prufrock* or Marianne Moore's *Observations* if they'd been filtered through the instant processing social network matrix. The pace of assimilation now thrives on the quick read, the surface glance, the exhilarated skim.

Given this situation, I sense a looming limit to basic paradigms: the integrity of an individual poet's work, and the virtue of an historical approach to the study of poetry. What we face today is a paradigm-changing state of affairs having to do with demographics. There are now so many widely published poets that it's no longer feasible to keep track of them. But they are very busy keeping track of one another, though at the risk of losing the historical sense altogether. In the realm of canonical statements on the subject of the canon, nothing is more canonical than "Tradition and the Individual Talent" by T. S. Eliot, particularly his pronouncement that "the historical sense compels a man to write not merely with his own generation in his bones, but with a feeling that the whole of the literature of Europe from Homer and within it the whole of the literature of his own country has a simultaneous existence and composes a simultaneous order" (1954, 14). Poets now write with a genuinely enlarged sense of their own generation in their bones, but with an attenuated sense of "tradition" in Eliot's sense. Their world is the *tradition of the moment.*

A plausible retort to my diagnosis is that the crises of the present are so unprecedented that the historical sense is of little account. The historical record obviously provides examples of environmental degradation, political travesties, tribal and racial rivalries, ghost dance religions, and the gold rush mentality of economic opportunism; but what's new is the global stage on which these depredations now play out. The role of tweets and instant messaging during the "Arab Spring" in the Middle East demonstrated the historical effectiveness of collective chatter; and why should poetry be immune from such a revolution in communication? Maybe poetry is entering a new planetary brain, a hive mind in which individual consciousness counts for little more than its immediate participation in the whole. The danger of herd mentality looms up in the face of linguistic collectivism, of course, but poetry still stands apart from the cynical platitudes of political discourse and the pabulum of journalism, whether state controlled or entrepreneurial (I think of Adrienne Rich's call for a poetry "not drawn from the headlines but able to resist the headlines" [2001, 108]). Kevin Young names this condition of forced proximity "Deadism," comparing the poet's prospect to that of the narrator of the Billy Wilder film *Sunset Boulevard*: "Deadism like those movies with voiceovers that sound not only dead, but by the end you find out are from a dead man: not ready for my close-up, but the one floating in the pool, the one who knows what he can't know but tells us anyway" (2007, 192). I like the enigma Young gets at here: *the one who knows what he can't know but tells us anyway* sounds like a real prospect for poetry—or, at least, commentary about poetry. In his statement for the same anthology, *American Poets in the 21st Century*, Joshua Clover writes: "Standing around talking to everyone isn't poetry, but I like a poem that makes that seem like a good idea" (2007, 163). Is this an instance of cynical hope? Hopeful cynicism? Or hope, plain and simple? Whatever it is, Clover may be onto something.

Standing around talking is old school, face to face, a respite from the lukewarm perpetual bath of "connectivity" in which we're all immersed, through the internet, cell phones, a network of constant "feeds." These multimedia feeds have induced a sense of expectation, investing the *moment-by-moment* with an unprecedented prominence. *Now* is always a neon now, with a cartoon *Pow!* hanging in a thought (or thoughtless) balloon. Never before in the history of our species has it been possible to know so much about the moment we're living in. The great and terrible temptation is to know nothing else but this, this very moment, now, filled with tweets and instant messages. This dramatic expansion of the bandwidth risks eradicating the historical sense, but at the same time it's a unique opportunity.

The challenge is: how to get out from under the traditional model of high and low that's now blended into the enormous smoothie of the cultural norm, the vast bland middle. The challenge for an artist is figuring out how to shed the peer pressure so effortlessly acquired by those generational holding cells created by education, by target marketing and all the cultural options that pinpoint you as baby boomer, Gen X, or whatever. And when human identity is tabulated by the numerical saturation of Facebook "friends," the *friend effect* now spills over into everything else, along with the "like" toggle. Reviewing two ecopoetry anthologies several years ago, I realized that as soon as I found a poem I liked I feel slightly defiled, as if I'd been shoehorned into a receptive frame of mind because of its topicality—as if the poem were a blinking sign saying Earth at Risk: Chip in Now!

The solipsism of ubiquitous communicability is something we see everywhere all the time, as the cell phone is on its way to becoming a cranial implant. Social networking is rendering the instant canonical—and perishable—moment by moment. For poets, the scope of the contemporary is enlarged to a previously unthinkable degree, while the past risks evaporation. But how is the past to be honored, respected, and retrieved without resorting to the old paradigm of a handful of titanic figures—especially when the new sensibility seems to have a healthy mistrust of that antidemocratic paradigm? This is the stirring challenge, and the only tool at our disposal is the past as such—not its monuments but its chastening diversity. Our condition "of being numerous" will always benefit from the vitality of the various, a vitality that rarely comes from the expected quarter, the appointed dignitary. For my part, I'll be on the lookout for any principled defense against the mesmerizing glamour and coercive eugenics of canon-mongering that seems always to be with us like that Mephistophelian poodle that follows Doctor Faust home. Unoriginal genius says: ditch the Faustian pact, and feed the dog.

Bringing in the Trash
The Cultural Ecology of Dada

THIS COMPOST (2002) was first drafted in 1980–1981 while I was living in an unheated cabin in northern New York, with a wonderful view over the broad Hudson River and the legendary Catskills on the far shore. Under duress as the weather turned cool in the fall, I began to harvest firewood from fallen timber. I had only a handsaw and an axe, Neolithic tools. This labor taught me the wisdom of the adage that a man cutting firewood warms himself twice. During the autumn months I spent most of my waking hours cutting and hauling wood. During the course of the year I kept a fire lit in my mind with the handful of books I'd brought east with me for the year. These were collections of poetry by Robert Duncan, Charles Olson, and Louis Zukofsky, works I loved and at that point thought I shouldn't be without, so I had them at hand.

A curious thing happened as the season progressed: I began to notice that certain passages by one poet might be imperceptibly slipped into the work of another. Passages from different poems could be transposed, sifted into an emergent palimpsest. Now this was very strange, since these three poets were as unlike as I could imagine: Olson's rhetorical bluster and bravado, and his fascination with anacolutha (a rhetorical technique for changing the grammar of a sentence midway), could hardly be farther from Duncan's propensity for mannerism and courtly imitation of verse traditions. And Zukofsky was another thing altogether. If Olson was a bear, and Duncan a flamingo, Zukofsky was an armadillo or a tortoise, flaunting his impenetrable shell. Nonetheless, I found sections of their poems slicing off of their own accord and falling like the Greenland ice pack into the North Atlantic.

What I had unwittingly discovered was the procedure that fuels my book: citing extracts of poems without identifying the authors, and composing (or *composting*) block or cluster citations as poem-extracts of their own, letting the lines of poems find affinities with others, giving them the same integrity and velocity that physicists accord atomic particles. As compositional practice, I was assenting to the magisterial labor of reallocation that works its magic on all perishable material on this planet. This is not only the grand theme but the mulching medium of *Finnegans Wake*, the greatest book the fewest people have read. In it, Joyce puts the question: "So why, pray, sign anything as long as every word, letter, penstroke, paperspace is a perfect signature of its own?" (1968, 115). This Joycean doctrine of signatures loosens the grip of personal identity, leaving in its wake a whole world to be regained.

My composting procedure was sanctioned in part by a word I coined around 1975:

w reading

in which the reader's share in the creative process was given a nod by borrowing the "w" from *writing*. In my devotion to poetry that was most meaningful to me, I couldn't help but participate in the composition rather than enshrine it, or put it under a quarantine of unassailable reverence. Composting poetry was a process of filtration that included infiltration, the uncanny experience of occupying another person's place and, as it were, mouthing their words. Of course this is what we normally do when reading a text. Poetry is hugely infested with tropes, and *tropos* means *turn*. Composting poetry is turning over, as well as overturning.

Now, what does this have to do with Dada? At the risk of going even farther afield, I want to approach the subject of Dada by way of an Emersonian theme. Ralph Waldo Emerson's first book bore the simple title *Nature*, but there's nothing simple about his understanding of it. "It is a mischievous notion that we are come late into nature; that the world was finished a long time ago," he observes in "The American Scholar" (1983, 57–58). A *mischievous notion*. His target here is in part the creationist myth of the religion he forswore after he decided he could no longer administer the sacrament. Attuned to the great geological discoveries of his day, Emerson was moved by the realization that nature has no primal or original condition. "Nature is a mutable cloud which is always and never the same," he observed in a later essay, "History" (1983, 113). *Always* and *never* are two chastening adverbs, especially paired like this. The planet is an ongoing metamorphosis, as likely to swallow up *Homo sapiens* as it did the dinosaurs. "Life is eating us up. We shall be fables presently," he remarks in his memorable essay, "Montaigne" (1983, 459). This is Emerson's version of memento mori. Think of the terms he uses here: it's not death that will claim us, but life that's eating us up—a thermodynamic observation. He has another formulation for this process in his essay on "Fate": "Life is an ecstasy," drawing on the etymological basis of the term ecstasy, meaning to get outside oneself. "Each creature puts forth from itself its own condition and sphere, as the slug sweats out its slimy house on the pear-leaf, and the woolly aphides on the apple perspire their own bed, and the fish its shell" (1983, 691, 692). Similarly, humans excrete or exteriorize what we call *culture*.

We tend to approach culture as a record of accretions, like a coral reef. And yet cultural history is conceived as a hierarchy. A symphony by Beethoven may be regarded as a preeminent event in cultural history, but not the invention of the poker, or the fermentation of milk to make yogurt. Much of what has passed for cultural history has been prejudicial, a reflection of the "old chronology of selfishness and pride to which we have too long lent our eyes," Emerson called it in *The Conduct of Life* (1860), observing: "The word of ambition at the present day is Culture" (1983, 721). He meant this in a derogatory sense at a time when upwardly mobile Americans (like Emerson himself) indulged in a European tour to acquire Culture, a term Ezra Pound would later spell "Kulchur" in his flamboyant *Guide* of 1938—a book as infused with "stream of consciousness" as that of his Irish friend's *Ulysses*. In it, Pound offers an intriguing definition of his subject: "Knowledge is NOT culture," he says. "The domain of culture begins when one HAS 'forgotten-what-book'" (134). That is, culture consists of everything we know without footnotes, without provenance, without authority, or authorization. Culture is the solution we paddle around in like fish in the sea, a completely encompassing environment that resists scrutiny as such. We tend to identify culture with the things we can detect and single out. But to do so is to neglect the holistic apprehension of an environmental totality. To speak of cultural ecology, then, is to summon the unseen, the inscrutable, the unnoticed, and overlooked.

But how do we perceive the undetectable? How do we comprehend culture as fully as it comprehends us? "Of what use is genius," Emerson asks, "if the organ is too convex or too concave and cannot find a focal distance within the actual horizon of human life?" (1983, 329). This horizon, as Emerson understood it, does not consist of village gossip and human affairs. The very term *horizon* suggests an outer limit. The "actual horizon of human life" is a strict reciprocity of organism and environment. When Emerson writes in *Nature* that "the whole of nature is a metaphor of the human mind," he's not denying the exterior world but insisting on its fusion with our minds, which may also be a source of *con-fusion*. "The ruin or the blank that we see when we look at nature, is in our own eye. The axis of vision is not coincident with the axis of things, and so they appear not transparent but opaque" (18, 41).

Emerson, like William Blake, was all about cleansing the doors of perception for the sake of this alignment whereby the vision is conversant equally with its source in human awareness and its resource in the encompassing world. The problem, Emerson perceived, is that we rely on culture to arrange the alignment and adjust the focus; but we turn to art to rectify the ravages that creep into the apparatus. But what's the cost of this instrumentalist supposition?

In *The Culture of Redemption* (1990), Leo Bersani observes that "art's beneficently reconstructive function in culture depends on a devaluation of historical experience and of art. The catastrophes of history matter much less if they are somehow compensated for in art, and art itself gets reduced to a kind of superior patching function" (1). Bersani is following a path staked out by Theodor Adorno. Railing against those "Sunday institutions that provide solace," clichés that "rub against the wound that art itself bears," Adorno insists on perpetuating the wound, not the Sunday consolation (1997, 2). The wound of historical catastrophe deflects the gaze of the artist like the head of the Gorgon pulsing with serpents. Art can only look in Perseus's deflecting mirror, not directly at the horror. But this is tantamount to saying art settles for the illusory rather than the real. The agony of modern art, wrote Adorno, "is largely that it wants to shake off its illusoriness like an animal trying to shake off its antlers" (102). Adorno was wary of that proud figure of the antlered buck, its head mounted on the hunting lodge wall. He repeatedly turns to the figure of the animal when he wants to clarify what's at stake in the artwork as a mode of sentience with a life of its own, not a prize specimen or a consoling Sunday institution. Against the massive accretion of success compounding success in a constant escalation of all stakes to one colossal end—utopia and/or Götterdämmerung—Adorno valued the intransigence of art, convinced that "Art is magic delivered from the lie of being the truth" (1974, 222). In "the open-air prison which the world is becoming," he wrote, truth is uttered only under duress (1981, 34). The poem, the painting, and the sonata converge (and take refuge) in the beast, an autotelic manifestation beyond coercion. "In existing without any purpose recognizable to men, animals hold out, as if for expression, their own names, utterly impossible to exchange. This makes them so beloved of children, their contemplation so blissful. I am a rhinoceros, signifies the shape of the rhinoceros" (1974, 228). This rhinoceros makes an encore in Adorno's uncompleted opus, *Aesthetic Theory*, contributing to this resonant definition: "Ausdruck ist der Blick der Kunstwerke"—Expression is the gaze of artworks (1970, 172; 1997, 112). Even though their creaturely properties are coveted, farmed, and bred, living animals remain *outsiders*, models for Adorno of the instructive intransigence of an artwork: intransigent in its animal sapience.

Intransigence means different things in different places. In the American context, given its compulsive fascination with outlaw figures, cultural conditioning has penetrated most deeply by means of mass media exhortations not to belong but to be different. This is the back door whereby *difference* has become a continuous investment opportunity. In this milieu it's exceedingly difficult to grasp Adorno's insistence that the function of the arts (its "functionlessness") is to provide an area outside commercial accountability: "The necessity of art…is its nonnecessity," he says (1997, 251). We're so accustomed to a rhetoric proclaiming the cultural benefits of an artistic legacy that art as such becomes tainted with the jargon of special pleading, reduced to a component of the service industry. Instrumental reasoning and commercialism have obscured our most unique endowment, which is a cultural reserve of vitality not dedicated in advance to specific application.

Of course, I'm not under the illusion that the arts are anywhere consigned to conspicuous applicability. But the humanities in general are accorded an honorific status as repositories of wisdom and insight, a status that renders them susceptible to institutional manipulation, procedures of rank and order; and this in turn filters down to the level of human ambition, the arousal of vanity, and the general syndrome diagnosed (1954) by the cantankerous Wyndham Lewis as the "demon of progress in the arts." At this point it will be useful to turn to Dada, with its reputation as an anti–art art movement.

Dada has gotten a bad rap, even if in some quarters having a bad rap is the best rep. If you check out definitions or characterizations of Dada, you'll often find it shackled to words like "nihilism," "cultural despair," "irreverence," and so on: "a feast of absurdity," writes eminent cultural historian Peter Gay (2008, 341). Such terms, suggesting adolescent peevishness, prejudicially ignore the perspective proposed by Marcel Janco. Janco was one of the founders of Cabaret Voltaire in Zurich in 1916, where Dada was haphazardly inaugurated. Fifty years later, Janco proposed that Dada had two speeds, the first involving revolt and negation, succeeded by the second speed, the creative. "Through an understanding of prehistoric art, children's art, primitive art, folk arts," Janco recalls, "we came to the conclusion that the crusade for the return to the Promised Land of creativity was Dada's most important discovery" (1971, 37). But notice the resources of this creativity: prehistory, the child, the demotic, and the vernacular. They all converge on anonymity.

The anonymous is what lacks or withholds a name; but if anything, our culture is obsessed with names. The taste for gossip permeates it from high to low. As pioneers of disinformation in the media complex that we still inhabit, the Dadaists include among their predecessors Henry David Thoreau, who lampooned the greed for gossip in *Walden*. "Hardly a man takes a half hour's nap after dinner, but when he wakes he holds up his head and asks, 'What's the news?'" (1992, 63). Consequently, Thoreau writes, "We are eager to tunnel under the Atlantic and bring the old world some weeks nearer to the new; but perchance the first news that will leak through into the broad, flapping American ear will be that the Princess Adelaide has the whooping cough" (35–36). The spurious "news" he ridicules has swollen incalculably since his time, and it can now be said that users of portable media devices have unwittingly become hawkers of "info-tainment." The circulation of newspapers has declined in tandem with the rise of Facebook and Twitter and YouTube. We're now de facto signers of an hourly manifesto attesting to the whooping cough of Princess Adelaide. The surfeit of linguistic garbage is no longer external, out there in the environment, whether as graffiti tags on railway trestles and subway conduits or as headlines on tabloids and the steady swag of political agitation on American talk radio. Instead, it circulates with a steady pulse through our hand-held gadgets. It's all in our hands. We're the gatekeepers—which is to say, we open the floodgates merely by pressing an *on* button.

Guilty as charged: this is how Dada understood its own complicity in the glut of media blather. In striking contrast to the highbrow disdain of the press adopted by their artistic peers, the Dadaists added the disarming aspect of a recognizable invitation to the traditional vanguard arsenal of invective and insult. To the timeworn vanguard gesture, *épater la bourgeoisie*, they added quintessentially bourgeois strategies derived from journalism, advertising, and finance. Dada arose in Zurich in 1916 as a convulsive response to the calamity of the First World War, which on all sides rode a wave of bourgeois self-affirmation fueled by self-delusion. Raoul Hausmann, addressing the bourgeoisie directly, offered this diagnosis: "You are the victim of your views, your so-called education, which your whole generation gets in great chunks from the history books, the book of civil law and a few classics" (2006a, 93). Exposure to heroic idealism from a standardized education, the Dadaists realized, was a recipe for war. Richard Huelsenbeck observed that in Germany "the most absurd idolatry of all sorts of divinities is beaten into the child in order that the grown man and taxpayer should automatically fall on his knees when, in the interest of the state or some smaller gang of thieves, he receives the order to worship some 'great spirit'" (1951b, 43)—the trouble being that in Germany the world historical agents of "Geist" were the Kaiser, the munitions industry, the bankers, and the general staff. At the Berlin Dada Fair in 1920, one of the slogans on the walls read: "DADA is the voluntary destruction of the bourgeois world of ideas" (Höch 1971, 72).

Worship of the "great spirit" in Germany had its local variants of course in each of the combatant nations. And this gave fuel to the Dadaist anti-art initiative. This has been somewhat misconstrued; certainly, the Dadaists did not desist from making pictures, though for the most part they did spurn traditional materials. They sold their works not as "art" but as "Dada products." These products were a send-up of the art market, which Hausmann described as "the barrel organ of pure poetry, painting and music [that] played in Germany on the level of an extremely efficient business venture." However, he thought, this was a debasement of anything he valued. Above all, he thought, art should not be "an aesthetic harmonization of bourgeois ideas of ownership" (2006b, 88). "The bourgeois must be deprived of the opportunity to 'buy up art for his justification.' Art should altogether get a sound thrashing," suggested Huelsenbeck. Accordingly, the Dadaists exposed the fraudulent role of art as "a moral safety valve"—"a large-scale swindle" (1951b, 44, 43). "Dada is forever the enemy of that comfortable Sunday Art which is supposed to uplift man by reminding him of agreeable moments. Dada hurts," Huelsenbeck clarified (1951a, 281).

Huelsenbeck and Hausmann were agitators in a Berlin milieu colored by street combat between rival political parties in the Spartacist uprising at the end of the Great War. But even in tranquil, pacifist Switzerland Hans Arp was outraged: "The conception of art that has upheld the vanity of man is sickening," he concluded (1971, 30). "The confusion of our epoch results from an overestimation of reason. We wanted an anonymous and collective art," Arp later recalled. In the catalogue of a 1915 exhibition (before Dada even existed) he wrote: "These works are constructed with lines, surfaces, forms, and colors. They strive to surpass the human and achieve the infinite and the eternal. They are a negation of man's egotism." For Arp, who would gladly have been of that anonymous tribe of medieval cathedral builders, the prideful domain of Art was a danger. For the modern art market, "Instead of anonymity there was celebrity and the masterpiece" (1971, 24).

The predicament identified by Arp and the other Dadaists was this: how can one make art when artworks are commonly understood (to use the title by Norman Mailer) as *advertisements for myself*? (Mailer had a predecessor in Johannes Baader, who used that title—"Reklame für mich"—in the second issue of the Berlin journal *Dada* in 1919.) In addition to being banners of personal egotism, the Dadaists knew quite well that artistic achievements are also held up as cultural triumphs, that they are compelled to signify on behalf of some constituency; so poems, paintings, symphonies become anthems of national soul, expressions befitting a particular race, class, tribe. But where other artists unconsciously or unheedingly submit to this process of collective vanity, the Dadaists emphatically did so, substituting for the masterpiece their empty cipher, "Dada," which they said meant nothing, insisting it was stupid and worthless, thereby pinning an ignominious bit of trash to the pinnacle of cultural striving, sullying the dignity of cultural institutions with the pretense that anything (a urinal, for instance) could be art. Not only was a Dada journal in Cologne given the title *Stupid* (in English, in occupied Rhineland), the Parisian Dadaists trumpeted themselves as "complete idiots": "All my friends…are every bit as stupid as me," wrote Philippe Soupault in a manifesto. "I am writing a manifesto because I have nothing to say," and he took care to add, "this manifesto is absolutely stupid" (2006, 185). "Dada is working with all its might to introduce the idiot everywhere," insisted Tristan Tzara (1951b, 94). Of course, these manifestos were read in public to a paying audience, which couldn't help but feel duped by open declarations of malfeasance, incompetence, and disinterest by the performers.

The art of public relations, that corporate outlook, was recognized by the Dadaists as a pervasively internalized code of expectations. As Kurt Schwitters affirmed, "Advertising is the sign of our times" (2006, 292). In addition to the usual subjects, "advertising and business are also elements of poetry," insisted Tzara (1951a, 78). In one of countless press notices on Dada we find the acknowledgement that "in the fine art of advertising their genius should be admitted even by their enemies" (Huelsenbeck 1993, 52). The entire edition of *Jedermann sein eigener Fußball*—seventy-six hundred copies—was sold in a single afternoon from a horse-drawn cart parading around Berlin, accompanied by a brass band and the Dadaists themselves hawking their individual contributions. In Berlin, Dada was pitched as an advertising agency: "Advertising is the road to success. . . . Your adverts must become more *psychological . . .* Our advertising *lacks any scruples . . . Bring your problems to us. Dada* is just what you need" (Huelsenbeck 1993, 162). This is simultaneously tongue-in-cheek and tongue protruding, in a gesture befitting the postwar calamity of hyperinflation in Germany, in which "dada is the only savings bank that pays interest for eternity," as the Dadaists pledged (Central Office 2006, 86). "When you are dead, dada is your only nourishment." In Tzara's appeal: "subscribe to Dada, the only loan that brings in nothing" (1951b, 96).

As my account suggests, Dada was a participatory staging of the motto *non serviam*, refusing to be of service even as it aggressively offered its services, confident that the public would find its services repugnant. What Dada offered, after all, was garbage, trash, refuse, the dregs of the social order. Reversing the conventional gesture whereby we take out the trash, benignly offering it to a public utility, Dada wanted to bring in the trash. What can we learn from this salutary impudence? First, it puts a spotlight on the system of compromises art undergoes as it enters the public sphere. In *The American Poetry Wax Museum* (1996), I documented what was at stake in the canonizing procedures whereby Great Authors are anointed—and, of course, how the preanointed jockey for position in the lineup. Between the *Wax Museum* and *This Compost* (2002) I charted two domains: one in which poetry is all about the proper name, the figure of the poet, and another in which the names dissolve, or sift into and out of one another—a realm in which the name Olson, say, sheds its transitory associations with the Democratic Party and Black Mountain College and even Gloucester, Massachusetts, and circulates instead like geological phenomena, a watershed or a seismic fault.

Letting the names go can be a liberating way to approach culture, because culture is in so many senses a constellation of names, like the quasi-astrological chart produced in Paris by Dadaists on the verge of becoming Surrealists (cf. "Erutarettil" in *Littérature* new series 11–12, October 1923). The names don't go away, however much we let go of them. Culture is a cenotaph; its mortuary ruins are nearly all we have of it, at least in its officiously documented versions. A museum, Adorno points out, is etymologically akin to mausoleum (1981, 175). Whether pondering paintings on a wall, sculptures on pedestals, or headstones in a graveyard, what do we see but a parade of names? The proper name is a pressure brought to bear on the exemplary (certified) artwork to radiate, in its sublime power, a salutary *compensation*. The work, then, is not only in certain circumstances answerable to the claims of instrumental reason; it is also burdened with an instrumental unreason, a pledge of charismatic entitlement. As we know from the case of Paul Celan, even the raw cry of anguish can be awarded a certificate in suffering, its unappeasable singularity rendered stereotypical the moment that claims of universality are made on its behalf. But there are no entitlements to significance, as Richard Poirier puts it, only enticements (1992, 146).

Consider as a superbly ecological enticement the following statement: "Dada devotes itself to nothing: not love, not work. It is unforgivable of someone to leave a trace of his time on earth," wrote André Breton in a manifesto called "Dada Geography" (1996, 44). This bracing recommendation to leave no trace is of course one that Breton himself didn't heed, leaving behind his own writings and spawning a broad swath of Surrealist activities spanning fifty years and impacting much of the developed world. But Breton made this statement before Surrealism, when he was an ardent proponent of Dada.

Ninety-two years later Kenneth Goldsmith opened his book *Uncreative Writing* with a gambit similar to Breton's:

> In 1969 the conceptual artist Douglas Huebler wrote, "The world is full of objects, more or less interesting; I do not wish to add any more." I've come to embrace Huebler's ideas, though it might be retooled as "The world is full of texts, more or less interesting; I do not wish to add any more." It seems an appropriate response to a new condition in writing today: faced with an unprecedented amount of available text, the problem is not needing to write more of it; instead, we must learn to negotiate the vast quantity that exists. (2001, 1)

Goldsmith goes on to criticize the fetish of originality and self-expression in the creative writing industry, offering procedural strategies for helping existing texts to resist the siren call of authenticity. In the end, human agency intervenes anyway. "The secret," he says, is that "the suppression of self-expression is impossible" (9). Copy a poem by Wordsworth and your typos or transcription errors can be chalked up to your account. Goldsmith is clearly venturing into the bold old world of Borges's symbolist poet Pierre Menard, who does everything he can to replicate *Don Quixote* except copying it verbatim. Menard's aspiration reveals a wish deeply inscribed in any aspiring writer, which is not so much to "express" oneself as to cohabit a proven sturdy vehicle. Writing a masterpiece isn't about gushing your soul—rather, it's like driving a champion race car. And any racing champion will tell you it's not about him or her, it's about the team that keeps the vehicle going.

Goldsmith's commitment to making do with existing materials can be regarded as ecologically sound. But it also has the virtue of pointing up a challenge intrinsic to ecological issues: namely, is there any room for the values that have defined the humanistic outlook in which anthropocentrism is the norm? If the cult of originality is consigned to unintended effects like transcription errors, is there no room left for a healthy pride? Does Goldsmith consign us to the vexatious domain spotted from atop postmodern continental theory by Foucault and Barthes, with individual works swallowed up in "textuality" like a spreading oil stain, haphazardly borne along by the rudderless ship of the "death of the author"? The ordinary consumer, eyeing the best-seller lists, cries *No way!* I want the author's name on my purchase like a seal of certification attesting to the integrity of the production process, as if a book were a pharmaceutical product. (Of course it is, as the late Friedrich Kittler tirelessly explained [1990].)

Goldsmith's case for making do with preexisting materials has a conspicuous precedent in Dada. Many of you may be familiar with a famous provocation by Tristan Tzara:

> To make a dadaist poem
> Take a newspaper.
> Take a pair of scissors.
> Choose an article as long as you are planning to make your
>   poem.
> Cut out the article.
> Then cut out each of the words that make up this article
>   and put them in a bag.
> Shake it gently.

Then take out the scraps one after the other in the order in
   which they left the bag.
Copy conscientiously.
The poem will be like you. (1951b, 92)

The beauty of Tzara's recipe is that originality is accidental, serendipitous; it just comes with the material, and the material can be anything at all. The collages and constructions of Kurt Schwitters were lovingly pieced together from debris gathered in the streets of Hanover. Friends remarked on his ceaselessly alert scrounging, his determined exultation upon snatching a cancelled tram ticket, a bottle cork, a wire spring, or a button from the gutter. This was urban litter in the strictest sense. Schwitters took walks to bring in the trash.

Hans Arp was equally steadfast in his embrace of material anonymity. "Modern times," Arp decided, "have consecrated men to megalomania" (1972, 232). So Dada creations "were meant to cure humans of the sheer madness of genius and to lead them back more modestly to their proper place in nature" (235). In contrast to cleverness and ingenuity, "the frenzy of intelligence" as Arp called it, "sometimes we learn to 'understand' better by observing the motion of a leaf, the evolution of a line, a word in a poem, the shriek of an animal" (165, 293). He longed for an elementary art in which "shapes arise, powerful as speaking mountains" (283). Arp would have shared Ezra Pound's quest for the "unwobbling pivot" (1947) but would have disavowed his megalomania. Arp's work is a pledge to innocence, radiating a vigorous simplicity. In contrast to the egotism of the masterpiece, Arp produced works that aspired to anonymity. There's a beautiful example in Carola Giedion-Welcker's *Modern Plastic Art*—published in 1937, the first book on modern sculpture. Photographs on facing pages juxtapose Arp's sculpture "Human Concretion" with melting snow on an Alpine creek. His marble could be imperceptibly deposited in the creek, blending into the snow, but it wouldn't melt.

Vacationing in the Swiss Alps with Giacometti in 1935, Max Ernst wrote to Giedion-Welcker that the two men were "afflicted with sculpture-fever" while extracting granite blocks from a glacial moraine. "Wonderfully polished by time, frost and weather, they are in themselves fantastically beautiful," he observed. "Why not, therefore, leave the spadework to the elements and confine ourselves to scratching on them the runes of our own mystery?" (Giedion-Welcker 1937, 300). Reading the runes was an enticing model for the outlook she favored, in which the ultimate task of art was to renovate human perception, not add to a lineup of aesthetic petitioners in search of approval. It's a prospect in accord with Victor Shklovsky's dictum: "Art removes objects from the automatism of perception" (1965, 13). Cleansing the doors of perception, the artist magnifies the commonplace, rendering what's beneath attention miraculously sturdy, rehabilitating it as a worthy basis for life. To apprehend the world so renovated is no longer to consign things to a static ensemble. Ernst's delight in glacial polish anticipates his own contribution of *frottage*, or rubbing, to the arsenal of Surrealism, which includes the pouring, or *coulage*, technique of Gordon Onslow Ford and the *fumage* smoke applications pioneered by Wolfgang Paalen. "Reminiscent of the prehistoric is this delicate awakening of the form from out the plane of stone, this swelling up and down of the plane," Giedion-Welcker observed of Giacometti, noting how in Arp too the apparent solidity of the material is infused with "something growing, welling, gliding which admits neither of formal nor mental frontiers and fixations" (1935, 200, 201).

Unlike many of her contemporaries, Giedion-Welcker was not threatened by the fact that "the human scale, the human angle, has ceased to be the universal norm," understanding the avant-garde dedication to the collective possibility of getting outside the anthropomorphic box by attaining this broader perspective (1937, 15). Giedion-Welcker readily recognized in James Joyce's "Work in Progress" a spirit similar to the Dadaist "rehabilitation of simple and quotidian qualities" (1935, 199). She found it disturbing, though, that a persistent but anachronistic fixation on proportionality impeded a proper recognition of Joyce. "Rounded-off existence, harmony, synthesis are just bluster, which we're still today filching from the past, for ornaments," she complained in a review of *Ulysses* (1973, 36). The criteria had changed. Mimesis was not an automatic standard: "The approximation of nature cannot be accepted as a requirement when the artistic aspiration is directed towards making visible a new independent organism," she wrote (1938, 342). Anthropomorphic scale is not the measure of the cosmos. The cunning of art is such that scale is always deceptive. A vast book may be simply a pirouette on a tiny proscenium, and a brief lyric may harbor an epic of vexing deliberations.

Giedion-Welcker was a friend of Joyce. At his funeral in 1941, watching his coffin lowered into the ground, she couldn't help but recall the last thing Joyce had said to her before his unexpected death: "You have no idea how wonderful dirt is" (1979, 277). She had many warm memories of Joyce, like his "moist word expeditions" on Lake Zurich to stimulate composition of "Anna Livia Plurabelle" (265); or his tipsy wish, after a night of partying, to be driven home on the hood of a car to get a clear view of the stars. "Tell me," he asked her at their first meeting, "what sort of an idea do you think the word 'automobile' would have aroused in the Middle Ages?" (273). Giedion-Welcker had known Joyce since 1928, when she published an appreciative review of *Ulysses*. "What does it deal with? Us. Our daily existence, our inner and outer reality, as overall rhythm, as detail" (1973, 27). By 1935 she was contributing regularly to *Transition*, the journal in which *Finnegans Wake* was being serialized as "Work in Progress." Surveying "New Roads in Modern Sculpture" in *Transition*, her opening sentence revisits the terms of her approach to *Ulysses*: "The plastic problem belongs to our life, to our daily life." To this end, "Modern plastic art wants to reconstitute the primal qualities" (1935, 198). From the kinetic contagion of the Futurist Boccioni and the embrace of refuse and found material in Dada and Surrealism, to Brancusi's elucidations of primal form, Giacometti's "prehistoric" sensibility, and Arp's "organic elementarism" in which the works appear to have been made by "a thousand-year-old glacier-polish" instead of by hand, Giedion-Welcker traces the sculptural path by which "objects were humanized, the human was objectified" (1935, 201). Her catholic understanding of literature and art suggests another approach to *Finnegans Wake*, so that it's not the ne plus ultra of literary gamesmanship but a fastidious agent in engineering the rudimentary building blocks of life: "linguistic revitalization," she called it (1930, 179).

Giedion-Welcker was not alarmed, perplexed, or ruffled by the purported unreadability of *Finnegans Wake*. But the issue of the unreadable persists, and the *Wake* has acquired the exemplary status of the unassimilable. A work often referred to, but infrequently read, it is rubbish of a sort. As Michael Thompson argued in *Rubbish Theory*, waste is a "sliding scale that relates private and public, informality and formality, expediency and principle" (1979, 93). *Finnegans Wake* not only reveals but revels in the fact that waste is bound up with vitality. In Thoreau's brilliant depiction in the "Spring" chapter of *Walden*, nature is known by its profligacy, its spendthrift surplus. Nature, in that sense, can be understood in terms Pound applied to culture: that which happens after one has forgotten which book. Maybe I'm going against that grain here by insisting on the pertinence of a book by James Joyce, but I think in its very excesses it surpasses the category of the book. Think of *Finnegans Wake* instead as a waste disposal operation.

Lisa Robertson pointedly writes: "A system is ecological when it consumes its own waste products" (2002, 25). By this definition, *waste* could be defined as *that which hasn't been used yet*. Thankfully we have Dada, and *Finnegans Wake*, as demonstrations of this ecology. In the *Wake*, the ludic continuum of Joyce's insubordinate polyglossia unsays everything it says. In doing so, it subjects the eternal dream of a transcendental signifier—a supersign—to equivocation, partaking of the perpetual motion of creative vagrancy, or "zigzag naturalism," as Arp called it (1972, 234). In the drama, and trauma, of starting from scratch with every letter, *Finnegans Wake* launches the reader on those "moist word expeditions" Giedion-Welcker admired Joyce for undertaking; and in the process we're bound (obliged, and destined) to hear "lettre" (letter) as "l'être" (being), opening up the manic prospect of all possible wor(l)ds compacted into a single (sacredly secular) text, undermining any distinction of inside from outside, essential from peripheral, literature from language, abstract versus concrete, or any similar pairing predicated on content/form distinctions. *Finnegans Wake* encouraged "all over" tendencies in Abstract Expressionist painting and, most importantly, served to induct a generation of artists and thinkers into a world of uncanny signs.

There's a passage from Heidegger worth heeding with the aromatic excrescence of the *Wake* in mind. "Thinking is not a means to gain knowledge," he says. "Thinking cuts furrows into the soil of Being." Then, quoting Nietzsche: "'Our thinking should have a vigorous fragrance, like a wheatfield on a summer's night.'" "How many of us today still have the senses for that fragrance?" Heidegger wonders (1971, 70). Heidegger's reference to fragrance evokes the incessant diminishment of our sense of smell, an attenuation of the biocentric horizon, diminishment of animal sapience. "I want the flower and fruit of a man," wrote Thoreau, "that some fragrance be wafted over from him to me . . . His goodness must not be a partial and transitory act"—not charity, in other words—"but a constant superfluity, which costs him nothing and of which he is unconscious" (1992, 52).

It's worth lingering over *superfluity*. It's a word that comes up in *Beasts of the Modern Imagination* by Margot Norris (1985), as she proselytizes for biocentric thought, a nonanthropomorphic prospect outlined by the eclectic assortment of Darwin, Nietzsche, Lawrence, Kafka, and Dadaist Max Ernst. These biocentric avatars exude animal vitality, with an unnerving indifference to cultural norms. "Since biocentric theorizing is an autotelic act," Norris explains, "it aims to reverse the traditional philosophical enterprise of substituting thought for life. And because it teaches nothing, explains nothing, and creates effects only by the most indirect and accidental means, biocentric thought is gratuitous: an excess, a superfluity" (238).

"Gratuity" is a term that dispenses with the salutary applications and obligations of "humanities." Instead of the dignities and dignitaries of the humanities, then, let's substitute the *gratuities*. *Gratuity* retains value while disposing of the *guarantee*, the false advertising of a redemptive "civilizing" influence—while also recalling that other meaning of gratuity as *gift*. "Existence is 'poetical' in its fundamental aspect . . . it is not a recompense, but a gift," Heidegger suggests (1949, 282–83). Likewise, Jean-Paul Sartre spoke of art as "a ceremony of the *gift*." "To write," he says, is "both to disclose the world and to offer it as a task to the generosity of the reader" (1992, 988, 990). Sartre is aiming for a delicate balance of exposure and commitment without making commitment a foregone conclusion and without coercing the world to appear in a familiar way. The concerned citizen may want to impart a message, but the artwork as life-form and social contract has to outlive its origins as an ego-derivative; it has to be generous, not legislative. And to be generous, it must be relieved of the odious obligation to be necessary.

This welcome condition is elucidated by Gertrude Stein in her cunningly simple pamphlet *What Are Masterpieces?* (1970). Stein concludes in her inimitably unpunctuated way: "A master-piece has essentially not to be necessary, it has to be that is it has to exist but it does not have to be necessary it is not in response to necessity as action is because the minute it is necessary it has in it no possibility of going on" (86). Rather than looking for a cause-and-effect relation between culture and society, it makes more sense to think of literature and the arts as arenas within which the very notion of efficacy—along with freedom—is puzzled over, tested, engaged, amplified, and necessarily left unresolved. This is not to say there's any lack of resolve on the part of individual artists; but nearly everything valued as art in the West has acquired that status not because it satisfies a function but because, given a nexus of possible functions, it equivocates between them in such a way as to suggest and even demonstrate the power of deviation, vagrancy, unexpected pilgrimage to improbable destinations. The improbabilities and the gratuities, with their waste motions and waste notions, are restorative nutrients in our cultural biomass.

Life itself is improbable, gratuitous. Theosophist and architect Claude Bragdon, in *The New Image*, extolling the need for "a new attitude toward life, a new consciousness," offers an anecdote that illustrates the future imperative:

> A biologist told me once that the form is created by, and follows the function, and that before the heart appears in the human embryo there is a palpitation in the place where the heart is going to be. So let us give over all this battle of the styles as a perfectly profitable employment, and strive rather to start that *palpitation* in the place where we want beauty to appear. (1928, 94)

Past the point at which phantom sensations call out from the work—as if probing the space around it for contact with a living body—the traditional activity of mimesis gives way to autopoiesis, a self-differential genesis without comparison, without recompense. But it's sentient in a sense gleaned by filmmaker Jean Epstein in terms of "the recoil before the leap, and the moment before landing, the becoming, the hesitation, the taut spring, the prelude, and even more than all these, the piano being tuned before the overture. The photogenic is conjugated in the future and in the imperative" (1988, 236).

This is the spirit I sense in Dada, tenaciously innocent in the face of the world's atrocities, "a play with shabby leftovers," as Hugo Ball put it, even as he compared Dada to "a Gnostic sect whose initiates were so stunned by the image of the *childhood* of Jesus that they lay down in a cradle and let themselves be suckled by women and swaddled." To which he pointedly added: "Dadaists are similar babes-in-arms of a new age" (1974, 65, 66). It's more than historical coincidence that the Great War that gave rise to Dada had a correspondingly devastating effect on Aby Warburg, the great art historian and founding father of iconography. Warburg's term *Pathosformel* (pathos formula) specifies the "dynamograms" or iconographic complexes that the discipline of art history overlooks or fails to grasp—the site of an agitation exceeding the parameters of those concepts by which art is conventionally understood. An artwork is a pathic receptacle, harboring a potential resuscitation and nurturing a posture of attentiveness owing as much to animal instinct as it does to social principle. As pathic receptacle, artwork harbors a biomorphic insistence, a biologically exigent extension of corporeality: the composer, poet, or painter is not trying to "say" something but to *make* something, and this generative impulse is profoundly embedded in a somatic manifold.

A footstep *impresses* the earth: this rudimentary imprint is the source of all signs. Carlo Ginzburg extols the "elastic rigor" involved in the conjectural paradigm encompassing hunting, divination, and semiotics: hunting after traces (1980, 28). "A baby does it in a dream to a star": a single line poem by John Thorpe that haunts me (in part because it's in his unpaginated 1972 collection *The Cargo Cult*, so it's only found by chance). These words too are traces of a life, tracks of a trek, whispers of reckoning. Life is eating us up, Emerson says, and all we can do about that is work on the fables, fitting together the parts of speech (Indo European *dhabh* + *bha I*), scratching out the runes and figures of presentiment. "Perhaps the most amazing sensation passed on to us by prehistoric man is that of presentiment. It will always continue," wrote the painter Giorgio de Chirico. "We might consider it as an eternal proof of the irrationality of the universe. Original man must have wandered through a world full of uncanny signs. He must have trembled at each step" (1938, 14). And may the tremors never cease.

Deep Image

An image is a stop the mind makes between uncertainties.
—Djuna Barnes, *Nightwood*, 111

IN HIS JOURNAL of literary Cubism, *Nord-Sud*, in an issue containing poems by Philippe Soupault, Louis Aragon, and Tristan Tzara, Pierre Reverdy published some reflections on the image. "L'Image" was one in a series spanning the run of *Nord-Sud*; other topics included emotion, space, syntax, tradition, and cinematography.

> L'Image est une creation pure de l'esprit.
> Elle ne peut naître d'une comparaison mais du rapprochement de deux réalités plus ou moins éloignées.
> Plus les rapports des deux réalités rapprochées seront lointains et justes, plus l'image sera forte—plus elle aura de puissance emotive et de réalité poétique.

> The Image is a pure creation of the mind.
> It cannot be born from a comparison but by bringing together two more or less distant realities.
> Insofar as the relationship between the two realities is distant and exact—the greater will be its emotional power and poetic reality. (1918, 3)

This is only the beginning of Reverdy's ruminations, but it's what André Breton chose to cite in his inaugural manifesto of Surrealism six years later, accompanied by enigmatic remarks about the author, from whom Breton had become estranged. Decades later, in 1952, he looked back on Reverdy with respect: "Once you knew him, nothing seemed as important as his theses on the image in poetry"—which, with his other pieces in *Nord-Sud*, "put forth several lasting principles and major themes on the subject of poetic creation" (1993, 30, 22). For the adventure of Surrealism, Reverdy's dicta offered a salutary provocation, foremost of which is the suggestion that the image is a pure creation of the mind. Mind (*l'esprit*), not *eye*. Furthermore, "poetic reality" demands that the bipolar forces conjoined in the image maintain their separation. There is no blending or merging, but rather a sustained tension in the electromagnetic sense. "It is, as it were," wrote Breton, "from the fortuitous juxtaposition of the two terms that a particular light has sprung, *the light of the image*" (1969, 37).

As it happened, the lyric effusions of Surrealist poetry rarely lived up to the incandescence of the image. In fact, despite the constant risk of pictorial anecdote, it was in the visual arts that the *deep image* of Surrealism was memorably achieved—albeit not strictly in optic terms but in the tactile provocations of Meret Oppenheim's fur-covered teacup, Man Ray's clothing iron studded with nails, or Marcel Mariën's monocular eyeglass, *L'Introuvable*. By 1950, in buttoned-down Cold War America, with its tweed-suited academy poets confident that a return to form was the order of the day, Surrealism seemed outdated. For young poets made uncomfortable by the spirit of conformism— David Antin and Jerome Rothenberg—the European avant-garde was news that stayed news. For Robert Bly and James Wright, too, it seemed absurdly premature to assume prewar vanguard provocations had been meaningfully assimilated. The Midwest of Bly and Wright converged with the metropolis of Antin and Rothenberg in a commitment to translation as *recovery* of untapped potential for English language poetry, rendering in a distinctively American idiom the enigmatic volatility of the subconscious and the prerational, manifested in work by poets like Federico García Lorca, Pablo Neruda, César Vallejo, Georg Trakl, André Breton, and Vicente Aleixandre. From about 1961 to 1965, "deep image" served simultaneously as spiritual intoxicant and technical principle; it was a way of embracing foreign poetry as a revitalizing tactic, attaining "more of the joy of the unconscious" as Bly put it (1959a, 47). In contrast to what Robert Kelly disdainfully thought of as the aridity of "craft" (1963, 24), deep image incited "a fertility of critical examination" (1965, 25). "To strip to the least," Kelly later recalled the fundamental initiative, "& the least was: image" (1968, 6).

Because discussions of deep image have been consistently riddled with error, it's important to establish a succinct chronology. Although the first use of the term was by Jerome Rothenberg, its subsequent association with Robert Bly makes it imperative to consider his magazine *The Fifties* (later *The Sixties*) instrumental to the dissemination of the concept, if not the term. Rothenberg, having appeared in *The Fifties* no. 3 with translations of Paul Celan as well as his own poems, published the first declaration of deep image in his little magazine *Poems from the Floating World* no. 2 in 1960. He regarded the magazine itself as "an on-going anthology of the deep image" (Alpert 1975b, 100), and the third issue in 1961 was given a title: "The Deep Image: Ancient and Modern." Key statements appeared in Robert Kelly's magazine *Trobar* in 1961: Kelly's "Notes on the Poetry of Deep Image" in the second issue (1961b), and Rothenberg's "Why *Deep* Image" (1961) in the third. Kelly's "Notes" had been privately circulated in late 1960, precipitating Rothenberg's lengthy correspondence with Robert Creeley on deep image, published in *Kulchur* in 1962. Also in 1962, the New York journal *Nomad* featured a portfolio of deep image work by Rothenberg, Kelly, George Economou, and Armand Schwerner, topped off by further position statements by Rothenberg and Kelly. The topic of deep image had become sufficiently public that when David Ossman (future member of the Firesign Theatre comedy troupe) conducted a series of interviews with poets—published as *The Sullen Art* in 1963—Kelly, Rothenberg, and Creeley were pointedly asked to comment on it. Bly's influential essay "A Wrong Turning in American Poetry" was also published in 1963 in John Logan's poetry journal *Choice*; and while Bly did not then (or later) use the term "deep image," he invariably extolled the archetypal virtue of *depth* and poetic necessity of *image*, thereby associating him with the term, particularly among readers unlikely to have seen fugitive publications like *Trobar* or *Poems from the Floating World*.

Despite close contact between Rothenberg and Bly in the late fifties, deep image was largely restricted to New York's Lower East Side scene. The conflation of this original initiative with Bly's circle, and the source of much subsequent disinformation, can be traced to Stephen Stepanchev's 1965 book *American Poetry since 1945*. By that point, Kelly and Rothenberg had adopted a retrospective posture toward deep image, and the term began its quasi-academic afterlife where it has persisted to the present, almost invariably used with reference to Bly and James Wright. To his credit, Stepanchev quoted extensively from Kelly's "Notes on the Poetry of the Deep Image" (hyperbolically declaring it the theoretical equivalent of Olson's "Projective Verse"), thereby making more widely available a central statement that had previously had very limited circulation. Misleadingly, he claimed that Kelly and Rothenberg had *collaborated* with Bly, Wright, and William Duffy (coeditor of *The Fifties*) in "launching a movement toward subjectivism in American poetry"—a movement, no less, that "denied any influence from the Charles Olson-inspired groups" (175). Far from denying such influence, Kelly was actively soliciting it from Olson himself (whose response—"not imageS but Image" was repeatedly cited by Kelly [1965, 26]), as it was in Rothenberg's exchange with Creeley. Stepanchev's focus on deep image, such as it was, served as prelude to a discussion of the work of Bly and Wright, thereby effectively consigning Kelly and Rothenberg to the role of theoreticians, since their poetry passed without notice. This bias is understandable, given that *Silence in the Snowy Fields* by Bly (1962) and *The Branch Will Not Break* by Wright were among the most widely reviewed poetry titles of the early 1960s, establishing the public face with which deep image has been associated ever since.

Why review this remote and apparently minor episode in literary history? After all, it's an affair in which the theoretical charter of deep image served largely as accompaniment to two inaugural collections published by Rothenberg's Hawk's Well Press, his own *White Sun Black Sun* (1960) and *Armed Descent* (1961a) by Kelly (neither of which has been reprinted, nor were they widely available in the first place)—an episode made even more tenuous in its significance because the original participants abandoned the term not long after they took it up, and the one figure most associated with deep image has always scorned the term. Given Bly's impatience when asked about it, there is little to be gained by persisting in the common application, even if "deep image" doggedly persists (as synonymous with "subjective" image) in criticism on Bly and Wright. Forced by distaste for "deep image," Bly came up with an alternative, "leaping poetry." If, as Daniel Kane usefully suggests, "the 'deep image' was as much a politics of dissent from mainstream poetics and what it suggested as it was an effort to find new uses for the poetic image" (2003, 91), is there any reason other than the foregoing clarification of its history to revisit it now? Before the question can even be addressed, it's useful to attempt some conceptual coordinates.

The coordinates are most accessible by way of Gaston Bachelard rather than the poets themselves. It's not clear that any of them knew his work; although his cycle of books on the imagination of matter appeared in the 1940s, the earliest translations appeared after the deep image publications. In *L'Air et les songes* (1943) Bachelard wonders, "Can the study of *fleeting images* be a subject?" (1988, 13). Differently construed: Can a deep image poem be composed? "We always think of the imagination as the faculty that *forms* images," he writes. "On the contrary, it *deforms* what we perceive; it is, above all, the faculty that frees us from immediate images and *changes* them" and, in this capacity, the imagination is "the human psyche's experience of *openness* and *novelty*" (1). To imagine, then, means nothing less than "to launch out toward a new life" (3). The theorists of deep image certainly felt the tug of this liberating potential, but they failed to extricate the created image sufficiently from perceptual material, as is evident from the reactions of David Antin, Robert

Creeley, and others at the time. Nevertheless, I suspect Kelly or Rothenberg would have been pleased with so clarifying a definition as this: "Both at the time of its birth and when it is in full flight, the image within us is the subject of the verb to imagine. It is not its direct object" (1988, *Air* 14)—to which might be added Aby Warburg's preoccupation with movement or rhythm in the image ("for Warburg the question of movement became associated with the subject's entrance into the image, with rites of passage, and with the dramatizations affecting his or her appearance" [Michaud 2004, 32]).

Rothenberg admitted with hindsight that, as far as deep image was concerned, the images "were probably in a Poundian way viewed as energy clusters" (Alpert 1975b, 142). If Pound's vortex was the tacit model, it was the image of Imagism that all too easily prevailed, despite repeated protests and disavowals. "The poetry we have now is a poetry without the image," Bly complained (1990, 20). In 1959 he declared the Imagists "misnamed: they did not write in images from the unconscious, as Lorca or Neruda, but in simple pictures" (1959b, 8). Of course it might seem ludicrous to malign the Imagists for something they never attempted, but Bly's charge replicates Pound's own shift in allegiance from *image* to *vortex*—which in turn has an intriguing historical parallel with Aby Warburg's critique of iconology, advocating that images in art might be better approached as "dynamograms" (Gombrich 1986, 244, 248). Robert Creeley shared Bly's concern that deep image risked subsiding into mere pictorialism. He took that to be the trouble with Imagism, which he felt was caught up in "the psychology of reference" and quickly becoming "a machine of manner" (Creeley and Rothenberg 1962, 28). Creeley was well aware of a deviant inflection of the image in Surrealism but thought that this tendency, implicit in deep image, could "make sensational reference over-valued" (28)—as, in a fashion, it soon would in the work of the Confessional poets.

In fact, in the history of poetry it's hard *not* to find abundant examples of the image as anecdotal illustration. In "Frost at Midnight," Coleridge offers such an image precisely so as to question its grip on the mind as "a toy of Thought":

> . . . Sea, and hill, and wood,
> With all the numberless goings-on of life,
> Inaudible as dreams! the thin blue flame
> Lies on my low-burnt fire, and quivers not;
> Only that film, which fluttered on the grate,
> Still flutters there, the sole unquiet thing.
> Methinks, its motion in this hush of nature
> Gives it dim sympathies with me who live,

Making it a companionable form,
Whose puny flaps and freaks the idling Spirit
By its own moods interprets, every where
Echo or mirror seeking of itself,
And makes a toy of Thought.
(1951, 63)

To what degree, then, are images putatively "deep" nothing more than "puny flaps and freaks"—suppositions of an "idling Spirit"? Creeley himself implied as much when, queried by David Ossman about deep image, he skirted the issue until, exasperated, he dismissively blurted out: "'Deep image' is 'deep'—ok" (Ossman 1963, 61). His prickliness may reflect some memory of Bly's recommendation that "Mr. Creeley should try to deepen his own imagination . . . by searching for more richness of language and image" (1959c, 21).

Deep image theory was haunted by the tautology its name insinuated. Like the emperor's new clothes, an image could be hailed as "deep" just because it was a "deep image." The liability was compounded by the terms most often used to evoke deep image: *visionary* apprehension, and the *unconscious*. Rothenberg aspired to a poetry in which "the unconscious is speaking to the unconscious" (Ossman 1963, 31). He suggested that a Zen koan was a more sensible analogy for the deep image poem "driv[ing] the mind into a *cul-de-sac*, in which it can only cry, 'Ah, this!'"—confronting "the perilous point where meaning is held in a tension on the sheer verge of meaninglessness" (1962, 52). Oscillating between vacancy and revelation, deep image was consistently thought to appear in a flash—sharing perhaps the messianic impulse, but not the historical dialectic, of Walter Benjamin's famous dictum, "The past can be seized only as an image which flashes up at the instant when it can be recognized and is never seen again" (Benjamin 1969, 255). An aesthetic of suddenness tends to dissolve continuity (provoking Karl Heinz Bohrer to ask, "Is the utopia of the moment a negative utopia?" [1994, 226]), but Kelly recognized that deep image registered a search for something determinate, like sonar scanning from a submarine. Deep image was not simply the 1912 Imagist image with depth as added value. Thus, Kelly spoke of "a kind of poetry not necessarily dominated by the images, but in which it is the rhythm of images which form the dominant movement of the poem" (Ossman 1963, 34; cf. Kelly 1961b, 15); and this dominant movement is disclosed as a kind of hologram. Andrei Bely, the Russian Symbolist poet, evokes the elusive domain sought by deep image theory: "In poetry the words are grouped in such a fashion that their totality gives the image" (1985, 97).

The original provocation behind Kelly's "Notes on the Poetry of the Deep

Image" (1961b) was the filmography, and film theory, of Sergei Eisenstein, who was keen on the cinematic potential of a "montage of attractions"—that is, the mobilization of "emotional shocks" deployed in "*a free montage with arbitrarily chosen independent . . . effects*" (Eisenstein 1988, 35). The important thing, from a poetic as well as a cinematic viewpoint, is the rhythmic dynamic correlating emotional intensity with images. "Image is the rhythm of poetry," Kelly declared, attributing the insight to Nicolas Calas (Ossman 1963, 37). Calas was a Greek poet initiated into the Surrealist circle in Paris in the 1930s, who later established himself as an art critic in New York during the war. In his first American book, *Confound the Wise* (1942), Calas discusses the "crisis of automatism" facing the Surrealist use of images drawn from the unconscious—a crisis typified by Rothenberg's early work, making it difficult in 1961–1962 for readers to distinguish deep image from Surrealism. Does Rothenberg's "rain that falls through my needle" qualify as one or the other, or both? Multiplied through the poem—with "an egg full of hours," "the rain of wet dollars," conveyed by burning eyes and hair taking root "like red trees" (Rothenberg 1960, 30)—the potential of deep image clearly collapses back into Surrealist dirge. As Calas observed, "The application in poetry of the great Freudian discovery of the role of the unconscious has helped Surrealism to understand all the poetic import of the image but it did not help us to grasp immediately the rhythm of the free association of words" (1942, 27). In the case of automatic writing, there is no structural distinction between beginning, middle, and end, so the reader is given no principle for absorbing the cadence of images. However charged with the dynamism of the unconscious, the images are static. "What was audacious in 1925 gave the effect of unbearable repetition"—resulting in what Calas calls "the crisis of rhythm" (28).

In the second issue of *Poems from the Floating World*, in which Rothenberg first ventured the term "deep image"—not as a theoretical platform, but as an evocation of the magazine's name—two epigraphs evoke the field (see p. 76). Supplementing the technical implications of Calas's proposition, Buber's exhortation to submit to the unknown validated the mystical potential of deep image. It's axiomatic in the tradition of visionary poetry that "vision" is independent of eyesight. Likewise, pursuit of the unknown may mean pursuit of the unknowable. Ironically (or mystifyingly), then, the deep image may not be an image at all, but a "sound" provoked by, or in attunement with, a rhythm. So Kelly imagines deep image not in retinal but in auditory terms: "The image, after its first appearance as dark sound, still lingers as resonance" (1961b, 15). "Sound is image. Touch is image" (1971b, 8). It was "dark sounds" that, for García Lorca, defined *duende*, the otherwise unnamable force he

POEMS FROM THE FLOATING WORLD

From deep within us it comes: the wind that
moves through the lost branches, hurts us
with a wet cry, as if an ocean were caged in
each skull:

There is a sea of connections that floats
between men: a place where speech is
touch and the welcoming hand restores its
silence: an ocean warmed by dark suns.

The deep image rises from the shoreless gulf:
here the poet reaches down among the lost
branches, till a moment of seeing: the
poem. Only then does the floating world
sink again into its darkness, leaving a white
shadow, and the joy of our having been
here, together.

"What can be learned does not matter; what
matters is the self-abandonment to that which
is not known."

Martin Buber

"The laws of the combination of images
constitute the form of poetry; the movement of
images is rhythm."

Nicolas Calas

associated with flamenco, bullfighting, and poetry at their perilous extremes. Duende is the dark side of creative endeavor. "Every image has its field of force, its shadow moving darkly through the poem, with which the poet must contend" (Kelly 1961b, 16). As with duende, deep image is a way of recognizing that ineffable point at which the work of creation intersects with—is pierced by—the work of destruction; and Kelly's concluding hope in his first proclamation is that deep image "restores the poetry of desperation" (16).

In a 1973 interview, Kelly discussed his earlier attraction to deep image in terms that suggest why it couldn't last: "I was concerned to find the image in the imageless," he recalled. "Deep image to me was the image that was not perceptible to the senses, and that could be arrived at finally only syntactically"—a proposition portending the "polysyntax" he pursued much later in *Sentence* (1980) and *Uncertainties* (2011) (Alpert 1974a, 20, 21). The *syntactic* contribution to the apprehension of images as such was crucial to Creeley's resistance to putative depth: "There is an 'image' in a mode, in a *way* of statement as much 'image' as any reference to pictorial element" (Rothenberg and Creeeley 1962, 26). Syntax means putting together; syntax is the arrangement of the parts, or rhythm in the sense Kelly drew from Calas. In his exchange with Creeley, Rothenberg singled out the older poet's "The Door" as a consummate example of deep image. At three pages, "The Door" is one of Creeley's longer poems; and I recall Kelly saying, in an appreciative reverie in 1973, that if you don't consult the clock, "The Door" is an epic. The poem deftly intertwines a rudimentary image with alternating passages of self-scrutiny and emerging dream vision, until "The Door" rivals the work of the medieval Pearl poet. If by deep image we mean "The Door," then deep image is a rarity. Despite the lucid image of "the door / cut so small in the wall" (Creeley 1962, 101), there's nothing uncanny or deep about it except through its cumulative effect in the poem, in which it operates as much as a musical refrain as an enhanced or augmented image. To pursue *deep* image, in light of "The Door," meant paradoxically superseding the image in what Rothenberg called a "pattern of the movement from perception to vision," as in *visionary*—a tradition of venerable apprehensions of imageless images. The sense of transfiguration implied is handsomely accessible through a cognate term, *imago*: an insect in its sexually mature adult stage after metamorphosis. A butterfly.

In addition to being a solicitous posture toward poetic vision and a petition to the unconscious, deep image harbored a potentially social aspect. Significantly, this went unmentioned by Kelly or Rothenberg but contributed much to their friend David Antin's decision to steer clear of any commitment to deep image (he refused to be included in the deep image group in *Nomad*). As he recalled in 1975:

The idea was that the image was a kind of primitive psychological semantic construct. A kind of instant response that wasn't contaminated by a conventional syntax that tended, because of its orthodox structure, to assimilate
all experience to what we used to call a "legislated reality," that was built up
out of a handful of conventional cultural metaphors. At least that's the way I
used to describe what we meant by an "image," and I think there was some
agreement among us that that's what it meant. (Alpert 1975a, 5)

As it happened, the issue of *Nomad* also included poems by Jackson Mac
Low, along with his essay "Poetry, Chance, Silence, &c." Mac Low was involved in the Lower East Side scene, and his performance work—together
with his chance-generated compositions—had a liberating effect on Antin,
particularly in the linguistic turn signaled by "definitions for mendy." Antin recalls reading this poem on an occasion on which David Ignatow and
James Wright were in the audience: "It must have sounded very aggressively
remote from anything like 'deep image' poetry . . . I know from others that it
sounded kind of fierce and antipoetic" (Alpert 1975a, 16). Antin's poem was
an elegy, so its tactical submission to a technical definition of loss (from an
insurance manual) spurned any trace of deep image.

> loss is an unintentional decline in or disappearance of a
>   value arising from a contingency
> a value is an efficacy a power a brightness
> it is also a duration
> (Antin 1991, 59)

Nonetheless, traces of deep image remain in the third page of the poem,
which is blank except for two lines: "is there enough silence here for a glass
of water" in the middle of the page, and at the bottom: "is it dark enough for
bread" (1991, 61). These are not the only images in "definitions," but *silence*
and *darkness* recall the aspirations of deep image to reach into, and engage,
the unimaginable in the image. Of Mendy, Antin said, "It was his death and
there was something about it I didn't understand and I knew I didn't, and
the one thing I believe a poet ought to do is respect what he doesn't understand, respect its unintelligibility" (Alpert 1975a, 17). But where deep image
was the pursuit of unintelligibility by means of images, Antin was exploring
instead the uncanny resources of linguistic banality drawn from professional
jargon and common speech.

In 1965 Rothenberg and Antin coedited the journal *Some/thing*. In the
inaugural issue, Antin provided a text that might be construed as its charter, "Silence/Noise" (printed mostly in full caps). The modernist aspiration

to purify the language of the tribe is reaffirmed, but with a shift of emphasis symptomatic of the Cold War/Vietnam era. Antin resists talk of a new aesthetics, urging instead: "WHAT WE NEED IS A SURVIVAL TOOL . . . I AM TALKING ABOUT LANGUAGE HERE   A HUMAN COMMUNITY CANNOT SURVIVE WITHOUT ITS LANGUAGE" (1965, 60). Rather than regarding poetry as a refinement of language, Antin affirms a reinvigorating embrace of the full potential of language, including its supposedly antipoetic aspects: "THERE IS NO NEED TO ASSUME THAT POETRY NEEDS TO RECOGNIZE ANY CONSTRAINTS BEYOND THE FUNDAMENTAL CONSTRAINTS OF LANGUAGE" (60). Rothenberg's agreement with this position is reflected not only in the procedural compositions he embarked on at this time but also in his later assessment of the danger "that one might move into a limited poetic vocabulary (a new set of image conventions as culturally controlled as the old) without ever exploring the full range of language that might also lead to the deep image" (Power 1975a, 141). Still, deep image was not altogether jettisoned in the context of *Some/thing*. Antin's concluding remarks link the magazine's title to utopian aspirations for *something* beyond reach, or deep: "THE FEELING THAT SOME/THING LIES OUT THERE THAT WE CANNOT LAY HOLD OF IS THE FEELING OF THE INADEQUACY OF THE EXISTING ORDER   IT IS THE DEMAND FOR A DIFFERENT ORDER   THE CONDITION OF POETRY" (1965, 63).

A coincidence of chronology invites consideration of the fact that *Some/thing* began in 1965, the year Jack Spicer died. Insofar as it's plausible to speak of a "linguistic turn" in American poetry, Spicer and Antin are among the poets most responsible. While Antin was clearly uncomfortable with the deep image theorizing of his friends, he concurred with them that poetic practice needed to somehow go down, to submerge itself in *prima materia* in the alchemical sense, to achieve a new distillation of its resources—resources Antin thought of as language itself in its broadest (fullest, deepest) capacity. Perhaps not coincidentally, Chomsky's theories of deep grammar were taking shape at this time, although Wittgenstein had an impact on Antin much earlier. Wittgenstein also evoked unfathomable depth:

> The problems arising through a misinterpretation of our forms of language have the character of *depth*. They are deep disquietudes; their roots are as deep in us as the forms of our language and their significance is as great as the importance of our language. —Let us ask ourselves: why do we feel a grammatical joke to be *deep*? (And that is what the depth of philosophy is.) (2001, #111, 41e)

Jack Spicer's work is a veritable carnival of grammatical jokes, stress marks of a surface irreverence disgorging "deep disquietudes"; he was a poet for whom "pathology leads to new paths and pathfinding. All the way down past the future" (Spicer 1975, 179).

Going down is an Orphic obligation; and Spicer's fixation on Cocteau's Orpheus provided him with the functional mythology of his work, the generative grammar of a poetics of fracture and what he called "disturbance." In the project initiating his cycle of composed books, *After Lorca* (1958), Spicer's gnarled receptivity to the Spanish poet is playful but also anguished, as if he'd glimpsed the prospect of deep image avant la lettre in its larval struggle with duende: "I would like the moon in my poems to be a real moon, one which could be suddenly covered with a cloud that has nothing to do with the poem—a moon utterly independent of images" (33). Of course, the moon and the cloud are images, and "I would like" remains a wish—unless, that is, it's elevated to theory, as it was for Goethe, for whom "the highest thing would be to grasp that everything factual is already theory. The blue of the sky reveals to us the fundamental law of chromatics. One would never search for anything behind the phenomena; they themselves are the theory" (Buck-Morss 1989, 72). Such pan-semiosis risks the suddenness of reversal from plenitude to poverty: all things signify something, or they signify nothing. The zero-sum game is implicit in Mallarmé's wager. Spicer rolled those dice and lost—a gamble addressed by Robin Blaser in "The Practice of the Outside," included in his edition of Spicer's *Collected Books* (1975). "It is within language that the world speaks to us with a voice that is not our own," Blaser writes in an insight germane to the developing poetics of his own "Image-Nations" sequence, in which the "strange unfamiliarity / of the familiar" resonates dexterously between the lure of the hermetic and the imperative of public discourse (1975, 279; 1993, 138).

Deep image theory, in light of linguistic considerations germane to American poetry prior to $L=A=N=G=U=A=G=E$ magazine—exemplified by Antin, Mac Low, Spicer, and Blaser—suggests aspirations alien to the practice and legacy of Robert Bly, unless Jungian archetypes are taken to be a kind of tribal deep grammar of the imagination. "On one level," suggests Kevin Power, "the deep image is a process that leads to the discovery of a universal language" (1975b, 154). Robert Bly was receptive to the universal cipher of nature in the doctrine of Jacob Boehme. Certainly for Rothenberg, as for Bly, the potential of the image had archetypal resonances. Rothenberg told Power that deep image "carried the hope, like poetry in general, of 'finding the center,' which is an activity the ancestors in the old myths of founding engaged in at the outset & that we have to learn to do again with all means at our disposal" (Power 1975a, 143). After *Some/thing*, Rothenberg went on to edit the anthologies *Technicians of the Sacred* (1968) and *Shaking the Pumpkin* (1972), and the ethnopoetics journal *Alcheringa*—all manifestly concerned with mythopoiesis; and he would also be instrumental in facilitating contacts between key participants in what emerged as "language writing." And while language writing inherited the procedural orientation of Mac Low and Antin, and expansively took in the challenge of Wittgenstein and Gertrude Stein, the issues surrounding deep image were left far behind. Or so it seems.

Should deep image be consigned to period connotations, understood as the selective integration of Surrealist-tinged duende into American poetry? That's how Edward Hirsch construes it in his study of duende, *The Demon and the Angel* (2002). Assimilating Lorca, Neruda, and Vallejo into the politically charged American milieu, deep image—"an image saturated with psyche that was both archaic and new" (210)—came to fruition, according to Hirsch, in the work of Bly and Wright, as well as in *The Lice* by W. S. Merwin, *The Book of Nightmares* by Galway Kinnell, *They Feed They Lion* by Philip Levine, and *The Sorrow Dance* by Denise Levertov. Certainly there's a familiar obsession with darkness: Merwin's "There are still bits of night like closed eyes in the walls" (1967, 79); Kinnell's "I, too, have eaten / the meals of the dark shore" (1972, 29); and Levine's young wife with "a gift / for the night that is always rising" (1972, 8)—not to mention the tone set, definitively, by Bly in "Snowfall in the Afternoon," the final poem in *Silence in the Snowy Fields:* "If I reached my hands down, near the earth, / I could take handfuls of darkness! / A darkness was always there, which we never noticed" (1962, 60).

Bly's subsequent turn to political poetry in *The Light around the Body* and *The Teeth Mother Naked at Last* mobilized deep image strategies for paradoxically public ends, the paradox being the wish that the unconscious might somehow be shared with an entire population in congregational rapport. In the form of Jungian archetypes the unconscious convenes a sacramental commemoration of images; and Bly went from being celebrated as the author of "newly discovered archetype[s]" (Libby 1984, 38) to being accused of practicing a "Jungian evangelism" (Kramer 1992, 214). Whether it's been consistently Jungian or not, evangelism defined Bly's career path. In retrospect, Bly's vigor as an advocate has had a more enduring impact than his poetry, particularly his advocacy of the poets he translated. The steady flood of Neruda in English, the ubiquity of Lorca, the availability of Vallejo, Trakl, Char, and Ponge in a variety of translations: these may seem like symptoms of a healthy interest in foreign poetry in America, but it was Bly who first called for (and often undertook) translations of their work in *The Fifties* and *The Sixties*. Only Rilke, among the many poets Bly promoted, had significant presence in English before Bly took up the cause. In the case of Tomas Tranströmer, his generational peer, Bly in effect discovered the poet most genuinely in touch with deep image; a poet whose life work fulfills the mandate of deep image theory, even if he never had any contact with it except remotely, through Bly.

In any case, Bly's wish came true, the wish for an American poetry milieu infused with the "depth" that only images conveyed from abroad could bring it.

And what of Kelly and Rothenberg? How did deep image shape their careers? Kelly was more peremptory in dismissing deep image than Rothenberg, for whom it implicitly remained part of an expanding arsenal of approaches to poetry and translation. In his innovative anthology *America a Prophecy*, coedited with George Quasha (1973), Rothenberg pointedly extracted from Kelly's "Notes on the Poetry of Deep Image" for an informative headnote. But he was also given to retrospective adjustments, wondering in 1965 if "it might not have been better to speak of, say, an *open* image rather than a *deep* one" (1965, 27). Kelly, too, attempted a terminological correction: "Where we were wrong was to speak of deep *image* when the word we wanted was *depth*" (1968, 9). Kelly dismissively recalled the formative period in which deep image theory emerged: "O how we talked too much, primitive & deep image & duende, blithering slogans & all the gimcrack foolishness of the articulate young"—pointedly acknowledging Rothenberg's warning, "we'll be sorry if we give 'em a slogan! & so we were" (1968, 6).

Despite the taint of slogan, for Kelly—who declared "the gateway is the visible; but we must go in" (1962, 58)—deep image was a serviceable charter of his poetics for at least a decade. *Armed Descent* inaugurated a quest guided by alchemical lore and other aspects of the Hermetic tradition, persisting through the sixties (most successfully in *Songs I-XXX, Finding the Measure*, and *Flesh Dream Book*) and culminating in the four-hundred-page poem *The Loom* (1975), a neglected masterwork that amply demonstrates an unexpected potential of deep image for narrative. As *The Loom* also reveals, Kelly was an adept practitioner in the *ut pictura poesis* tradition (culminating in "Arnolfini's Wedding" in *The Mill of Particulars* [1973]), raising the question of whether deep image could have a manifest iconographic content. Does poetic meditation on a painting qualify as "deep" if, rather than simply pondering the image, it renders it slightly creepy? Certainly, this possibility arises in much post-1960s poetry, of which James Tate might be taken as a consummate practitioner; but the case of Tate suggests another aftereffect of deep image—the seemingly motorized production of poems emitted from a kind of deep image popgun. Such a prospect seems to have been on Kelly's mind in 1965 when he denounced "phony primitivism and the decades-old search for discordant images," while conceding of deep image: "It is deeply painful to me to see its name applied to incompetent bourgeois romanticism" (1965, 26). Was it the incompetence, I wonder, or the bourgeois romanticism that rankled?

During an epidemic proliferation of creative writing programs in the 1970s, deep image poems (understood by way of Bly and Wright) became the privileged idiom of a "bourgeois romanticism" more competent than Kelly would admit. But there was an aura of carnival tents nearby—a happy carnival, not the monster midway of William Lindsay Gresham's novel *Nightmare Alley*— a carnival where the ball always hits the bull's-eye and the girlfriend takes the teddy bear home, stopping for a soda on the way. Such kitsch moments abound in the work of the most dominant figure in American poetry of recent decades, John Ashbery. *The Double Dream of Spring* (1970) resonates throughout with an almost olfactory hint of deep image; and the title poem of *Self-Portrait in a Convex Mirror* meets the challenge of iconographic meditation; but the campy pop cultural foundations of Ashbery's swelling body of work give a very different inflection to suppositions about what one encounters in the "sieved dark" (Ashbery 1970, 66)—an inflection possibly more attuned to the American psyche than the archetypal panorama of Bly or the episodic homespun Polaroid surrealism of the creative writing programs in their first flush.

What Ashbery made available, at least as supplement to deep image, is a complex apparition of "the loose / Meaning, untidy and simple like a threshing floor" (1970, 18). Insofar as Ashbery's readers are disoriented, the patently simple is haunted by some peripheral worry, deep image as shark's fin—or is it just a trick of light on the waves? Surface or depth? The sense that surface and depth may be snug against one another is even more insistently pursued by Michael Palmer, a beneficiary and agent of the linguistic turn in American poetry. Palmer, like Creeley, bears allegiance to the syntactic rather than the pictorial promise of poetry; and such images as do emerge ("A headless man walks, lives / for four hours" [Palmer 1988, 59]) are enhanced (or rendered "deep") by syntactic perturbations rather than by rhetorical framing.

Syntax—that labor of joining or putting together—has turned out to be a more fertile incitement to poetic possibility than the reassuring parade of images. As early as 1965 Rothenberg admitted as much, locating the incentive behind the deep image debate in a "freedom for the mind to move among words and things, to *invent* . . . relationships without finality" (1965, 27). To invent relations without finality has been a worthy prospect for poetry since being theorized by the German Romantics in Jena. Rothenberg's explorations of procedural composition (like Gematria) and performance strategies (infusing Dada with ritual chant) released him from the trap of deep image as somnambulistic automatism. It's by way of his fusion of a performative transfiguration of "found" material that deep image came to fruition in Rothenberg's long poem "Khurbn" (1989), arising from his visit to a concentration camp in Poland (the term *khurbn*—the "dark word"—is a Yiddish alternative to "holocaust": "too much smacking of a 'sacrifice'" [1989, 5, 3]). This forty-page poem (anticipated in "The Presence of the Dead Is in Every Corner," a poem immediately following "Deep Image: Footnote" in *Nomad* in 1962) consists almost entirely of litanies and lists, but the historical context renders them not only accessible but even suspenseful, unencumbered by any sense of automatism. In contrast to Bly's tendency to replenish the waking world with dark archetypes, "Khurbn" is a cry of pure loss, following the hypnagogic instruction "practice your scream" (1989, 11): "Let a picture begin to form with every scream / Let the screams tell you that the world was formed in darkness that it ends in darkness" (34). It is only by its exuberantly declamatory means that "Khurbn" emerges as an affirmative encounter with the blackest of black suns; and, in the process, suggests that deep image continued to beckon Rothenberg for decades after he abandoned the theory.

In conclusion, what can be said about the life and afterlife of deep image? As a concept abandoned by its creators, even as they held on in practice to the hopes it awakened, it remains unsettled, a trail of clues leading to an abandoned worksite. The short career of deep image was plagued by a sense of overbearing advocacy, not because Rothenberg and Kelly were prone to issuing edicts but because the term was quickly associated with Bly, who was. Nonetheless, an injunction remains in the form of a lesson learned: there can be no program of deep image, no programmatic relation to the composition of deep image, any more than one might choose duende from a flamenco menu. One can only be aware of deep image in peripheral vision, as it were: thwarting direct scrutiny, it cannot be assimilated to a program.

Because deep image was a misleadingly concrete specification of the unspecifiable, Walter Kalaidjian claims that in Bly's case it was an "essentially conservative aesthetic" draining his poetry of its "discursive power" (1992, 197). Bly's commitment to the redemptive power of the unconscious is an act of faith, where Kalaidjian wants self-awareness. The two have rarely been united, let alone reconciled, in poetry. In contrast to the novel, that eminently modern genre, poetry is archaic. Bly and Rothenberg both went tribal in their own ways, notwithstanding the irony that the original provocation of deep image was the poetry of cosmopolitan Europeans. Deep image aspired to renew the archaic resources of poetry, and such a quest could not help becoming ontological rather than aesthetic. "The basic enigma of 'deep image' poetry," wrote one critic in 1973, "is that it is not so much a technique as it is a state of being" (Piccione 1992, 53). Compounding the ontological enigma, suggested Charles Altieri, is that deep image is "man's way of experiencing the nonsubjective depths of his own being alive" (1979, 85).

The existential imperative that drove deep image—this feeling around in the dark for something without predetermined shape or dimension, but which by that very indeterminacy (openness, "without finality") belongs to the darkness—was an act of faith that it (whatever it was) would be recognizable when it appeared. But recognizable to whom? After all, "the unconscious speaking to the unconscious" bypasses consciousness altogether: so one might be engaged with deep image and know nothing whatever about it, like a sleepwalker oblivious to a nocturnal ramble. The valedictory aspect of the poet's commemoration of the stream of images lost to the dark is memorably put by Robert Kelly:

> I once had a deep intuition of . . . a place in us in which the images die, in which they mount up and falter to the back, almost literally going over the pons, over the bridge in the brain, back into the back and die, die there, the images die. And our obsessions die there too, the hundreds of thousands of perceptions that we have every minute go there and become washed clean, and some few of them become redeemed along the way. (Erwin and Rasula 1974, 135)

In the end, deep image is the reader's share, not the author's prerogative; the deep image is the one that sucks you in under the ongoing flow.

In its search for a tropological trapdoor, deep image was clearly a belated inflection of Surrealism: not only the surrealism of associative discontinuity and cultivated perceptual mutation—not only a *style*—but Surrealism as understood by Octavio Paz, whose lucidity on the subject derives from a unique combination of participation and distance. "The surrealist adventure is an attack on the modern world because it tries to suppress the quarrel between subject and object," he wrote, in a passage that might equally apply to deep image. "The same acid that dissolves the object disintegrates the subject. There is no self, there is no creator, but rather a kind of poetic force that blows where it will and produces gratuitous and inexplicable images" (1973, 153). The mystical assent is ominously at hand in the presence of this gratuitous force, as Paz well knows. "Inspiration is manifested or actualized in images. By means of inspiration, we imagine. And as we imagine, we dissolve subject and object, we dissolve our selves and suppress contradiction" (154); and as Paz infers from Reverdy's definition, "every image approximates or unites realities that are opposite, indifferent, or far apart. That is, it subjects the plurality of the real to unity" (85). And yet, surmised Roger Caillois, the ex-Surrealist, the poetic image must not contritely submit to some consolatory mission: "The terms it connects must summon each other on one level, and repel each other on another" (2003, 317). There's much to savor in unity, even when it's achieved by suppressing contradiction, but there is always the morning after, the new day when contradiction and variety are reborn. That is a world that can, and must, be discussed, not hailed in the narcosis of deep image. We don't live in our dreams, but (and this is the persistent allure of deep image, this reminder) our dreams do live in us, after all, loaded with all the darkness we pack into them.

Flesh Dream Books

I FIRST READ work by Robert Kelly nearly fifty years ago, in 1972. It was my third year in college, and I'd found a hearty friend in Mike Erwin, who shared my absorption in Pound but knew more about contemporary American poets than I did.[1] Visiting my parents during Christmas, I took a stack of his recommendations: *The Maximus Poems* by Charles Olson (the Corinth reprint of 1960), *Bending the Bow* by Robert Duncan, *Gunslinger* by Edward Dorn (again, just the first installment as issued by Fulcrum in England), and *Flesh Dream Book* by Robert Kelly (1971a). On my own steam I'd also brought along titles by Pablo Neruda, Fernando Pessoa, George Seferis, and Eugenio Montale. Olson and Duncan I'd already dabbled in (*The Distances* and *Opening the Field*), so I had some sense of what I was getting into, and Dorn had made a legendary appearance at Indiana University where I was studying (I missed it, but my ears were full of the reports). Kelly, though, was a shot in the dark, fueled only by Mike's obvious and almost liturgical reverence for this intriguingly named book—a book, moreover, that was almost two hundred pages and made a show of containing only two- or three-years' worth of writing.

Flesh Dream Book was the fuse that lit the dynamite cluster of the other books. I didn't expect that an apparently tossed-off gathering of poems by a guy in his early thirties would claim the exalted heights charted by Olson and Duncan; but there was something deeply insinuating in that title, something leonine in the yellow-tawny cover, to say nothing of the bardic-bearded countenance of the poet himself in the photo provided by Black Sparrow in its author profile. It's hard now to imagine the impression made by a book like that, because its impact came with the full force of its moment in tow. For a (or *this*) twenty-year-old white male that moment reverberated with the seemingly endless ignominy of the Vietnam War (my draft number was just two digits above the draft threshold in 1970), the squalid Nixon presidency, and the quaintly named generation "gap" that felt more like an abyss—to say nothing of that estimable triple crown (sex, drugs, rock 'n' roll) with which the sixties has been branded and which by the seventies provided an inescapable hedonistic countenance to countercultural life. Against that backdrop, contemporary poetry, *real writing by real living people*, was tantamount to the discovery of long-lost Atlantis. *Flesh Dream Book* waved its obscurely ceremonial wand—its freak flag, to use the idiom of the time—over this hidden domain.

I need to be precise about the magical procedures involved. I don't quite mean Magick in Alastair Crowley's sense, though that was much in the air and certainly courted by the references and vocabulary in Kelly, Gerrit Lansing, and others. The most succinct way to specify the aura is to challenge the term "recreational drugs": my point being that, for us anyway, there was no such thing. Drug use was part of a hieratic engagement, a spirit quest. An acid trip was a carefully choreographed itinerary of unabashed soul searching. And while smoking dope was more casual, it too contributed its share to one's discovery of the *calling*. Call it quaintly period specific, but there it is; and arched over it all, like an inscription above a portal, those words, that mantra: *flesh, dream, book.*

So what was it in that book, in Kelly's writing in general, that led us on— led us *in*? Right there on the surface was the look of the poems, ranging expansively across the page. Where Olson had insistently expanded the visual coordinates of the poem by occupying the space of the page as force field, Kelly took an additional lead from Duncan's elegance (to clarify my coordinates: I hadn't yet encountered Mallarmé's *Un coup de dés*). The result was that a poem by Kelly made a subcutaneous impact before it was read, like a hermetic barcode scanned with an adroit alchemical flourish over the alembic. Striking through the lines of "The Separations" from *Flesh Dream Book* gives you the poem's visual template, deftly released from margins, gently cantering left and right over the page (see figure 5.1). The lines seem to swish back and forth as if panning for gold. Such pages were paradigms of whatever "open poetry" connoted. (*Open Poetry* was an anthology edited by George Quasha).[2] It meant, above all, openness to experience. What's more, in this book the poems were printed continuously; a poem had no privileged claim to commence on a page of its own. This novelty had the effect of leaching a cornucopia surreptitiously into the textual sum. Furthermore, Kelly's mind was so sharp, his ear so refined, that this effortless resistance to the staple tug of the left-hand margin revealed a ballet of pure creative intuition. It constantly courted the moment-to-moment of a diary or journal with the tacit grail quest of processual poetics. Robert Duncan's "Structures of Rime" and "Passages" sequences were evident models, but they were procedural gambits whereas each Kelly poem seemed the charter of some potentially new genre unto itself. In all of them, though, there was a characteristic melody of a

THE SEPARATIONS

150

Figure 5.1. Strikeout of lines from Robert Kelly, *Flesh Dream Book* (1970), "The Separations"

mind on the move—portending glimpses of what he called (echoing Wallace Stevens) "The Stream on the Other Side of the Mind."

The code words in Kelly's title speared three related fish. *Flesh* suggested the incessant immediacy of desire, but also the corporeal envelope of the world that Olson had anatomized in his "Human Universe" essay (1967). *Book* was what you held in your hands as you read, and while reading it became the palpable emblem of desire, the residuum of foreknowledge in an almost alchemical sense: scriptural, without the scriptures. *Dream* was the crucial hinge. Where *flesh* and *book* seemed to rotate their respective beacons without overlapping, *dream* dissolved the Euclidean geometry and parsed everything in a fabulous nimbus of potential connectivity. *Tat tvam asi* (thou art that) has been a constant underpinning of Kelly's work—revenant of childhood Catholicism no doubt, but also a trip-lever of perpetual discovery in the flow of analogies (re)inaugurated by Baudelaire. The book, scaled back, was a dream of flesh; skin, probed lightly, was a dreaming book. The dream folded flesh onto flesh and the book took flight.

I don't want to make too much of a single title among Kelly's sprawling oeuvre. *Flesh Dream Book* was a portal for me, but it was shaggy and uncouth in a way befitting my own condition at that moment. Returning to Bloomington (Indiana) after the holidays, I quickly laid hands on anything else I could find by Kelly, and it was as if the very title (to say nothing of the contents) of *Finding the Measure* became my compass. Dig deep and open your mouth as wide as you can: that was the portent, or "permission" in Duncan's sense. Although I was far from realizing it then, Kelly's mouth-to-the-measure momentum constituted a poetics very close to Gertrude Stein's way of laying hands on the moment, as she describes it in "Composition as Explanation." This may be hard to see because of Kelly's thematic straining after orgasmic epiphany—whereas Stein, one might say, is all about multiple orgasms. But taken more broadly, Kelly's abundance is as *continuous* a composition as "Lifting Belly" or *The Making of Americans*. "There is no end to a Kelly poem," wrote Guy Davenport in 1974. "It is a cataract of energy" (164).

Just as important as the energy, though, was the flotsam of curious lore dispensed with the casual gesture of some herculean fund of esoterica. Other poets in a more conservative lineage might make the appreciative nod to Mozart or Beethoven in a poem, but with Kelly you stood exposed to *Die Frau ohne Schatten*—one of the lesser-known operas of Strauss—or even more obscurely, "Mare Nostrum: A Sequence from the Piano Music of Frederic Mompou," a Catalonian composer better known now, but whose very existence I could not verify until long after this initial exposure in *Flesh Dream Book*. Kelly's work took the spark from Olson's patchwork bibliophilia in "A Bibliography on America for Ed Dorn" and "Proprioception" (1974); and *In Time* seemed achingly poised on a threshold where any proper name or title could become a poem unto itself. This Olson Effect went well beyond Kelly, encompassing Howard McCord's *Gnomonology*, John Clarke's *From Feathers to Iron*, Ed Sanders's *Investigative Poetry,* and much else. It infused a broader discourse evident in *Io*, Richard Grossinger's journal of bioregionalism and poetics in which the first translation from Foucault's epochal *Le Mots et les choses* appeared, as well as Jerome Rothenberg's *New Wilderness Letter* and his numerous anthologies. In many ways the slap-happy culmination was *America a Prophecy*, edited by Rothenberg and Quasha, a singular apparition all too quickly forgotten.[3] Looking back now, it's apparent that this venturesome initiative of poets following the lead of Pound as grand wizard and grammar-school headmaster was spurned in academia, which insisted on a strict division of labor whereby poets would supply product and critics seal the packages. It was this factor, more than anything, that made Kelly such an attractive portal to a poetry counterculture with its own presses (e.g., Black Sparrow, City Lights, Auerhahn, Oyez, Four Seasons, Jargon, Coach House in Canada, and Fulcrum and Cape Goliard in England), its singular bibliomania, its cultural eclecticism, its grand sense of adventure.

An important factor in the glow Kelly emitted was the "company" in Robert Creeley's sense. Olson and Duncan, like Zukofsky and Pound, were conspicuous coordinates, but Kelly's own contemporaries were crucial portents of very different destinations. As companions in esoterica, Gerrit Lansing, Stephen Jonas, and Kenneth Irby were promissory notes of their own. Clayton Eshleman's journal *Caterpillar* netted these and others with clear deference to the force of gravity Kelly exerted—a milieu in which Paul Blackburn also held court. On a somewhat different track were Jerome Rothenberg and David Antin, comrades from the beginning of Kelly's career who, by the late sixties and the journal *Some/thing*, were heading off in procedural directions owing more to John Cage and Jackson Mac Low than to Black Mountain poetics. That Kelly could serve as a roundhouse from which conceptual trains embarked on such variable destinations says something about his charisma at that time. Through Kelly you could get to—get *into*—all these poets, along with a younger generation (often but not always his students: Harvey Bialy, Thomas Meyer, Charles Stein, Bruce McClelland, Pierre Joris, and others), and even, through that curious Anchor anthology he edited with Paris Leary, *A Controversy of Poets* (1965), back into the conservative Hall-Pack-Simpson crowd. As dense and impenetrable as Kelly's own work could seem at times, Kelly the phenomenon was an agreeably accessible conduit to adjacent worlds. Certain of his works pointedly cohabited their sources as well: *Axon Dendron Tree* is the best poem Zukofsky never wrote.

And this is where the touted delirium of the long poem comes in. I can't overemphasize the aura of the long poem at the time of Pound's death in 1972. I'd only been reading *The Cantos* for a few years at that point, but in the life span of a twenty-year-old that felt like a big chunk of my life. Although Olson died in 1970, acolytes had to wait until 1975 for the final volume of *The Maximus Poems*. Zukofsky's *"A"* was a momentous perplexity: we knew of it, of its decades in the making, but it was unavailable until I nabbed the two-volume Jonathan Cape edition in London in November 1973—and it was only after the revelatory publication of *"A" 22-23* in 1975 that the spigot turned full throttle for me. But these were ancestral examples. The long poem was a fixture of *Caterpillar*, in which Theodore Enslin's *Synthesis* was being serialized, amid a steady series of long poems by others.[4] As *Caterpillar* shepherded the sixties into the seventies, it seemed as if the whole mission of poetry was intent on abolishing the discrete private lyric moment, not denying it but enfolding it into a phenomenological continuum. For the prescience of that trajectory, consider that Michael Palmer and Ron Silliman first appeared in the pages of *Caterpillar*.

And then came *The Loom*. It was like nothing before, and nothing since (although it was clearly beholden to the installments of Dorn's *Gunslinger* that had immediately preceded extracts of Kelly's epic in periodicals). If there is a lost grail of American poetry in the twentieth century, *The Loom* is self-nominating. To be a partisan participant in a certain poetry world of the early seventies meant being exposed to installments of *The Loom* in *Caterpillar* and elsewhere. There was no mistaking the spellbinding insistence with which they came across as portents of another mission in poetry altogether. In time, I would recognize *The Loom* as an assiduous assimilation of alchemy, and a poetic companion to C. G. Jung's *The Psychology of the Transference* and his other studies in the hermetic tradition. Yet even as I came to appreciate the intertextual resonance *The Loom* carried impetuously along like a tidal wave, its own unique duende was unmistakable.

Lore had it that the vastly overweight Kelly (obese when the concept was a distant gleam in the lecherous eye of fast-food franchises) had been told he wouldn't live past forty, which would be 1975, the year *The Loom* was published. Written during Kelly's sojourn in southern California, 1971–1972, it was an acutely ontological reckoning with looming mortality. As it happened, Kelly survived—"you will not die," the Nurse confides in the poem (*Loom* 98)—and he eventually shed so much weight as to appear a different person altogether. In the process, his poetry changed as well. It's hard to tell at this distance whether the physiological transformation or the deflation of the sixties played the greater role. By the time Reagan took office, Kelly's poems had largely returned to flush left margins, as if chastened by former indulgences into a penitential compliance with Official Verse Culture. It was during those years that the clamorous challenge of Language poetry began to infiltrate the discourse, and while Kelly steadily plied his vigilant intelligence in poems and tales, he drifted away from the discursive edge he'd pioneered in the charters of *In Time* and "On Discourse" (in the Biopoiesis issue of *Io* edited by Harvey Bialy). He became, in other words, a recognized practitioner, no longer an obstreperous agent of the broad poetic Awakening of the New American/

Black Mountain lineage—a lineage subsiding into dubious relevance in the long interregnum after Olson's death in 1970, Duncan's principled refusal to publish another book after *Bending the Bow* in 1968, and the ongoing obscurity of figures like Robin Blaser, Kenneth Irby, Ronald Johnson, and others.[5] Kelly became just another poet, then, among all too many others, eventually disappearing altogether from the radar of younger poets.

An unkind attitude might peg Kelly's case up to the late seventies as that of a preposterously fluent instinct finding a voice, as the expression has it. In turn, this suggests that a recognizable Kelly voice is evident in everything since. The seeds for such a response were planted by Barry Alpert in the Kelly issue of *Vort* in 1974, in which he suggested that "many resent the quantity of work he's published" (1974b, 166). Many since then have simply shrugged in defeat, acknowledging Kelly's impeccable ear while insisting that his publication record was unmanageably vast. There's merit in this view, but what I want to draw attention to here is the cornucopia, the vagabond potentiality, in that delirious mass of publications from the sixties, when Kelly could toss off as if it were an aside a book-length sequence like *Songs I-XXX*. The phrase that comes to mind is *possibilities of poetry*—a potential intelligence—for that's what it all amounted to. But these were not possibilities as in false starts, shots in the dark; rather, they were thoroughly habitable instances in the life of poetry as *the truth and life of myth* in Robert Duncan's title, or *going down in the world's books*, as Melville so sportingly puts it in *Moby-Dick*.

In the long poem "The World," Kelly unabashedly stakes the largest possible claim for the ethos of that time:

> there is no
> form not
> organic no
> mind not mine
> (1973, 129)

Organic form was the rallying cry behind the New American poetry, and Kelly here affirms it while abolishing it in the mode of Hegel's Aufhebung—cancelled in preservation/preserved in cancellation. Even more boldly, his declaration of omniscience insinuates a cohabitation many readers might not want to share and leads directly to Kelly's characteristic sex obsessions, flamboyantly expressed in "Ode 6":

> Every branch I pick up's a cock
> & wants to come I rub the wet bark
> rainblack opulent with crumble. Come!

Aither light & shade & spurts
the glad rollicking masturbant of earth
disguised as human love & harvest.
(1981, 211)

This emphatically male orientation smacks in hindsight of the sexism insidiously rampant in the heyday of free love and patchouli oil—despite which the poet's fecundating vocabulary proves irresistible.

Deep in the inner sanctum of these reveries played out under the tutelage of the Great God Pan, there was the androgynous model of the alchemists, one of the grand themes of *The Loom,* and also strikingly evident in Charles Olson's final days when he surmised that a sex change operation might save him, transforming the liver cancer that was killing him into Lady Live Her. As if under the spell of Olson's last hope, and with explicit guidance from alchemical tracts and the renegade Thomas Gospel, Kelly envisions a gender switch as the grand finale of terrestrial matter in *The Loom*:

> *when the male*
> *becomes female & the female*
> *male, & we move*
> *naked at last*
> *beyond the garments*
> *male & female one*
> *& none.*
> (1975, 19)

The path forged by this revelation is what Kelly calls "polysyntax," "the permission to take any or every word or phrase as linkable with what comes before, or with what comes after, or as capable of bearing meaning while standing alone" (1995, 395). In light of the above, I note the pressure of the otherwise innocuous verb *comes* (Kelly wrote a book-length poem called *Comes,* which I aspired to publish at one point). But there's more: "So any continuous text," he suggests, "is in fact rife with moves, forward, backward, stopping and recovering—syntax reaches as far as our lust for meaning lets it. And that's the joy of it." Joy: *jouissance,* that opulent word Roland Barthes never stopped fondling. And *lust,* that *must* to which Kelly's polysyntactic aspirations aspire— on which they expire? The passage I cite concerns *Sentence,* a 1980 portent of the book-length cycle concluded in 2018, triumphantly brandishing polysyntax as procedural equivocation in the deictic domain, where "there is only you / and what I guess as me / is the smallest measurable part of you" (2018, 146). Does polysyntax answer to all that was promised so long ago? I'll resist a conclusion, but in its depths I hear the old Wagnerian hammer hearkening in *armed descent* (the title of Kelly's first book):

> the sun is your mother's hand
>
> held high to shield you from the dark
> like a hammer grieving for its nail.
> (2011, 122)

I've opted in the foregoing pages to address the crystallization of a moment in a mind—a mind seemingly capable of moving through language with sinuous serpentine ease, a moment at once vexed and privileged, a moment when the vectors of historical possibility had not yet become unilaterally *global* as they are now, a moment in which the palpable residue of the past hung enticingly over those alert to its potential. That moment ended, and its termination ushered in the age of self-perpetuating contemporaneity. The internet and cell phones and unalleviated connectivity were all far in the future, but around the time *The Loom* appeared, an entire initiative in poetry culminated and vanished all at once. Kelly's epic was squeezed through the doorframe along with the final volume of *Maximus*, *"A" 22–23*, Spicer's *Collected Books*, Dorn's *Gunslinger* and his *Collected Poems* (1975a), and most consequentially for what has followed, *Self-Portrait in a Convex Mirror* by John Ashbery, which won all the big prizes (deservedly, if oddly, considering the competition), crooning a deep and unsettling new tune into the inner ear of poetry's body politic. What I'll always recall as the signature event marking that cusp, however, is a reading by Kelly that I arranged in conjunction with an exhibit I organized in spring 1975 at the Lilly Library, the rare books collection at Indiana University. *The Loom* wouldn't appear until that fall, but it formed the core of his reading to an audience of about thirty, only a few of whom had ever read his work. It was the only reading I've ever attended that could be called spellbinding in the strictest sense: when Kelly stopped, after forty minutes, people applauded, but not a soul left the room. Spellbound.

Panorama, Sentence by Sentence
The Alphabet *by Ron Silliman*

"THERE ARE SAID to be certain Buddhists whose ascetic practices enable them to see a whole landscape in a bean." So begins a famous book published in 1970. After a few methodological issues are stated, the author declares his purpose: "The goal of literary work (of literature as a work) is to make the reader no longer a consumer, but a producer of the text" (*S/Z* 3, 4). This may seem a familiar credo of language writing, but the author is Roland Barthes and the book is *S/Z*, known for its bravura microanalysis. A thirty-three-page tale by Balzac is consecutively distributed, sentence by sentence, throughout two hundred pages of Barthes's exegesis. This procedure is followed, with autobiography replacing semiotic analysis, in Ron Silliman's *Under Albany*, in which he subjects the two-page poem "Albany"—first in *The Alphabet*—to a hundred pages of backstory that is as wistful and heartfelt as Barthes's text is clinical and diagnostic.

In "The World as Object," an early essay on Dutch painting from 1953, Barthes notices that an art so stuffed with minutely registered detail ends up conflating painting with inventory: "Every definition and every manipulation of property produce an art of the catalogue, in other words, of the concrete itself, divided, countable, mobile. The Dutch scenes require a gradual and complete reading: we must begin at one edge and finish at the other, audit the painting like an accountant" (1972, 7). But all these works of still life are supplemented by the portrait genre, and Barthes ponders the collective faces of all these upstanding Dutch burghers gazing out of acres of paint. Then, he suggests, the table is turned and the viewer becomes the subject of—or is subjected *to*—the painting. "Depth is born only at the moment the spectacle itself slowly turns its shadow toward man and begins to look at him" (12).

So how about Ron Silliman's *Alphabet*? It offers up a vast inventory of discrete moments and things, seeming to solicit a scrupulous account, an audit of its contents. Such an audit would reveal a plenitude of dogs barking behind fences; a holocaust of neglected houseplants; a sizeable population of homeless people alongside a diverse retinue of urban types; a spectrum of birds rendered with increasing ornithological exactitude; a steady thump of newspapers hitting the sidewalk or porch, along with the beep and whirr and shudder of garbage trucks, microwaves, fax machines, and dishwashers; constant trips on public transport, from subways and buses to airplanes; and weather with a lot of fog and rain, punctuated with bouts of weightlifting and episodes of sexual relief. But is this an art of inventory? Or do all these things gaze out at us like Dutch merchants, sizing us up for some purpose unknown to its author? How does the retinue make its impact?

The initial impact of *The Alphabet* is its sheer size (Amazon.com lists the shipping weight for the paperback as 3.1 pounds—nearly a pound heavier than *The Maximus Poems*, *The Cantos*, or *"A"*). Classical aesthetics included a category for the monstrously large, and a single book of poetry exceeding a thousand pages would seem to fall into the category of the sublime. In *Critique of Judgment*, Kant associates the grandeur of the sublime with whatever seems likely "to do violence to the imagination" by virtue of its scale: *"the sublime is that in comparison with which everything else is small"* (1982, 386, 388). Certainly from the perspective of those who take their poetry in modest doses Silliman's opus is an unsettling prospect. But given the precedents Silliman would avidly align himself with, there's nothing grim about page length, so another model is needed. Philip Fisher, doubtful about the sublime, calls it "the aestheticization of fear," an "intricate theory for a type of art that we do not actually have and would not care for if we did have it" (1998, 2, 3). He advocates supplanting the sublime with wonder, "the most neglected of primary aesthetic experiences within modernity . . . the aestheticization of delight" (2). Fisher insists that wonder is predicated on the instantaneous apprehension of a whole, for which the rainbow serves as his model. This privileges visual arts, of course, handing writing a distinct disadvantage. He even calls syntax and grammar "the enemies of wonder" (22). But Fisher doesn't want to dismiss poetry's potential for the experience of wonder, so he imagines that a dense, clotted language (like Zukofsky in *"A"* 22–23—albeit not among his references), by impeding the smooth temporal flow, forces a puzzled confrontation with linguistic instantaneity, inducing wonder. "Modern poetry since Mallarmé," he writes, "has weakened the part played by grammar and syntax and crossed a critical threshold in the use—one after another—of unexpected words and references until expectation itself ceases to work and the experience of wonder can take over" (Fisher 1998, 23). *The Alphabet* demonstrates another possibility. It meets Fisher's criteria for wonder, but without availing itself of "unexpected words and references"; furthermore, it proceeds precisely by means of the syntactic unfolding of time.

While *The Alphabet* would obviously confound the so-called common reader, whose reading relies on formulaic models, any literate person could plausibly read the whole book. It abstains from the obscurantism of its own lineage: no word salad à la Gertrude Stein, no esoteric references like those in Pound and Olson, nor the elliptical concentration of Zukofsky and Bunting, just accessible American speech. It is massively invested in the everyday, the pedestrian realm to which the poems of William Carlos Williams adhere with comparable devotion. Silliman's corporeal orientation also merits comparison with Frank O'Hara, but the latter's pledge to what he called "personism" is not really integral to the autobiographical persona of *The Alphabet*, which is personal in a matter-of-fact way when the personal is of note, but in many instances is simply a register of the recording apparatus. Not "I because my little dog knows me," but "I" because grammar predicates identity, sentence by sentence. By adopting the obscurantism of Mallarmé as a precondition for the experience of wonder in poetry, Fisher oddly forfeits any prospect of finding a poetic corollary of the rainbow, which may be rare but is utterly familiar. He may be right that expectation impedes the experience of wonder, but the reader of Mallarmé *expects* to be taxed to the limit no less than the reader of Carl Sandburg expects plain speech. If thwarted expectation is a criterion, then, it would seem that a *structural* solution would be best, and *The Alphabet* is a good example of how a thoroughly familiar world may be defamiliarized by the arrangement of parts. Can this arrangement be called an inventory? Certainly, *The Alphabet* teems with the sort of details that make comparisons with the inventory plausible, especially because it accommodates so much repetition. In everyday life, acts of attention are not hierarchical: you see what appears, mixed in with what you might be on the lookout for, and Silliman's book itemizes such acts of attention without arranging them into the sort of order an inventory would allocate. And yet the very title suggests a familiar order.

The familiarity of a world registered so scrupulously throughout Silliman's opus, however, is precarious. The look of things as well as deep structures change over time. But these transformations are projected on a screen of continuity in the social imaginary. The San Francisco Bay area chronicled with observational exactitude in the earlier portions of *The Alphabet* has by now receded into a penumbra of fantasy, fueled by the ubiquity of media images still in circulation, like the Dirty Harry flicks and the TV series *Streets of San Francisco*. Against this debased backdrop, *The Alphabet* is no compendium of naïve inscriptions but an act of semiautobiographical vandalism. That is, its brazen intermingling of public and private shares more with graffiti than with, say, "Autumn Begins in Martins Ferry, Ohio" by James Wright, or comparable lyrics that salt and pepper the personal with decals from the so-called public sphere. The role of the participant-observer is always open to charges of subjectivism, and for all the architectonic integrity of his overall design, Silliman permeates the text as a temperament—cf. Émile Zola's famous characterization of the artwork as "a corner of the world seen through a temperament" (1998, 550). Zola's commitment to documentary fiction as an experimental enterprise is a useful precedent for Silliman's method, although the prism of temperament in *The Alphabet* is more conspicuous and imposing than in even the most insistently moralizing novels, but with this Whitmanian difference: a body consistently appears, while attitudes are intermittent.

The Alphabet might be construed as "a poem including history" on Pound's model. But no historical figures are called on to serve as models of statesmanship, like Adams and Jefferson in *The Cantos* or John Winthrop in *The Maximus Poems*. Still, *The Alphabet* does carry its history within it like a virus: most of the history that ends up in it has become so during its composition. The text is a weave of its times. The characteristics of this history are evident in details that may prove increasingly esoteric to future readers, beginning with the very first page: "I decided not to escape to Canada" (1). Americans, perpetually underinformed about their own history, may not recognize as well as Canadians the demographic profile of draft age men during the Vietnam War. Other references will seem recognizable, if anachronistic: "Sooner or later you will have to get up to change the record" (3); "I remember when everything was a western" (141); "Trigger stamps out a haiku" (370)—Trigger being Roy Rogers's horse. A reference to a "cordless phone" (571) now sounds quaint, as does the reference to a jogger "Turning / the tape in her Walkman over" (772).

Thanks to corporate strategies, entertainment media keep recycling old content, so Silliman's references to TV shows like *Charlie's Angels*, *Miami Vice*, and *Hill Street Blues* may not require footnotes; but there are embedded references that will. The conclusion of "Paradise"—"Listen. Be careful out there" (431)—was the warning delivering by the briefing sergeant in the opening scene of each *Hill Street Blues* episode. Here's another: "There you go again" (229), Ronald Reagan's crafty rebuke to Jimmy Carter in a presidential election debate (it now has its own Wikipedia entry). At this late date, even the infamous line "If it does not fit, you must acquit" (943) from the O. J. Simpson trial may be receding into Trivial Pursuit lore. How many younger readers will notice its conflation with the scandal leading to the impeachment of Bill Clinton in 1998? "Johnnie Cochran holding aloft the long cigar before Miss Lewinsky / Then turning to the entire Senate, shouting / If it does not fit / You must acquit" (959). There's a historicity even in the simplest references: "Jose Canseco twitches his neck" (364). For those indifferent to major league baseball, this is just a guy with a Hispanic name. But for those in the know, does the reference evoke the glory days of an Oakland A's slugger, or the cutting edge of steroid fueled achievement? This sentence is followed by another: "The hang time of telling," which pinpoints the equivocation of the reference to Canseco hanging over differently informed readers. The hang time of telling is also a good temporal marker for this long poem written from 1979 to 2004, half the time it took Pound and Zukofsky to write their epics, but longer than either *The Cantos* or *"A."* "Any text is a time capsule," we read near the end of *The Alphabet* (1035). Another line, "The past emerges vast enough to swallow any present" (947), may well address the passing years (Robert Duncan's title *The Years as Catches* becomes "The years as batch files" in *The Alphabet* [456]), while it also registers the biological accumulation of years on the part of a then fifty-eight-year-old author.

In the hang time of telling, the reader is drawn into the author function, as author and reader emerge together in the paradigmatic role of someone who reads an environment. The author—a typological agent of the author function—is a conspicuous figure throughout *The Alphabet*, even if not all its first-person formulations can be assumed to be autobiographical. The authorial persona has its roots in Whitman, and maybe more significantly in the cameraman in Dziga Vertov's 1929 film *Man with a Movie Camera*, repeatedly shown dashing around an urban milieu filming everything. Silliman constantly places himself at the scene of writing, though that scene is first set by way of *Peanuts*: "Atop a small house, the cartoon dog types away" (4). But soon enough the itinerant poet appears:

> Half-haunted, it seems, to walk so briskly, aimlessly,
> changing direction many times, sitting every few
> **blocks** on a bench **or** stoop to scrawl—more accurately
> half print, half draw—words into the notebook. (213)
> I crouch against a wall to write. (15)
> I kneel / at a light post to write this. / Hunker against it
> really. (797)
> Putting the *Privacy Please* sign **onto** the hotel room door, I
> pull out my notebook. (216)

There's a cost to peripatetic composition that recurs like a thematic thrombosis: "Heart pounds, thinking I've misplaced this notebook" (388); "Instant at which, imagining this notebook lost on the airplane (or, worse yet, may still be in Dallas or Houston, anywhere), wave of panic, nausea, bathes you" (443). This anxiety is periodically revisited until a portable electronic device

overtakes the notebook, and "Forced to write more slowly, pocket computer's tiny keyboard touch-typed by thumb, sentences unfurl differently" (989).

Another factor of writing in public is that it's "a form of performance, on
buses, say, or here amid sunbathers" (151). So, "Big-eyed child stares over his
mother's shoulder on the bus, silently watching me write" (388)—and even
"The fly pauses to watch me write" (233). Is it the reader to whom this sentence is addressed: "You stop to stare, / to watch me write" (849)? Regardless,
there *is* the inevitable question put by the old Puerto Rican man: "Why do I
write?" (75). Fused into these scenarios of composition is a primal scene as
answer to that question: "I began to write at the age of ten as a means (and
a good one) of making a safe place for myself in a house ruled by madness"
(147); "When I was a boy I would go to my room, shut the door, sit on the
bed and write in a notebook" (429); "After dinner they would clear off the
table and I would bring in my grandfather's massive typewriter and work
for hours" (431). Writing needn't be so strictly compensatory. Its viral insistence suggests a generalized enthusiasm, like speaking in tongues. In one improbable scenario worthy of Whitman's absorption of multitudes: "Everyone
on the bus / is writing furiously into notebooks" (776). But elsewhere we read,
"Everyone on the bus is wearing headphones" (369), equating a scene of poetic production with a consumerist solipsism. Writing has to face its effortless
commingling with any act whatsoever: "Preparing to write, I touch my cap,
hitch up my pants and reach for the bag of resin" (377). Silliman urges himself to "Shake off that metaphor," but only, I think, because *The Alphabet* is a
work conspicuously resistant to metaphor. But it does occasionally indulge in
allegory, sometimes heavy-handedly, as in: "At the base of the heroic // sculpture, in the shadows of / the Federal Trade Commission, / the homeless man,
sleeping // looks so small" (887).

The figure of the writer, carefully situated, begins to accrue a bodily dispo-
sition, and this is important to distinguish from personality traits. The person
in *The Alphabet* is personal without extending into persona and personality
like, say, Allen Ginsberg. There is most consistently a body that hears and
sees, touches and is touched, rendered with somatic specificity. The temporal
duration involved in the composition is poignantly registered in a mantra
borrowed from William Carlos Williams's lines opening *The Desert Music*.
These lines—"The descent beckons / as the ascent beckoned" (245)—run in
tandem with Robert Creeley's "The plan is the body," amounting to a useful
credo for anyone embarking on a twenty-five-year composition in the prime
of life. In the 1876 preface to *Leaves of Grass*, Whitman concedes that his self-
presentation as robust everyman in 1855 was bound to yield to "the pathology
which was pretty sure to come in time from the other" (1982, 1108). Unlike
Leaves of Grass, with its prefatory or ancillary matter to which the profile of

decline is confined while the poems themselves perpetuate the image of radiant physiology, *The Alphabet* integrates physical decline into its ongoing portraiture. Throughout the text teeth are lost, arthritic conditions flare up, and vision is impaired, accelerating a downward spiral toward the "wounded animal stage of life" (941) as the ophthalmologist's question looms to allegorical proportions ("How many fingers am I holding up?" [916]). In sum: "My body, my archives" (956).

The long poems with which *The Alphabet* is bound to be compared, like *The Cantos* or *"A,"* were burdened with a certain mystique or mystification of design, implying some revelatory totality. Part of the mystification about Pound's design was by way of W. B. Yeats:

> Certain typical books—*Ulysses*, Virginia Woolf's *The Waves*, Mr. Ezra Pound's *Draft of XXX Cantos*—suggest a philosophy like that of the *Samkara* school of ancient India, mental and physical objects alike material, a deluge of experience breaking over us and within us, melting limits whether of line or tint; man no hard bright mirror dawdling by the dry sticks of a hedge, but a swimmer, or rather the waves themselves. (1962, 373)

Because of the clarity of Silliman's images and observations, and because they're transmitted insistently in the medium of the sentence, *The Alphabet* illuminates the borderline Yeats evokes between reflective clarity and participatory enthusiasm. The clarity is registered moment by moment, while the sense of a swimmer engulfed in palpable waves is more evident in the vast temporal scale of a text that sedulously chronicles its author being engulfed by its design. The design is structural, not thematic, however. In its title, *The Alphabet* evokes a labor of rudiments seemingly disinterested in the big picture. Or to be precise, the theoretical model of "the new sentence" suggests a panorama, sentence by sentence. Multum in parvo. Each sentence a cell, as in celluloid. But is each sentence the equivalent of a close-up? Is the relation between sentences analogous to the jump cut in film?

In the 1950s childhood I share with Silliman, we had modular building toys marketed as Lincoln Logs, Erector Sets, and Tinkertoys (corresponding to a folksy frontier, an industrial, or a Bauhaus design template), all of which are anticipatory models for *The Alphabet* as a complex structure built up of prefab units. The modular form establishes potentially meaningful links even between parts where no coordinated meaning is intended. As parts, each bears a stress load, and as in architecture, stress loads are transmitted contiguously from part to part. But in Silliman's text, is there anything equivalent to load-bearing walls? Because the compositional unit is the sentence, that cellular pulsation, and because the principle of accumulation is paratactic not hypotactic, there's nothing one could call a "controlling argument." You might then think that the gist is in the details, but *The Alphabet* marshals a prodigious array of details while resisting the urge to make details exemplary. Exemplarity of detail, after all, is a characteristic strategy of the essay, the argument, the sales pitch. The challenge is how to impart a sense of immediacy without a conspicuous labor of mediation. *I see this, I see that* like O'Hara's lunch poems, but without the perpetual run-up to a conclusion, a revelation, a parting shot.

Another problem of any large-scale form is that the individual contributing elements may be effaced as soon as they're assimilated. Details, once used, are used up, reverting to anonymity. The principle of subordination and hierarchy endemic to military organization remains intact. Parataxis hands the baton to hypotaxis, and hypotaxis lights the torch. The challenge is to puncture the grand form so its grandeur drains off, reinvesting the droplets with their own scale of incident. Bruce Andrews puts it succinctly: "The parts need not *refer* to a whole; they can implicate the whole by implicating its constitutive processes" (1996, 81). The great nineteenth-century precursor for such a form is *Leaves of Grass*, the very title of which proclaims its orientation. Whitman's catalogue rhetoric, as it's called, harvests a maximum of individuating detail as a processional, or parade. If Whitman's object libido remains fixed on the military, it's not the top brass but the rank and file he cherishes. But there is a *rhetoric* underlying the catalogue, and that rhetoric so prizes the individual, the unique instance, that one and only one of each is allowed. *Leaves of Grass* is an ark from which the biblical pairs are turned back at the gangplank, and propagation stalls, given over to reverie rather than reproduction. It may seem counterintuitive to say so, but nothing in *Leaves of Grass* is ever repeated, even though it creates a mood of perpetual familiarity. *The Alphabet*, on the other hand, revels in repetition; this is a lesson retained from *Ketjak* (1978)—and it's appropriate that *Ketjak* itself makes an encore here, in what you might call the rhythm method of presentation.

A familiar way of understanding repetition inside a long work is by way of the leitmotif. *Ulysses* is filled with them, from the pocket soap Bloom carries around all day to the racing horse called Throwaway; and Silliman shares in these spoils. But there's a sense in which the writer of *The Alphabet* is an autopilot device, registering observational sentences with the mechanical persistence of a surveillance camera in a bank lobby, with a soundtrack mumbling a mantra from Wittgenstein:

> The world is all (the word is all) / that is the case (is false). (75)
> The world is all that is your face / isn't it exactly either. (82)
> The world is all that floats through space. (96)

Poem is all that is the case. (199)
The world is all that's in your face. (350)
The word is all that is your face. (345)
Do not / cop to all that is the case . . . (820)

The emphatic registration of details becomes autistic, or takes on the characteristics of autism, as observations submit to the compulsive rhythm of repetition—especially when adhering to Ginsberg's prescription to drop articles ("Ginsberg's right: strike / articles out" [797]): "Clogs announce person" (228); "Smell of piss in rear of bus" (762); "Blue plastic wrap of the *New York Times*" (919); "Belt that missed one of the trouser's loops" (333); "How dry the peanut butter gets at the bottom of the jar" (381–82); "Bees swarm around my hotdog" (574); "Moving the teabag to the trash can without dripping" (953); "Secretly conscious of huge pimple under my beard" (150); "Syrup forms **pools** in the sunken squares of a waffle" (174). Cumulatively, a commuter-transit attention span settles into place.

What I'm calling an autistic attention to detail is also germane to investigative work by police, journalists, private eyes, archaeologists, historians, and scholars. Because such procedures build toward a conclusion, details have little wiggle room; they always submit to a higher authority so as to count for something. Considering the profusion of *The Alphabet*, determining the status of detail is tantamount to determining the function of the sentence. If there are moments in which a few sentences build consecutively, they are soon leveled out by the vast horizon of parataxis—which should not, however, be understood in terms of the burden of history as *one damned thing after another*. How many (how few) sentences are in fact consecutive? Only a reader can say, and each reading and rereading will be different insofar as it supplements the inertia of a printed text with the attention span projected by an embodied agent. The wreader becomes the performer of the text, but without the implication of a musical template with bars, rests, and other performance cues. Reading/performing *The Alphabet* unfolds in another space altogether.

The relation of one sentence to another in *The Alphabet* mimics proximity in public and semiprivate space. Just because I happen to be standing next to you doesn't mean I have to talk to you. On the other hand, since we happen to be within earshot, we might as well pass the time of day. So there's an ongoing conversational potential among details, sentence by sentence, sometimes explicit, sometimes tacit; but there's always a relationship of *proximity* even when there's no outward exchange. Think of it as a bird's eye view, like looking down from an upper story of a building at an intersection and noticing the convergence of two pedestrians and three cars. It's a coincidental convergence, but to the observing eye it's as if some design is unfolding, bringing together a concentration of elements against all probability. So, too, consecutive sentences in *The Alphabet* may seem responsive to some magnetic compulsion drawing them together even in their randomness and anonymity. This effect is not precipitated by consecutive sentences, but by the repetition and variation of sentences and motifs throughout the whole, a reminder that part calls out to part, often far apart, clamoring for synthetic coordination by the reader.

On the other hand, the paratactic repetitiveness of sentence upon sentence threatens to assign the reader a mechanical role in a recording apparatus, like the camera at the opening of *The Man Who Left His Will on Film* by Japanese director Nagisa Oshima (1970), so everything is apprehended in a fixed aspect ratio. Values of scale have to be calculated after the initial exposure, because there's no consistent intervention of a controlling point of view. The same sense of ambiguity applies to location: *The Alphabet* provides no establishing shots in the cinematic sense. So the cowpies (377) suddenly signal a trip to the countryside, just as the milieu in which "dogs / wander amid the diners / without interest" suggests this must be a restaurant in France (347). The impedance of narrative at the level of consecutive sentences is not globally applied, however; the very nature of repetition imparts a cumulative dimension to the text, and when such repetitions have a personal character a story is convened, albeit in larger temporal arcs of ocular degeneration, marriage, children, and the constancies of everyday life adapting to a changing American environment.

Repetition also serves as an invitation to the reader. It's first of all an invitation to note the fact of repetition as such, and to assess how the text is coordinated in a series of interlocking moments, all of which are repetitive inasmuch as they reiterate the pledge of syntax. From the simplest acts of subliminal recognition—raised to prominence by being the subject of sentences—to momentous or consequential events, sentences tacitly accord equal opportunity to each and every subject. The bowl of soup and the car crash are given equal weight. By doing so, they are revealed as cohabiting a common world. There's no discontinuity between major and minor. All is a steady state in which the emergence of some perception or event into prominence reflects a motivated *act* of attention on the part of the reader—and accompanying that act is the recognition of its arbitrariness, or the circumstances of its motivation. *The Alphabet* is not so much a text that tells you to pay attention as it showers you with its own acts of attention, and then lets you hazard what paying attention might possibly involve. It achieves this utopian state by creating a platform or an assembly area in which the reader must *unlearn* reading habits that incline them to comb through texts in search of messages. What I'm describing here makes *The Alphabet* sound aleatory, like a gargantuan semantic feedlot from which you can pluck your personal text for an astrological reading. In fact, *The Alphabet* extends constant invitations to discriminate, heed, adduce, but without the inducement of ranked finality. It imprints a physiological outlook on the reading process, so you can read without fear of "missing" something, because it will find you again. I think of John Ashbery's line: "You get lost in life, but life knows where you are" (1984, 16).

Each sentence bears the whole (or is it *lays bare*?), albeit a whole in motion. Cumulatively, Silliman's sentences contribute to a sensation Proust's narrator has as he looks back and forth out of opposite windows of a train at sunrise.

> [as] the train turned, the morning scene gave place in the frame of the window to a nocturnal village, its roofs still blue with moonlight, its pond encrusted with the opalescent sheen of night, beneath a firmament still spangled with all its stars, and I was lamenting the loss of my strip of pink sky when I caught sight of it anew, but red this time, in the opposite window which it left at a second bend in the line; so that I spent my time running from one window to the other to reassemble, to collect on a single canvas the intermittent, antipodean fragments of my fine, scarlet, ever-changing morning, and to obtain a comprehensive view and a continuous picture of it. (317)

This resonates with the experience of reading *The Alphabet*, a work that runs back and forth from one window to another on its own, on our behalf, extending this invitation: "You're free to move about the text" (1053). There's a stroboscopic feel to the episodic reappearance of phenomena in *The Alphabet*—an implicit justification of its length. Details are not lost but circulate like currency from hand to hand and place to place. They're individuated in the process. All beer cans look alike until they're crushed, at which point each assumes a singular shape. This is precisely the fate of words and phrases, slogans and proverbs in *The Alphabet*. "Stop—pay troll" (217), "Vanilla envelope" (818). This procedure transforms abstract repetition into recognizability. "Haven't I seen you somewhere before?" one feels invited to ask of a sentence.

This rejuvenation of worn parts—vernacular castoffs—is put into play by means of word games. These range from simple phonetic combinations ("Hobo oboe" [147], "Eye designs / I.D. signs" [796]), and puns ("The buck shops here" [844], "polyvocalic want a closure?" [34], "Note to typesetter: you can't always get what you font" [534]), extending to treated proverbs ("Cactus makes perfect" [519], "You can lead a horticulture but you can't make it thick" [163], "Seeing is deceiving" [748]), vernacular expressions ("trope or treat" [23], "Asleep at the real" [379], "Margin of terror" [747]), and retouched quotations ("Let them each tech" [146], "Tune in, turn on, log out" [166], "I link therefore I am" [188]). Eventually it's just a matter of time before self-portraiture blossoms in this fecund soil: "I rose at dawn to write these words, going from bed to verse" (1029). Corny puns are in abundance throughout *The Alphabet*, naturally or preternaturally forming semantic boogers—a characterization that comes to hand with the motif announced by "Baby finger roams in nostril // up to the second knuckle" (62). This punning proclivity vacuums up everything in sight with almost alarming dedication, extending to song, book, and movie titles.

Film titles:

Terms of enjambment. (17)
Terms of endowment. Gravitational fields forever. (769)
The **silence** of the limbs. (219)
Science of the lambs. (220)
"Silence of the Looms" (598: title)
The silence of the yams. (951)
All this and heathen too. (71)
Sodfather III. (187)
Bride of spatula. (205, 586)
Days of rhyme **and** noses. (211)
Splendor in the graphs. (214)
A **mall** runs through it. (220)
The singing defective. (219)
The bottle of Algiers. (221)
Desperately seeking Godot. (345)
A fistful of linebreaks. (383)
When words collide. (558)
Thin blue linebreak. (599)
A day at the / traces. (848)
The name who named Liberty Valence. (905)
Readers of the lost art. (908)
Rubble without a cause (1020)

Song samples:

This brain is bound for Concord, this brain. (104)
This brain is bound to story, this brain. (105)
This train is bound for Fremont, / this train. (517)
I'm going to sit right down and writhe myself a bladder. (207)
Gonna sit right down and write myself a ladder. (441)
You must remember this—to dis is just to dis. (171)
You must remember this (a bris is just a bris). (215)
Words at the end of a decade (this hand is your hand). (171)
This brand is your brand, this brand is my brand. (180)
Chestnuts roasting over an open wound. (151)
Lucy in the sky with **macros.** (145)
Pineapple fields forever (321)
Gravi- / tational fields forever. (769)
You make me Lizzy, Miss Dizzy. (154)
Stand by your bland. (178)
Void **in**, void out. (188)
Can I get a whatness? (191)
Send in the **clones.** (196)
Wild form, you make my heart storm. (208)
Swamp thing, you make my heart sink, you make every think Post-X. (442)
What a long strange text it's been. (223)
Bead it. (227)

Where the beer and the cantaloupe play. (417)

Old Butterick sky. (418)

They call the wind Toshiba. (547)

It's a long way to topiary. (586)

I dream of e-mail. . . . Twilight of the bods. (591)

It's mah / purdah and I'll cry if I want to. (821)

The brain in pain falls mainly on the plane. (911)

The yellow rose of praxis (974)

This is medicated / to the one I / lu-uh-uv (981)

Plan's flan is grandly in the van (986)

To everything turn (990)

To shining C's (996)

Harlem Truffle (1016)

If I had a Hummer (1050)

Book titles:

Prism house of anguish. (570)

Prism mouse of language. (599)

Prism house of luggage. (769)

Hard of darkness. (333)

The art of darkness. (849)

The pressure of the **text**. (172)

Dog star boy. (177)

My sentence, my self. (180)

The ill-wrought **worm**. (191)

Paradox lost. (216)

The shock of the **normal**. (218)

The hero with a thousand feces. (344)

Waiting for Conan. (365)

sometimes a great lotion (367)

give 'em enough trope (494, 991)

The unbearable whiteness of being. (529)

The joy of looking. (562)

I dream of e-mail. . . . Twilight of the bods. (591)

The old man & the alphabet. (598)

The gangster theory of poetry. (639)

The Mao of physics. (775)

Let us / now raise famous hens. (779)

Freud's garden: / Case studies in wisteria (968)

Visions of Brody (998)

Of being timorous (1000)

Glove songs (1000)

Stanzas in medication (1007, 1045)

Blood on the floss (1037)

Hitchhiker's guide to the fallacy (1037)

The tacit instruction behind all these substitutions is a command: *RESET*—followed by another: KEEP IT GOING. Silliman, it turns out, has the stamina and the ingenuity of Sonny Rollins, whose colossal tenor sax explorations accommodate the Woody Woodpecker theme, an operatic aria, and a Tin Pan Alley chestnut in a seamless continuum. The structural design of each of the sections in *The Alphabet* also provides a sort of *RESET* function: think of it as operating not with a table of contents but with a playlist.

Word substitutions are an inherent feature of language learning, regardless of whether they partake of the punning propensity Silliman delights in. *The Alphabet* is a great hive of alphabetic mutations, constantly reminding me of my own childhood version of the manger scene with what I heard as

"Round John Virgin, Mother and Child." Before the alphabet, there's sheer orality, acoustics without inscription. But within an alphabetic order, vigilance to detail has to be provoked, especially in a longer work, which simply won't be read like a sonnet by Mallarmé. The incentive here, however, is to be on alert not for word games but for the extended premonition words convey in syntax. Silliman has taken to heart Pound's reiteration of Mallarmé's poetics—to purify the language of the tribe—by adding, in effect, the *language of the tribe*. *The Alphabet* constantly engages a politics of tribal utterance. It chronicles the permeation of entertainment media and entertainment criteria into all aspects of public discourse in the late twentieth century, a process deftly infusing vernacular speech with ideological prompts and reflexes—a paradigmatic example of which is the Nike slogan "Just do it" (199) generalized to a narcissistic American model of behavior conflating personal and public will. Automated speech, permeating the technological environment, provides a steady low roar of prosthetic vocabulary standing in for public discourse. This is the "society of the spectacle" diagnosed by Guy Debord. "The spectacle is essentially tautological," he observed, "for the simple reason that its means and its ends are identical. It is the sun that never sets on the empire of modern passivity" (1994, 15).

The Alphabet undertakes a frantic enterprise of resistance in its constant permutations of familiar slogans, ads, and other raw (if commercially refined) language matter, as Silliman practices the Situationist strategy of *détournement*, "a negation of the value of the previous organization of expression" redirecting the raw material of the spectacle to other ends (Debord 1981, 55).[1] Silliman shares the Situationists' outlook in his observation that "most of the language we consume is forced upon us involuntarily" (2008, 386). Examples roll and tumble through *The Alphabet* with the mechanical resonance of buttons in a dryer:

> Lucky Strike means fine tobacco. (428)
> Helping pets live longer, / healthier lives. (814)
> Factory direct to you. (937)
> But first this word from our sponsors. (382)
> Safe when taken / as directed. (Less filling! Tastes great!) (394)
> Live here and you / could be home by now. (757)
> The pet food cats ask for by name. (53)

We recognize, because we share, Silliman's exasperation when he discovers "I imagine the words 'Cool Mint Gel' even before I realize I've read them" (455). As a defensive strategy, these jingles are subbed out: "Wake up and smell the copy" (172); "This flood's for you" (205); "Coming soon to a paragraph near you" (7). These in turn are assimilated into an environment of automated speech: "If you have a touch tone phone, press one now" (926); "The time at the tone / will be 8:35" (790); "We will begin preboarding at this time" (103); "Please return trays to the full upright position and fasten your safety belts" (379); "Flight attendants, prepare to cross check" (1032).

The steady patter of administered jargon leaves a subliminal ringing sound in *The Alphabet*, smearing the text with these directly applied parasitic droplets of everyday American life—the sound of "Infomercials in the sky" (970). Silliman has a diagnostic approach to this legislated condition, but like everything else here there's little in the way of pontification. "Film of victims, over *Tubular Bells*, called news" (209) we read in one seemingly neutral appraisal. A bit more forcefully, "a reporter wades through rubble stringing clichés into a 'think piece'" (579). In a satiric jibe (though maybe the names are real), we get the familiar local television station line "News, / Ken and Barbie / weeknights at eleven" (487). This is, of course, the world of *infotainment*, which has left Silliman and the rest of us "wondering where the news went" (824). It's the world of the twenty-four-hour news cycle, with "CNN pumped into the hotel lobby as though it were background music, too low to focus on, but a familiar, almost comforting prosody" (566). It's also, in part, a world with pioneering social agents like American presidents: "As tho / he were a rock star, Reagan names Asian trip / 'Winds of Freedom Tour'" (810). Considering such provocations over the decades, Silliman has managed to keep indignation largely in check. Near the end there's a rare outburst: "At night Republicans jump on the outstretched hands of the frail and needy with a resounding thump" (1051). Could a Republican read *The Alphabet* without feeling personally implicated? To pose the question is to wonder how a poetic aptitude comports itself over time, bearing political commitments on one shoulder while leaving the other free for all the agility requisite to the unfolding composition. Commitment without tendentiousness is one way of describing *The Alphabet*.

Resisting the urge to editorialize, however urgent it may seem, Silliman's outlook is manifested almost furtively: "On the radio, Timothy Leary speaks of 'the glorious revolution of virtual reality.' Next slide, please" (557). It's an effective put-down, determined to resist the irony that passes so often for informed response—an underplayed retort evident in another pairing: "'One needn't read the whole of Pound when Mr. Kenner has so ably provided us with a selection.' The thought of what America" (639)—the latter phrase being the beginning of Pound's "Cantico del Sole," vividly recorded on the grounds of St. Elizabeth's with the pugnacious poet rolling his rrr's to great effect. The poisonous milieu of infotainment effortlessly absorbs whatever lies outside its own programmatic fertility, and there are moments in *The Alphabet* when you sense a sudden helpless relevance to the text itself. "Why Vanna **claps** while the wheel is spinning" (153): the *Jeopardy* question could well be, What is the alphabet? Another sentence reads: "Image, after image, spin control" (216). In a book filled with image after image, *spin control* applies not only to public relations in the customary sense but to the interplay of text with reader, which is another kind of public relation. To look into that, we have to ask what the reader presumes to be reading.

Today, when the novel is a default setting for most writing practices, readers from the so-called "general public" confronted with *The Alphabet* would wonder: How do you write that many sentences and have it *not* be a novel? It's certainly an immense database for novelists to plunder, filled with the sharply observed details that make novels seem realistic to their readers.

> Door bashed in on the driver's side // roped shut. (64)
> Out an open window, the radio broadcasts applause. (569)
> Scuffbearded oily street wino's sidekick a curiously healthy
>   and muscular bulldog. (89)
> From the bowling alley, even at dawn, the rolling clatter of
>   pins. (137)
> Half-curled, stained orange, a maxi-pad / lies on the walk. (850)
> Fog this thick gives one the sense of forever being indoors. (375)
> Loud funk rhythm in the too-bright falafel shop, red formica
>   table top. (112)
> Dreadlocks on her left side, crew cut on her right. (380)
> A homeless man struggling with his shopping cart, one of
>   its wheels out of whack. (547)
> Smell of fast food chicken / permeates elevator. (827)
> Tinny rock beat leaking from the headphones of that
>   Walkman. (387)

Such precise registrations of detail pack a distinct ratio of social text into seemingly neutral descriptions. Consider: "Young woman alone, asleep in the doorway of an abandoned porn theater, not even a sleeping bag" (907). In one sentence we're reminded of a preinternet venue for pornography— architectural staple of any metropolitan core in those days—along with the social destitution that was a surrogate conscription service for the industry. In another vignette, as sharp and wan as an Edward Hopper painting— "Hooker / in hotpants framed in the light of / the automatic teller" (828)— pinpoints the fiscal opportunities launched with the ATM (after all, hookers could not previously congregate in front of banks). Like so much of the social content of *The Alphabet*, analysis can be found in the text but rarely where the examples appear. In this case: "That which is capital intensive (porn) is legal, that which is labor intensive (prostitution) is not" (292).

So we have the makings of a novel without a narrative frame: a strategy adopted by novelist David Markson under the defiant title *This Is Not a Novel* (2004), composed like *The Alphabet* in lapidary lozenges disbursing specific information. (Another novelist, Padgett Powell, published *The Interrogative Mood* in 2009, revisiting the cascade of questions pioneered in "Sunset Debris" without apparently knowing of Silliman's precedent.) By resisting the siren call of the novel, *The Alphabet* taunts the domain called "novelism" by Clifford Siskin (1988), which might even be called *novelitis* to give it the character of a virus. In 1965 the French writer Philippe Sollers lamented the conditioning effects of the novel at that crucial juncture when a literary form was being engulfed by broadcasting media: "Men will more and more ask machines to make them forget machines, and the apotheosis of the civilized individual may someday be to live in an entirely novelized manner" (1983, 188). Novelism exhorts its consumers (*consumers*, note, not readers) to buckle up, play it safe, take it on the chin, let it all hang out, get with the program, trip the light fantastic—promptings that Samuel Beckett pillories in his early book on Proust: "'Live dangerously,' that victorious hiccough in vacuo . . . the national anthem of the true ego exiled in habit" (2006, 8–9). The narrative treadmill is spurned at the very beginning of *The Alphabet*, as the section "Blue" opens with the line reported by Breton in his *Manifesto of Surrealism* as Paul Valéry's example of a deplorable opening for a novel: "The Marchioness went out at five o'clock" (Breton 1969, 7).

If it were published by Dalkey Archive rather than in the University of Alabama Press series Modern and Contemporary Poetics (where it nonetheless stands apart as the only nonscholarly title), Silliman's opus might well be acclaimed as a novel. If it merits attention as a novel, though, it's in a special sense: it fulfills a promise of the novel as conceived by the German writers associated with the journal *Athenaeum* from 1798–1800, who called themselves Romantics to reflect their dedication to the novel, *der Roman*. But for them the novel was not yet the industrial literary medium it became in the next century. It had only a few examples, like *Don Quixote* and *Tristram Shandy*. These were not models, though, but provocations. The German Romantics (the Schlegel brothers and Novalis, mainly) set in motion a crucial trend that persists to the present, in which the novel is most sensibly realized in the antinovel. However, I don't imagine that any of this served as an incitement to *The Alphabet*, which wears its poetic patrimony on its sleeve, its lapels, or wherever it can find room to fasten a prodigious heraldry. Has any poetic work made such a concerted effort to include the names of so many other poets, I wonder? "Rodefer / has referred to me / as a romantic / which I'd deny," Silliman writes (764–65), and probably in the sense intended by Rodefer he's got a point. With respect to German Romantic theory it's accurate. But what did Rodefer mean? My guess is that he sniffed out a sentimental attachment to poetry. Not only the names of poets, but lines from poems form a kind of arterial pathway through the text. Consider the sampling of other poems (though *fetishizing* might be the more accurate verb). The opening lines of Pound's *Cantos*, Olson's *Maximus Poems*, Zukofsky's *"A,"* Williams's *Desert Music*, Ginsberg's *Howl*, and Eliot's "Prufrock" are replicated throughout like so many product unit rejects, in that the constant punning deviations render them unfit for their original service even as they're retrofitted, here, to new purposes:

> And then went down to the chips, set wheel to gambit,
>   forth in the Reno night. (5)
> And then bit down on the chops. (228)
> And then went not down to the ships, old image of
>   conquest. (380)
> & then went down on the ship. (424)
> Let's write of kids and kitchens / and what spills down bibs:
>   and then went down / for chocolate chips. (759)
> And then / went down on the snips / of old lines parodies. (813)
> & then went down w/the blips (1045)

> Repetition flogs the theme / the intent thickens / as the
>   cement hardens (129)
> The syringe **beckons** as the doobie beckoned. (163)
> the descent beckons so slowly (317)
> the descent beckons / trays returned to their "full upright
>   locked position" (318)
> the dissent beckons as / the assent beckoned (514)
> the dissent bickers / as the assent battered (515)
> The dissent bickers as the assent hunkered (memory is a
>   kind of astonishment). (443)
> The lights flicker, // the dissent beckons. (900)

> Let us go then, I & I, / outward. (365)
> Let us jog then / you and I / through fluorocarbons in the
>   sky (521)
> Let us go then, / you and I, like bananas / baked in a pie,
>   gone soft and mushy. (836)

I saw the best minds of my generation trying to figure out why
the network crashed each time they tried to log on. (150)
I have seen the best texts of my generation, starving, hysterical,
unfunded. (214)
I saw the best faces of my generation starving, hysterical, covered
with paint. (642)

Offload by islands / hidden in the traffic (65)
These islands / (not hidden in the blood) . . . (405)
offshore, by context / hidden in the head (496)
Offhand, / by comments hidden in the brain, / we reiterate
an old refrain. (751)
(offshore / by subtexts hidden in the margin . . . (866)

the round of fiddles / playing rock (371)
A round of crickets playing back. (937)

Snatches from other poems get integrated as well, suggesting Silliman's allegiance to a short-wave Spicerian radio set on a twentieth-century American
poetry wavelength. Most of them are thematically appropriate. Williams's line
from *Spring and All* about the pure products of America gets a treatment resembling the declension of a verb in Latin grammar:

The pure products of America are introduced by Ed
McMahon. (170)
The pure products of America seek market share. (207)
The pure products of America are made in Hong Kong. (386)
The pure products / of America are not made for sale. (777)

Silliman likes to revisit lines from Frost's "Stopping by Woods on a Snowy
Evening" and Olson's "Kingfishers" and worries Ginsberg's famous dictum
"first thought, best thought" like a dog with a bone:

first desk, best desk (44)
First botch, best **botch**. (162)
First bought, best bought (gag reflex at the OK Corral). (441)
First dot, best dot. (481)
First fear, / best fear: that mom's tit (the world) / might be
withdrawn. (790)
First dot, best dot. (945)
First bought, best bought (liar's remorse) (971)
First bought, best bought (1005)
First wipe, best wipe (1012)

Apart from an affectionate nod to Lyn Hejinian ("Writing is an aid to friend-ship" [154]), the sampled lines from poems mainly are by men. The one omi-nous exception is by Christina Rossetti:

> When this you see (cup of tea). (103)
> Micro to mainframe: when this you feel, stop and kneel. (149)
> When this you see, justify right for me. (333)
> when this you see / hold the bus for me (336)
> When this you feel, start to squeal. (345)
> When this you see, apple tree, there's a blight. (537)
> When this you see, hit and run / for me. (760)
> When this you see / duck and cover. (777)
> When this // you hear the time for fear / is hard upon us. (878)
> When this you see / Xmas tree. (900)
> When this you see, remember. (903)
> Stein to Hook: when this you see, remember Smee. (909)
> When this you hear, so much to fear. (925)
> When this you see, RFP (992)

I say *ominous* because I suspect this comes not from reading Rossetti, but from Robert Aldrich's film noir rendition of the Mickey Spillane novel *Kiss Me Deadly*, where the line "When this you see, remember me" inaugurates a plot that eventually leads to a nuclear explosion. (The line from Rossetti isn't in Spillane's novel: it was added by screenwriter A. I. Bezzerides, who also took the liberty of naming the woman who speaks the line Christina.)

These multiple mutations of other people's lines disclose a tactile depen-dency at the heart of *The Alphabet*, in which the very paradigm of habita-tion, the household, is being gradually overcome with books—stacked, we're told, not shelved (though there *are* shelves: recounting his move from Cali-fornia to Pennsylvania, Silliman reports an "Old deep purple bookcase still has original 'Impeach Nixon' sticker not entirely faded" [918]). In a moment of abject self-portraiture, he writes: "With a patch over one eye and ordered by the doctor not to read for three **days**, I stagger into the local bookshop" (221). There is undoubtedly a vast amount of autobiographical information in *The Alphabet*—*Under Albany* confirms it, as well as the retread of *Ketjak* as section "K"—but I'd caution against easy assumptions. The line "Always stop to talk to a cat" could be autobiographical (417), but it also applies to Leopold Bloom, and *Ulysses* is a book Silliman prizes.[2]

Like *Ulysses*, *The Alphabet* is played out largely in the public domain. Silli-man's determination to explore the possibilities of poetry in public was com-memorated in an issue of the *San Francisco Review of Books* in October 1978, where he was featured alongside Kathleen Fraser (see figure 6.1). Inside, Bob

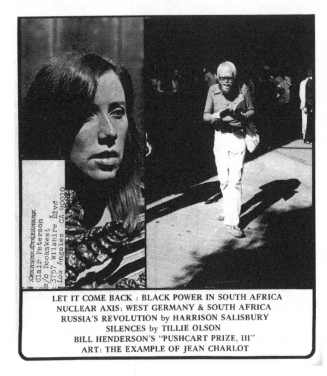

SAN FRANCISCO
Review of Books
VOLUME FOUR NUMBER FOUR / ONE DOLLAR

LET IT COME BACK : BLACK POWER IN SOUTH AFRICA
NUCLEAR AXIS: WEST GERMANY & SOUTH AFRICA
RUSSIA'S REVOLUTION by HARRISON SALISBURY
SILENCES by TILLIE OLSON
BILL HENDERSON'S "PUSHCART PRIZE, III"
ART: THE EXAMPLE OF JEAN CHARLOT

Figure 6.1.
Ron Silliman,
on cover of *San
Francisco Re-
view of Books*
(October 1978)

Perelman's review of *Ketjak* doubled as a report of Silliman's reading of the entire book on September 16, 1978, in San Francisco at the intersection of Powell and Market Streets—"spectacularly dramatic," in Perelman's account, "with the poet belting out this encyclopedia of sentences for four and a half hours at the top of his voice in an effort to make himself heard above the noise of traffic sirens, street musicians, Hare Krishnas, shoppers, tourists, and even, at one point, a corps of drummers and dancers from Chinatown. He couldn't have picked a spot where the work would have received less special pleading as 'literature.'" Oral graffiti, then. "It is greatly to Silliman's credit," Perelman concludes, "to have focused such a wide panorama so clearly, and to have sounded it so publicly" (1978, 23).[3]

The Alphabet has taken this panoramic potential to another level. It's an epic that has managed to slough off the snakeskin of previous epics, infiltrated the pleasure dome of the novel with impunity, and revitalized the Romantic aspiration of a book without precedent that nonetheless manifests a convivial attachment to everything anywhere that has given rise to it. The great criterion of the Romantic book in that German sense is that it should be the book and the theory of the book in one. Operating instructions are macroscopically issued from each and every part. In conclusion, I offer a synoptic assembly kit from *The Alphabet* itself.

> Poem conceived as a marathon, a life. (170)
> Poem as gradual as weather. (919)
> Gradually the poem begins to circle itself. (947)
> You could start almost anywhere and find anything. (200)
> Image follows image / just because. (820)
> What I say / is what I saw. (858)
> Yes, I'd repeat that / if I saw it again. (827)
> "Write often, write upon a thousand themes, rather than
>   long at a time." (262–263: Thoreau)
> Words spill forth, / adjuncts of a mind that won't quit . . . (844)
> I follow my thoughts, trailing / a little behind. (850) . . .
> Words whip past, faster than thought. (857) . . . Pages fill
>   all too quickly. (912)
> Details / articulate a structure // otherwise not seen. (68)
> Not "stream" of consciousness / but "blocks" of writing. (773)
> Sentences don't "flow" from this pen but rather are built up,
>   patched together, the junk sculpture of found objects. (582)
> Pick a sentence, any sentence. (148)
> If you don't like that sentence, here's another. (142)
> One sentence for every reader. (378)
> Simple sentences, again and again. (411)
> Your perfectly typical Silliman sentence. (418)
> Your sentence here. (442)
> For each and every sentence an equal but opposite sentence. (139)
> For each and every sentence there is an equal but opposite
>   syntax. (144)
> Each sentence understood as a dialog box. (943)
> Think of paragraphs as bricks. (558)
> Burma Shave parataxis. (190)
> Everything written according to the rules of the infield fly. (200)
> Why is this poetry? (570)
> What is a poem and where can I find one my size, extra large? (571)
> Is it poetry yet? (584)

You want to describe everything, she said. (418)

A woman in blue shorts (I can describe anything), fog over
the far hill. (21)

Develop a procedure, then violate. (428)

The system here / is there is no system, tho one might
discover / the cumulative pattern . . . (850)

This is not the sequence of composition. (51)

A book is a gift you can open again and again / especially
when you're writing it yourself. (767)

I don't think of myself as a thief of language, but as a
value-added remarketer. (150)

Why / am I telling you this? (813)

I worked as a short order book. (845)

This was not the book I intended. (843)

This is the alphabet. (208)

Anarchy in an Environment That Works

NORMAN O. BROWN got a contact high from the sixties, which propelled him into a Dionysian pledge to poetry that would sustain him for the rest of his life. But what do we mean by that much-touted period reference? To refer to a period is a way of exercising imaginative control over something otherwise out of reach. For poets, such an exercise transforms the historians' fallacy of essence into patterns of incidence (narrative) and coincidence (trope). This is tantamount to saying that historical periods are poetic visions, constellations of images: imaginary gardens with real toads in them. In Thomas Carlyle's pungent characterization in his 1830 essay "On History," history "is an ever-living, ever-working Chaos of Being, wherein shape after shape bodies itself forth from innumerable elements"—or in strictly human terms, "the Message, verbal or written, which all Mankind delivers to every man." Carlyle objected to the tendency to parse this message along progressive or narrative lines: "Narrative is *linear*, Action is *solid*," he cautioned (1984, 60). So he favored terms like *palimpsest* to evoke the density of history, "a real Prophetic Manuscript" that "can be fully interpreted by no man because such interpretation would be "more suitable for Omniscience than for human science." Carlyle sensibly reckoned that the profusion of evidence, where history is concerned, is unwieldy. Ironically, "History, then, before it can become Universal History, needs of all things to be compressed." Compression is an art; "DICHTEN = CONDENSARE," Ezra Pound insisted (1934, 77). Even so simple an exercise as "stating the facts" relies on the rhetorical devices involved in making and arranging sentences (and deploying tropes, as Nobby's friend and colleague Hayden White patiently elaborated in *Metahistory*, *The Content of the Form*, and other works). Facts may be *reported*, but sentences are *made*, and the honorific model of the maker is *poet*. "History" is the term we use for vast collective forms of life that are literally inscrutable, beyond the grasp of an observer except in figurative or poetic terms.

A quintessential artifact of the sixties is a book called *Blueprint for Counter Education*, published in the fall of 1970. It was actually a box with three large posters (each roughly 3' x 4'), along with a book titled *Shooting Script*, in which the authors provided thirty pages of guidelines for readers—or what they envisioned as "the reader-looker-rioter"—followed by 150 pages of a table of contents of recommended reading, including *Life Against Death* and *Love's Body*. The authors were Maurice Stein and Larry Miller, both at the newly launched Cal Arts, where Stein was dean of Critical Studies, and Miller associate dean; true, Stein's tenure was short-lived, ending when he drew the ire of Roy Disney with his very public effort to recruit Herbert Marcuse to the faculty. But at the time of publication, Stein and Miller could confidently declare that "during the last years of the sixties an alternate culture began to appear. This fact is documented in almost any radical bookstore where . . . mythopoeic authors like Norman O. Brown nestle alongside communitarians like Allen Watts and Gary Snyder. . . . There is a new tribe and the Woodstock Music and Art Fair may have been its single most massive manifestation" (unpaginated, in *Shooting Script*).

The *Blueprint* is a time-capsule artifact of the sixties. Two of the posters were organized around two influential figures, Marcuse and Marshall McLuhan, as magnetic polarities. But in one you'll find Norman O. Brown placed in a pivotal position, as if he's both the engine driver and the crossroads of major issues of the time. He's flanked by the peculiar pairing of George Steiner and Eldridge Cleaver and on the other side by Harold Rosenberg and Susan Sontag. Lurking in the depths below him are Black Mountain College and the Bauhaus, and those sites of significant upheavals: the Sorbonne, Berkeley, and Columbia. The list of "little mags" might look peculiar, including as it does the *New Yorker* and *New York Review of Books*, whereas the only genuinely little magazine listed is *Caterpillar*, edited by the poet Clayton Eshleman from 1967 to 1973. The inaugural issue of *Caterpillar* featured "From Politics to Metapolitics," a lecture Nobby had given at Harvard six months earlier.

In his Harvard address, Nobby provocatively took on the role of Merry Prankster, asking "What have I learned in my bizarre psychedelic trips, I mean my books?" (1971, 7). Surveying the fraught political landscape of 1967, he conceded, "It is possible that the future is a contented humanity / without neurotics like me / but I don't think so / I don't think the future is behavioral engineering." He touched on the themes of *Love's Body*: Dionysian communion, madness, and poetry as the beyond of the reality-principle and suggested that "the real action in *Love's Body*, / is to find an alternative to systematic form," which he found in aphorism, or "instant dialectic," "fragmentary moments which bring something new into the world." The essence of the aphorism as fragmentary form is that "there isn't anything we can count on or accumulate." No surplus, no stockpile. Nobby was in effect preparing himself for his encounter with Bataille's theory of unproductive expenditure central to "Dionysus in 1990," the last chapter in *Apocalypse and/or Metamorphosis* (1991).

The Harvard talk closes by promoting aphorism as sacrificial agent, emblem of "brokenness" and "dismemberment." Nobby's conclusion suggests he was about to embark on *Closing Time* (1973): "The great revolutionary intellectual of the 20th century," he decided, was James Joyce. Earlier in the talk he had spoken of utopia in terms that sound scripted for *Finnegans Wake*:

> My utopia is
> > an environment that works so well
> > that we can run wild in it
> > anarchy in an environment that works
> > ("Metapolitics" 13)

Beginning with *Das Kapital* and ending up in the thickets of *Finnegans Wake* is an unparalleled trajectory worthy of Nobby's theme. "A metapolitical solution to the problem of madness," he declared, "would see politics as madness / and madness as the solution to politics" (1971, 12).

Rhetorically, this is a chiasmus (chiasmus means "crossing" in Greek). Nobby thought in terms of the figures of classical rhetoric (and I'm grateful that he told me where to put the accent on the term *clinámen*, which became a crucial element in my anthology with Steve McCaffery, *Imagining Language* [1998]. In *Closing Time* he proclaims the return of the barbarians and finds in Joyce's *Wake* "polyglot turning into glossolalia," such that barbarism means speaking in tongues (1973, 63). As a corollary, then,

> God does not speak good English.
> Not atticism but solecism.
> Barbarism.
> Instead of the sentence, the sounddance. (*Closing Time*, 63)

In this instance he was reiterating a passage from *Love's Body*, in which he wrote glowingly of the way *Finnegans Wake* "restore[s] to words their full significance" (an aspiration Brown shared, albeit unwittingly, with Hugo Ball, founder of Dada). To achieve this "is to reduce them to nonsense, to get the nonsense or nothingness or silence back into words." Nobby saw it as nothing less than the "destruction of ordinary language, a victory over the reality-principle, a victory for the god Dionysus; playing with fire, or madness; or speaking with tongues; the dialect of God is solecism" (1966, 258–59).

Most provocative from Nobby's rhetorical arsenal is this, from *Closing Time*: "History is paronomastic" (85). Often cited as another word for pun, paronomasia is more specifically a play on words that sound alike but mean different things (like *there* and *their*). Observing that "the texture of history is the texture of *Finnegans Wake*," Nobby recognizes that in Joyce's frothy turbulence everything puns with itself, as if demonstrating the primal meaning of pen pal. And as we learn from Hayden White, history is not what really happened but what was really said about it, and saying anything at all is to find oneself prancing around in the costume (the clown suit) of rhetorical figuration.

Nobby's embrace of poetry arose in what he called "the surprising turn taken between *Life Against Death* and *Love's Body*" (1991, ix). This turn was made public in the Phi Beta Kappa address he gave at Columbia University in 1960, titled "Apocalypse: The Place of Mystery in the Life of the Mind." "Mysteries display themselves in words only if they can remain concealed; this is poetry, isn't it?" he wonders (1991, 3). He then turns to Pound, who would remain not only a touchstone from then on, but a conduit to other poets as well.

One of those poets was Robert Duncan, who became a friend and guide to Nobby on contemporary poetry after he came to Santa Cruz in 1968. Duncan attended Nobby's lectures on Vico and Joyce in 1970. Shortly afterward, he wrote the long poem "Santa Cruz Propositions," in which we find him puzzling out Nobby's new-found faith in poetry

> Poetry! Would *Poetry* have sustain us?   It's lovely
> —and no more than a wave— to have rise
> out of the debris, the stink and threat
> —even to life— of daily speech,   the roar
> of the giants we begin from,
> primordial Strife,   blind Opposition,
> a current that sweeps all stagnant things up
> into a torrent of confidence   beyond thought.
> (2014, 470)

Did Duncan think Nobby's faith in poetry had caught him up in a torrent "beyond thought": a blind faith?

"There is only poetry": this is the resounding conclusion of *Love's Body*. But Nobby didn't stop there. He kept repeating the dictum in subsequent books and lectures. He couldn't let go of it. Or it didn't let him go. "I am sentenced by my own sentence," he later said (1991, 159). Sentenced—as for a crime? And what would the crime be? Trespassing? Purloining? Indecent exposure perhaps? He came to recognize himself sentenced, in custody. I think the most apt expression is *captivated*. He was captured by the thought, "there is only poetry," captivated, mesmerized.

So what does it mean, and what was in it for Nobby? By *poetry* he didn't mean versification. It's not a literary genre to which he refers, but a far broader matrix of *making*. Nobby, ever the classicist, knew and made frequent reference to the root meanings of words, their derivations, the "etyms" of etymology he paired with *atoms* in *Closing Time*. So poetry is *poiesis*, Greek for making. "There is only poetry," then, is the charter of a fundamental anthropology. What do humans do? They make. There is only the making; there is only poetry.

But what about that seeming diminutive, "only"? Its meaning is dramatically adjusted by a twist of the grammatical key: only poetry means *nothing but* poetry. The statement is absolute, and Nobby was like a woodpecker perennially hammering away at absolutes. He once asked me if I was a fox or a hedgehog. I was unfamiliar with the pairing, which he said was from Isaiah Berlin (his tutor at Oxford). The fox is polyphemous, in search of many things, while the hedgehog knows One Big Thing. I immediately recognized myself as fox, and Nobby as hedgehog. Where he says *only*, I say *also*. A similar conundrum seems to have aroused poet Susan Howe to wonder, "How could someone so completely not care and yet bother to care so completely?" (2005, 159).

Of course Nobby was polyphemic insofar as he was a polymath. His mind made many even of the big things he took on one by one. There was Marx. Then there was Freud. Then Vico, *Finnegans Wake*, and Islam. All big things. His habit was to put them in congress with each other. "Is it optical or optional?" he asked of one of Joyce's portmanteau puns: both, he decided. "Two words get on top of each other and become sexual." Nobby had the instincts of a punographer, reading Marx and Freud in light of one another, like two words getting on top of each other. Or Vico and Joyce in *Closing Time*. His method of pairing authors is best put by Canadian poet—and, like Nobby, a classicist—Anne Carson. In the preface to her own treatise *Economy of the Unlost*, on Simonides and Celan, she outlines a method that could apply as well to Nobby:

> To keep attention strong means to keep it from settling. Partly for this reason I have chosen to talk about two men at once. They keep each other from settling. Moving and not settling, they are side by side in a conversation and

yet no conversation takes place. Face to face, yet they do not know one another, did not live in the same era, never spoke the same language. With and against, aligned and adverse, each is placed like a surface on which the other may come into focus. Sometimes you can see a celestial object better by looking at something else, with it, in the sky. (1999, viii)

In Nobby's hands such a prospect becomes a mating ritual. It's all *making*— "making love"—it's all poetry. "Nothing but poetry" gets a boost from poetry's mutual aid society:

> The making is poetry, *poiesis*
> *Dichterisch wohnet der Mensch auf dieser Erde*
> there is only poetry (*Closing Time*, 79)

"Poetically man dwells on this earth" is what the German says, Hölderlin quoted by Heidegger who, like Nobby, was a thinker consulting poets for mutual aid.

There's more to his poetics than method. Consider *Love's Body*, a book visibly displaying its compositional medium. Nobby copied out quotations from his sources—his resources—or else paraphrased them on 5" x 7" note cards. But rather than being assimilated into a stream of expository prose (as was the case in *Life Against Death*), the template of the cards persisted, so the whole book reads like a stack (I estimate the total to be about 630 cards). It's inviting to imagine a new edition of *Love's Body* printed on cards, which could then be shuffled and the reading emancipated from the programmatic arrangement he devised for its contents. (Not that I have any doubts about the prosecutorial tenacity of his arrangement, brilliantly condensed to sixteen key words as chapter titles.)

Nobby offers an intriguing augmentation of his faith in poetry when he characterizes poetry as "impossibility made credible" (1991, 151). This is not so much blind faith as a leap of faith, a gymnastic devotion. "Acrobatics is involved whenever the aim is to make the impossible seem simple," writes German philosopher Peter Sloterdijk (2013, 196). As he elaborates in *You Must Change Your Life*, acrobatics is predicated on the "practicing life," practice understood by way of asceticism. Asceticism generally suggests withdrawal from worldly things, embracing spiritual exercises in the contemplative life. But Sloterdijk takes asceticism in its most literal sense, from the Greek *áskesis*, or *training*. The artist and the tightrope walker alike are acrobats. Sloterdijk is reasserting a basic precept of modernism. The propensity for pursuing art as exploratory gymnastics inspired Karel Teige, the Czech leader of Poetism, to resist the ornamental and the devotional in art. "Let art be a spiritual hygiene just as sport is a physical hygiene," he wrote in 1922. "May it be equivalent and commensurate with sport, or perhaps with acrobatics, rather than with mysticism, metaphysics, religion" (Winner 2015, 51).

Love's Body is a work of spiritual hygiene, an acrobatic promenade. It was also a brandished ember setting flammable tinder at the midpoint of the sixties as the world began to burn. Watts, August 1965; Newark and Detroit, July 1967. Riots with references, the way John Coltrane was adopted as an ancestral spirit hovering over the conflagration (he died on July 17, 1967, the last day of the Newark riot). *Love's Body* did not cause these events, but it's important to remember that in the sixties, causation was polymorphously perverse, to use a favorite expression of Nobby's. In that light, everything took on a faintly causal glow, *Love's Body* no less than the Beatles' "Helter Skelter." It was a time when "information assumed increasingly peculiar shapes. The quality of news was measured by its grotesqueness," writes Geoffrey O'Brien in his wonderful book *Dream Time* (1988, 178). But of course, the sixties ended, and many of us are its orphans, or survivors.

Nobby characterized himself as a survivor in 1989, addressing the conference on "Revisioning Historical Identity." "Revisioning as I have experienced it is not a luxury but life itself, a matter of survival," he said, "trying to stay alive in history; improvising a raft after shipwreck, out of whatever materials are available" (1991, 158). The shipwreck had been broached the year before, in a talk he gave at Wesleyan on John Cage:

> Broken heaventalk, poetic diction
> that ocean
> in which the Apollonian ship capsizes (2005, 87)

Although it's Cage he places in the shipwreck here—a man who had embarked on a long voyage of acrostics in his own negotiation with broken heaventalk—Nobby saw himself as a fellow Ishmaelite, adrift on the sea of history. In "Revisioning Historical Identities," he characterized himself as "a premature post-Marxist," foundering not in open water but "in the frozen landscape of the Cold War" (1991, 158).

It was from that Arctic-sized ice floe that Nobby became fixated on fire, and finally found "the historical process, the Last Judgement, the great, the everlasting bonfire in which we are all consumed, all the time" (2005, 91). This was the vision he arrived at, concluding his lecture on Cage. Cage embodied the shipwreck of the Apollonian, while Nobby held fast to the Dionysian furor, fanning flames wherever he found them:

Dionysus is all fire
not Apollonian light but Dionysian fire
not purified by Buddhistic extinction of desire
but Thunder of Thought and flames of fierce desire (90)

A rhyming quatrain. If there's anything to catch the attention of a younger generation now, eyeing with dismay the indifference and incompetence with which their elders are facing climate change, it's Nobby's fiery urgency, his sense of palpable emergency. Especially because he invariably thought of it in collective terms:

The rabble, the revel, the rebel
crowd psychology, mass psychology, is Dionysian
    psychology
Canetti says: Suddenly it is as though everything were
    happening in one
and the same body. (89)

In the collective body, everything is a symptom of something else. It's all symptoms, metaphors, poetry.

After Marxism, seasoning his outlook with Freud, the incendiary flare of politics took precedence for Nobby, a prospect rekindled in that "one and the same body" of Dionysian psychology he found in the sixties. For he understood that "human culture is human sacrifice, together with symbolic substitution" (1991, 31). This is also the basis of Roberto Calasso's ongoing work on the sacrificial foundation myths of human cultures. For Calasso, myths are "actions that include their opposites within themselves" (1993, 280). And in a passage that (unintentionally) applies to Nobby's reckoning with the sixties: "We enter the mythical when we enter the realm of risk," Calasso writes, "and myth is the enchantment we generate in ourselves at such moments" (278). Nobby lived out that enchantment.

Always one for vaulting out of the ice into the frying pan, Nobby was not "Norman" but *nabi*, Arabic for prophet, and "prophecy is the perception of potentialities," he wrote as he embarked on his study of Islam in the early eighties, embracing "the Prophetic Tradition, including Judaism, Christianity and Islam; and heresies in Judaism, Christianity and Islam" (1991, 46). It's characteristic that he'd insist on the heresies as a component of the Prophetic Tradition. For he was a true heretic in the end, a paronomastic prophet— and prophet of paronomasia—in his perception of potentialities.

From Verse Narratives to Documentary Poetry

Enhancements—and Enchantments—of the Poetry Book

IN 1917 EZRA Pound confided to James Joyce, "I have begun an endless poem, of no known category," broadly indicating it was "all about everything" (Cookson 2001, xxiii). Fifteen years later, after several installments of his *Cantos* had been published, Pound offered a much-cited definition: "An epic is a poem including history" (1935, 19). With this, he set a certain tone for future aspirations in poetry, with the ongoing *Cantos* clearly modeling the prescription. And then, in 1948, *The Pisan Cantos* shifted the equation. It was a document of being *included in* or contained *by* history, written as it was in captivity while Pound was awaiting return to his homeland to stand trial for high treason. The controversy surrounding the award of the inaugural Bollingen Prize to *The Pisan Cantos* is a bracing culmination of the "modern movement" Pound had been nurturing since 1914. Because that's an episode I've profiled at length in *The American Poetry Wax Museum*, I'll pass over it here, as my concern instead is with the long poem more broadly, and the potential for poetry to adjust to and expand upon the documentary mission at the heart of *The Cantos*.

Pound's *Cantos*, in their "all about everything" propensity (enabled by principles of collage), bore no resemblance to other long poems. So what were the available models that poets and readers would have associated with such an enterprise? Examples from Greco-Roman antiquity had served for many as literary and grammatical training texts, which Pound dutifully sampled in the first Canto, revisiting the *Odyssey* through a Latin translation of 1538. In the English tradition, *The Faerie Queene* and *Paradise Lost* held pride of place in their aspirational updates of the epic. Wordsworth's *Prelude* is quasi-narrative, and Blake's longer prophetic books *Milton*, *Jerusalem*, and *The Four Zoas* convene epic possibilities on a different plane altogether. Tennyson's *Idylls of the King* and Longfellow's *Hiawatha* achieved a cultural eminence that, however anachronistic, made the long poem appear contemporary. And then there was Robert Browning, the immediate incentive for Pound to ponder the prospect of a long poem even as an undergraduate.

As it happens, the decade in which the *Cantos* began their first installments saw a singular and forceful manifestation of verse narratives, thanks to the achievements and precedents set by Edwin Arlington Robinson and Robinson Jeffers. Fugitive poet Donald Davidson observed in an omnibus review essay in 1931 that, after the "pyrotechnics" of debate following vers libre and *The Waste Land*, the American scene had been characterized by a turn "away from lyric to narrative verse, or at least toward extended poems, philosophical or loosely epical," citing "Jeffers' dithyrambic recital of horrors; the sprawling, half-lyrical, half-epical *John Brown's Body* of Benét; the Yeats of *The Tower*; Robinson's *Tristram*" (1931, 433). After positive appraisals of two recent verse narratives, *Green River* by James Whaler and *Jonathan Gentry* by Mark Van Doren, Davidson speculated that "some of the modern novelists, in their nervous experiments with the texture and structure of the novel are attempting, in prose, effects that are rightly poetical and that can be more advantageously handled in verse" (440).

Robinson's star was in the ascendancy when his *Collected Poems* was awarded the first Pulitzer Prize for poetry in 1922 (edging out titles by Amy Lowell and Edna St. Vincent Millay). Consisting mainly of shorter lyrics, it also included two verse narratives, "Merlin" and "Lancelot." In 1921 he published *Avon's Harvest*, his first non-Arthurian verse narrative (with some resemblance to Poe's tale "William Wilson"), presaging a direction that would consume most of Robinson's output until his death in 1935. Robinson subsequently received Pulitzers for two more verse narratives, *The Man Who Died Twice* (1925) and *Tristram* (1928). Pulitzer files suggest that the only reason he didn't win more was the committee's sense that the award needed to be passed around. Three in seven years was enough. In addition to the titles already mentioned, Arlington published seven other verse narratives: *Roman Bartholow* (1923), *Cavender's House* (1929), *The Glory of the Nightingales* (1930), *Matthias at the Door* (1931), *Talifer* (1933), *Amaranth* (1934), and *King Jasper* (1935). Thanks to this prodigality, narratives take up eleven hundred pages of his posthumously published *Collected Poems*, with the lyrics filling four hundred pages.

The Pulitzer recognition of Robinson's narratives presaged a burgeoning field. The year after *Tristram* took the prize, Stephen Vincent Benét's *John Brown's Body* was the recipient—and a best-seller, with over one hundred thousand copies sold even before the award. Archibald MacLeish's *Conquistador* was the sole verse narrative to win the Pulitzer during the next decade. The next to receive the award was William Rose Benét's autobiographical *The*

Dust Which Is God in 1942. His brother Stephen's posthumous *Western Star* in 1944 was his second Pulitzer. Archives of the Pulitzer committee's deliberations indicate that numerous other verse narratives were runners up in years in which the prize went to collections of lyrics.

Was it the eminence and output of Robinson that elevated the verse narrative to the high profile it sustained during the decades between the world wars? That can't be discounted, but the tremendous success of Robinson Jeffers needs to be factored in as well. The explosive impact of *Roan Stallion, Tamar and Other Poems* in 1925 launched his career. *Tamar* had been published in a small edition the previous year, with half its 128 pages taken up by the narrative title poem. The successor added more lyrics and another narrative, "The Tower Beyond Tragedy," bringing the total to 250 pages in a closely set smaller font.[1] The reception accorded the book may be measured in reviews of the time. Percy Hutchison wrote appreciatively in the *New York Times* of the earlier *Tamar*, finding "many, many pages, which are equaled only by the very great," marveling at Jeffers's supple long lines but warning that he is "not a poet for the adolescent; he is not a poet for the Puritan; he is not a poet whose conception of poetry is confined to the honeyed lyric and to conventional themes" (*NYT*, January 3, 1926).[2] "Terrible imaginings conveyed in hard bright images and deliberate restless rhythms that transfix and hold. Not for babes of any degree," opined an anonymous reviewer in the *English Journal* (January 1926, 86). *For adults only* is the message, which clearly applies to the narratives, drawing a prurient reproach from *Poetry* editor Harriet Monroe, for whom "it is doubtful whether even the most accomplished artistry would excuse the deliberate choice of so revolting a subject" (1926, 160–61). Yet after quoting appreciatively from the shorter poems, Monroe concludes: "A poet of extraordinary power is Mr. Jeffers, with perhaps a purple pride in the use of it" (164).

These examples mark the parameters of the response to Jeffers from *Tamar* through the thirties, acknowledging the visceral power of the lyrics while registering discomfort or outright alarm at the savagery of the narratives. The muscular insistence of Jeffers's verse, combined with his thematic material, struck Mark Van Doren as proof positive of "a certain maturity in the American literary mind" (1928, 102). Among the strengths of the decade, he also singled out Robinson and the autobiographical narrative poem *Two Lives* by William Ellery Leonard ("correctly hailed as a major contribution to American letters" and "a specimen of the grown-up poem" [103]). It was Jeffers, though, who garnered the most attention during the years that Robinson's verse narratives poured forth, and the California poet was equally prolific. As Jeffers recalled in the preface to his *Selected Poetry* in 1938, "Long ago, before anything included here was written, it became evident to me that poetry—if it was to survive at all—must reclaim some of the power and reality that it was so hastily surrendering to prose." Facing what he felt to be a widespread attenuation of possibilities for poetry, Jeffers felt compelled "to write narrative poetry, and to draw subjects from contemporary life; to present aspects of life that modern poetry had generally avoided"—subjects like incest, sourced from Greek myth, unsettling many reviewers. "It was not in my mind to open new fields for poetry," Jeffers explained, "but only to reclaim old freedom" (1938, xiv) (see figure 8.1).

The *New York Times* published reviews of at least eighty verse narratives from 1920 until they disappeared at midcentury, with Percy Hutchison alone contributing reviews of thirty-three, including five on Jeffers and seven on Robinson. He clearly held the latter in highest esteem, as after his initial enthusiasm for *Tamar* he quickly soured on Jeffers. Of *The Women at Point Sur* he griped that "to be muscle-bound is not to be beautiful. And Jeffers's poetry is, in the present volume, not muscled, but muscle-bound" (*NYT*, September 22, 1927). The athletic analogy served Hutchison again the next year, as he complained of *Cawdor* that "Jeffers is dominated by his material; he is not master of it. The Titan's strength is waning; but he still goes through the motions of lifting and heaving from force of habit" (*NYT*, December 16, 1928). *Give Your Heart to the Hawks* moved him to acknowledge that Jeffers "so often writes with such searing power and such flame of emotion that his poetry as a whole is something to be reckoned with." But it was spotty, he found, and "when the power lags his verse can be as raucous as the voice of a calliope." In the end, he decided, "Jeffers is a novelist, a teller of tales," and while as a poet "he is lineal descendant of the bards of old," he was infected "with every modern virus," a kind of versified D. H. Lawrence (*NYT*, October 15, 1933). Two years later, Hutchison decided that despite the poet's "modernism, perhaps even Freudianism, Jeffers is truly Elizabethan" (*NYT*, October 20, 1935). Hutchison was not alone in reviewing Jeffers for the *New York Times*. In 1932 Jeffers was featured on the cover of *Time* magazine when *Thurso's Landing* was published, and an anonymous reviewer in the *Times* declared it the poet's "crowning achievement to date," minting "a very terrifying sort of beauty in the lines that flow molten from his pen" (*NYT*, April 3, 1932). Such was Jeffers's prominence that in their *History of American Poetry 1900–1940* Horace Gregory and Marya Zaturenska declared that "Jeffers' position as a poet among his contemporaries became one that can almost be compared with Victor Hugo's eminence in France of the mid-nineteenth century" (1946, 407).

In 1929 Alfred Kreymborg chose Jeffers to conclude his monumental history of American poetry, *Our Singing Strength*. In it, the phenomenon of the verse narrative got no special attention, though he did discuss a few examples.

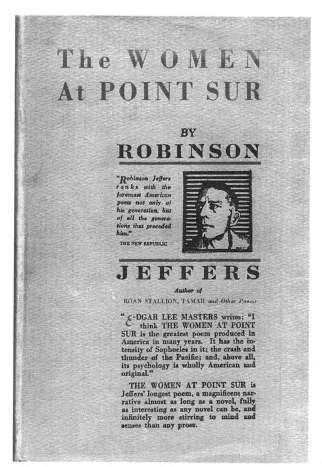

Figure 8.1.
Robinson Jeffers,
*The Women at
Point Sur* (1927)

But in 1933 Kreymborg provided an overview of "American Poetry after the War" for the *English Journal,* with nearly half of the space given to narrative poems, Jeffers in particular (E. A. Robinson was omitted, as Kreymborg had already expressed a preference for his lyrics in *Our Singing Strength*): "Jeffers can write whole passages, long thrilling passages, whose sheer power and impact have few peers in modern American literature" (1933, 267). Although he had modest reservations about *John Brown's Body,* Kreymborg was particularly keen on *Temptation of Anthony* by Isidor Schneider, with its "fire of language surpassing Benét's." Above all, he appreciated his "forthright gusto and enjoyment of life rare among Americans at any time and all the more rare after *The Waste Land*" (269). Joseph Moncure March's *The Wild Party* and *The Set-Up* (1928a and 1928b) also comes in for much praise, "written in an amazing staccato reflective of the rhythm and spirit of the post-war age." These

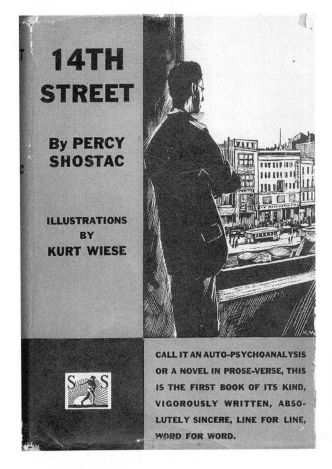

Figure 8.2. Percy Shostac, *14th Street* (1930), dust jacket illustration by Kurt Wiese

poems had all been discussed in *Our Singing Strength*, but by 1933 Kreymborg realized that, taken together, they revealed a growing trend.

By the early thirties the vogue for verse narratives was on the rise, remaining a format favored by publishers for the next two decades. By this point, Eda Lou Walton could lament that "so many very bad narrative poems are being written" (*NYT*, April 17, 1932), while for another *Times* reviewer, "one is always glad to find narrative poetry on the publisher's lists" (*NYT*, June 1, 1930). But this new vogue was of somewhat uncertain provenance. Publishers vacillated on the question of what to call them. Percy Shostac's *14th Street* (1930) bore the subtitle "A NOVEL IN VERSE," while the dust jacket cover offered other options. "CALL IT AN AUTO-PSYCHOANALYSIS OR A NOVEL IN PROSE-VERSE, THIS IS THE FIRST BOOK OF ITS KIND, VIGOROUSLY WRITTEN, ABSOLUTELY SINCERE, LINE FOR LINE, WORD FOR WORD" (see figure 8.2). The concluding references to lines and words conveniently split the difference, ge-

Figure 8.3. Helen Wolfert, *Nothing Is a Wonderful Thing* (1946)

nerically speaking. Call it what you will, novel or verse. Many verse narratives were published during the period in which Robinson and Jeffers were pre-eminent, but few ventured to call them novels, exceptions being *Each to the Other: A Novel in Verse* by Christopher La Farge (1939), and two by Robin Lampson subtitled "A Novel in Cadence." Others hedged their bets. Henry Chapin's *West Walking Yankee* (1940) was "A Narrative Poem of the American Frontier," and Selden Rodman's *Lawrence: The Last Crusade* (1937) was billed as "A Dramatic-Narrative Poem."[3] In several instances the title page refrained from the generic indicators blazoned on the dust jacket, which was the only way one would know that Helen Wolfert's *Nothing Is a Wonderful Thing* (1946) was "a story poem" (see figure 8.3), Helene Magaret's *The Trumpeting Crane* (1934) "a narrative poem," and La Farge's first publication *Hoxsie Sells His Acres* (1934) "An American Novel in Verse" (see figure 8.4).

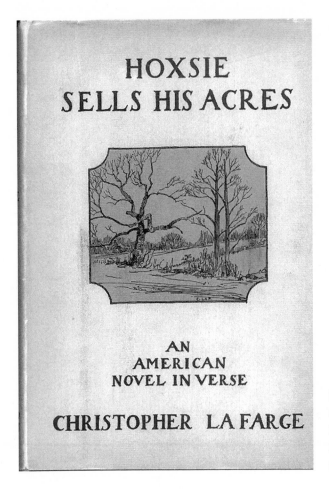

Figure 8.4. Christopher La Farge, *Hoxsie Sells His Acres* (1934)

One reviewer characterized Edwin Arlington Robinson's *Roman Bartholow* (1923) as "a problem novel raised to the high plane of poetry" (*NYT*, March 25, 1923), while the poet himself called *Avon's Harvest* a "metrical dime-novel" (1921, 596). Generic considerations notwithstanding, Robinson's success provided a formal solution for many. As Harriet Monroe wrote of *Matthias at the Door*, "Robinson's blank verse is a perfected instrument, developed exactly to his needs" (1932, 216). It was therefore with approbation that Josephine Young Case could be described as writing "a commendable, and dependable, blank verse" in *At Midnight on the 31st of March* (*NYT*, November 13, 1938). For some, Miltonic blank verse updated by Robinson was suitable, but others had no such pretensions. In his boxing melodrama, *The Set-Up*, Joseph Moncure March (a former student of Robert Frost) deployed the same colloquial idiom as his previous outing, *The Wild Party*, with line breaks applied strictly to heighten the intensity. Percy Hutchison accordingly advised the reader that March surely did not "desire to be classed among the poets. He is attempting something else, namely, to tell a story in such a nervous and rapidly moving fashion that the reader is kept at high tension, and swept irresistibly to the climax"—by means "midway between Masefield and Ernest Hemingway" (*NYT*, October 28, 1928). Hutchison valued the strategy of Christopher La Farge in similar terms, suggesting the poet "clearly entertains the conviction that verse lends itself more effectively than prose to the portrayal of degrees of emotional tension" (*NYT*, June 17, 1934). Poet Margaret Walker was likewise appreciative of La Farge's ability to balance verse with narrative obligations. "Poetry serves a definite purpose here," she wrote, "heightening and intensifying the various effects of the novel, as well as maintaining unity by the use of leit-motifs running through the lyrical passages" (1940, 281). Appraising *The Trumpeting Crane* by Helen Magaret, a reviewer found that "verse heightens the sentiment and enhances the dramatic intensity" (*NYT*, December 2, 1934). Josef Fox, assessing *Glory for Me* by MacKinlay Kantor, was more specific: "Power-loaded understatements, striking syntax, studied casualness, tags, repetitions, mystical refrains," he found, were "devices Kantor would have to forego if he wrote in prose, and these devices make for a greater intensity and greater glory" (1946, 54).

Various critics cited intensity as justifying the role of verse in furthering a narrative. Done with deliberation, the verse novel "is a medium that can be used colloquially enough to give a sense of actuality and brisk movement and which can rise with the dignity of the action and the significance of the emotion," wrote Mary Colum (*NYT*, November 30, 1941). But it was always a question of balance. As Hutchison observed, "An author who thus attempts to ride two horses has daring in his make-up, for he lays himself open to judgment both as novelist and poet" (*NYT*, October 7, 1934). Reviewers were consistently preoccupied with which role should be stressed when appraising a new publication. Donald Stauffer took pains to advise the prospective reader not to be put off by the verse format of Norman Rosten's *The Big Road*, a chronicle of the construction of the Alcan highway, replete with maps and documents: "Certainly the poetry should not throw the reader off, for it flows along easily and without contortion" (see figure 8.5). And as if to provide further assurance, Stauffer suggests that "it is too easily written to be great poetry: there are few memorable lines or phrases" (*NYT*, July 7, 1946). But it was possible to swing too far in the other direction. Of Edgar Lee Masters's *The New World*, Harold Rosenberg scathingly wrote, "It is 'narrative'—with a vengeance" (*NYT*, January 1938). Yet story-driven poems could be valued for the way the variable versification propelled the narrative. Accordingly, "It is not as poetry that *Morgan Sails the Caribbean* is to be judged, but as head-

Figure 8.5.
Norman Rosten,
The Big Road
(1946)

long, vivid story, borne along with a swing on Mr. Braley's nimble measures"
(*NYT*, January 27, 1935). A good yarn could even entice those leery of poetry. Mabel Langdon wondered, concerning his Gold Rush tale, whether "Mr.
Lampson has not beguiled many people who like a good story, but who are
firmly convinced that they 'can't read poetry' into spending several enjoyable
hours with *Laughter Out of the Ground*" (1936, 320). Percy Hutchison particularly valued La Farge's studious deployment of "different verse-forms" in
Hoxsie Sells His Acres, "assigning them not by character, as costumes might
be assigned, but selecting whichever has seemed to him best fitted to express
a mood" (*NYT*, June 17, 1934). The optimal equation would be Hutchison's
recommendation of *Westward under Vega* by Thomas Wood Stevens: "good
poetry, good drama, good narrative" (*NYT*, June 12, 1938), an assessment
with which I concur.

"Book-length verse is to book-length prose what grand opera is to the drama," suggested Ralph Thompson of Rodman's *Lawrence: The Last Crusade* (*NYT*, February 26, 1937). At a time when radio broadcasts of opera performances were readily found on the dial, this was a recognizable distinction for those who might never set foot in an opera house but recognized the sound of high drama. But by 1944 poet Robert Hillyer had had enough: "It may be my own personal taste which has increasingly convinced me that verse is no vehicle for a modern novel. For example, E. A. Robinson's tales of contemporary life seem to me to creak on wooden wheels down a bumpy road" (*NYT*, December 10, 1944). Five years earlier, Peter Monro Jack lauded *Each to the Other* by La Farge for the ease with which he rendered contemporary speech idioms in verse, a welcome advance, as "any reader of the late E. A. Robinson's stories in verse will remember how he went into incredible huddles with his muse when he wanted to give his character a Scotch-and-soda" (*NYT*, April 9, 1939).

In many instances, reviewers found much to admire in the tale despite the verse. A reviewer of *Snow Covered Wagons* conceded that "with all the admiration in the world for Mrs. Altrocchi's zeal in reconstructing the Donner story one cannot praise her verse. It is prevailingly pedestrian" (*NYT*, March 15, 1936). Eda Lou Walton dismissively remarked of Stanley Burnshaw's *The Iron Land* that some of it "might just as well have been written as prose sketches," a response predicated on its proletarian subject matter (*NYT*, June 21, 1936). Contemporary urban locales seemed to invite more skepticism about the medium than did historical settings and adventure stories. Percy Shostac's *14th Street* was felt to be narrated in "broken prose rather than in fluent verse" (*NYT*, July 6, 1930); while *Efficiency Expert* by Florence Converse "isn't really poetry, but just verse" (*NYT*, April 15, 1934). But it's not as if the frontier was ideally suited to lyrical effusions either. Historian Bernard DeVoto, reviewing Benét's posthumous panorama of the opening of the American frontier, *Western Star*, wrote that the result "is less poetic than its predecessor"—*John Brown's Body*—and for that reason, "it is a better poem" (*NYT*, June 27, 1943). Mary Colum felt, concerning Harry Brown's *Poem of Bunker Hill*, that "at times the versification cannot be distinguished from prose," but this was a mere "drawback" in the work of a young poet who "shows surprising maturity in his conception of the action and in the models he has taken"—listing Homer, Eliot, Pound, MacLeish, and Auden (*NYT*, November 30, 1941). Other positive reviews also included qualifications about the poetry in passing comments, not as overall judgements. Maurice Swan observed of William Rose Benét's *The Dust Which Is God*, "a work of this kind is veined heavily with prose whose only distinction from common prose is the arrangement of the lines" (*NYT*, December 14, 1941).

When MacKinlay Kantor was tapped to write a treatment for an MGM movie about the challenges facing demobilized veterans, he inexplicably wrote it in verse. "It is undeniably verse," Orville Prescott wrote, "but it might as well be prose" (*NYT*, November 16, 1945). Prescott was more impressed by another military venture in Peter Bowman's *Beach Red* (a Book of the Month Club selection), presented in verse stanzas, heavily and often insensibly enjambed (see figure 8.6). But lest readers take this for poetry, the publishers indicated on the dust jacket (front flap) that "the typographical arrangement of lines and sections was devised by the author to represent the rigid timing by which each step of such action is governed"—the action being an amphibian assault on a Pacific island. *Beach Red* (1945) emphatically invents an idiom of its own, one that the author seems to have studiously designed for an audience of combat veterans, wise to the necessity of hyperbole, irony, and mixed messages.

> Talk, talk, talk. You like to listen to men talk
> at a time like this, because their lips seem to
> bloom into ponderous slowgaited poetry and it is rich and
> wholesome. (41)

It's in that spirit of jaunty existential dread that Bowman pitches many of the combat descriptions:

> Heavy guns blare out their syncopated jazz and abruptly
>   stop
> and there is a short pause while the warring spirits
> terminate their jitterbugging and stand around to applaud
>   the number.
> Then someone puts another nickel in the same old jukebox
> and havoc selects a partner and the dance goes on. (17)

> Beyond is the jungle's steaming pie, fresh from the oven,
> with a stinking coagulation of mud and water as filling
> under a hard, unyielding crust of firmly tangled tropical
>   foliage. (18)

These broadly elaborated analogies, fortified by plus size irony, gradually recede from the narrative as the action unfolds, and the reader realizes these are meant to replicate the peculiar aura of self-distancing the soldier adopts in the first flush of the assault landing.

Such passages are gradually succeeded by more carefully explicit accounts

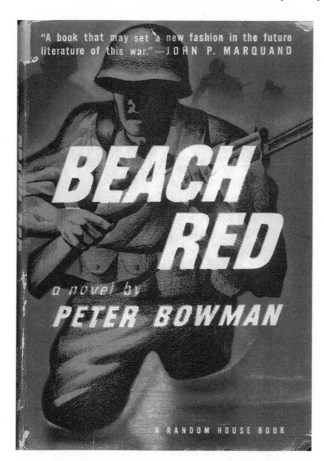

Figure 8.6. Peter Bowman, *Beach Red* (1945), dust jacket illustration by H Lawrence Hoffman

of the carnage. And at this point Bowman's use of second person narration becomes more penetrating. Watching a medic in action, "you watch the clumsy geometry of a body suffering" (24). Checking a fallen comrade, "there is only the sodden dampness of his sweat / and the thin tingle of human warmth turning to coldness" (93). In a pause in the combat, "you" rummage through your billfold, "a pocket cemetery for the things you once thought important" (45). It's a menacing and potentially fatal environment with "all your frail inadequacies / constantly pursuing you in thoughts that refuse to remain unthinkable" (59). And here analogy returns, bearing news that only analogy can hold:

> Battle is a huge clockwork and your squad is one
> of its little wheels and every time the hands meet
> they pinch off another bit of existence. (23)

> Your whole body is battered by little shocks of instinct
> and your mind is loose and unbuttoned and all your
> thinking is drained from you in disjointed blobs. (91)

Another way Bowman achieves a balance between doughboy wit and observational wisdom is in the single line that concludes each two-page narrative unit: "You have stumbled into history and can't get out again" (14); "Murder is your sixth sense. You lost the other five" (16); "You want to be brave. You also want to be" (94); "Life's a luxury. You can't afford luxuries on Army pay" (96); "Patriotism means allowing the enemy to die for his country" (64); "Battle doesn't determine who is right. Only who is left" (106). And, upon encountering the enemy dead: "War is a Japanese industry. And these are the unemployed" (72). These nuggets cumulatively prepare the reader for the somewhat editorializing tone of the finale, as the main character slowly dies from a wound sustained in combat, while thoughts of mortality, memories of the past, and projections of a receding future set the tone: "Birth seems to have been goodbye to some inanimate entity / and only the logical end of living is hello again" (97).

> There will be words spoken and words left unsaid. It
> will be a peacetime war that will go on and
> on and on and you will never really get it
> out of you. (117)

Beach Red concludes with chastening reminders of the cost of war: "others should remember / and should be periodically reminded that when the world owed / them a living they sent somebody else to collect it" (118). "Peace is an interval created by / killing those who disagree" (118). Bowman even extends the reckoning to democracy in a way that continues to resound today:

> They have what they call
> democracy and they are content to let it muddle along
> like a spoiled child, wasting its time and money and
> making mistake after mistake with amiable caprice but
>   preserving its
> health by declining to worry. And the only reason it
> survives is that it is inherently optimistic and no matter
> how bleak the outlook, it would never contemplate its self-
>   destruction.
> (109–110)

Beach Red is fairly typical of American poem-novels, or verse narratives, in that its author was not a poet. Robinson and Jeffers were rarities, both in being poets and in terms of the number of narratives they published. Of those known mainly as poets, only Witter Bynner, Stephen Vincent Benét, Mark Van Doren, Theodore Morrison, and Selden Rodman published more than one entry in the field. In the case of Archibald MacLeish, William Rose Benét, Robert Hillyer, Robert Francis, Lola Ridge, Harry Brown, Boris Todrin, Isidor Schneider, and Norman Rosten, only one of their books was a narrative poem. The same applies to Jeremy Ingalls, though hers is an interesting case. Her first book, *The Metaphysical Sword* (1941), was a Yale Series of Younger Poets pick by Stephen Vincent Benét. A native of Gloucester, it's intriguing to consider whether she knew Charles Olson, a fellow native less than four months her senior. Ingalls's *Tahl* (1945), the most extravagant of all the verse novels at over six hundred pages, was denounced by Orville Prescott in the *New York Times* as "pretentious flummery" and "the most exasperating and infuriating book that I have read in many years," comparing this "monstrous freak" to *Finnegans Wake* (*NYT*, June 11, 1945). Perhaps chastened by the savagery of this response, the *Times* followed up with a more appreciative review by F. Cudworth Flint (*NYT*, June 24, 1945). Coleman Rosenberg's review in *Poetry* carped that *Tahl* gave the feeling of "the manipulation of innumerable file cards" (November 1945, 108), while young Robert Lowell ridiculed Ingalls as "the typical emancipated graduate student, [who] wears her scholarship on her sleeve" (1946, 146). To have these male reviewers unleash their venom on a young woman's ambitious work offers revealing insight into the postwar masculine braggadocio about to descend on the poetry scene. As for Ingalls, she had a long career as a professor of Asian Studies, spent three years in Japan, and kept her distance from the sexist enclaves of the American poetry establishment.

The other contributors to the idiom are relatively fugitive figures in literary history, and in some instances the only books they published were verse narratives. Some were well known authors, like James Norman Hall, co-author of *Mutiny on the Bounty* and other Pacific Ocean novels by the time he penned *A Word for His Sponsor: A Narrative Poem* (1949). Frank Ernest Hill was a man of letters, as was Christopher La Farge, author of three of the more highly regarded verse narratives: *Hoxsie Sells His Acres* (1934), *Each to the Other* (1939), and after an interlude in which he published books in other genres, *Beauty for Ashes* (1953). Among lesser-known authors, Robin Lampson was a California native who wrote on the Gold Rush in *Laughter Out of the Ground* (1935) and went on to produce a biographical account of General William Gorgas's triumph in eradicating yellow fever, *Death Loses a*

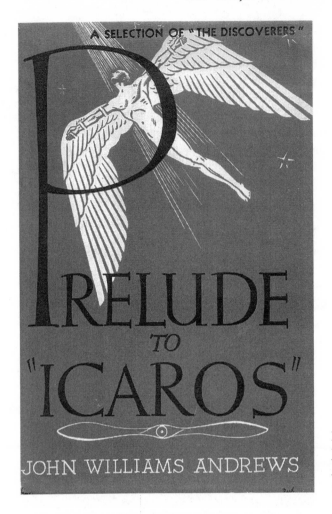

Figure 8.7. John Williams Andrews, *Prelude to "Icaros"* (1936)

Pair of Wings (1939). *Death* was hailed in the medical journal *Bios* (Cockerell 1940) for its prodigious research (Lampson says he consulted over twenty-seven hundred newspaper issues, in addition to compiling a prodigious bibliography). Henry Chapin published two verse narratives, *Leifsaga: A Narrative Poem of the Norse Discoveries of America* (1934) and *West Walking Yankee: A Narrative Poem of the American Frontier* (1940). Leighton Brewer's *Riders of the Sky* (1934) was based on his experience with the American Flying Service in the First World War and was one of several homages to the flying spirit, with Selden Rodman's *Airmen* (1941) and *Prelude to "Icaros"* (1936) by John Williams Andrews, a lawyer who returned to poetry in later life after retiring (see figure 8.7). James Whaler's only books were *Green River, a Poem for Rafinesque* (1931) and a collection of shorter narrative poems, *Hale's Pond*

(1927). Oscar Brynes did a master's thesis at Cornell on English poet John Clare, and while he published numerous poems in *Poetry*, his only book was *The Day's Work* (1938), which Sol Funaroff characterized as "a horselaugh at the expense of the New York City police department" (1938, 231). Although a heist tale, Funaroff demurs on some of Brynes's jargon: "My objection to the use of slang as verse is that it inclines towards rhetoric rather than poetry and tends to read like a lexicon of racketeer dialect" (232). But he was enthused overall. "If poetry in general were to approach the level of entertainment of *The Day's Work*, there might be some hope of diverting the book public's interest from the Crime Book Clubs to sampling the thrillers of poetry" (233).

The verse narrative was a genre attracting the talents and aspirations of numerous women. Decades after *Nothing Is a Wonderful Thing* (1946), Helen Wolfert published two collections of poems. Belle Turnbull was a Colorado poet, whose only other book besides the narrative *Goldboat* (1940) was the collection *The Tenmile Range* (1957). Turnbull was a lesbian, as was Florence Converse, a novelist whose *Efficiency Expert* (1934) was followed by a *Collected Poems* in 1937 (see figure 8.8). In *Snow Covered Wagons* (1936), Julia Altrocchi narrated the cannibalistic tale of the Donner Party. Her *Poems of a Child* was published in 1904 when she was ten, another collection in 1917, and a final collection in 1964. World Cat indicates three other poetic narratives: *Chillon* (1929), *Black Boat* (1946), and *Chicago: Narrative of a City* (1973), but I haven't been able to see any of them. Nebraska native Helene Magaret, author of *The Trumpeting Crane* (1934) and *The Great Horse* (1937), as well as a collection of lyrics, was possibly African American, as she published in *Opportunity* and was fondly remembered by Audre Lorde. *At Midnight on the 31st of March* (1938) by Josephine Young Case is one of the more imaginative plotlines, about a New England village enduring an odd space-time erasure of the world around it. Case, like Joseph Moncure March, published one collection of poems apart from their narratives, and both were far more visible in other vocations (March was a screenwriter, and Case the head of RCA).

The terms by which verse narratives were scrutinized were inconsistent. During their heyday, it's clear that reviewers got used to seeing them on publisher's lists, and while they could at times be savagely dismissive or full of exclamatory admiration, fitful attempts to scrutinize metrical resources and plot points could take surprising turns. Henry Wells, for instance, took Mark Van Doren to task for *The Mayfield Deer*, "a poem nearly as long as the *Aeneid*, based on a narrative as simple as a folk ballad." The poet "does not compress a potential novel into verse; he elaborates a short story into a long poem" (1942, 430). As a result, "His deer lies floundering in a pit between the real and the symbolical, convincing neither zoölogically nor allegorically" (431).

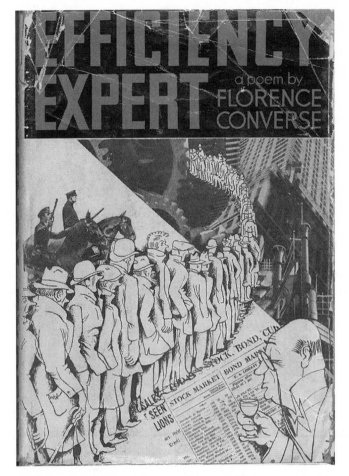

Figure 8.8. Florence Converse, *Efficiency Expert* (1934), dust jacket designed by Georges Schreiber, with photographs by Margaret Bourke-White

It's perplexing, then, to find Wells commending the book as "among the finest long narrative poems produced in our own times" (432). By comparison, when Mary Austin declared MacLeish's *Conquistador* "quite the most successful piece of narrative verse, the most freely inspirational, that has been done in English," she didn't contravene her analysis (1932, xvi).

Reviews of verse narratives, unlike novels in prose, went out of their way to examine formal strategies employed. Yet I can't help feeling the vogue for these books was not driven by those who normally read poetry. The difference is registered in the venues of reviews, with the *New York Times* providing a steady chronicle from 1920 to 1950, during which the coverage in

Poetry was only about a tenth of what the *Times* produced. It's not because Harriet Monroe and her successor, George Dillon, were wary of such efforts; rather, their sights settled comfortably on lyric modes that have always been the predominant content of that magazine. Furthermore, they recognized that the authors of a great many entries in the form were not contributors to *Poetry*. They were not aspiring poets who happened to reach for the stars, but authors—Christopher La Farge being a prime example—who tried out their storytelling abilities in verse and were just as likely to go with prose. Their poem novels were aimed at a prose market, essentially. And here's the other side of the equation as gleaned from reviews: in the end it was subject matter that counted. Why read *Riders of the Sky, Prelude to "Icaros,"* or *The Airmen* unless you were interested in aviation? The Wild West could give you *Snow Covered Wagons, The Westward Star, Western Star,* and for a contemporary jaunt over the same landscape, you could read *Westward under Vega,* not to mention Helene Magaret's account of the westward crossing of the Mormons in *The Great Horse* (1937). Then there's the Christ theme in *Eden Tree* and *Firehead,* the urban settings of *Nothing Is a Wonderful Thing, Efficiency Expert,* and *14th Street,* and history in the making courtesy of *The Big Road, Green River, The Poem of Bunker Hill, Jonathan Gentry, West Walking Yankee, Goldboat, Lawrence: The Last Crusade, John Brown's Body, Conquistador,* and *7 Days.* You could even find hard-boiled if you like: *Hell in Harness* by Joseph Auslander, Oliver Brynes's heist tale *A Day's Work,* and those doozies by Joseph Moncure March, *Wild Party* and *The Set-Up.* In fact, the subject matter of these narratives aligns rather closely with Hollywood films. *The Westward Star* pointedly opens with a precise evocation of familiar cinematic techniques:

> The wagons that had threshed the sand all day,
> Or jolted over rock or rutted clay,
> Lurched to a stop at the command.
> Spent oxen drooped,
> Sweating beneath their yokes; dust settled languidly.
> Past the two wagons leading hers
> Sarah could see three horsemen grouped
> At the train's head, one with a lifted hand.
> They searched the westward prairie; so did she,
> And found near the horizon
> Dots moving—little blurs
> Of shadow on the farthest swell of land.
> Antelope there? Or bison?
> Or were they— With fixed eyes that smarted

From dust and heat,
And cracked lips parted,
She traced their motion from the wagon seat. (Hill 1934, 13)

All the elements of a John Ford western are convened here in vista, wagon train, and physical strain combined with wary alertness. It's against such narrative backdrops that John Wheelwright cheekily subtitled *Mirrors of Venus: A Novel in Sonnets 1914–1938* (1938). The publisher's prospectus announcing the book omits the phrase "A Novel in."

The very existence of this poetic activity has been forgotten, if it was ever known, by scholars. Robinson's once shining star has not only dimmed but, it seems, been snuffed out altogether. Jeffers's lyrics have continually circulated in reprints like Robert Hass's selection, *Rock and Hawk* (1987), while the narratives have faded into obscurity. Apart from the graphic novel treatment of March's *Wild Party* and Ingalls's *Tahl*, none of the verse narratives cited above have been reprinted. In fact, a majority of poetry titles from the period when the "story-poems" thrived are increasingly hard to come by, too recent to be available in digital format due to copyright law, and often relegated to remote storage facilities by university libraries or demoted to discard status by regional libraries. Not surprisingly, then, critical attention to verse narratives lapsed at midcentury when the publishing industry dropped them. What's disarming—yet maybe predictable—about the one exception, "The Verse Novel: A Modern American Poetic Genre" by Patrick D. Murphy, is that he seems unaware of the prodigious number of long forgotten publications relevant to the topic. Jeffers, whose narrative poems are the subject of another article by Murphy (1987), clearly prompted the latter's deliberations. In the end—reflecting the theory-dominated milieu in which the article appeared—Murphy provides a structural profile but no substantive genealogical research. But he does offer this handy synopsis of the genre:

> A large number of modern American long poems are best defined as forming part of a new poetic genre, the verse novel. In terms of length, the work must have a sustained duration and intensity of reading experience with the line length a contributing but not determining factor of this. In terms of structure, it may have a variety of structural shapes from continuous narrative to fragmented sequence of units of varying lengths, but it must have an underlying plotted narrative involving characters and events occurring in time. (1989, 67)

Murphy's reference to a "large number" suggests that he may have known of many titles he didn't mention, or he may simply have figured that those by

Jeffers and Robinson alone amounted to numerical consequence. Another matter of which Murphy was apparently ignorant was a recent surge of attention to verse narratives. The *Kenyon Review* had hosted a special topic issue on the subject in 1983, with contributions by Mark Jarman, Dana Gioia, Dick Allen, and Frederick Feirstein. The articles in *Kenyon Review* were reprinted in a Story Line collected volume, *New Expansive Poetry* edited by R. S. Gwynn (1999), with three other reprinted essays. Yet none of the authors made mention of the bounty of verse narratives I'd cited here, other than Jeffers and Robinson, seemingly being more intent on then-current possibilities like Frederick Turner's sci-fi epics and titles by Vikram Seth, Jarman, and Feirstein.

In addition to the profusion of book reviews that greeted publications of verse narratives from the twenties to midcentury, there was extensive discussion in the academic quarterlies. One has some bearing on the recent turn to documentary poetry, namely, Edwin Honig's "History, Document, and Archibald MacLeish" in the *Sewanee Review* (1940). It was a reckoning of sorts with tendencies in poetry that had arisen during the previous decade. At the time MacLeish, nearing fifty, was the recently appointed Librarian of Congress, and Honig was a brash twenty-one-year-old poet (known now for his translations of Fernando Pessoa). Honig contrasted MacLeish with Hart Crane to characterize responses to *The Waste Land*, with the latter attempting a "complete artistic antithesis" while MacLeish sought "a consciously social program, with more or less affinity for the current ideals of a socialist society" (Honig 1940, 385).

In *Conquistador*, Honig, suggested, "He has taken the history of the Mexican conquest not as imaginative idea but as story, as written *document*, and with the instrument of eclectic poetic sensibility has fashioned it into a romance, presumably inviting to the tastes of the modern reader." But, he charged, "The deception is not in his having followed the *document* of history at all, but in his having had to supply it with an *added* document of his own" (387). Deception is a harsh assessment. For Honig, recruiting the historical past in order to nourish contemporary sensibilities was fraudulent, insofar as it refused to acknowledge history as commensurate with present sensations and needs. The vocabulary of his title is a bit confusingly applied to the predicament facing a poet who would engage the historical record. One could be "*objectively* critical" by according equal validity to past and present. But by contrast, "The poetry which is circumscribed by primarily technical, impressionistic, and eclectic concerns can only be *subjectively* critical. It is the difference between an 'historical' poetry and a 'documentary' poetry" (395). Because his article was mainly about MacLeish and the false hopes of his "'documentary' poetry," Honig refrained from fully examining what a more honorable

Figure 8.9.
Archibald
MacLeish,
Conquistador
(1930)

path of "'historical' poetry" might consist of. But it would not be "the colossal documentary compendiums of Ezra Pound" (396). One can only infer from his repeated and often parenthetical mention of Blake, Baudelaire, and Yeats what an "imaginative" engagement encompassing past and present on equal footing would be.

As for Honig's critique of *Conquistador*, it's admittedly the case that MacLeish's book defies narrative parsing. One would be hard pressed to discern the actual course of events as given in his source text, the *True History of the Conquest of New Spain* by Bernál Díaz del Castillo, a participant in the conquest (see figure 8.9). This is not to say the poem lacks narrative momentum; in fact, Walton suggested in her review that "those who read 'Conquistador' for the story told will find it perfectly handled, vivid, clear" (*NYT*, April 17, 1932). It's propelled forward by methods MacLeish adopted from Pound's "The Seafarer," even to the extent of using old Anglo-Saxon words (thills, reeved, glibbed, chocks, etc.) and syntactical inversions: "We that to west now: weirdless: by fates faring / Follow on star-track" (1932, 52). Above all, MacLeish milks velocity out of the article "and," just as Pound launched *The Cantos* ("And then went down to the sea in ships . . ."). On page forty-five, for instance, eleven of the first fifteen lines begin "And . . ." On pages seventy-two to seventy-three there are twelve consecutive lines beginning with "And," with six of the preceding nine lines also commencing that way. So the spell of *onward* is relentlessly cast for more than a hundred pages, with "the roll of the / Drums like the thud in the ear of a man's heart" (70). Formulations like this continually embellish the text with a "poetic" accent (at times defying sense: "we heard the wind in the / Shrill nipple of stone as a wasp" [104]), conjuring an acutely sensory atmosphere:

> We woke scenting the slot of the heat on the air:
> We rinsed our mouths in the sun (90)

Character profiles can also be swiftly registered in this manner, as when Montezúma lies dying, "His eyes were lewd with the strange smile" (106).

Conquistador combines verse narrative with the documentary tendencies that have emerged more recently—but there's another genealogical forerunner to consider. Muriel Rukeyser's "The Book of the Dead" has become a touchstone for poets working in a documentary mode, and while it initially appeared as the first half of her book *U. S. 1* in 1938, it has recently been reprinted as a book by itself (see figure 8.10). In her *New York Times* review of *U. S. 1*, Eda Lou Walton singled out "The Book of the Dead" for comment. Acknowledging that "a report on a village dying of silicosis is the material for poetry," Walton complained that Rukeyser's poem "is not poetry. This is reporting and not the imaginative vision" (*NYT*, March 27, 1938). This response would sound blasphemous now; after all, "The Book of the Dead" has been canonized precisely as a model of imaginative vision applied to unbecoming and potentially recalcitrant documents. But a clue as to the reason for Walton's dismissal is at hand by way of Honig's imputation to MacLeish of a poetry circumscribed by "technical, impressionistic, and eclectic concerns." There's little in "The Book of the Dead" that could pass as impressionistic, but Walton, I imagine, was put off by something like technical and eclectic concerns.[4] Rukeyser's fastidious handling of actual documents did not assimilate them into rhetorical and dithyrambic recapitulation or "imaginative

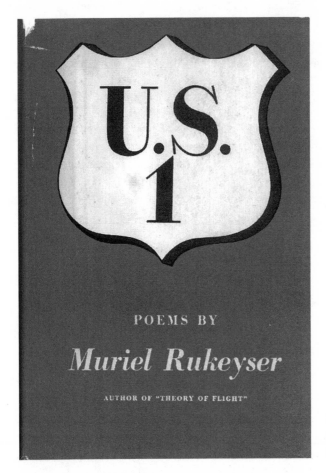

Figure 8.10.
Muriel Rukeyser,
U. S. 1 (1938)

vision" as Walton would have it. Instead, the poem stays close to the ground, palpably immersed in the documents, warily eyeing "this fact and this disease" descended upon "These citizens from many States / paying the price for electric power"—going so far as to include a facsimile of stock prices and dividends (68, 64, 57).

In a note, Rukeyser suggests that "The Book of the Dead" was planned as part of a much longer work to be titled *U. S. 1*, but the two dozen other poems in the 1938 volume show little evidence that they might contribute to "a summary poem of the life of the Atlantic coast of this country, nourished by the communications which run down it." Most telling is her curt concluding sentence: "Poetry can extend the document" (146)—and "The Book of the Dead" signals a specific approach. Rukeyser visited the site in West Virginia

LAND OF THE FREE
BY ARCHIBALD MAC LEISH

Figure 8.11. Archibald MacLeish, *Land of the Free* (1938), dust jacket photograph by Willard Van Dyke

with a photographer friend, Nancy Naumburg. As a collaboration it came to nothing, but if it had, it might have been along the lines of *You Have Seen Their Faces* by Margaret Bourke-White and Erskine Caldwell (1937) and *An American Exodus: A Record of Human Erosion* by Dorothea Lange and Paul Schuster Taylor (1939), though the texts of those classic photo books were in prose. In fact, a closer model was by none other than MacLeish: *Land of the Free*, with each page of text facing a photograph, many by Lange and the rest sourced from newspapers and Federal Resettlement Administration projects (see figure 8.11). Like *U. S. 1* it was published in 1938, written as "the opposite of a book of poems illustrated by photographs. It is a book of photographs illustrated by a poem. The photographs," MacLeish acknowledged, "existed before the poem was written" (89). The text was presented as "The Sound Track," with a recurring refrain: "We wonder / We don't know / We're asking," each time accompanied by a photograph of despondent Depression era faces (88). Inasmuch as film soundtracks are musical, MacLeish adhered to the principle by providing as steady pulse of observational quandary a "wondering" commensurate with the refrain. Unlike documentary film, he offered no facts or figures, no data, other than an itemization of photographic sources and subjects.

The notion of documentary poetry—or what Joseph Harrington calls "docupoetry"—would have been perplexing until fairly recently, simply because "document" suggests preexisting material from which the poem draws. Wouldn't that qualify virtually the whole legacy of European poetry as documentary in nature, insofar as it repeats and re-encodes Greek myth and Biblical lore and a host of typological scenarios? Isn't *Paradise Lost* a documentary poem of the Christian primal scene? There's also the natural history of Erasmus Darwin's book-length poems *The Botanic Garden* (1791) and *The Temple of Nature* (1803), which have their distant ancestor in the pastoral legacy of Hesiod's *Works and Days* and Virgil's *Georgics*. So documentary poetry is by no means unprecedented.

It's intriguing, then, to find a notable increase in documentary poetry in recent years. The trend may be an unintended byproduct of anthologies. When the anthology industry was at its hectic steady state—particularly from the sixties into the nineties—an anthology served as a kind of standing incentive for poets to get the nod, be included, "represented." And as any consultation of anthologies reveals, the bulk consists of certain lyric types, self-sufficient and not too long. It's hard, and probably pointless, to consider extracting from a documentary project for an anthology, just as excerpts from long poems are rare. The decline, or outright collapse, of the anthology as a career incentive has opened the way for poets to embark on ambitious, book-length works and heterogeneous projects, foremost of which are those making use of documentary materials.

For documentary poetry in its purest form, consider Canadian poet Moez Surani's ةيلمع *Operación Opération Operation* 行动 *Операция* (2016), a hundred-and-fifty-page list of four thousand code names for military operations conducted by United Nations member states between 1945 and 2006. From 1965, as an example:

> Riviera
> Big Drum
> Choc Ice
> Peter
> Short Trek
> Ox Trail
> Dagger Thrust V
> Tiger Hound
> Charger Sweep
> Give Up

Gladiator
Feline
Harvest Moon (59)

The purity is in Surani's decision to list the code names and nothing else. No arrangement but chronology. The poetry had already been applied in the choice of code names by the United Nations, so this is found poetry as well as documentary.

It's plausible to regard Ezra Pound's *Cantos* as documentary. This massive "poem including history" is a logjam of proper names, and Pound does not shy away from printing historical documents verbatim. Yet for all his aspiration to fortify the *Cantos* with primary sources, it raises the question of whether documentary poetry merits consultation: does one read a poem to get verifiable information? Pound characterized poetry as news that stays news, but of course news is a precarious category. Thoreau infamously suggested that the trans-Atlantic cable would not enlighten but simply plug Yankee ears with news of a royal whooping cough. News that stays news may come perilously close to rumors that influence public opinion. In any case, a formidable body of scholarship suggests that readers of *The Cantos* are not in search of revisionary history. Pound's poem is valued for other reasons altogether.

Are the documents in documentary poetry, then, merely inspirational resources for the poet, no different in status than a flock of sheep, billowing sails on a frigate, or rumpled bedsheets? Or does a documentary approach entail some fundamental recalibration of resources, a change in modus operandi? These are questions with a considerable history, actually, albeit in another medium. Photography has been used for documentary purposes almost from the beginning, from surveying distant places around the world to capturing historical events. It took on an investigative role in chronicles of the ghetto in New York around the turn of the century by Jacob Riis and Lewis Hine. Clearly, identifiable subject matter could provide raw material for documentation. But what was the appropriate technical means? That was a question taken up in the pages of *Camera Work* and other venues promoting photography as an art form. At issue was what was called the "straight print," an option claimed by some photographers as an alternative to the heavily "treated" prints favored in the aesthetic practices of Pictorialism. A straight print was printed straight from the negative, and as such presumed to be untreated, though of course anyone who has done darkroom work knows that even such a prospect brings with it a range of optional manipulations, like the tonal range from light to dark. There is, in short, no demonstrably "straight" print. In his 1907 article "What Is a 'Straight Print'?" Frederick H. Evans made precisely this point. He was willing for his own relatively unretouched prints to be called straight, but added that "I should object to being classed among the documentary photographers (though what higher praise could one desire for one's portraits than that they should be described as 'human documents'?)" (119).

Evans's distinction between straight print and documentary photography reveals something pertinent about documentation in poetry, where there's obviously no equivalent of the straight print, but there is a parallel history of advocacy for a straight, uncluttered presentation, thanks to the tenets of Imagism. The Imagists made no claims about subject matter. Anything was suitable, so long as the "treatment" eliminated rhetorical afflatus and decorative obfuscation. An Imagist poem, like an Evans print, was a "human document." The prospect of documentation, then, appears to arise exclusively from the subject matter. Slums and silicosis alike were subjects begging to be exposed by artists committed to documenting them in whatever medium they practiced. Well, not so simple. The photographic dictum popularized by Kodak, pitching simplified cameras for a mass market, was "point and shoot." It there a poetic equivalent? "Tell it like it is"—to quote the title of an Aaron Neville hit from 1966—sounds like a formula, but it's really an emotional appeal, and even the courtroom pledge to "tell the truth and nothing but the truth" skirts the issue of what might constitute a *straight* verbal account. Documentary poetry always already entails procedural logistics. Eda Lou Walton's claim that Rukeyser's "Book of the Dead" was reporting, not poetry, crudely but usefully suggests that performative parameters in a given art must be heeded, no matter how urgently the subject matter may impose itself.

Rukeyser regarded her poem as reportage and saw no conflict in accommodating poetry to such a task. In that respect she was in step with political art during the thirties. In 1939 Margaret Bourke-White—whose photographs had defined the look of *Life* magazine from the start (the inaugural issue in 1936 featured her photo of the Fort Peck Dam)—gave a lecture to the Photo League in New York, urging her peers to pursue a documentary mission with the goal of disclosing more than the major media outlets were willing to cover. She emphasized that "the most important task of the documentary photographer is to dig into the background of spot news and show how these things happen" (Hill 2018, 133). Similar initiatives had been undertaken in many other countries as the political stakes escalated through the decade. Photo books like those by MacLeish, Bourke-White, and Lange were part of the trend, and the fact that the words were subordinate to the images indicates an advantage that photography and cinema had in disseminating political content. Words could convey messages, but an image was more suggestible, like a poem in fact. Yet poets resisted the documentary impulse. Openly political poetry in America by Edwin Rolfe, Kenneth Fearing, Robert Gessner,

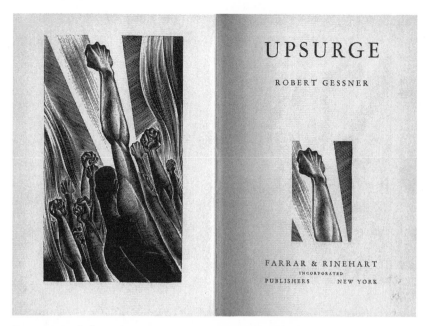

Figure 8.12. Robert Gessner, *Upsurge* (1933), uncredited frontispiece

John Beecher, and others was a poetry of advocacy (see figure 8.12). It could name names, evoke the Spain of the Lincoln Brigade, rally to the cause or, like Beecher in 1940, address fellow citizens:

> Americans
> let's think about this Negro problem a little bit.
> I don't know what you happen to think about Negroes
> but I was raised with them
> and I know them
> and I am of the opinion
> that they are human beings. (*And I Will Be Heard*, 40–41)

This is getting it straight, as it were, from a poem, but no doubt Walton would insist that plain unadorned speech broken into lines was not poetry. Rukeyser, by contrast, was emphatically lyrical at many points in "The Book of the Dead," even while being prosecutorial. Joseph Harrington makes a telling point about the mimetic deficit at the heart of documentary poetry, and how it impinges on political objectives. "The modesty of the poets' political aspirations for their work," he writes, "stems from their simultaneous belief in and mistrust of referentiality—a conflict that makes for a poetics at odds

with itself" (2016, 67). If lyric wins out over documentation, then, a fundamental discrepancy is revealed between political mission and the artistic integrity of the poem.

After Rukeyser there's little in the way of documentary poetry until recently. A notable exception is Charles Reznikoff. Intimations of a documentary impulse in his work actually date as far back as 1921, in his self-published
Uriel Accosta, with its sequence of poems under the collective title "Jews"
(1926, 12). Each is a vignette of some domestic circumstance, registered in a
dry laconic style. One begins,

> He had a rich uncle who sent him to a university and
>   would have taken him into the firm; but he went off and
>   married a girl, the men of whose family were truckmen.
> His uncle would have nothing to do with him, and he
>   became a cigar pedlar; but his wife was beautiful.
>   (1927, 51)[5]

These portraits are documentary in the sense Evans meant by a photographic
portrait being a human document. It was only many decades later that
Reznikoff—who'd been trained as a lawyer, though he largely avoided practicing law—returned to the format he'd devised in "Jews." The results were
published in *Testimony: The United States 1885–1890; Recitative* (1965), followed posthumously by a complete text in two volumes (1978–1979). Many
are narratives of several pages, others are short; nearly all end in death or
mutilation.

> The bell did not ring nor was the whistle blown
> and his view of the train was shut off
> by the waiting shed—
> until the train was right on him:
> he hadn't time to snap his fingers.
> (*Testimony*, 85)

In most cases the documentary aura is a byproduct of the legal implications
of the actions, or as in the one cited here, a post-mortem forensic report.

If documentary suggests investigation, Reznikoff's work refrains from this
undertaking. The poems are closer to the "straight print" of photography.
Where a documentary poetics is concerned, Edward Sanders's *Investigative
Poetry* is a founding manifesto of sorts. Published in 1976, based on a lecture given at Naropa the previous year and written with his affable wit, it's as
much a genealogy as a propositional chart. He credits Hart Crane's *The Bridge*

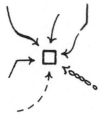

Figure 8.13. Edward Sanders,
The Z-D Generation (1981),
data cluster

as "a ziggurat of scholarship" and finds in Pound's *Cantos* "melodic blizzards of data-fragments. History as slime-sift for morality" (7, 9). Charles Olson is the major compass and progenitor for Sanders, with *The Maximus Poems* setting the bar for "poetry as history, or history-poesy, or Clio come down to Gloucester in a breeze of High Energy Verse Grids, or Data Clusters" (8). He even provides a winsome illustration of a data cluster, slightly augmented in a follow-up booklet, *The Z-D Generation* (1981) (see figure 8.13). *The Z-D Generation*—adopting Denis Diderot and Émile Zola as progenitors—refrains from addressing poetry altogether, turning its sights instead on the political investigation of what Sanders calls The Right Wing Nut. To that end, one must "Demand to infiltrate the National Security grouch apparatus!" (unpaginated). As in *Investigative Poetry*, Sanders advances his propositions with line breaks and verse units. "The Right Wing Nut in its heart of hearts wearies of the concept / of voting, and longs for a rigid boss with / powers of Total Spank." Taken together, these two booklets reflect Sanders's own investigative work on Charles Manson and his followers, *The Family: The Story of Charles Manson's Dune Buggy Attack Battalion* (1971).

Sanders's foray into documentary poetry commenced with the book-length *Chekhov* (1995), followed by *1968: A History in Verse* (1997), an autobiographically infused chronicle of that turbulent year, then most ambitiously in the multivolume *America: A History in Verse* (2000, 2002, 2004) covering the years 1900 to 1970 and still ongoing. He also published *The Poetry and Life of Allen Ginsberg: A Narrative Poem* (2000). Sanders's mode in these documentary books can be terse—as this from *1968* on the aftermath of Martin Luther King's assassination:

> The sword stabbed blacks
>   in their hoping hearts
> & big riots began in D.C., Baltimore, Chicago
>   Detroit, Boston
>   and 125 other places

> where 46 died
>   with over 20,000 arrested
>   55,000 troops sent to quell
>   stats that do not tell the pain (84)

He can also be frankly personal:

> I was feeling a little guilty
> for urging Janis all that spring
>   to go out on her own
>   (though many others also urged) (232)

—and, as so often in this book, the personal is public, the "Janis" here being Joplin, a friend of Sanders's on the rock circuit he frequented with his band The Fugs. *1968* works because its lived experience personalizes the public chronicle.

One could imagine that the volumes of *America* lack this inflection of personal involvement, as their data clusters replicate material readily found elsewhere. Sanders's investigative outlook is similar to Howard Zinn's revisionist *A People's History of the United States* (1980). Yet what differentiates *America: A History in Verse* is Sanders's whimsical phraseology. Amid a bald recitation of facts and events we come across an aside like "Com-fear is always a face-brace for the moaning bemoneyed" (2000, 105). But then, more facts, more lists, which as they accumulate over hundreds of pages begin to feel like notes for an unwritten book. In the end, the rationale for charging poetry with investigative potential fails to account for the basic question, why poetry? "Interrogate the Abyss!" Sanders exclaims in *Investigative Poetry* (23), but abyssal as American history can seem, it's a far cry from the capitalized Abyss of Pascal or Baudelaire.

There is, though, something indispensable in Sanders's prognostic aspiration, something that poses a challenge to that which casually falls under the rubric of documentary poetry: the key concept, *investigation*. For it's clearly the case that documentation by itself may be little more than a stand-in for lack of imagination. It can be a way of suggesting importance or relevance without any corresponding effort at delving and discovering. Document as decal, yet another turn in bumper sticker culture, that longstanding American enterprise in righteous (or sassy) signaling. Is the turn to documentary a repudiation of the modest lyric with its fawning disclosures of private life? Even as that grandee, Robert Lowell, slips farther into the past, it seems that the private correspondence from which he derived his last books is now fair game for public perusal, so the personal lyric is not dust yet. Can documentary engage the lyricism of personal disclosure? To answer in the affirmative is tantamount to saying that the traditional subjects of lyric are "documents" of some sort, documents of sorrow, exaltation, despondency. Document your emotions and emote over your documents.

Documentary poetry as it now thrives is something else altogether. Perhaps the most reliable indicator of a documentary project is a list of credited sources, and even bibliographies befitting scholarly research, as in Tyehimba Jess's *Olio* (2016), or *American Anger* by H. L. Hix (2015) with its seventeen-page Works Cited list. A bibliography needn't be so extensive, of course. In *Coal Mountain Elementary* (2009), Mark Nowak's Works Cited only runs to three pages, but one online source consists of sixty-three hundred pages of testimonial transcripts from the West Virginia Office of Miners' Health and Safety. Nowak's documentary book details mining disasters in China and West Virginia, with its contents directly lifted from such sources, refining the way in which *found* poetry can be redirected to maximum impact by scrupulous research, selection, and arrangement. The poetry is in the arrangement of requisitioned elements. *Coal Mountain Elementary* is one of a number of contemporary books discussed by Lynn Keller in *Recomposing Ecopoetics: North American Poetry of the Self-Conscious Anthropocene* (2017), nearly all of which entail considerable documentary components or at least preparatory research, suggesting that ecopoetics has been a major stimulus to the recent rise in documentary poetry.

One of the more audacious debuts by a poet in the twenty-first century is *Styrofoam* by Evelyn Reilly (2009), which might be characterized as poetry-against-the-odds, as a considerable portion of the book consists of technical data and chemical formulas: "Enter: 8,9,13,14,17 -ethynyl-13-methyl- / 7,8,9,11,12,14,15,16-octahydro-cyclopenta-diol" (9). In a cheeky note at the back of the book, Reilly writes, "Some chemical formulas have been slightly altered in the cause of poetic rhythm. Apologies to my entirely hypothetical chemist readers" (67). Styrofoam is the trade name of polystyrene, and this book never for a moment strays from documenting its uses, its makeup, its consequences in the modern world, from the tiniest thermoplastic polymers coursing through the bloodstream to the vast swirl of plastic flotsam in the Pacific Ocean. *Styrofoam*, however, is not a manual, however much technical information it marshals. In a sense, it's a rhapsodic chatter of recognition, alarm, solace, accommodation, curiosity, stress, yet somehow as buoyant as plastic in water. Asked to write a blurb for the book, I characterized it as "a piece of functional social anatomy ranging from roadkill to the ecstasy of Saint Teresa, effortlessly sweeping up everything from thermoplastics to cancer cells as if they were the dice tossed by a vast, remote croupier. You don't so much read a book like this as feel it strapped onto your brain like a phantom limb."

Styrofoam is so immersive a reading experience because the text itself is a vast cartography of information, yet the poetry mimics a survival strategy in its ability to assimilate any- and everything without recourse to hectoring rhetorical afflatus. It's a recombinant artifice, in strangely gentle alliance with the plastics overrunning the planet, "this intimate.multitude mixed with authentic.faux.art.products" (16). Reilly uses typography from patented products and web browser formulae like domain names to enhance the sense of being immersed not just in plastic materials but in the *plasticity* of a material poetics:

> Thus the common.experience   to bear
> moreandmorewitness.to
>
>   this apoplexy apocalypse incantation
>   this devastation deflection invocation
>   this reflex context perplex
>
>   (Perspex®!   (63)

Perspex is the acrylic known as Plexiglas, and the registered trademark symbol here is a stark reminder that the paraphernalia of everyday life is not innocently at hand, like trees and rocks, but *put* in place by complex legal and technological means. "Reilly's collage poetry," writes Keller, "indicates that art in the contemporary mesh is thoroughly interwoven with the marketing and consumption of products that threaten environmental health." Keller points out that "much of the text is online detritus," effluvia eligible for the proverbial dump (2017, 82). If "we humans have gotten ourselves in deep trouble by letting so much of this metamorphic material, plastic, loose upon the world," she elaborates, "the desire that led us to do so seems as based in aesthetic sensibility or social and economic ambition as in scientific curiosity" (95). Reilly, then, far from insulating her art from the toxicity she surveys, deliberately exposes it to the means and rhythms of an ongoing torrent. Plastic (bad) and plasticity (good) are inseparable.

Keller's reflections on the way *Styrofoam* contaminates itself, as it were, with viral potentiality, raises a question germane to documentary poetry: namely, what are the self-validating parameters of a text that would responsibly document some sphere of human activity while also aspiring to aesthetic accomplishment? Poetry is not reportage. To call it poetry is to make an *enabling* point, but documentation impinges on that prospect. The documentary works of C. D. Wright offer a way of thinking this through. The very title of *One Big Self: An Investigation* (2007) flashes a provocative claim on Sanders's "investigative poetry," though Wright makes no reference to him in the book's framing paraphernalia. She's concerned, instead, to register her sense of unpreparedness for a project initiated by a friend:

> I am going to prison.
> I am going to visit three prisons in Louisiana.
> I am going on the heels of my longtime friend Deborah
>   Luster, a photographer.
> It is a summons.
> All roads are turning into prison roads.
> I already feel guilty.
> I haven't done anything. (xv)

The guilt of an inmate—perhaps claiming innocence—and a poet who, as an artist, might well feel guilty about not having achieved a desired result, converge here. *One Big Self* follows a compositional design Wright had worked out earlier in a travel book, *Deepstep Come Shining* (1998), in which ripe phrases and proper names plucked from the environment were subjected to a periodic cycle of recurrence, mixed with the poet's own observations.

In *One Big Self* much of the material is presumably quoted directly from prisoners, though no quotation marks are used in the book.

> Nobody here for spitting on the sidewalk
>
> I am the seventh child of Sister Rose. She put her life in
>   JEOPARDY to come see about her son Aaron. A God-sent
>   woman, born with the double veil, foresight.
>
> Wherever you find knots of men
> you will find the charisma of violence
>
> American as pie
>
> Poetry   time   space   death   (46)

Elsewhere, spitting will be slightly modified ("no one here for urinating in public" [53]), and three or four spaced words recur throughout, reinforcing the sense of déjà vu in the correctional facility environs. For the most part, though, the reader is implicitly asked to read between the lines, to somehow discern lives in their uniqueness although proper names are withheld (except when inmates are referring to others). Rather than individuation, the composite portrait is precisely named in Wright's title, one big self.

In fact, individuation in the project was concentrated in the photographs of Deborah Luster, only one of which appears on the cover of *One Big Self*. Four years before Wright's book was published, the poem accompanied the photographs in a glossy, large-format limited edition with Luster as primary author, *One Big Self: Prisoners of Louisiana*. Apart from minor formatting differences, the text is the same, though the volume also includes text by the photographer. The photographs are interspersed throughout the book, bisecting Wright's poem every few pages. Each of the 149 photos depicts a convict (sometimes two), with name, location, birth date, number of children, prison work, and sentence. It can be startling to match a given visage with specifications ranging from "3 years," "21 years," "50 years" to "life." Some of the photos are head shots, others are full body with elaborate postures and costumes, and a few omit the face altogether. They conjure a haunting in which Wright's poem arises, and with which it must coexist. None of this atmosphere is apparent without the photographs. In this context, reading between the lines becomes literal: at any point you turn the page and find a row of faces, and often you need to turn several pages before the poem resumes.

Another "one" returns in Wright's next documentary project, *One with Others* (2010), in which the compositional strands are interconnected yet maintain their individual integrity. The book is in part an elegiac reflection on the author's friend, called V. But it weaves in a 1969 civil rights "March against Fear" in Arkansas, Wright's native state, in which V took part. Additional events involving racist reprisals in a public school are also interwoven, along with time-capsule phrases from the sixties that recur like the ringing of a small bell, such as the Dear Abby advice columns, generally concluding: "Everybody has a problem. What's yours" (29, 62, 88, 106). Repeated speech tics—"You get my meaning," "You get what I'm getting at," "You got me there," "Come again"—reinforce an air of orality. And the civil rights refrain is mordantly sustained by a bracketed cancellation—"[N-word]"—the frequency of which is a stark reminder of its ubiquity in that time and place. As Wright concedes, "Hateful words survive in sticky clumps" (108, 121).

Suggesting that Wright is "loading up lyric with evidentiary fact" Dan Chiasson (2010) may be placing undue emphasis on *lyric*. Is lyric the appropriate term for a rotary processional of words, phrases, and images sustained for over 150 pages? Certain aerated passages might pass for lyric, as the expansive spacing draws attention to the images:

Vines protect the copperhead from the hoe

Cottonwoods flutter as one

Bats at the cell tower

The tub in which James Earl Ray stood (*One with Others*, 49)

The formatting varies throughout the book, sometimes with wide spacing as in this extract, sometimes in prose paragraphs with unjustified margins, and lineation mostly flush left. Overall the appearance of space makes it possible for anything to appear without explanation or cause, as snakes and trees and bats slide into the assassin of Martin Luther King Jr. Although the strategy is to braid diverse storylines, they are mostly contemporaneous but not entirely. The poem has regular infusions of geographic and cartographic scene setting, albeit gestural, thumbnail. There are also patches of what Sanders would call data clusters.

> The only sure thing in those days were the prices:
>
> Jack Sprat tea bags only 19¢.
> A whole fryer is 59¢.
> A half-gallon of Purex, 25¢.
> Two pounds of Oleo, 25¢.
> Ivory Soap 10¢ a bar.
> Cherokee freestone peaches, 5 cans for $1.
>
> And the temperatures:
>
> Los Angeles enters its sixth day of rioting, 32 dead;
>   Chicago's
> rebellion ends in two.
> KKK's lawyer dies in Birmingham.
> Hurricane Camille sacks Pass Christian.
> The president of the Cosmos Club holds a tea.
> Soybean cyst nematode puts the county's crop under
>   quarantine.
> Three Brinkley children die in an icebox.
> It is time to pick the cotton. (39)

It may well be that Chiasson's reference to lyric was a gesture, not a specification, as he precedes it with a substantial summary of Wright's method. He observes of the sixties that the decade is readily conjured for us through documentary film footage and concomitant techniques (voice over, news footage, soundtrack, etc.), yet notes that "there are no such ready conventions for documentary writing."

> The available prose genres would miscarry the subject in one way or another: "oral history" is too scattershot, memoir too tender-headed, investigative reporting too bound up with evidence and judgment.

It turns out that the literary genre least likely to get in the way of this story is poetry, which, despite its reputation for gilt and taffeta, comfortably veers close to "documentary" conventions. It comes especially close in Wright's angular strain of postmodern poetry, which draws on refractive techniques now a hundred years old: collage, extensive quotation, multiplicity of voice and tone, found material, and, often, a non-authorial, disinterested stance.... these conventions feel very natural. No longer disorienting, not yet shopworn, they are, for the reader, transparent, like a documentary camera: you can see right through them to the subject matter. (Chiasson 2010)

This useful synopsis of Wright's methods is somewhat misleading, ending as it does with the assumption of total transparency. As I discovered when teaching *One with Others* in an upper-level undergraduate course, everything itemized by Chiasson as contributing to the operative ease of the postmodern reader has, in fact, to be learned. That they are "no longer disorienting" applies only to frequent consumers of the modernist strategies he lists.

So we're back to "lyric," a term pointedly applied to two of her own books by Claudia Rankine, *Don't Let Me Be Lonely* (2004) and *Citizen* (2014), each of which is subtitled "An American Lyric." *Citizen* in particular has been heralded as a defining publication of the new millennium: its sobering chronicle of racism smoldering just below the surface of everyday civility was the corollary in poetry of Ta-Nehisi Coates's bestselling *Between the World and Me* (2015). Like *One with Others*, Rankine's book recycles salient phrases, in this case centering on the emotional experience of racism at the personal level. "Move on," as in: get over it, "Let it go" (2014, 66, 151); "Did I hear what I think I heard?" (9, 63). The locales are benign—school, office, airplane, restaurant, coffee shop, subway, therapist's office—making the incidents that emerge all the more unsettling. Rankine also uses a number of images to maximum effect. Tennis star Serena Williams is at the center of the book, struggling with her rage as she tries to play through an umpire's miscalls, and it's her game (in many senses of the word) that concludes the book: "It wasn't a match, I say. It was a lesson" (159). What holds everything together in *Citizen* is not the interweaving narrative strands, a strategy Rankine shares with Wright, but the fact that most of the incidents are reported in the first person singular, leaving the reader with a horrendous sense of being witness to persecution. This strategy of anchoring reportage in the first person singular prompted Cole Swensen to note an irony: "Most people find her 'I' convincing, and yet it turns out that, in fact, it's not true" (2011, 62). That is, Rankine assimilates anecdotes and narratives from various sources, collectivizing them in the mode of personal disclosure, making the impact more direct than if she'd used such anecdotal locutions as "a friend told me," "I've heard it said," and so forth. It's an old legacy, in fact, from Whitman's claim to contain multitudes. Rankine's multitudinous "I" is disarming in its deft concentration of plurality in the least likely receptacle. For an African American, even so simple an act as speaking is swollen with uninvited testimony.

Swensen's observations are from her essay on documentary poetry, "News That Stays News," in which she makes some discerning observations about the genre. As she notes, "Documentary poetry has a paradox at its core, a clash between two, contradictory relationships to truth" (2011, 54). One relation to truth is testimonial, involving facts and verifiable information. But the medium of poetry itself is not reportage; its purpose is not juridical, though it may of course provide evidence. Rather than making truth claims about the world, Swensen suggests, poetry adds itself as another fact *to* the world even as it is a factor *in* the world. As such, a poem "cannot make truth claims because it is itself a true act" (54). Swensen disputes the notion that poetry is incapable of telling the truth, however. Not only is it "perfectly capable of conveying the truth," she contends, "it can also attain a unique relationship to truth because it implicitly acknowledges and interrogates the limitations of language" (58). True enough, though I'd suggest that poetry is not so much testing the limits of language as enlarging its possibilities. That's what I hear, for instance, in C. D. Wright's elegiac reports on her Arkansas friend in *One with Others*: "If religion, she liked to say, is the opiate of the masses, fundamentalism is the amphetamine" (2010, 35). "Language is at the service of information," Swensen says of documentary poetry, which has "devised ways to make the language of information even more informative by subtly augmenting it with the language of art" (64).

Documentary poetry, then, seesaws back and forth between the mission of conveying news of the world and positioning itself *as* news in that world. This suggests a potential opportunism on the part of a poet choosing subject matter. But it's also the case that by engaging a particular subject, poetry can make it matter in ways that another kind of report might miss. *One with Others* is an elegy for a friend, but that friend's life opens out on civil rights and racist events in Arkansas in the sixties, and neither the friend's life nor the historical events are subordinate with respect to each other. Both are primary. And, as Swensen says of the work of Susan Howe, "while the primary goal of Howe's research may be to create a base for her poetry, the goal of that poetry is, in turn, to constitute an alternative mode of knowledge, a mode in which truth has nothing to do with clarity, but rather with novelty. It's a different kind of news in which only the unprecedented is true" (2011, 65–66). This, she claims, is the difference between "thought" and "thinking" in the poem. Thought is propositional, invested in persuasion, whereas thinking is open ended and speculative. The distinction has a long pedigree, one that goes back to Wallace Stevens's "Metaphors of a Magnifico":

> Twenty men crossing a bridge,
> Into a village,
> Are twenty men crossing twenty bridges,
> Into twenty villages,
> Or one man
> Crossing a single bridge into a village. (1990, 35)

You choose, the lines seem to suggest, while also allowing, *Why bother?* After all, this is a poem, neither a report nor a plan of action. So you can have it both ways.

As documentary poetry has been adopted by many poets in the form of research projects, the impulse behind it has cast a certain halo on other book-length poetic compositions. Brenda Hillman's four volumes addressing the four elements are neither long poems nor documentary projects like those by Nowak or Wright, but the thematic focus makes them feel like an information epic. Kimiko Hahn's *Brain Fever* (2014) and *Toxic Flora* (2010) would appear to the casual browser to be collections of shorter poems, but each book's immersion in scientific information exudes a documentary aura. Nearly all of Cole Swenson's output as a poet consists of projects. What at first appears to be simply an indicated theme, like *The Book of a Hundred Hands* (2005) or *The Glass Age* (2007), turns out to be speckled and striated with assiduous research. The most successful may be Swensen's *Gravesend* (2012), which involves research into something that cannot be researched, life after death. So it's a book of folklore in a sense, and as the work of a good folklorist would do, *Gravesend* draws material directly from the folk, in this case residents of the town of Gravesend in England, who Swensen interviewed in local pubs, asking them about ghosts. The title poem concludes with an eerie image that, thanks to the investigative elements Swensen has deployed, seems almost like a technical observation:

> A grave
> is a door laid flat in the earth, worked into a hinge, which articulates
>   a gulf
>
> without being a bridge. (*Gravesend*, 47)

Swensen thrives on writing to a set theme, and as with many of her peers a theme becomes a point of engagement with document and research.

This sort of engagement is forcefully registered in the book-length projects *100 Notes on Violence* (2010) and *Real Life: An Installation* (2018) by Julie Carr. Neither claims a thematic template—though the titles are clearly viewfinders—but, by setting up a porous relationship to the news cycle, certain themes announce themselves with a kind of mordant insistence. Gun violence being so pervasive in American society, it becomes an inescapable backdrop in both books. Columbine High School, Virginia Tech, Binghamton, Fort Hood, Aurora, Sandy Hook, San Bernardino, Orlando, Las Vegas, Sutherland Springs, and Stoneman Douglas High School are strewn through the pages of *Real Life*, even as it tracks data on childhood poverty in America. Of these titles it could be said, "The stink of the real lay like a scum on the pages of the poems" (Carr 2018, 72).

The stink of the real has clearly been a primary incentive behind the spread of documentary poetry in recent years. As I mentioned earlier, declarations and effusions of the lyric have waned somewhat, in part because of the decline of the anthology market as an incentive to produce eligible poems, but also because the lyric can seem compromised by rosier sentiments from innocent times. Whether a West Virginia mining blight or a mass shooting in a Colorado Cineplex, the world keeps issuing urgent bulletins. Today and tomorrow seem equally imperiled. Even the urge to sound a bucolic note faces the doom of the Anthropocene. Poetry, ever on the lookout for fresh material, may now be entering a time when just *being on the lookout* is enough. Confronting the "Urizenic mindset with its irreversible mitigation-propagation-snarling-release of toxicity," Anne Waldman's vast trilogy *Iovis* (2011) escalates what's at stake in poetry as the art of subtle defiance (xiv).

The vogue for verse narratives was unique to its time and place, owing its momentary ascendancy to the impact of Edwin Arlington Robinson and Robinson Jeffers when the challenges of modernism were fresh and, for many, too menacing to absorb. Narrative was safer. And then it faded rather abruptly at midcentury. There have been narrative poems since then—and the best of them all may be *The Long Take* by the Scotsman Robin Robertson (2017), a surprise finalist for the Man Booker Prize—but a vogue for such works seems unlikely to recur, although Robertson's success has been followed by raves for Stefano Massini's massive *The Lehman Trilogy* (2020), so who knows? In contrast, documentary poetry has grown slowly in and because of the larger potential of book length projects, particularly by women. Lyn Hejinian and Alice Notley, to name two of the more influential poets of recent decades, publish almost exclusively book-length poems, though neither has done documentary work. Anne Carson, equally influential, has been quite resourceful in her irreverent recalibration of poetry as imaginative prowess unleashed and unprecedented. But like Hejinian and Notley, she has refrained from documentary prospects (though she has produced two well-received poetic narratives, *Autobiography of Red* [1998] and *Red Doc>* [2013]). Her profession as a classicist of course provides her with a rich store of "documentary" material, so Sappho and Thucydides are as innate to her sensibility as Robert Lowell's ancestors were to him. They're part of a toolkit, not subjects of special investigation. The examples of other intrepid masters of the composed book and the long poem like Harryette Mullen and Eleni Sikelianos suggest that a compelling and inescapable incentive is at hand for continuing adventures in expanded scale, with every possibility that a documentary spirit will be at its core.

EXCHANGES

Global Scale and Transient Occasions

An Interview with Evelyn Reilly on This Compost

EVELYN REILLY'S BOOKS include *Styrofoam, Apocalypso,* and *Echolocation.* Her work has been widely anthologized. She has taught at the Poetry Project at St. Marks Church, and has been a curator of the Segue Reading Series. Portuguese translations of *Styrofoam* and *Echolocation* will be published in 2022.

Reilly: What led you to write *This Compost?* How do you see it connected to other activities by poets who are exploring the notion of "ecopoetics"?

Rasula: *This Compost* is an example of an emergent occasion. I didn't set out to write a book, it just came over me. For a year living in rustic circumstances in upstate New York in 1980–81, I'd brought a handful of books to reread with some care: *The Maximus Poems,* "A," and *The Opening of the Field.* The links between Duncan and Olson were familiar, of course, but I was surprised to see how readily Zukofsky contributed to their open field matrix. The field kept expanding as I periodically took out the manuscript to revise it (1985, 1990, 1995, 2000). Because I was out of touch with contemporary American poetry during the 1990s (when ecopoetics emerged), I didn't foresee any connection to contemporary practice at all. So it's really serendipitous that what began as an utterly idiosyncratic exercise in 1980 found a welcoming environment when it was published in 2002.

Reilly: What, if any, is the relation between ecopoetics and so-called experimental or innovative poetry? You've written that "the bulk of modern poetry suggests a calamitous abandonment of the legacy of Whitman and Dickinson." Do you see any more hope in the so-called "experimental" wing of the poetry scene today? Are there any current trends that seem interesting to you in this light?

Rasula: Whitman and Dickinson were experimental. That was the point of singling them out from, say, Longfellow and Whittier. They were like soil bacteria breaking down dead matter, rearranging the contents—standard procedure in nature, but a cultural experiment. In their case the biodegradable material was poetry. I tend to regard, as ecologically wholesome, any activity in which decomposition is germane to composition. There is, of course, a completely different legacy in this respect, with Mallarmé as resident guru ("Destruction was my Beatrice," he said), the urbanity of which is probably more immediately related to the experimental poetry of the past couple decades.

Jen Bervin's *Nets* is an encouraging instance of something that would be widely regarded as experimental, though I think the more accurate term is "procedural" for this rigorous trawl through Shakespeare's sonnets. I guess it might qualify as an experiment if her approach was, "Ronald Johnson succeeded in reducing the word count of the first four books of *Paradise Lost* in *RADI OS*, so let's see if I can do the same with Shakespeare." Likewise, Jenny Boully's *The Body* consists entirely of footnotes, clearly a compositional ordinance, not an experiment. But I'm probably beating a dead horse, insisting on this semantic distinction, because the whole category of procedural operations tends to get lumped into the zone of experimentation.

Insofar as there's any reason to speak of experiment, it's best to take an ecopoetic outlook. The danger is in looking for analogies from nature, assuming that cultural terms should be resolved with reference to natural cycles. I think culture as a whole is an extravagance, and an exorbitant experiment. And I mean, by culture, all human production, including the byproducts of natural functions (e.g., waste disposal). We make things: What are the consequences of our making? What do we make? From this perspective, possibly the most honest approach is Giacometti's insistence that he had no interest in producing sculptures, he just persisted because the more he did it the less competent he felt. Or, the more clearly he understood how unprepared he was to handle that material. To me, that sounds like the very definition of being experimental. It also rings true to my own experience as a poet, which revealed itself long ago as that point of engagement I have with dysfunction where I am otherwise most functional: in language. I really hear Beckett when he says, in one of those dialogues with Georges Duthuit, [that] "to be an artist is to fail." For the artist, "failure is his world" (a thesis tirelessly worked out by Blanchot). Beckett brandishes failure in this triumphant declaration, as if to embody the very condition he characterizes as: "Total object, complete with missing parts, instead of partial object."

Reilly: Although you have reservations about the use of the word "experimental," can you talk a little about the Lucretian concept of the *clinamen*, the swerve or the deviation that might be compared to the genetic variation that potentially results in better adaptation to a changing environment?

Rasula: I do have reservations about the use of the term "experimental," which is so casual and ungrounded as to be senseless, at least if it's to be understood as empirically derived from the verb "to experiment." As things stand, anything is called experimental that won't be included in a forms and craft textbook. But by my reckoning, it's experimental to write a sonnet or a sestina: as in a laboratory experiment, you have carefully delimited parameters and a clear set of instructions. If these kinds of experiments have not interested legions of practicing poets, it's because it's a very old and familiar experiment, the results of which strike many as incapable of bearing news. Without a wholesale determination to reoccupy the form (I'm thinking of Berrigan's sonnets), a sonnet says little more than "author X can write a sonnet," which is about as interesting as claiming the ability to walk through a doorway as a personal accomplishment. If you can attenuate statistical probability, though, so that getting through the door is a real challenge, then something interesting occurs—at least in a Charlie Chaplin movie. The clinamen is a wonderful concept in this respect; it opens the door on chances. It adds, to the confident expectation of going through the door, the propositional incertitude "I'll chance it." I'll take that risk, I'll bear the brunt of serendipity. Serendipity and catastrophe are twins in the domain of the clinamen.

Although the concept of the clinamen was just a shot in the dark, conceptually, on the part of Democritus (and propagated by Lucretius), it has very precise application in, say, genetics. Growth hormones in the embryo are synchronized with a molecule called IGF-1 (for "insulin-like growth factor"), but this molecule—which is like a green light on a traffic signal—can't promote growth all the time. It needs to be curbed by a protein (called PTEN). But if this protein "swerves"—or, in genetic terms, is defective—then we end up with that medical condition called the Proteus syndrome, famously associated with Joseph Merrick, the Elephant Man. Unchecked by the PTEN protein, the IGF-1 molecule continues to promote cell proliferation (particularly in bony matter—hence the huge skull) until the person is more or less suffocated by becoming a skeletal catastrophe.

When Steve McCaffery and I decided to use the clinamen as the defining concept for *Imagining Language* (2001), we tended to think of it in its more positive, benign, or serendipitous aspect. But the multitude of "monstrous" examples included in the anthology retain some sense of malignant, catastrophic potential (e.g., the whole section called "Mania," as well as Francis Lodwick's "Forms of Distinctional Marks," or Urquart's universal language "Naudethaumata").

Reilly: Maybe the question of so-called "experimentalism" is really a matter of more-or-less used or overused "forms"—so that certain writers find themselves deadened by the use of the sonnet or sestina but can embrace, say, Oulipean "constraints." As for catastrophe, I've always thought that aesthetically the greater the risks taken the worse the potential catastrophe, but also the greater the chance of "bearing news." Your description of author X who can write sonnets brings up the problem of "craft" as a way of thinking about the poem as well-made object, rather than, say, Lyn Hejinian's notion of poetry as "the language of inquiry." Is one or the other more or less likely to help in revealing our language's complicity in the abuse of our habitat?

Rasula: While I'm wary of the reverence accorded to "craft" in the creative writing world, it is an important term with broad associations. Craft, handicraft (Walter Benjamin links storytelling to handicrafts), manual labor, tilling, and harvesting: these terms provide a continuum leading back to how we handle the earth. One school of poetic formalism (cf. anthropologist Victor Turner's son Frederick Turner, whose book *Natural Classicism* I wrote about in *Syncopations* [2004]) regards craft as an investment in those integral biological structures of hand-eye coordination that constitute our ancestral heritage as a species. There is something to be said for strict metrics as a means of coordinating manual labor of a predictably repetitive sort, like chain gang hollers. But I resist the notion that 4/4 time is more "natural" than any other meter. It's instructive—and in 1913 it was revelatory—that Stravinsky's *Rite of Spring* is a cascade of self-differentiating time signatures. The primal scene demands it. And this is in accord with Jerry Rothenberg's longstanding insistence that primitive means complex. So on these grounds it makes sense to affirm Lyn's model of poetry as the language of inquiry with the understanding that "the language" is never a neutral term, nor a given artifact, but the medium in which to craft inquisitiveness.

Your reference to "language's complicity in the abuse of our habitat" implies that language operates as an independent agent, a bit like Chris Dewdney's specter of language as parasite in *The Immaculate Perception*, or Jack Spicer's deathbed declaration "my vocabulary did this to me." Does language really pull the wool over our eyes? Is language an ideological toxin? If one were to believe that, then surely one would have to adopt music or visual art as preferential media—and, what's more, regard them as necessary antidotes to the poison of words. But then, the visual arts would have to go, ecologically speaking, for their use of toxic pigments. Anyway, "language" is too general for our sociologically inflected modes of complicity, for which the more accurate term is idiolect. Consider the ruckus over global warming: I can't help but think that the term is close enough to "global warning" that the nay-sayers are motivated to protest because of the surreptitious provocation hanging over the whole thing.

Reilly: In *This Compost*, you put a particular emphasis on the Black Mountain school and its descendants even though the notion they embraced of "organic form" now seems rather naive to us. How useful are "organic" or "natural" metaphors in thinking about what an ecopoetics might be? I'm thinking not just of the notion of "poetic compost," but Retallack's "fractal coastlines" also come to mind. Are we risking a new kind of pathetic fallacy?

Rasula: I think it's important to distinguish between the implications of organic form among Black Mountain poets and the protocols of explication generated by the New Critics, from whom we derive the somewhat debased notion of organic form to which you refer. Black Mountain poetics understands organic form in a broader context extending to cybernetics. (Somebody should write a big survey of the liberating effects of cybernetics on postwar American thought in the sciences and the arts, culminating in the sixties. You get a lot of it recapitulated by Pynchon in *Gravity's Rainbow*, but of course that's a phantasmagoria, not a chronicle.) In any case, I don't think you can dispense with organic form as long as poems have beginnings, middles, and ends, the terms of organic form spelled out by Aristotle. When you think you've finished a poem, how do you know? Whatever hunch is operative there is "organic"; that is, it arises from your nature, your being. Unless you're dealing with a prix fixe menu or formal prosody—here's the dessert, here's the fourteenth line—how do you recognize where the end is? Organic form permeates every possibility except those indebted to chance operations. Even being arbitrary, in the psychologically willful sense, drags the organic along behind it, even if only as an unwanted third leg.

  As for risking fallacy, let's consider ecologically what "pathetic fallacy" means: it signifies pathos, the feelings that are a necessary precipitate of their time and circumstance. I haven't seen any footage of it, but I'm pretty sure that the memorial in Blacksburg, Virginia, following the shooting at Virginia Tech was full of pathos, and that the pathos on display took many forms, from convulsive tears to the calculated rhetoric that Bush and any other delegated officials felt obliged to provide. The "fallacy" in John Ruskin's term is the attribution of feeling to the mechanical operations of "nature." It's basically an objection to anthropomorphism run amok. For the time being, anyway, I don't see any danger of organicism run amok. There are always instances of ideological fury, of course, holier-than-thou postures of rebuke and recrimination that pride themselves on their terminological choices. But here we get into the perennial problem of associating a concept with someone who espouses it (Hitler was a vegetarian, therefore vegetarians are pathological).

As to the use value of organic metaphors: any such use is limited to those for whom it's meaningful, and when the circumstance is ripe. I've deliberately put this in a colloquial form that makes an appeal to the organic, in order to remind you how metaphors are not always chosen, they can be inherited in the vernacular. We're exhorted to "strike while the iron is hot," but how many of us are blacksmiths? This is the raw linguistic material Derrida anatomizes in his early essay "White Mythology." The danger, for ecopoetics, is to deliberately systematize analogies and metaphors and frames of reference in strictly organic terms, and then attempt to legislate those terms. Whereas I think the more responsible ecological approach is to be aware of the balance of passive and active in the choice of terms—that is, to be aware of all discourse as the promotion of what Kenneth Burke called "terministic screens" (1989, 114–25).

Reilly: Well it's certainly true that there is no escaping the organic. And even chance operations connect to the random processes of nature. Although it strikes me that some entirely nonorganic metaphors could potentially be just as useful as organic ones in helping us understand how language use feeds into environmental abuse. As you say, it's a matter of circumstance.

Can you say a bit more about the connection of organic form to cybernetics and also about Burke's notion of terministic screens?

Rasula: To speak of the organic is to refer to the conditions favorable on this planet for the propagation of carbon-based life forms. Cybernetics (from which we get the term "feedback") examines the interplay between organism and environment, which is such a rudimentary yet pervasive structure that cybernetics became the supreme science for a decade or so after World War II. Olson's poem "The Kingfishers" is a record of his encounter with Norbert Wiener's presentation of cybernetics (Wiener is quoted in section 4 of the poem). Adapted to the Central American setting, Olson comes up with this formulation of the principle of feedback [in "Kingfishers"]:

When the attentions change / the jungle
leaps in
      even the stones are split

I can't offer anything more precise than Don Byrd's (1994) observation, "Cybernetic thought is not a new paradigm. It is rather a science of
paradigms. . . . In light of it, no paradigm or archetype carries more than
local significance." He's aware that this sounds dangerously like an incentive to solipsism: "Representations of the world are pragmatic, related to
particular purposes, ideological. There is no common picture of the world."
But his point is that "the limit is not epistemological but environmental.
Organic dignity is now founded neither on a transcendental source nor on
the immediate intuition of being itself. Organisms are to be valued for their
autonomy, for their existence through themselves, not for their origination
in something Other. This is to say, organisms are the other."

To return to your question, "organic form" is a red herring where cybernetics is concerned. Rather, everything we know as form is to be ascertained
in the cybernetic subject, organism-plus-environment. You don't get one
without the other, and their mutuality means that neither can be regarded
as a stable term. This is where facile exhortations like "back to nature"
come undone. Back to what nature? Much of what people would identify
as nature in California, for instance, consists of the ubiquitous eucalyp-
tus, a tree imported from Australia in the nineteenth century. Humans are
by no means the only species that migrates; and any large-scale migra-
tion rearranges the habitat opportunities for other species. The impact of
human behavior, given the imposing scale of our species population, is obviously of urgent concern because of the way local nudges expand exponentially into global consequence. Buzzards that used to be indigenous to
the American southeast are now found in abundance in Ontario. Why?
Because the interstate highway system gives them an updraft of warm
negotiable air currents along which to travel, and the roadkill gives them
plenty to dine on during the trip.

Global warming has become an acceptable ecological topic (one of the
few, in fact), I think because it rather comfortably succeeds previous paradigms of global malady like nuclear holocaust. Such paradigms invite, in
turn, Big Fix solutions: nuclear détente via the SALT treaty, global warming via the Kyoto treaty. In both cases we have available agents that can be
approached like criminal culprits, nuclear powers and greenhouse gases.
There's every reason to deal with them, of course, but the Big Fix options
serve as terministic screens in Burke's sense, deflecting attention from the
multitude of other contributing factors. The elimination (or at least stand-

down) of the nuclear threat has done nothing to abate militarism around the world; and the scale of environmental impact related to human activity is almost incalculable. "Impact" is constant, and it doesn't necessarily mean bad except from a romantic longing to live lives that can be easily mapped onto those of our predecessors. We live in a world that dates back only about two hundred years, the point of a dramatic increase in human population (coincident with the industrial revolution) that Fernand Braudel calls the collapse of a biological ancien régime. So our biogenetic makeup is, historically speaking, an anomaly we drag around in the big sack of cultural anachronisms.

Reilly: To return to poetics, is there any reason to think that in ecopoetic terms metonymy, as a relational figure, might be preferable to metaphor?

Rasula: Of all the rhetorical tropes itemized by Quintillian in his immense catalogue, metaphor has no rivals (and he singles it out as most beautiful); the closest contender would be irony. Is it because we take pleasure in conversion? Is it symptomatic of human intelligence to delight in metamorphosis? Is metaphor grounded in nature in some way—arising, for instance, by observing tadpoles turning into frogs, caterpillars becoming butterflies? If so, then the allure carries with it more than the simple act of comparison. As the tadpole becomes the frog, the metaphor suggests that X might actually become Y. (Wallace Stevens's poem "The Motive for Metaphor" concludes with an ominous evocation of "the vital, arrogant, fatal, dominant X" [1990, 240].) The figural reckoning we as a species bring to our engagement with the world is of momentous consequence on a planetary scale. We can make a pewter spoon and we can make a hole in the ozone layer. Metaphor may fluctuate in poetic practice but it's a steady constant in vernacular speech, and this may reflect the propensity of the species for bending and shaping and changing things.

Metonymy raises different considerations altogether. Richard Lanham intriguingly suggests, "Perhaps metonymy has received attention in postmodern critical thinking because it is an affair finally of scale-manipulation, and manipulating scale in time and space undergirds much postmodern art and music." This strikes me as a fairly accurate characterization of a world increasingly known in the interplay between miniaturization and gigantism. That is, the global consequences of our species life are ever more apparent as a precipitously ad hoc collectivism that lies far beyond any inherited notions of political economy. By the same token, another form of globalism is evident in the internet, which is based on microtechnologies. All this is unpremeditated or unintended, but when intended it does seem to reflect Lanham's notion of metonymy as scale manipulation.

Reilly: Isn't there also a "proximity aspect" to metonymy that might connect to an ethics of "coexistence"?

Rasula: Good point. But where humans are involved, it seems that coexistence within our own species is a challenge. Scale manipulation is something we're in the process of confronting in terms of population growth. In the past two centuries, each doubling of the global population has taken place in half the time of the previous doubling; and since 1960 we're getting an increase of a billion people every twelve years. North America remains one of the less-populated regions, but for someone of my generation the increase is palpable. No matter where I go now, I can't help asking myself where did all these people come from? A century ago you'd have to attend a World's Fair to experience the throngs we now have in a suburban mall. Then it was part of a singular spectacle; now it's the public face of the inscrutable. I tend to hear certain tendencies in public discourse in a diagnostic way. So, for example, the preoccupation with "the other" is really an exercise in nostalgia, when the other could be identified by way of superficial immediate indicators (race, gender, class). I don't mean to suggest that theorists of otherness long for a return to that: rather, the profusion of others now presses the issue of how one responds, and a reasonable response is to preach coexistence. But population growth hits us in unreasonable ways—it seems to provoke social attitudes notably based on fight-or-flight responses, while reinforcing religious fundamentalism. In the natural world there are recognized patterns of collective suicide or species abortion, as if a species were an incipient organism recognizing its inability to persevere on a certain scale. The global phenomenon of terrorism may have little to do with politics in the long run; rather, it might be an early warning signal of the stress of coexistence in the close-proximity environs facing people whose cultural heritage is of no help in thinking about population growth.

Reilly: In *This Compost* you write of "the ability of humans to know themselves as their own matter," with the emphasis on *matter* as material substance. Can you discuss the implications of this kind of knowledge, including its implications for poetics?

Rasula: It's a question that clearly relates to what I've just been saying about population. We're approaching some limit at which humans numerically become sheer matter, and certain kinds of behavior reflect a panic response. It's like when you're hiking (here in Georgia, anyway) in the heat of the summer and keep walking into cobwebs. It gradually goes from aggravating to faint panic to potential freakout; and I think that "other people"

(I'm thinking of the line in Sartre's *No Exit*: "Hell is other people") increasingly provoke that response now.

But to return to your question: the passage in *This Compost* refers to Charles Olson's observation, in the wake of Buchenwald and Hiroshima, that the war had reduced people to so much raw material, and for him this led to a moral obligation whereby the ancient dictum "know thyself" had to include, in that knowledge, the expendability of yourself in the strategic reckoning others might bring to bear on you. The moral part of it, for Olson, is reflected in his use of the first-person plural: it's "we" who need to attain this perspective. And I think that informs his poetics very precisely, in that the figure of Maximus is himself (Olson) plus all possible others. An impossible challenge, but a necessary undertaking. It's quite a contrast from the studious replication of the Oedipal family you get in Zukofsky's *"A,"* not to mention the transhistorical paint by numbers bombast of *The Cantos*.

Reilly: In earlier essays you've expressed discontent about the nature and dynamics of the contemporary poetry scene. To what extent is *This Compost*, with its vision of a multigenerational "composting community" (manifested graphically by the juxtaposition of unattributed quotations from numerous poets across its pages) a call for a new kind of poetry society? Does this point to a more collaborative, communal notion of how poetry happens, in contrast to the more hierarchical notion of individual genius?

Rasula: Careerism is the real bête noir in my observations on the contemporary scene. It's a byproduct of the success of creative writing programs, which have now been around long enough to have become thoroughly integrated into the institutional apparatus of the university system; so the bottom line is the annual report to the dean on professional accomplishments. Just as you could observe procedural and thematic surges in scholarship in the past by looking at syllabi and publications—deconstruction in the eighties, postcolonialism in the nineties—it's now possible to discern holomovements in the body politic of poetry. It's a way of detecting a somewhat different kind of "composting community" than I focused on in *This Compost*. The alliance between Olson and Duncan and Creeley on the issue of open field composition, for instance, was deliberate but not programmatic, a matter of elective affinities that could extend to others without any question of membership, allegiance to party line, or even personal acquaintance. The poetry scene today constitutes an archipelago of sites where various alliances are made along similar lines; although, as far as I can tell, these sites don't seem to be broadcasting identifiable slogans like "open field" and "deep image" were forty years ago. It's at a higher demographic level, in the university system, where we can see clumps of unelected affinities coagulating, disclosing trends and filtration patterns that radiate from a collective practice despite which, curiously, the issue of individuality seems not to suffer. As far as I can tell, your generation seems fairly comfortable with group dynamics, with a poetry scene from which the alpha male ego has been detoxified, to some extent. I'm pretty sure this reflects the increased involvement of women poets. As I suggested in *Syncopations*, this is a decisive demographic transfiguration that has and will continue to create a very different sort of poetic community.

Reilly: At the beginning of your book, you quote Jerome Rothenberg's description of the poet as "defender of biological and psychological diversity" in the context of parallels between ethno- and ecopoetics. Does this view of the poet necessarily connect ecopoetics to an activist stance? You also write that "poetry is unique in favoring utopia as a transient occasion not universal city," which might imply the opposite.

Rasula: Why not see activism as the promotion of transient occasions? It's probably a consequence of utopian thinking that we tend to think of activism as pursuit of the greater good over the long haul, instantiating governance as transhistorical plebiscite without really considering what it's in our power to accomplish. Of course the key term is "our." Who are we? How many can "we" accommodate? To think on behalf of other people is, at one level, generous. It can also be presumptuous and, at another level, paternalistic (I know what's best for you).

This spectrum, from the egalitarian to the controlling, is evident in debates about ecology. To fully embrace the prospect of a planet in peril seems to lead to an absolutist response, in which "take it or leave it" merges into "America: love it or leave it"; so it's understandable that people seek some moderate position (think globally, act locally). At the largest level, ecology is tantalizingly close to the Archimedean position: that is, in order to know all we need to know in order to act, we'd no longer be in or of this world. So it's useful to remember that the Greek root of ecology links up with economy in *oikos*, household management.

In that Confucian tag revered by Pound, if a man has not order within him, he cannot spread order about him. That's a little dictatorial, so let's make it more descriptive than prescriptive. The Confucian adage has conspicuous consequences for this society, simply in the fact that public life is dominated by television. The tremendous growth in forms of interactive media may be a reaction to the enforced passivity of the television legacy, but unfortunately that legacy remains the paradigm, the surrogate host, of the very models of interactivity that some see as replacing it. (For one thing, interaction invariably comes with a visual screening device, for which a TV screen is the template.) The diversity of transient occasions I'd advocate are not to be confused with the kind of diversity (viewing options) specific to a medium, and that means poetry as well as television. I have a certain phobia about generic experience as such, probably stemming from the expression "watching TV" which spooked me as a kid, when I realized that for most people it really was watching TV, rather than watching something specific, making a choice ("watching TV" meant no choice, submitting to whatever was on). I continue to feel wary in the same way about, say, reading poetry, as if it were all the same. In the ecology of elected habitats, it may be beneficial to write poetry, or read it, but I disapprove of the urge to be a poet, which for many is the driving force. This is a posture almost indistinguishable from "watching TV"—as in, first I'll be a poet, then I'll find out what kind of poetry I'll write (or, again, read). As a defender of psychological diversity, I'd like to expunge the word "poet" from our vocabulary. Wouldn't it be wonderful to commend a piece of writing without the special pleading of genre marching alongside like the change of guards at Buckingham Palace?

This is why I've found it so expedient to draw on the literary theory of the German Romantics (the Jena group, especially Friedrich Schlegel), in which every venture in writing inaugurates its own species—the poem is at once an instance of poetry and "the poetry of poetry": that is, the act that includes reflections on its nature as act—amounting to a kind of evolutionary continuum in which the possibilities for change are accommodated to the medium without necessarily being the raison d'être. From that prospect, there's no need for "experimental" poetry because poetry is the name of an inevitable experiment in living.

Reilly: Having thus dispensed with the issue of "experimentalism," perhaps we can turn to another question: Is an ecologically informed poetics necessarily a reaction against the Western rationalist tradition? A few of the essayists in *Eco-Language Reader* take that stance (Iijima). I'm thinking of your phrase "the sanguine narcissism of the cogito."

Rasula: Merely to refer repugnant habits of behavior or styles of thought to the Western tradition has always struck me as a cop-out, a way of admitting, in effect, the problem is too big to think about, so dismiss something big as a kind of mental bait and switch. When I was twenty, "Don't trust anyone over thirty" was the slogan; denigrations of "the West" (and its variants) derive from the same mindset. In both instances you willfully cut yourself off from your own experience, or potential. For baby boomers, it was an historically specific way to "go native" in one's own juvenescence (which is not the same as adolescence, it's not juvenile: it was a fascinated response to the demographic swell). We got over it, merely by virtue of biological consequence. But can we "get over"—let alone overcome— Western civilization? Far better, I think, to understand its complexities and not be swindled into thinking it's one big package deal. It's not a matter of either/or. What more instructive paragon of the Western rationalist tradition than Thoreau? The beat he heard emanating from a different drummer was as much indebted to Latin authors and Enlightenment botany as it was to Native American lore.

It's true that my phrase "the sanguine narcissism of the cogito" evokes Descartes, and Cartesian dualism can be held accountable for modern varieties of discourse that, pushed to a limit, provoked Lyotard's instructive question, "Can thought go on without a body?" (1991, 8–23). But, prodigious as the Cartesian legacy has been, I wouldn't conflate it with Western rationalism as such (is Hegel, then, part of Western rationalism?—it's a question to be heard in the spirit of David Antin's remark that if Robert Lowell is a poet, he's not interested, but if Socrates is a poet he'll consider it). So there's no way an ecologically informed poetics is a necessary reaction against Western rationalism, because "Western rationalism" is a figment of the impatient imagination. Somewhere in *This Compost* (maybe in draft, so it might not have made it into the published book) I referred to Western civilization as something one might plausibly characterize as a series of "gang related incidents" in police lingo. I think that's much more accurate than talking about rationalism. In the end, it's not about what we "know," but what we do and what we've done that makes a difference. "Here error is all in the not done, / all in the diffidence that faltered," Pound wrote at the end of Canto LXXXI (1972, 522), and I can never hear these lines without this juxtaposition from Canto CXVI: "To make Cosmos— / To achieve the possible—" (1972, 795). The em dashes extend, conceptually, all the way to the horizon. And they join the Cosmos with the possible in a gesture of unavoidable engagement.

At Work on the Incalculable

A Radio Interview with Leonard Schwartz on This Compost

Leonard Schwartz is the author of, among other books, *The New Babel: Towards a Poetics of the Mid-East Crises, Heavy Sublimation,* and, most recently, *Actualities: Transparent, to the Stone.* From 2003 to 2018 he hosted and produced the radio program *Cross Cultural Poetics.*

Schwartz: I've been reading your work and your critical thinking for quite a few years now. I wondered if we could talk about *This Compost: Ecological Imperatives in American Poetry,* about which Guy Davenport wrote, "Jed Rasula's insights are fresh and often exciting. This is an important book." Guy Davenport so recently passed away. It figures in the book—he's mentioned or quoted from in your section "On the Library." In a way *This Compost* seems related to the ideas he explores in his book *The Geography of the Imagination* (1981). Could you speak a little bit about Davenport as a potential influence on your sense of what an essay does?

Rasula: Certainly—and you're quite right to recognize that *The Geography of the Imagination* played a kind of formative role in *This Compost. The Geography of the Imagination* was published in 1981, and it was an extraordinarily stimulating book for me, especially the title essay, which just covered so much territory. That title essay is a kind of deep reading of the Grant Wood painting *American Gothic,* which everyone knows in bastardized form from calendars and things like that. But in this essay, he looks into the painting and sees that, for instance, the farmer is wearing overalls that were only available mail order from Sears Roebuck. He also notices that the guy is holding a pitchfork, which he connects with the ancient Greek God Zeus. It was that wide-ranging, encompassing, and kind of freewheeling sense of handling a lot of diverse details all at once that was very instructive and liberating. It gave me a way of moving toward talking about the variety of things I felt compelled to talk about but had very little precedence for, other than poet's prose like the essays by Charles Olson, Robert Duncan, and people like that. So Davenport's essays were absolutely vital and hit me at the right time because when that book came out I had already produced a very early draft of *This Compost* and it was such a challenge to me to figure out what I could possibly do with it or where it could go. Davenport's writing made a lot of possibilities appear. So it was serendipitous that the press asked Davenport to review the manuscript, which was something I didn't know at the time. I think I would have been trembling in my boots if I'd known.

Schwartz: In Davenport's book he can do anything from an extremely close reading of Olson's "The Kingfishers," all the way over to picking up a Carolina phone book and finding the names of the hobbit folk. I think it's something in that tradition that happens in *This Compost*. Could you say a little bit about what I take as your central term in the book, which is the spelling [of] "reading" as "wreading"—that kind of conflation or insistence on the reading/writing continuum that is confirmed by such a spelling?

Rasula: It was a concept that I had been dallying with for a number of years in the seventies, largely in the wake of reading Roland Barthes. I really liked his essays in general. I edited the poetry magazine *Wch Way* from 1975–1984, and in one of the issues we had sort of a round table discussion of *The Pleasure of the Text*. I think it was in that milieu that I started thinking about how important it is to recognize that we are not passive consumers of material that is completely finished and closed off in a book that we open and devour like a box of cereal. I wanted to figure out ways of talking about how the reader can be motivated to strategically reassemble a world of the text that is not necessarily the world that the author intended. And I don't mean to suggest something along the lines of a misreading, or a deliberate violation or travesty of the original, but rather that any original work has more going on than the author could have possibly recognized. That is what I was interested in preserving. That term is also related to a kind of personal malady that many friends have noticed and remarked over the years, which is that I take particular delight in registering my misreading of things, especially in public spaces, where you glance at something and think "wait a minute" before you realize "no, it doesn't say that." But what you mistook it for, or what I mistake it for, is often much more interesting than what it says. There is a little bit of a personal signature in that kind of reading. So to do that I just took the w from our verb "writing" and appended it to the beginning of "reading" to suggest that—if "write" is five letters—at least one-fifth of the labor of writing is invested in the written product of the reader, not the writer.

Schwartz: I really love that term as a way of thinking about the relationship or interdependency of the two. And it is that kind of notion of the inter-dependent, which I think is important in certain kinds of ecological dis-cussions leading to the prime metaphor of this book, which is compost. I know there is the Walt Whitman line. Maybe you could comment on *This Compost* and its sourcing, or the kind of things you are doing with the metaphor of quotation or text as compost, which is so central to the book.

Rasula: That aspect of the book, as I said in the preface, has a dual identity, On the one hand it's a monograph or a long essay, and on the other hand it functions as an anthology. "An anthology of mutilations" might be one way of putting it because I think there is only one poem in the book that is quoted in its entirety. In the seventeenth and eighteenth centuries people used to put anthologies together by taking whatever they wanted out of poems, and you can find curious anthologies in which there is no respect for the original text. Whatever segment they wanted to anthologize they would just carve out and enshrine it in its own way. Now that isn't the model I was following, but it is a way of saying that it's not completely un-precedented to assemble extracts in this way. And the reason I think it functions partly like an anthology is that the bulk of quoted material is far greater than what is normally the case for a critical book or anything along those lines. Once I made the decision to preserve that much of the origi-nal material, I had to think about why I was doing it and what the conse-quences of doing that might be. And that arose, naturally enough, out of the book itself. It really came about by my noticing overlapping bits of dic-tion and thematic concerns in various poets, and I was thinking that if you didn't respect the integrity of a given poem, but imagined that over time it decayed the way leaves decay in the forest, you're going to get that palimp-sest effect, like seeing one thing while also seeing something else appearing underneath it. They form a kind of composite identity. So I was working with the sense that in composting you get composite identities being formed, and in that process you see links and connections between things that you wouldn't otherwise see, like if you're thinking in terms of the in-tegrity of a poem by itself. So in the process that meant having to get past the notion that a given poet is the controlling identity or mastermind be-hind a body of work. The specific poets who form the core of this book—who are generally associated with the Black Mountain College in North Carolina—spoke in terms of composition by field. And one of the implications, for me, was that they were collaborating in the same poetic enterprise, the same poetic universe. That sense of implicit collaboration meant that it might be possible to read a poem by Robert Creeley as if it were authored by Charles Olson, or a poem by Olson as if written by Robert Duncan, and see what it did to the mindset of reading that poem. So in a sense, it sounds like my way of approaching these poet's works is by deliberate misattributions of authorship.

Schwartz (laughs): There is so much I want to respond to there. Of course, as a reader one does note with great pleasure the way in which Black Mountain Poetics is so central here. To me, Charles Olson seems to be central to this book. Robert Duncan is there in a very important way. As well as Jonathan Williams and Louis Zukofsky, who are not Black Mountain but are also important figures. I also see a lot of Ann Waldman's work and a lot of thinking about her work in your book. I wondered if I could read you a passage of your own writing from toward the end of your book and ask you to comment on compost as a way of getting at poets you are interested in, or what kind of composting is happening in those poets. You write:

> The poets in *This Compost* have affirmed the poem as a space possessed of a nature, which absorbs "symbol detritus" like the photosynthesis of light in chlorophyll. They confirm the poem as a passage, akin to the elaborate cave passages leading to Paleolithic image sanctuaries, leaving the temporarily of the wreader's experience of it as the orientation, as the Orient of one's own good nature stands revealed. Such poetry is esoteric in this time when nature is no longer analogous to inner ecology, in this space where the topos of the tropics is not inclined to trope or apprehend anything other than opportunistically. (197)

There is also a sentence I thought quite powerful earlier: "Imagination is the organ of inner ecology" (159). Can you comment on the moves you're making there?

Rasula (laughs): The passage you read is so packed with the sense of everything that's going on in the book that I'm stupefied at the prospect of responding to it. It does remind me of how much condensation there is in the book as a whole. It's a two-hundred-page book, but if I had written it in the standard language of scholarly exposition it would probably be about eight hundred pages.

Schwartz: That's the influence of Creeley there. You get it all so tersely condensed that you get it all in there. You already cited one of the great things about this book—that, to me, it's more of a philosophical essay than a work of scholarship, as you're taking the poems you're working with and seeing what those poems make it possible to say, or what they make possible to think. And some of the philosophical passages, like the one I quoted, have a lot densely packed in there. So maybe just pick one possible route through the forest.

Rasula: I like your term "philosophical" in that it's a reminder of how the stakes in the type of poetry that I was interested in are literally world forming. I've long had a sense that the kind of poetry I look at in *This Compost* is written by people for whom writing poetry is a way of creating an entire world. And I don't mean "creating a world" in the novelistic or fictional sense, like a place in which you immerse yourself as a refuge from reality. It's rather that there is literally an incalculable effort involved in the active imagination, which is concerned with actually addressing the world, figuring out how it works, what goes on and what the consequences of our actions are. I tend to be inspired by people who just roll up their sleeves and set to work on the incalculable. And that means that there is always going to be a lot of rough edges in the work of people with that propensity—a lot of the sense that they are a little bit rude or unmannered. Certain of these are characteristics that people originally identified with Whitman, that is, as someone who probably shouldn't be let in the front door but be coming in the back door to deliver whatever it was presumed he was delivering.

Schwartz (laughs): Doesn't Ed Dorn have that line: "Too far-gone on thought to ever look good," or something along those lines?

Rasula: It was also important to me, and this is going back to your point about philosophy, that in American culture, it's been far too easy to create a dividing line between poetic complexity and poetic insolence. The role of poetic insolence was played very effectively by the Beats, but I think that's too easy a distinction. Poets of the Black Mountain orientation, like many of the people that I was interested in, and poets like Zukofsky, who were not involved with Black Mountain at all, were really embarked on a very different enterprise. That is, their lack of decorum or propriety was not related to any kind of truculence or adolescent confrontational spirit; rather, the assembled vehicles of cultural investigation of the world just seemed to be rickety, old fashioned, unusable, or inept from their point of view. So as poets they were not particularly interested in performing in the venue of inherited verse traditions. They were interested in investigations in a philosophical or, you could almost say, Wittgensteinian sense, in that they wanted to find out what difference it made to say certain things about the world and then have to live up to the propositions that came about as a result of that.

Schwartz: That's intriguing. You know I am not impartial as Robert Duncan and Robert Kelly were really important teachers to me, and they figure very importantly in this book as Black Mountain or as poets who were influenced by that. So when you privilege Black Mountain over the Beat, or simply suggest that there is something in terms of adolescent impudence burns out pretty quickly, unlike the sustained meditation that you find in the possibility of another world, or the possibility in the poets you write about. I think it's really the argument that needs to be made in American poetry, rather than a certain kind of nostalgia for something good that might have happened in the fifties, but long since came to an end. Am I right to think that Olson is the central figure here?

Rasula: Yes, there's no doubt about that, and for two reasons really. One is because of his poetic stance and his investigations as a poet, but also because he wrote such a voluminous amount of prose, or gave talks and lectures that were transcribed and gave me a lot of material to think about and engage with. For instance, one of the central pieces that I draw on is a series of lectures at Black Mountain College in 1952 or '53 called "The Chiasmus" about the Paleolithic imagination. In these lectures he's trying to imagine what was going on thirty to forty thousand years ago in these caves in the southwest of France and northern Spain, which are filled with this extraordinary extravaganza of visual art that we have otherwise no way of knowing anything about, as there are no documentary records going even remotely back that far. And he takes it on. He takes it on as something that is imperative for a person living in the wake of World War II to think about, because it's thinking about roots. Where do people come from? What's on their minds? What are our deepest legacies as hominids? It was that kind of provocation that made Olson a central character in the book.

Schwartz: That is also interesting to follow out on in terms of origin, which you spoke of, but of course *Origin* is also the name of Cid Corman's magazine, which was such a crucial one of that period. You have a chapter on origin, meaning not Cid Corman's journal but the idea of origin and the various attractions and pitfalls of origin. You say:

> The babble of origin; the talkative manner in which "origin" is itself a discursive construct to begin with rather than a metaphysical drive, the contingency of origin as acts of perception; means that . . .

And then you quote from Foucault and his idea that

> surface is marked by that "collateral contemporaneity" in which William James found the whole universe knocking at the door to be let in.

Again—packed passages, but I wondered if you could say a little bit about your sense of the way in which origin is always present.

Rasula: In that particular chapter (or rather than calling them chapters it might be more accurate to call them episodes because most of them are very short, none longer than ten pages), origin is, if you think of an onion, something that if you take off one layer you do not get to some primordial layer, you just get to another layer that used to be the surface. And it's part of the natural process I think related to composting. That is, when you go deep down in the earth, you're not getting to the origin of things, you're just getting to things that used to be the surface, used to be the most recent, and that's a figure that interests me in cultural terms because there's so much emphasis, culturally speaking, put on precedent, and so much investment in the original of something. It's the kind of thing you encounter all the time when you read, for instance, music criticism, especially rock criticism, in which people bring tremendous powers of investigations to bear on who laid down the first of a certain kind of blues lick, and how other people transformed it. I think it's a little misguided because it ultimately doesn't really make much difference where it comes from. The leveraging of difference is applied to what people are doing in any circumstance with the resources of what they have available to them. So origin is constantly present as the thought, not of what happened before or where something has come from, but present as a sort of *inaugural* possibility, which is the way I approached it in the book. Whatever act we undertake at any given moment is the origin of the next thing that follows from it.

Schwartz: As if we were looking forward to our origin instead of looking backwards.

Rasula: Yeah, that's a good way to put it.

Schwartz: That's also really intriguing in terms of the ecological metaphor of depth being what was once surface. To do the archeology or to do the digging but not hierarchically arrange depth and surface. We're up against time—I wish we had more of this, Jed, to keep our conversation going. I know you've published a book since *This Compost* that I haven't read yet. What was that one?

Rasula: That is a book that's almost entirely about contemporary poetry really of the last twenty years or so. The title is *Syncopations* and the subtitle is "The Stress of Innovation in Contemporary American Poetry." The University of Alabama Press publishes that. And I'm just now finishing a book—I actually just finished it earlier today—called "Poetry's Voice-Over" [published as *Modernism and Poetic Inspiration*], which derives in part from an essay I published about ten years ago.

Schwartz: On the muse, right? That's the piece that involves the problematic of the muse, right?

Rasula: Yes, exactly. It's a more extended investigation into those provocations that would appear to be the cause of poetry, but are often the goad, the agonizing itch, or stimulus to something that is helplessly transmitted. I'm interested really in the helplessness, or the figure of helplessness, in the composition of poetry, which has been a consistent attribution of poetic inspiration from the beginning. So how do we help ourselves into helplessness?

From *Ripley's Believe It or Not* to *Finnegans Wake*

Interview with Tony Tost on Imagining Language

TONY TOST IS a screenwriter and television producer in Los Angeles. He is the creator of *Damnation*, a Netflix series of the labor wars of the 1930s. He was also a writer-producer for *Longmire* and *The Terror: Infamy*. He is the author of the poetry collections *Invisible Bride* (2004) and *Complex Sleep* (2007).

Tost: *Imagining Language* strikes me as a fairly unique approach to the anthology project, or at least compared to how it's often done in poetry (where anthologies as often as not are occasions for solidifying reputations and careers, leaving any and all underlying assumptions about notions like poetry, reputation, and career unaddressed).

What were the circumstances that led to Steve McCaffery and yourself collaborating on this project? Or, to be a little more specific, what drew the two of you together as collaborators and/or what were the underlying motivations for doing this kind of project?

Rasula: First, I'd want to correct the widespread perception that *Imagining Language* is a "poetry anthology." I suppose that may be a helpless association, given my own protracted ruminations on poetry anthologies in *The American Poetry Wax Museum*. But despite the publication dates (*Wax* in 1996, *Imagining Language* in '98), the anthology had a much earlier inception. *Imagining Language* started off as a projects file folder for television. From 1982–85 I worked for *Ripley's Believe It or Not*, the ABC TV show hosted by Jack Palance. My job was to come up with story ideas, pitch them to the producers (mostly Mel Stuart—director of the original *Willie Wonka and the Chocolate Factory*—but also Jack Haley, producer of *That's Entertainment*, son of the Tin Man in *The Wizard of Oz* . . . and at the time I was working with him he was recently separated from Liza Minnelli, so theirs was a mismatch made in Oz heaven), and shepherd the stories through the production process. It was an interesting job, with extraordinary resources. The research support I had at Ripley's exceeded anything I've encountered in academia. My office mate there was an itinerant scholar named William Moritz, who died a few years ago but who was executor of the estate of filmmaker Oskar Fischinger, and also one of the premier authorities on the phenomenon of "visual music." It was Bill who introduced me to the work of Fischinger and the Whitney brothers, pioneers of this phenomenon I've recently been writing about in my forthcoming book *Oblique Modernism* [*History of a Shiver*]. Bill and I shared the same approach to the job, as we found that we could get most of our week's work done on Monday, and really only needed to be on call after that to respond to emergency (in Hollywood it's always emergency) script meetings, rush cuts, translation needs (Bill was enviably multilingual), and prepping documents for the network censors (one of whom, astonishingly, was Freud's great granddaughter). We therefore had lots of time, not to mention resources, to work on our own projects. Nearly all the articles and reviews I published during those years were written at my Ripley's desk, including a little diatribe called "The American Poetry Wax Museum" published by Lee Hickman in *Temblor* (and by Ben Friedlander and Andrew Schelling in *Jimmy and Lucy's*) a decade before it became a book.

Now, all this may strike you as anecdotally evasive. But, truthfully, *Imagining Language* wouldn't have happened without *Ripley's Believe It or Not*. "Imagining Language" was the name I used for one of my project file folders (to give you a sense of scale, at any given time I had about fifty such file folders going). In the context of commercial television, the topic was the longest of long shots. I tried in vain to interest the producers in a segment on *Finnegans Wake*, for instance. But they did bite on the phenomenon of Boontling, an argot local to Booneville in northern California (see *Imagining Language*, 50). They also did a segment on Benjamin Franklin's spelling reform proposals. What really went over well, though, was sound poetry. In fact, Mel Stuart was so captivated by it that he went out to shoot the segments himself (normally, he dealt only with scenarios involving Jack Palace; all other footage was either stock or else produced as needed by hired "stringers"). These included George Quasha and Charles Stein, who didn't perform that much in public but had developed a striking buccal symbiosis. After that was broadcast, Mel went to Toronto to film the Four Horsemen, the seasoned sound poetry quartet that included bpNichol and Steve McCaffery. It was filmed on the roof of the loft Steve was living in at that point on the east side of the city next to the Don Mills Parkway. The one other byproduct of my "Imagining Language" file at *Ripley's* came later, when Marie Osmond became cohost with Jack Palance. In the format of the show, little topic clusters (like "weird language") were introduced by one of the hosts. In this case, the frame was Cabaret Voltaire. Marie was required to read Hugo Ball's sound poem "Karawane" and a few script lines. Much to everybody's astonishment, when they started filming she abruptly looked away from the cue cards directly into the camera and recited, by memory, "Karawane." It blew everybody away, and I think they only needed that one take. A year or so after it was broadcast, Greil Marcus approached me, wanting to use Marie Osmond's rendition of Hugo Ball for a CD produced in England as sonic companion to his book *Lipstick Traces*; so I was delighted to be able to arrange that.

It was after *Ripley's* expired in 1985 that I applied to graduate school, ending up in the History of Consciousness Program at UC Santa Cruz. The "Imagining Language" dossier from *Ripley's* continued to haunt me— it was gradually swelling, like an accordion file, with new sightings—and I remember talking to my supervisor, Hayden White, about the feasibility of an anthology as a dissertation. Not possible, so that was that. Back into hibernation. By the same principle, I assumed, tenure and promotion would be insecurely grounded on an anthology, which is the main reason *Wax* preceded *Imagining Language*. But when I had moved to Canada in 1990 to teach at Queen's University I renewed contact with Steve McCaffery. We went back a ways: he'd stayed with us in Los Angeles in February 1977, and I remember how excited both of us were to find the new translation of Derrida's *Of Grammatology* in a bookstore out near UCLA. On that trip he also scored a bunch of first editions of Gertrude Stein—my first intimation of his spectacular antiquarian library, which came in handy years later for the anthology. So, when Steve was hired as a sessional teacher at Queen's, his proximity made me realize, with the force of that proverbial lightbulb in the head, that the only way I was ever going to move forward with *Imagining Language* was with a collaborator, and who better than him? The first thing we did was apply for a grant, which we didn't get. But the feedback was useful, so we succeeded the next year (1994), at which point we had to start work in earnest. By the time we got that grant we had no clear organization in mind, just a huge stack of photocopies, maybe two thousand pages. Since *Finnegans Wake* had been at the center of the anthology concept since *Ripley's*, the timeliness of the grant enabled Steve and I to present papers at the International James Joyce Symposium in Seville that summer, launching ourselves into some of the writing that ended up in the introduction and section prefaces to the anthology. I was also able to do some extensive research in London at the British Library, turning up things like the Chladni diagrams, and that curious Welshman Rowland Jones.

To speak to the "underlying motivations" of the project: I think what we shared was a long foreground of immersion in continental theory. That was evident from Steve's publications in the journal *Open Letter* (some of which were reprinted in his book *North of Intention*), which I discovered in 1974 at the time I was first reading Barthes, Foucault, Lacan, and Derrida. In retrospect, I imagine anyone reading *Imagining Language* now might feel put off by the heavy diesel odor of theoretical jargon in our prefaces. Steve was more of a tar baby in that respect than I was, as you can see by comparing his *Prior to Meaning* with my *Syncopations* (more or less parallel projects reflecting, to some extent, our work on the anthology); but that's an indelible material trace, I think, that communicates in the same olfactory/tactile way that the aromatic effusion of patchouli oil and hashish reanimates the sixties. It's that aspect, curiously, which makes such fossilized jargon somehow commensurate with Walter Benjamin's remark in the *Arcades Project* (1999) that the eternal "is far more the ruffle on a dress than some idea" (N3,2).

Tost: One of the aspects of *Imagining Language* that I was most immediately entranced by was the selection of work drawn from Eugene Jolas's *transition*. It's astonishing to see just to what extent things like *Finnegans Wake* and Gertrude Stein's works appeared in a journal surrounded by other, now obscure, writers exploring similar territory. Can you talk a little about what drew you to the work of writers like Jolas, Abraham Lincoln Gillespie, Bob Brown, and other folks connected with *transition*? Were there any other specific groups or journals considered for the kind of spotlight focus *transition* enjoys in *Imagining Language*?

Rasula: The prominence of *transition* was strictly related to the central place accorded *Finnegans Wake* in the anthology. Right from the beginning at *Ripley's*, the *Wake* was like Wallace Stevens's jar in Tennessee, gathering all else around it. When I started thinking of *Imagining Language* as an anthology—around 1985—I characterized it in conversation as a project in which *Finnegans Wake* would be normative and central rather than eccentric and peripheral. Since Joyce's book, as "Work in Progress," played a similar role in *transition*, it seemed natural enough to highlight that legacy in *Imagining Language* by placing our extract in a section drawn exclusively from the pages of Jolas's journal. Another factor contributing to this framing device (for me, at least) was a sense of dismay *In Transition: A Paris Anthology*, edited by Noel Riley Fitch [and] published by Doubleday in 1990. The design was handsome, and the contents couldn't help but be astonishing, but Fitch confined her selections to the first couple years of the journal (1927–1930), with an emphasis on works by famous authors (like Gide, Hemingway, Kafka, Rilke). This presentation completely obscured the often-zany thematic strategies deployed by Jolas and Elliott Paul, particularly from 1930–1938 when the bulk of *transition*'s run appeared. A more enduring sense of the "revolution of the word" had long been available by way of Jerry Rothenberg's anthology of that name from 1974. The contents of that anthology, and the innovative format of *America: A Prophecy*, coedited by Rothenberg with George Quasha (1973), had always provided me with the compass points of how an anthology could be both innovative and serviceable at the same time.

Because the role played by *transition* in *Imagining Language* was predicated on *Finnegans Wake*, we never considered other magazines as framing devices or germinal contexts. For the "Sound Effects" section, however, we had a keen sense of a specific legacy, the traces of which could be found in vanguard periodicals. It was while working on *Imagining Language* that I embarked on what has now become a decade long crawl through the whole repertoire of modernist avant-garde journals, providing indispensable perspective for *Oblique Modernism* and lots of material ripe for translation and/or reprint for the anthology projects I'm still working on [eventuating in the anthology *Burning City*, 2012]. These journals constituted a sort of international lingua franca. They tended to be polylingual; they took their marching orders, as it were, from Apollinaire; they pioneered sound poems and concrete poems as practical means of surmounting language barriers; and by their commitment to visual arts they substantiated this translinguistic zone. I've gone page by page through the contents of over a hundred of them at this point—too many to list except by a baker's dozen: *Bleu* ed. Gino Cantarelli (1920–21), *Contimpuranul* ed. I. Vinea and Marcel Janco (1922–26), *Devĕtsil* ed. Jaroslav Seifert and Karel Teige (1922), *Grecia* ed. Isaac del Vando-Villar (1919–20), *L'Italia Futurista* ed. Bruno Corra, Arnaldo Ginna, Emilio Settimelli (1916–18), *Ma* ed. Lajos Kassák (1917–1925), *Mecano* ed. I. K. Bonset [Theo van Doesburg] (1922–23), *Merz* ed. Kurt Schwitters (1923–1932), *Noi* ed. Enrico Prampolini (1917–20, 1923–25), *Nord-Sud* ed. Pierre Reverdy (1917–18), *Orpheu* ed. Mário de Sá-Carneiro and Fernando Pessoa (1915), *Het Overzicht* ed. Berckelaers [Michel Seuphor and Josef Peeters] (1921–25), *Portugal Futurista* ed. José de Almada-Negreiros (1915), *SIC* ed. Pierre Albert-Birot (1916–19), and *391* ed. Francis Picabia (1917–24).

In the milieu of these and other journals and books, an expansive typographic field was cultivated from which we compiled the potential for yet another section in *Imagining Language*. Amédée Ozenfant used terms like "psychotypie" and "typométrique" to speak of this tendency, and Marius de Zayas defined the psychotype as "an art which consists in making the typographical characters participate in the expression of thoughts and in the painting of the states of soul, no more as conventional symbols but as signs having significance in themselves." A critic writing in *Les Soirées de Paris* in 1914 thought it imperative that humans begin to conceive the world "synthetico-ideographically instead of analytico-discursively" (Naumann 2009). The graphic and typographic liberation of the word in the wake of Mallarmé and Marinetti established a dimension in which poems might rival—or, less aggressively, participate in the milieu of—the visual arts. Because we ended up with so much in the way of typographic compositions, Steve and I realized it would be too intrusive to the structure of the whole if we were to attempt any kind of documentary overview—which had never been our agenda, anyway, with respect to the topic areas of the anthology— so we settled on the very thin profile in "Words in Freedom" and left it at that.

Tost: *Imagining Language* is such a unique project, and it occupies this odd place in my imagination, as a foundation of so many possible bodies of knowledge. Part of the thrill is simply accessing these figures, such as Edna Sarah Beardsley and Benjamin Paul Blood, who seem to point to previously unsanctioned systems for using language. When contacting various people to get approval for doing this supplement, or to inquire about possible leads, without fail, each person responded enthusiastically upon mention of *Imagining Language*. What's your sense to the reaction the book has received? As an editor, did you have specific intentions as to how the anthology could be utilized?

Rasula: Although *Imagining Language* received grant support from the Social Science and Humanities Council of Canada and was enthusiastically embraced by MIT Press, I honestly can't say what we expected in the way of reader response. It was a whacky project, really; an artichoke of eclecticism held together mainly by sheer profusion. It was instructive, to me, when a reviewer characterized it as a carnival. I hadn't actually thought of it that way, but it fits. Of course, a carnival only works if there's structural integrity to the different attractions, and at that particular editorial level I knew we'd done our job. The variety of the material meant that the nature of editorial labor was continually changing. For the extract from Judge Schreber's memoirs, for example, I carefully prepared an abridgement of the whole text, which was an incredible experience. Steve spent a while with the book by Alfred Kallir, contemplating similar strategies of holistic reduction and ended up choosing a single letter (B) as a suitable extract. Because the nature of these editorial tasks varied according to the source material, it seemed to refract possibilities off each text in a prismatic way;

and that registered most beguilingly in the assembly process. The five parts with their various subsections were really generated by the material; but the closer we got to finalizing it the more hectic it became. It was as if texts were revenants seeking proper burial, or petitioners out of Kafka attempting in vain to have their case files reviewed. If you think of the "Sound Effects" section, for instance, and then look at the table of contents, the anthology buzzes with alternate possibilities. I think what made it all come together in the end was the fifth section, "Matter and Atom," anchored by the "Clinamen" conclusion. And here's one of the little enigmatic things about collaboration: we didn't hit upon clinamen as a solution until after we both spoke at the large symposium for Robin Blaser out in Vancouver in 1995 where, serendipitously, the clinamen concept was a major feature of our talks. We'd been on parallel tracks the whole time without even knowing it, mulling over "clinamen" without ever thinking of it in relation to the anthology. We were lucky to have that conference, since it revealed a long-awaited editorial solution—applying which, the whole structure of *Imagining Language* seemed to quiver into place.

This has been a roundabout way of answering your question. But it affords the best purchase I can offer on prospective uses of the anthology. It's prismatic by organization, and the sheer number of items overall is just enough so that the whole thing creates the apparition of a steady flow of atoms drizzling through the void in Lucretius's sense, in which the clinamen as serendipitous swerve inaugurating deviant destinies comes into play. You could call it an autopoetic structure, an immense cross-referencing playpen, a fractal arbitration of glee.

Tost: One last question. If you don't mind, could you give us a sense of what your forthcoming book, *Oblique Modernism*, is about? Do you see it as a continuation of previous projects?

Rasula: Like *Imagining Language*, *This Compost*, and *Syncopations* (*The American Poetry Wax Museum* being the exception, written 1992–94), *Oblique Modernism* is another long-time-coming book.[1] Its inception goes back to my application to the History of Consciousness Program at Santa Cruz in 1986. I ended up writing a 550-page thesis on "The Poetics of Embodiment" instead. Still, *Oblique Modernism* is not what I envisioned twenty years ago, and it's really the fruit of long archival prowling. But there is a link to its inklings in the past—particularly to materials in *Imagining Language* drawn from the modernist avant-garde—that it shares with my other projects in general: a conviction that prevailing attitudes (on topics like modernism, contemporary poetry, linguistic diversity) are little more than platitudes. I've always been astonished by how much

in the way of general knowledge and opinion is absorbed second hand—
and, concomitantly, how we're institutionally enjoined to make a little go a
long way. It's just a hair's breadth away from frivolous to generalize about
modernism on the basis of Pound, Eliot, Woolf, Joyce, and—in the idiom
of dissertation-cum-first book—another figure of your choice. In that respect, at least in English departments, "modernism" has largely been a way
of talking about a slender portfolio, with little support for innovative research or even adequate background preparation. How many Eliot scholars
have ever really read Laforgue? I doubt that Poundians even know about
Henri-Martin Barzun, whose multivoice epic aspirations Pound surmised,
in 1913, might be the poetry of the future. Thankfully, the situation has improved in the past decade with the Modernist Studies Association and the
journal *Modernism/Modernity*. And a salutary interdisciplinary banner has
been held aloft for decades now by Marjorie Perloff.

The basic premise of obliquity in *Oblique Modernism* can be put in
the form of an anecdote. Tristan Tzara tells of how he once met a man
who claimed to have spent time in Paris where he knew a famous Dadaist, none other than Tristan Tzara. Bemused, Tzara asks the man what he
looked like. Tall and blonde he's told (Tzara himself was short and dark). I
take this as a paradigm of misrecognition upon which so many presump-
tions about modernism are predicated. The familiarity of modernism is
now its stigma. The artistic push that gave rise to the principle of defamiliarization (Shklovsky) and the alienation-effect (Brecht) needs now to be
defamiliarized in turn. Rather than full frontal encounters (i.e., normative textual and iconographic exegesis), I rely on a more oblique reckoning,
apprehending modernism from peripheral vision as it were, overhear-
ing rather than listening, following scents to hidden lairs rather than bar-
reling down the interpretive thoroughfare. This has meant that I've spent
a lot of time become acquainted with figures like Carola Giedion-Welcker
(who was prescient enough to recognize that what Joyce was doing with
language matter in *Finnegans Wake* had a plausible corollary in what Hans
Arp was doing with plastic matter in his sculptures), Louis Lozowick (the
only American artist, as far as I know, who visited the USSR at the height
of Constructivism; and who, knowing Russian, produced the most lucid
accounts of that scene in the early twenties), Thomas Wilfred (a Danish
folk singer who devoted his life to pioneering "lumia," misleadingly called
"visual music"—several of his works were on view at the Visual Music exhibit at the Hirshhorn last summer, one of them with a running cycle of
more than a year!)—and Frederick Kiesler (known, if at all, as "the greatest
unbuilt architect of the twentieth century" in Philip Johnson's estimation).
Other important figures in *Oblique Modernism* are slightly better known,

like Maurice Maeterlinck and Aby Warburg (the art historian who spent a lot of time in an insane asylum, until he petitioned for release by preparing a lecture on the Hopi snake ceremonies he'd witnessed thirty years earlier). I also look at Wagnerism—the "ism" that preceded, and prefigured, the more familiar vanguard *isms* of the early twentieth century—and "jazzbandism," so named by that curious Spanish writer Ramón Gómez de la Serna in his fascinating and odd book *Ismos* published in 1931. As you can infer from these references, the "modernism" that emerges under the gaze of this obliquity is not restricted to literature. To dig into any of the periodicals of the time, like those I listed earlier, is to encounter a consistent and ready reciprocity between all the arts. You find a poem in Czech, say, next to a concrete poem by Schwitters, followed by some architectural photos and section plans, a celebration of Charlie Chaplin, and a portfolio of Archipenko, and then maybe a sample page of music by Bartok. After a while, Pound's immersion in music seems almost obligatory, not a quirk of his character.

So *Oblique Modernism* will be a book much in the spirit of *Imagining Language*, I think, in that it is nourished by a lot of fugitive figures carefully intermingled with a familiar spectrum (from Mallarmé to Abstract Expressionism), in a structure designed to animate the encounters.

Glut Reactions

An Exchange with Mike Chasar on
the Demographics of American Poetry

MIKE CHASAR IS the author of *Poetry Unbound: Poems and New Media from the Magic Lantern to Instagram* and *Everyday Reading: Poetry and Popular Culture in Modern America* and, with Heidi R. Bean, is the coeditor of *Poetry after Cultural Studies* (2011). He has received grants from the National Endowment for the Humanities and the Kluge Center at the Library of Congress and is an associate professor of English at Willamette University.

Rasula: Yesterday Ron Silliman was here, visiting my classes and giving a reading, and he mentioned the figure of twenty thousand poets actively publishing in the US. This figure presumably excludes those coasting on vanity presses, etc. (though who's to tell, these days?). Ron also mentioned he gets a thousand books a year sent to him, gratis, just for the potential notice in his blog I assume. So how do we deal with this glut? Is it "glut," in fact? And how do such figures stack up against two profiles: 1. Official Verse Culture, and 2. the cornucopia of the demotic, as you so assiduously track it?

Chasar: Ron isn't the only one using more than fingers and toes to count up poets and poems recently. In "The New Math of Poetry," David Alpaugh estimates that every year more than one hundred thousand poems are published in online and print journals. Seth Abramson has calculated that M.F.A. programs graduated twenty thousand poets in the last decade alone. And in his *Harriet* blog posting "It's Too Much," Stephen Burt writes, "I think I can keep up with [poetry] books, more or less, which are countable, finite sets of things . . . but if the proliferating, ramifying, exciting discourse about poetry now takes place in a million web journals, at all hours of the day and night, I'm not sure I can keep up with them." And "if I can't keep up," continues Burt, citing his stable job, leisure time, and professional obligations, "who can?"

I agree with the upward trend in people's accounting, though I think that, large as their figures seem, they're actually quite conservative and far more people are writing, reading, or hearing poetry than we'd expect. (I don't have exact figures for how many people saw the moving recitation of Whitman's "I Heard the Learn'd Astronomer" on Season 3, Episode 6 of AMC's *Breaking Bad*, for example, but it's a lot.) But this is hardly a new phenomenon; to some people seventy-five or a hundred years ago—when poetry was appearing regularly in magazines and newspapers and was being broadcast on national radio shows devoted exclusively to poetry and appearing on business cards, postcards, pin-up girly posters, billboards, and even souvenir pillows—it felt like there was a similar sort of poetry glut as there is now. You yourself have noted that, in 1911, Davenport, Iowa, lawyer and poet Arthur Davison Ficke wrote, "Just now there appear to be more writers of verse than there have been at any time in the history of literature." Fifteen years later, Iowa novelist Ruth Suckow wrote in the *American Mercury* that her state's literary culture "is snatched at by everybody— farmer boys, dentists, telegraph editors in small towns, students, undertakers, insurance agents and nobodies." The first edition of *Granger's Index to Poetry* appeared in 1904 and contained thirty thousand listings of poems appearing just in books and anthologies; the second (1918) edition of *Granger's* grew to fifty thousand listings, and its third (1940) to seventy-five thousand. Its 1940 subtitle alone (*A Practical Reference Book for Librarians, Teachers, Booksellers, Elocutionists, Radio Artists, Etc.*) suggests a much more active—and demotic—poetry-reading culture than we typically associate with the age of High Modernism. But as much as these examples are suggestive, perhaps my favorite is the one Heidi Bean and I use in our introduction to *Poetry after Cultural Studies*—and that's the case of the Auxiliary Poetry File constructed by librarians at the Public Library of Cincinnati and Hamilton County in Ohio. In the early 1900s, right after *Granger's* appeared, the librarians realized that *Granger's* was only indexing poems printed in books, not in local and daily newspapers and magazines, so they started their own supplemental index, making three-by-five-inch index card entries for the poems they selected and then filing them by author, title, and first line. Whenever possible—which was about 40 percent of the time—they actually cut out poems from their source publications and pasted the verse to the back of the appropriate card. By midcentury, their index alone had sixty thousand cards in it!

So I agree there's an astonishing amount of poetry in circulation, and it's partly astonishing because the high numbers don't square with the various "death of poetry" arguments that get rehearsed every other decade or so. That said, I think there's been a poetry glut for a long time and that at certain times—probably during periods when people are gaining more access to new media or communication technologies, just as they were when Ficke and Suckow were writing, and just as they are now—it comes into view more strikingly than at others. My gut reaction (you could maybe call it my glut reaction) is to say that questions like "Is it a glut?" or "Is it a problem?" aren't nearly as interesting as questions like "Who is it a problem for?" and "Why do those people think it's a problem?" For critics like Burt, it's a problem because it challenges what it means to be an "expert" in American poetry. Whenever someone's status as expert is predicated on knowing everything—all the good poems (i.e., a canon), what everyone is saying, etc.—a glut is going to be a problem because, as Burt puts it, "I just can't keep trying and failing to get myself to read everything," and thus the governing paradigm for what it means to be a poetry expert is put into crisis; how can you be an arbiter of taste if you can't read everything to pass judgment on it? Insofar as the centrality of Official Verse Culture is affected by a period of glut—where there is no longer an official center—then Official Verse Culture has a stake in the matter. But so does the avant-garde (a profile you didn't mention in your question above), since terms of distinction and debate like "quietist" and "avant" are incapable of describing the nature of the glut, which appears to have no inside for the outsider to react to, and no outside to shock the inside; there are more types of poetry than any binary (raw or cooked, high or low, etc.) can fully account for. Finally, a glut is problematic for anyone who benefits from an economy of scarcity—or a perceived economy of scarcity—because that person's status, prestige, or perceived self-importance, is suddenly devalued by the glut, which goes by the name of "surplus" in other conversations. That's the point at which governments start burning crops and paying farmers to let their land lie fallow.

For me, the glut isn't a glut so much as a fundamental condition of poetry in the long twentieth century, a period when—thanks in part to the emergence and maturation of the culture industries, the development of mass media as well as personal communication technologies, and the expansion of consumer capitalism and the consumer marketplace—more poetry was written, distributed, circulated, and consumed than at any other time in history. Realizing that means reassessing our histories of American poetry, the maps and guidebooks we produce about it, and the way it gets measured and recorded. I'd expect that, for someone like you—who lived through, studied, and participated in the canon expansion of the 1970s and 1980s—some of this would sound familiar. Does it?

Rasula: The canon expansion as you call it was only fitfully demographic in the ways your mind-boggling statistics suggest. On one side there's sheer mass, in which "poetry" means anything with line breaks—and then some. The other side is dominated by various versions of Pound's Sagetrieb, or cultural force, high and abiding. Anything goes versus quality control, you could say. But then here's where it gets sticky. The canon expansion was predicated on the recognition that "quality control" applied only to a small cadre of certain types, white men mainly, Ivy League educated for the most part (even Robert Bly, who otherwise made his reputation as a principled outsider, went to Harvard).

Looking back, it's clear that the famed "anthology wars" of 1960 set in motion various kinds of expansion. At one level, it was relatively conservative, in that the incursions of the Donald Allen crowd mainly added more male contenders: Creeley, Ginsberg, Snyder, Baraka, Dorn, O'Hara, and Ashbery in particular, along with the older Duncan and Olson. It's revealing, however, to look back at anthologies from the sixties even into the seventies that tried to pretend these guys weren't serious options: it tells you a lot about the even longer odds of adding women. In the end, though, the real force of the New American group had to do with the counterculture in general, and the clutch of progressive social movements that made the *counter* politically efficacious. The deployment of poems in the antiwar movement, the women's movement, the black power movement, prisoner's rights, gay rights, education reform, and more was pervasive; and, until the political gains were enfranchised (slowly and unevenly), all this poetry can be described as *for use* rather than *for consideration*—this latter term meant to suggest something like the Oscars, since that's how the consumption of poetry was legislated. A world of poetry, avidly consumed and circulated on the one hand, and a "poetry world" on the other hand, an industry unto itself, with its anthologies, prizes, fellowships, endorsements.

Calling it an industry rather than an institution draws attention to its public profile, but I wonder whether it's gone the way of the rust belt economy in general? Certainly, the institution(s) chugs on, more adaptively expansive, so it's shed the sense of being a protective phalanx of privilege. And yet, I'm sure to lots of younger people it would seem that even C. D. Wright, Nate Mackey, and Rae Armantrout signify "establishment" even if not as self-serving as the old boys' clan (e.g., John Hollander, Mark Strand, Richard Howard). One thing for sure is that the vast domain of "for use" poetry is still a world apart from institutional viewfinders. Wouldn't you agree? But then, what could be gained by having a completely porous, ecumenical *institution* of poetry? I'm curious about the continuing role of institutions in keeping populist poetry at bay, in the dark, under wraps, consigned to obscurity and potential inconsequence. But the moment I put it that way, I think of the obviously *consequential* uses to which poetry is put in all those private and semipublic ways you've documented. Which raises the question, then, in a different light: do the institutions of poetry (to give a collective name to everything from AWP to the Poetry Foundation to the Academy of American Poets—maybe even Small Press Distribution) have any relevance to "poetry" in the expansively heterogeneous and ultimately democratic sense?

Chasar: I agree that, broadly speaking, the culture of popular poetry is still a world apart from most institutional viewfinders, and it's important to remember that many of those viewfinders aren't very old. The Poetry Society of America was founded in 1910. Pound and Harriet Monroe fought over who should win *Poetry*'s first Guarantor's Prize in 1913, when Pound lobbied (successfully) for William Butler Yeats's "The Grey Rock" over Monroe's favorite, "General William Booth Enters into Heaven" by the more populist Vachel Lindsay. The Pulitzer was first awarded for poetry in 1922. The Academy of American Poets formed in 1934, and the University of Iowa Writers' Workshop was founded in 1936. The Poet Laureateship was more or less established in 1937. And what Joseph Harrington has called the "poetry wars"—in which the high/low distinction was a major front—took place in the 1930s.

I think the formation of this modern literary economy emerged partly as a way to replace and deal with the prominence of the popular Fireside Poets and the "crisis" that their deaths and poetic models precipitated in some spheres of US poetry. (For one take on this crisis, see John Timberman Newcomb's *Would Poetry Disappear: American Verse and the Crisis of Modernity*.) And its lasting influence, in which there have been generational changes in emphasis (i.e., Stephen Vincent Benét to John Hollander to Rae Armantrout), but not paradigmatic ones, is one reason why Modernist studies are so relevant to studies of contemporary poetry. The effects of that period's discourse—which pushed popular poetry out of institutional viewfinders even as popular verse persisted "for use" in many other institutions and other spheres of American culture (cf. work by Cary Nelson, Joan Shelley Rubin, and Maria Damon, among others) is difficult to understate. Many books are waiting to be written on these and related topics, such as a critical history of the Laureateship; a history (or exposé, perhaps) of poetry contests and their politics and economics; and a study of poetry and public libraries that would have to be rooted in the 1,689

Carnegie libraries built in the US between 1883 and 1929 just as the long twentieth century's dominant poetic institutions were taking shape. I could go on, but you get the idea.

Assessing the relationship between institutional and popular or "for use" poetries is difficult. The question you pose—do the institutions of poetry have any relevance . . . to "poetry" in the expansively heterogeneous and ultimately democratic sense?—is enormous because poetry is put to so many different uses and because so many interfaces or middle men facilitate relationships between institutions and what we might imagine as "uncredentialed" readers, especially now that the Web gives people access to large online libraries and many more people attend college than fifty or a hundred years ago. Are we talking about the possible relationship, for example, between those institutions and the trained writers of AMC's *Mad Men* who had their lead character, advertising executive Don Draper, reading Frank O'Hara in a couple of episodes? Or about the recent television ads for Levi's, Nike, and Chrysler that were designed by the Portland-based advertising firm Wieden + Kennedy and that incorporate poems by Walt Whitman, Charles Bukowski, Maya Angelou, and Edgar Guest? Or are we talking about socially, culturally, or politically marginalized and disenfranchised people reading and writing poetry much farther from poetry's institutions (what Audre Lorde called "poetry as illumination" and "the skeleton architecture of our lives")? Or high school poetry slams and "Poetry Out Loud" competitions? Or are we just talking about my mother-in-law who at one point clipped out several Edgar Guest poems from the newspaper and saved them because they reminded her of her son?

I'm not trying to avoid your question. The relationship between institutional power structures and the demotic, or between the supply side and consumer side, is fascinating and complicated, and I find Michel de Certeau's description of the nomadic or "poaching" reader in *The Practice of Everyday Life* to be helpful when thinking about it. (Other cultural theorists in this vein include Walter Benjamin, Pierre Bourdieu, Dick Hebdige, John Fiske, Constance Penley, Janice Radway, and Henry Jenkins.) For de Certeau, in order to make their lives "habitable," readers and writers who lack "a 'proper' (a spatial or institutional location)"—which I want to read here as a location in poetry's institutions—use or repurpose institutionally sanctioned texts in unexpected and creative ways. They find them, they use them as raw materials, and they transform them sometimes very deliberately in the process. Consider, for example, a couple of pages from a poetry scrapbook that I refer to in chapter 1 of *Everyday Reading: Poetry and Popular Culture in Modern America*. This album was assembled in the late 1920s or early 1930s by Doris Ashley, an aspiring writer and unmarried sawyer's daughter in her late twenties living in Massachusetts, and on these pages she pieces together six poems cut out of newspapers or retyped by hand—two poems by popular poets Frank Stanton ("A Rain Song") and Helen Welshimer ("And So Are You") and four by "modernist" writers that I'm certain were copied from Louis Untermeyer's third revised edition of *Modern American Poetry: A Critical Anthology* (1925), including H. D.'s "Oread" and Pound's "In a Station of the Metro." This is what supply-side cultural reform theorists would have hoped to see, as Ashley's "taste" is clearly being improved by having access to the institutions of good poetry (here represented by Untermeyer's anthology), right? Well, not exactly. In combining these poems, Ashley is picking up on their repeated tree motif (Millay's "Pear Tree," H. D.'s "firs," Campbell's "maple tree," and Pound's "wet, black bough") and using that motif and its associated springtime connotations to surround an article on H. L. Mencken's late-life marriage to women's activist and writer Sara Haardt—no doubt a marriage that the unmarried and aspiring writer Ashley was thinking about as a model for her own life. Her logic in combining the poems is unassailable even though she's treating *for consideration* poems as *for use* poems and reading in a way that would have probably frustrated Pound. From my perspective, then, it isn't the poetry that's transforming her so much as she's transforming it. That is, Pound (or the institution) isn't turning her into a different type of reader; in a sense, it's more like the other way around—Ashley is turning "In a Station of the Metro" into a popular poem!

So there is a relationship between the institution that produced Untermeyer's anthology, on the one hand, and the expansive, heterogeneous world of *for use* poetry represented by Ashley's scrapbook on the other. But this is only one example, and the nature of that relationship—between the "spatial or institutional location" and what de Certeau calls the reader who is "migrating and devouring [his or her] way through the pastures of the media"—was one of the major impulses for me in writing of *Everyday Reading*. That said, I shudder when I think of the challenges of tracking these types of activities or relationships in today's world of online and social media, even though the base practice of publishing, circulating, cutting, pasting, and repurposing may not be all that different.

Rasula: The role of the critic, as the word in Greek means, is to judge. The critical validation of vernacular uses of art is a belated and much needed corrective to the metropolitan intellectual vandalism that has often passed for criticism, but doesn't it also risk abandoning the critical role altogether? Are all privatized scrapbook memorabilia of poetry consumption equal? (Your example of Doris Ashley suggests that her discovery of Pound and

H. D. somehow lifts her above mundane peers.) Let me offer a grim parallel from the art world. The most famous and best-selling artist in the history of the world is apparently Thomas Kincade, which means there are literally millions of "users" out there whose homes are graced with his creepy Hobbit cottages lit by kitsch tonalism. Obviously, there's a thriving commercial enterprise that drives this consumption, but Kincade started as a vernacular special-niche artist: he certainly didn't deviate from a prospective career in Manhattan galleries. However you spin the tale of volition at the level of consumption, the taste that has made Kincade rich is surely applicable in its own diminutive way to the poetry that washes up in sanctuaries of private use, whether scrapbook or blog or community paper.

While I'm sympathetic to your faith in the Situationist *dérive*, or what you call repurposing—as well as your commitment to "uncredentialed" readers—I have to wonder where that leaves the work of poets committed to another scale that would seem far removed from being recognized, let alone *used*, in the "everyday" valorized by de Certeau. And I have in mind here a body of work written by poets committed to these very values. In other words, where does your account leave *The Iovis Trilogy* by Anne Waldman, or *The Alphabet* by Ron Silliman (each more than a thousand pages), or even the long if not supersized works by Alice Notley, or Lyn Hejinian? These are poetic events, really, not just collections of poems from which the motivated reader might excerpt a bezel of wisdom or a consoling moment.

A poet writing a long poem tends to be hyperaware of the legacy of long poems, a legacy that *cultivates* the practice. It's hard to imagine such a practice sustained by the ad hoc appetite of the everyday, which is responsive instead to a more streamlined criterion of use. This raises a pertinent distinction between the transitive and the intransitive in the arts. The body of poetry amenable to notebook clippings is unambiguously transitive: I clip this poem because it's (a) meaningful to me right now, (b) beautiful or moving, (c) fits into the thematic or emotional design of my personal compilation. But *A Border Comedy* by Hejinian, say, is intransitive. It resists *application*—although one could say that its applicability applies to another scale altogether: slow simmering. This perspective of course is familiar from Adorno, who regarded the flagrant uselessness of artworks as a mote in the eye of global capitalism, which is constitutionally blind to any value that's not "for use." One way to think of poetry and literature, then, as institutions, is in terms of this balance between use and uselessness. An anecdote from a recent *New Yorker* (October 3, 2011) spells out the difference. The founder of Lexicon, a firm specializing in developing product names (one of which was Blackberry), discovered the futility of telling clients

"Hey, what we're creating here is a small poem": "You can see people sort
of get concerned," he observes. "Like, 'This isn't really about art here. This
is about getting things done.'" (As I'm sure you know, Marianne Moore was
approached by Ford in 1957 to come up with a name for the car that ended
up as the Edsel, after Ford's son, passing up the poet's suggestions like
Utopian Turtletop, Mongoose Civique, and Pastelogram—an instance of
going from bad to verse, in a pun Ron Silliman keeps recharging throughout *The Alphabet*.) As this anecdote suggests, the distinction between transitive and intransitive isn't fixed, and that which is anathema to marketplace mentality at one time may become iconic later on—think of the
Beats!

Chasar: Since you brought him up, and since he might be the best parallel we have to the phenomenon if not force of nature that the unstudied
poet Edgar Guest was in the first half of the century (among other things,
Guest wrote a nationally syndicated poem every day for thirty years for the
Detroit *Free Press* newspaper, was known as the "people's poet," and was
probably the most widely published poet of the century), Kinkade might
serve as a good point of illumination. If the hermeneutic I apply to Ashley's
album doesn't reveal anything about Kinkade's fans or users—and who's
to say it *wouldn't*, as we haven't done the research that would tell us one
way or another how and why those hobbit houses have been so appealing and used—then that doesn't mean it's not worth studying him in other
ways. In fact, given the ubiquity of his art, we'd probably be remiss not to;
to not study him (or the phenomenon that has become "Thomas Kinkade,
Painter of Light") would be like saying we're going to seriously assess the
nature of twentieth-century food consumption but then limit ourselves to
five-star French restaurants without any reference to the economic, cultural, nutritional, and commercial impact of McDonald's. If we don't have
data on how and why people have "used" the Happy Meal of Kinkade as
they've done, then certainly—and especially now that cultural studies has
been thoroughly mainstreamed—we have the resources to find other ways
of assessing and judging him as a hobbit-cottage industry based in an appeal to, manufacture of, and probable circumscription of vernacular tastes.
There is probably a very informative dynamic at play in Kinkade's prints
that may have less to do with the kitschy tonalism of the art per se than
with how that tonalism effectively mediates between ideological, commercial, religious, and consumer interests. (Kinkade bills himself as an explicitly Christian artist.) As Stuart Hall has explained, "Alongside the false appeals, the foreshortenings, the trivialization and shortcircuits" of mass
cultural products, "there are also elements of recognition and identifica-

tion, something approaching a recreation of recognizable experiences and attitudes, to which people are responding." If Kinkade doesn't yield to one analytical rubric, that's not his problem; it's ours. And if we want our scholarship to be engaged—according to Wikipedia, "one in twenty homes in the US feature some form" of his art—then we need to come up with another rubric or set of rubrics for it to be so. Simply dismissing him and his users, which I know you're not advocating, is not good enough unless we're content with letting "Thomas Kinkade, Painter of Light" do its cultural, religious, and ideological work unremarked and unobserved.

By presenting Ashley's poetry scrapbook—and her inclusion of Pound, which, in some people's eyes, would lift her above her peers—as an example, I'm using her strategically, hoping by way of her proximity to "legitimate" culture to gain a hearing and provide a gateway for other scholars beyond high/low binaries and into the complex and compelling world of popular poetry more broadly. It's bait, right? I could just as easily have cited another scrapbook, one that I pair with Ashley's in the beginning chapter of *Everyday Reading* and that was assembled by someone who was far more distant from literary institutions than Ashley was, but that album would have had far less appeal in today's world of poetry criticism. That collection is meant to show how not all privatized scrapbook memorabilia are equal to each other; they're different from one another, for sure, but each might be complex in different ways. I don't think that I, or anyone else at the moment, knows enough about the culture of popular poetry to begin making definitive judgments about it (or, heaven forbid, creating a "canon") even though we can, and must, make particular judgments as we go forward as the scholars who most specialize in language use. I think Wieden + Kennedy's citation of Angelou's "I Rise" in the appealing and spectacularly produced LeBron James Nike ad is a reprehensible co-optation, for example—far worse than Rick Santorum's 2011 attempt to hijack Langston Hughes's "Let America Be America Again" as a slogan for his presidential campaign. The engaged critic is responsible for saying so, be it in regard to "high art" (not all of which is on the side of the angel) or the mass and the popular (not all of which is ideological).

I think it's also important to remember that not everything that is "useful" is instrumentalized in the way that the marketplace instrumentalizes things, and not all things that are fetishized are fetishized as capitalism fetishes them. For instance, when I send you a Thomas Kinkade print for your birthday this coming year—and when you then hang it on your office wall—we are certainly using it but hardly, I think, instrumentalizing it; rather, we are packing it with additional meanings and embedding it in exchange and value economies in which capital is not paramount and that may intersect with a capitalist value economy but hardly replicate or reduce to it. The print is thus fetishized not because of its abstraction from social relations, as Marx's analysis of commodity fetishism would have it, but because of its *proximity* to social relations. The same thing possibly goes for the poems that Doris Ashley saved and likely exchanged with other readers. (Other scrapbookers recorded in their albums whom they got poems from and how.) Use is not a bad thing: the moral or ethical component depends on what use things are put to.

Many elements of popular or vernacular culture value the uselessness, apparent uselessness, or noninstrumentality of things—poems, puns, wordplay, ornaments, gifts, linguistic and artistic performances, recreational play, and evasions of work of all sorts—and so it might be interesting to talk about continuities between these things and the long, deliberately useless motes in the eye of capitalism that you mention; certainly, bringing language poetry theory into a consideration of Burma-Shave advertising jingles wasn't fruitless from my point of view. Personally, though, I don't have a lot of patience for the types of long texts you mention, so I'm not the best person to ask. Maybe it's the residual working class in me that finds them a bit silly (read "useless," I suppose); or maybe I'm a corrupted child of the MTV age with a short attention span; or maybe I already have enough to simmer about without having to simmer in those projects; or maybe I'd just rather write a poem to my grandmother—I don't know. That said, I don't see any reason why a study of those long poems can't happen in the same disciplinary field as a study of popular ones (it's why Heidi Bean and I use the term "poetries" in the plural and with a lowercase "p," rather than "Poetry" in the singular and with a capital, in our introduction to *Poetry after Cultural Studies*), and I'm always surprised at the implication that they *can't* coexist, or that the field can't be capacious enough for it all. I mean, fiction studies manages to acknowledge its genre's plurality pretty well, so that we aren't all that surprised to find that someone writing about literary fiction also writes about Harry Potter—or a western, romance, serialized, dime, spy, book-club, or science fiction novel. So why can't poetry studies do this too?

Rasula: What's tantalizing about your research is the discovery of a hidden zone of poetry buried deep in the mass like a stratum of precious metal in a rock formation. To go on with that analogy, here's my sense of emergent prospects. One is like industrial extraction, removing the precious substance and purifying it of residual dross from the excavation site. This is more or less standard practice in Poetry World. The other prospect is to do core samples of the substance in situ, parsing what "poetry" means along a continuum of adjacent materials and practices. A long time ago my friend Don Byrd remarked that poetry had so diminished in terms of its cultural prestige that it occupied about the same social status as tatting and ring tossing (demographically, I'm sure he was right). It was meant as an alarming observation, but I've always been haunted by another prospect, which is to imagine poetry as part of a continuum of creative responses to the world that can seize upon any medium whatsoever. It's routine for sports writers to refer to the "poetry" in a basketball layup or a soccer pass (*Bend It Like Beckham*); and I have no doubt that any devotee of a specific practice, whether it be golf or crossword puzzles, thrives on a sense of the "poetic" (ingenuity, justice, or sheer luck). Yet these sports examples disclose all over again the problem that dogs poetry, which is the glamour and power of the exception, the unique instance. But then the analogy collapses: Michael Jordan beats John Ashbery hands down when it comes to general appreciation of what they do and how they do it. So the "poetry" of poetry (as opposed to the "poetry" of sports) is muffled in obscurity and inconsequence. The consequences are so private as to be invisible (nobody's ever going to hear about Ashley except from you).

Whatever else it's been accused of being and doing, official verse culture purported to be about quality control: it's a kind of semiofficial regulatory agency. But thinking back to Mathew Arnold's famous yearning for the best that has been known and thought, I wonder: how does this not capitulate to the blandishments of the marketplace? How is it to be distinguished from the shopper's outlook, the bargain hunter mentality, or the five-star rating system? How will the quest for quality avoid the perils of solipsism? Aren't we all motivated, to various degrees, to legislate our personal tastes as general criteria? What do we *do* with our value judgments once we've made them? Taking delight in some obscure artist, do you resign yourself to solitude in your pleasure? The Nick Hornby novel (and movie) *High Fidelity* pinpoints the conjunction between private neurosis and the canonical instinct. It has its pulse on a common urge to mete out personal fate in the form of a playlist, a canonical seal of approval on an otherwise private experience—moments *in drag* as monuments.

There was a moment (and in retrospect it was little more than a moment) when poetry really seemed to be news that stays news, in Pound's sense. I associate that moment with the sprawl as well as the unbinding of aesthetic corsets put into play by Jerry Rothenberg's anthology co-edited with George Quasha, *America a Prophecy* (1973). That initiative was promptly squashed (e.g., Helen Vendler in the *New York Times Book Review*, an infamous piece I discussed in *The American Poetry Wax Museum*), with the consequence that everything started being tidied up,

with poets themselves subbing as the cleaning crew. It turned out this presaged the demographic tsunami of the writing programs, in which an entire generation or more squandered the potential of the art by making it
all autobiographical (from the bestselling *I'm OK, You're OK* to "I'm *not*
OK..."); and that all too easy target was what Language poetry trained
its sights on. But all of that now seems a distant fight in the OK Corral,
doesn't it? To go back to that moment of *America a Prophecy*, though, is to
revisit some lost potential that seems a bit like the Zone in Pynchon's novel
Gravity's Rainbow (published around the same time, in fact), where all bets
are off. My hunch is that, for you, that's always been the case with the sorts
of *détournements* you document in the private sphere. My worry, though,
is that popular culture, so penetratingly commercialized, has poisoned the
well, and the Situationist moment in America amounts to little more than
another T-shirt logo, and the uses of poetry amount to little more than
broadening the waveband of greeting cards. Cynical, I'm sure it sounds.
So if I can belt out my plea with the help of Fontella Bass's early sixties hit,
"Rescue Me"!

Chasar: I have a private theory—a feeling, rather—that the term "poetry"
has become, in the age of capitalism, a discursive category into which all
things that in one way or another resist or escape complete regulation, ra-
tionalization, instrumentalizaton, description, or measure by the logic of
the commodity are projected: emotion, magic, uselessness, intimacy, hopes,
dreams, love, utopian urges of all sorts, beauties, elegances, difficulties,
nonsense, mysteries, etc. Thus, the category of poetry is not a continuum
from bad to good or amateur to pro like baseball is (where players move
from little league to college to the majors) but profoundly heteroglossic—
something of a Lower East Side, perhaps, where the value of sentimental
worthlessness (cast as "it's only poetry") and the value of what you call
"the glamour and power of the exception, the unique instance" (cast as "it's
sheer poetry") both reside. "Poetry" has, as you indicate in your example of
Michael Jordan, become a sort of floating signifier in the process—a term
to describe those aspects of experience that we don't have much language
for and that capitalist ideology doesn't want us to have a language for, because it would then call those things into being and make them real and
more powerful. Any threat to rational utilitarian discourse—anything that
can't be "read" or completely instrumentalized, ranging from *The Alphabet*
to the sort of obscure beggars' chants that Daniel Tiffany explores in parts
of *Infidel Poetics: Riddles, Nightlife, Substance*—ends up here as a victim of
capitalist damage control: poetry gangs, and the various human experiences that are not satisfied or accounted for by capitalism, turn their spit on

each other, and the administrators of capitalism can reach in and select any of these values for strategic use as the occasion requires.

For example, it can be hard to figure out why poetry is frequently pitched as the most democratic of literary genres (third graders are taught to write haiku, not novels or screenplays) even as it's pitched as the highest of human achievements ("the glamour and power of the exception"). Regardless of whether we want it to be one or the other, functionally it's *both*, a floating signifier that gets attached to any phenomenon that potentially reveals or reminds us how capitalism does not account for all aspects of human existence and experience. Thus, poetry is simultaneously made out to be the most trivial and worthless thing one could pursue (it has no value because even a third grader can do it) and something that only the very few can pursue (only the exceptions); and everything it represents— the mystery of life, the limits of knowledge, utopian impulses, and urges to social justices of all kinds—is either diminished, distanced, or constructed to be self-contradictory, irrational, or unresolvable in the process. Capitalism 1, Poetry 0.

Instead of trying to pin down and reduce the capacity of this floating signifier, I feel like we need to embrace it and liberate it, along with the human experiences it represents and yet contains. You're right: probably, the well has been poisoned, but let's not, for example, throw out the impulses or motivations that find expression, however poorly, in the commercially penetrated language of greeting card verse, because that's precisely—so my feeling goes—what capitalism wants us to do. For me, then, cynicism isn't the answer. I'm by no stretch of the imagination an expert in Derrida or deconstructionist theory, but I'm inclined to say, along with Derrida, "On the contrary we must *affirm* it [the floating signifier of "poetry"]—in the sense that Nietzsche brings affirmation into play—with a certain laughter and with a certain dance." Given the regime we are faced with, maybe we don't have any other choice?

Rasula: Given the fatalistic tone of your question, I can't help but wonder whether (and when) a "floating" signifier can sink—a question implicit, it seems, in your suggestion that it needs rescuing. Isn't it the case, though, that capitalism engineers *everything* as a floating signifier? The logic of the commodity permeates everything. It's well known that people don't buy cars, they purchase mobile cocoons, clan heraldry, emotional armor, and a spirit of adventure all in one. The tendency promoted by capitalist commerce is to make choices on the basis of anxiety if not outright fear, for which the mild old plum "keeping up with the Joneses" was coined. This is altogether distinct, I think, from that bracing dictum by Laura Riding: "To go to poetry is the most ambitious act of the mind." I dwelled on that in the preface to *Modernism and Poetic Inspiration*, so I won't reiterate it here, other than to add Riding's cautionary reminder that "in poem-writing and poem-reading the stirring up of the poetic faculties has been a greater pre-occupation than their proper use; the excitement of feeling oneself in a poetic mood has come to be regarded as adequate fulfillment both for the reader and the poet." I can't think of a better description of how poetry serves as floating signifier, than as a vague "stirring up" of latent faculties.

Because I think you're right to identify the role of poetry now as a float-ing signifier, I'm just adding Riding's diagnosis to suggest that a floating signifier is neither a sanctuary nor a vehicle. In vehicular terms, it may float but it can't sting; it may get around promiscuously, but as you suggest it's always dogged by the sense that a third grader can do it. That's a hard knock, so I think it may be more accurate to observe that poetry in the public sphere—in a way that clarifies the sense in which a poetic "feeling" is stirred up—is predominately anecdotal. Poems are very short stories, with line breaks. (And the line breaks seem to have shed all traces of Olsonian vocalism: this really comes across on radio, where it can be heard by practi-cally every guest on New Letters on the Air.) This is the functional transfer-ence point from "poem" to personal access; it's the "aha, I get it" that aligns, culturally, with everything from water cooler jokes to televised product ads. I suppose in the most ecumenical view we could say that this little foyer of accessibility is a good thing for poetry: after all, peculiar behavior needs an explanation, and we've certainly had no end of poets eager to contribute to the poem-a-day, cultural vitamin building mentality. Besides, slap-happy populism is *American*; and now the anecdotal palliative is being reinforced by YouTube on a monstrous scale, where the "poetic" and the "cute" alter-nate with spellbinding rapidity. It's a media blender in which compulsive attention and indifference are spun into an unprecedented psychological alloy.

I've sometimes thought what's been simmering under our exchange is the tension between poetry as something approachable, welcoming multi-tudes, and poetry in Riding's sense as "the most ambitious act of the mind," which clearly invites charges of elitism. Are these positions necessarily op-posed? As cultural studies has revealed over time, extraordinarily ambitious acts of the mind can be applied to trivial phenomena—and, more impor-tantly, the mind is not rendered trivial in the application. That's because, in the act of scrutiny, the context is permitted to carry a signifying weight that the "text" cannot. Is it the case, then, that the sort of ambition Riding called for in poems is a vain attempt to jettison context, to speak as Stevens often aspires to speak in "ghostlier demarcations"? But then, isn't it *also* the case that "repurposed" poetry in the demographically expansive sense is just as intent on setting any messy adjunct considerations aside? Any answer to these questions dangles in the wind, for the time being, because *every* conceivable context that might be used to explain and/or justify the use of poetry is defined with reference to some model of the commodity.

One of the intriguing disclosures of research like yours is that it provides a much broader demographic profile of poetry users, historically speaking. And that takes us back to a nineteenth-century heyday when poetry in its most official capacity was *also* the most commonly consumed. Since then what's happened is not, as so many assume, that poetry consumption declined, but that the demographic alignments shifted beyond recognition. In the United States the role of poet laureate has changed over the past decades; where it used to be an awkward honorific, it's become a bully pulpit in the marketplace. So there's now a steady audience in the tens if not hundreds of thousands (not an audience of fellow poets, I should add) who have "poetry" on their viewfinder when it comes to high profile figures and events, i.e., poet laureate, Pulitzer, and once in a great while Nobel. Is this a distant perpetuation of that nineteenth-century taste for poetry, or evidence of the capitalist infiltration of market share?

However diversely poetry is debated, celebrated, and deplored, the one thing that can be said about it is that it now conforms to an escalating pattern of consumption we see across the board, from politics to chatrooms. Every tendency and constituency has its little (or big in some cases) homeland, and all intellectual discourse haplessly revolves around (usually surrogate) issues of homeland security. I use this tainted Bush Era term to evoke the xenophobia behind it. In the old OK Corral domain of Beats vs. Squares, dismissive attitudes were common, but to dismiss something you had to at least be aware of it. Now, by contrast, the mountain of poetry has grown exponentially, but without a corresponding sense of scale. Enclaves remain enclaves, but the total number of enclaves has outpaced the ability to enumerate them. Withering contempt has been supplanted by withering indifference.

Chasar: As Doris Ashley's scrapbook is partly meant to suggest—and as her incorporation of Pound is echoed in various ways by the recitation of Whitman on *Breaking Bad*, the reference to Hughes in Santorum's campaign, and the quotation of Maya Angelou in the Wieden + Kennedy Nike advertisement—the tension between poetry as "something approachable, demographically welcoming" and poetry as "the most ambitious act of the mind" is not necessarily a primary tension structuring the reality of poetry's social or cultural lives. Ashley, *Breaking Bad*, Santorum's people, and Wieden + Kennedy all found poetry approachable enough to suggest that maybe approachability isn't a key issue in some spheres; they've approached it, and people will continue to approach it. Thus, it's what they've *done* with it, admirable or not, that interests me. And in this sense, perhaps, all poetry is anecdotal or occasional. That's not to say that that tension you discuss doesn't exist, just that I don't feel it is as crucial as literary critical conversations like ours oftentimes want (or need) to make it out to be. From my perspective, if there is a tension simmering under our exchange, it is rather the tension between the literary critical tradition we have inherited—one in which discussions of poetry are implicitly or explicitly framed by binaries like Beats vs. Squares, quality control vs. anything goes, for use vs. for consideration, art vs. the marketplace, the "mind" vs. the "heart," "demographically welcoming" vs. "the most ambitious act," anecdotal vs. something more—and the possibility of augmenting or moving beyond those binaries to find analytics to help us judge and assess poetry in a greater variety of ways.

I'm not put out by all the enclaves—in fact, I'm thrilled by them (*Write* it!) and by how they frustrate or evade measure by a critical center or dominant historical narrative produced out of oversimplified antagonistic relations (high/low, genteel/modern). Nor do I think that "withering indifference" describes much more than the "expert's" jaded or defensive response to those enclaves. Certainly, the people in those enclaves aren't indifferent to the poetry they read and write; certainly, they perceive the stakes to be real and of consequence. Nor am I going to assume that one enclave is indifferent to the poetry read and written in another; I simply don't know. And all that being said, I don't think I agree with you that, in our world, the "logic of the commodity permeates everything" totally, inevitably, or evenly. Part of our job is to untangle and understand the real poetry and the commodity "poetry" wherever and whenever we can.

Serendipities

An Interview with Joel Bettridge on Critical Practices

JOEL BETTRIDGE IS the author of four books of poetry, *Ligatures*, *The Public Life of Chemistry*, *Presocratic Blues*, and *That Abrupt Here*, as well as two critical studies, *Avant-Garde Pieties: Aesthetics, Race, and the Renewal of Innovative Poetics* and *Reading as Belief: Language Writing, Poetics, Faith*. He coedited *Ronald Johnson: Life and Works*. He is a professor of English at Portland State University.

Bettridge: One of the most engaging strands in *The American Poetry Wax Museum* was your attention to the history and legacy of the New Critics; I was very compelled by your account of what they tried to do and where they put their focus (Tate in particular)—poetry as a practice of knowledge, which draws them close to a poet like Charles Olson. I had the sense that you too had some sympathy with aspects of their initial project. Do you think any elements from their project (however diverse in practice) might still be useful? I'm thinking about what they thought it meant to be poet-critics, which seems interesting with the dominance of "creative" writing now.

I am also interested in how Tate conceived of the role of criticism in particular, and wonder how relevant that seems to you now? I think this is especially sharp for me coming off reading your exchange with Mike Chasar, where the critic's role is central. One passage I have marked with emphasis comes on page 97: "Tate, on the other hand, was unwilling to consign criticism to a secondary role because he was not prepared to concede that *any* conscientious act of imagination, reason, or faith was subordinate. That he refused to assign a role to criticism (as well as to poetry) is attributable to his anti-instrumentalism. But New Criticism had become English department functionalism—the antithesis of everything Tate valued—and he was not happy with the results." I would count *Wax* a very Tate-like book, in these terms. Would you agree?

Rasula: I share with Tate an unwillingness to concede any form of discourse to automation, including responses to student essays and letters of recommendation (the pro forma exercises I see in job application files are alarming). I suspect Tate inherited this determination from Pound—the "good job" mentality of frontier culture. It's notable that the New Critics identified themselves with criticism first, even though key figures like Tate and Ransom were poets. They were following the lead of Pound and Eliot, who were inveterate essayists, but the New Critics had a precise domain in which to operate. They were assaulting what passed for criticism in academia. When I was writing *Wax* in 1994–95, it was a good moment to take cognizance of the cyclical nature of intellectual trends, since the heyday of Continental theory was clearly dissipating. What the New Critics preached was *applied* criticism, stressing exegesis over judgments of taste; they wanted to abolish the shower of biographical and cultural data then prevalent in literary studies. Theirs was a practical agenda, in that they wanted to pioneer methods of reading contemporary work, like *The Waste Land*, and rightly felt that the biographical and sociological methods that made sense when addressing historical phenomena were misleading when applied to the present. The most conspicuous criticism on contemporary writing then (in the thirties) was for them tainted with commitment, engrossed in what the Germans call Tendenzliteratur, the literature of political advocacy and engagement. For all their political opinions, the New Critics refrained from an ideological stand. Of course, my approach in *Wax*—openly partisan, with great dollops of biographical and historical detail—is precisely what New Criticism spurned.

The origins of *Wax* go back to my realization, circa 1975, that books on contemporary poetry were not credible: they were unimaginative, and intellectually flimsy. The contrast was immediate if you turned to books in other fields. So in anthropology I'd be reading Levi-Straus and Clifford Geertz; in sociology, Erving Goffman and Jacques Ellul; in philosophy, Adorno and Heidegger and phenomenologists like Erwin Straus and Helmuth Plessner (and from there to early Derrida); all this augmented by the meteoric impact of Foucault and Barthes and Kristeva. The only *interesting* writing about poetry came from mavericks like Hugh Kenner and Harold Bloom. Because that was a moment when the repudiation of New Criticism was in the ascendancy, it was easy to let it go. Once in a while I'd come across a book or an essay by someone like Blackmur, glance at it, and be perplexed by its sagacity. Eventually, after a numbing cascade of dismissals had washed over the deck—"New Criticism: we know all about *that!*"—I realized it was being stigmatized second- and thirdhand, so I decided to read the originals. What a revelation, to find there'd been a generation that brought some smarts to the table. There was still much to rankle at—peremptory judgments, an air of snobbery verging on smugness, and the Southern agrarian background—but what emerged was that the New Critics were distinct individuals. That had been covered up by programmatic dismissals, dismissals reflecting an institutional backlash—after all, by the seventies the orthodoxy of New Criticism had prevailed for a quarter century or more. Since then, of course, the replacement orthodoxy of Continental theory has run its cycle, though it's been succeeded by nothing as comprehensive. Now, it seems, academic protocols follow the mantra of English magus Aleister Crowley: "Do what thou wilt is the whole of the law."

Bettridge: Your answer gets at something I'm repeatedly drawn to, which is the question of criticism as a literary and creative act. This proposition of the critic as artist has a long history, but I'm eager to hear you address your sense of how such criticism might work for poet-critics now, especially those working in or alongside the university, or in the company of literary theory. Maybe a simpler way to put this question is to ask what you think *Wax* shares with Kenner's *The Pound Era?* I don't want to anticipate your answer, but when reading *Wax* I was struck by how much the two books share a kind of texture, maybe even tone; I was amazed, for one, by how much yours, like Kenner's, undertakes a project reminiscent of Pound's *Cantos*, of getting everything in.

Rasula: It's true that the "poet-critic" model has a long pedigree, though the "critic" portion is often consigned to the closet. Would Wordsworth or Whitman be described that way? No matter, their prose fits the bill. What the New Critics introduced was advocacy in prose, for which they settled on a recognizable *belletristic* style, a legacy reflected in its French appellation, with Saint-Beuve huffing and puffing behind it. Or think of Pound's adulation for Remy de Gourmont. What do we have in English? A lot, actually, but little of it would pass as "criticism": Emerson's essays, Thoreau, Carlyle, Ruskin (whose *Fors Clavigera* was a thrill to discover by way of Guy Davenport, who characterized it as the *Cantos* of the nineteenth century). A strong seasoning in these writers was amplified by *Human Universe* and *The Truth and Life of Myth*, which cast imposing mythopoetic shadows for me, and the effect was enhanced by that anthology Don Allen did with George Butterick, *Poetics of the New American Poetry*. So it seemed perfectly normal when *L=A=N=G=U=A=G=E* came along, a poets' journal of theory and criticism. At the same time, late seventies, academic writing was becoming so loaded with jargon it was often unreadable. But careers blossomed, catastrophically promoting an aura of *faking it* that continues to this day. We now have a billowing heap of academic writing, most of it produced by people under duress for the purpose of job security, and even much of what's written with passionate interest in a subject is indifferent to considerations of style. The book is reduced to a grotesquely inflated memo—and few scholarly books amount to more than the one or two journal publications they started out as. The lapse of the old Greco-Roman heritage of rhetoric as a *discipline* of articulation is all too apparent.

The current plight would have astonished the New Critics. Being anti-"academic," their books were published by Random House, Doubleday, Harcourt Brace, Scribner's, Regnery, and smaller literary houses like Swallow and New Directions. Men of that and succeeding generations had similar careers in the public eye: Kenneth Burke, Northrop Frye, Marshall McLuhan, Frank Kermode, Hugh Kenner, Roger Shattuck, Denis Donoghue, Edward Said, George Steiner. I'd mention Susan Sontag but she wasn't in academia. Harold Bloom eventually muscled his way into the limelight. There are of course plenty of academics publishing in the trade market in history, politics, and other subjects, but literary criticism has been sucked into the inner sanctum of academia. What little market there is for literary topics goes to people like Geoff Dyer, Alain de Botton, Jane Smiley, James Wood—novelists and *New Yorker* columnists (and often English—as if that were a qualification rather than a nationality). Sociologically speaking, though, it's less a matter of critics being edged out of the market than simply abandoning it, and that's a reflection on the ferocious cycles of fashionable research that have prevailed ("prefailed" I wrote, exquisite typo!) in humanities fields. Once a junior prof's sights have been set on mastering the intellectual gestures expected by the leading journals, it's hard to crawl up out of the oil slick.

So what's to be done? I'm reluctant to don a legislative tone here; after all, writing theoretical and critical prose is not a natural vocation for poets. But I have the continuously pleasurable experience of reading the (generally mandated) prose of doctoral students in creative writing, marveling at their fertility of imagination and stylistic resourcefulness. It's dispiriting to think that after grad school these folks may confine themselves to poetry. Since Eliot and Pound were among the first poets I was drawn to, it seemed natural that poets would write lots of prose, reflecting a healthy and unstoppable sense of commitment rather than some onerous chore. So I'm generally alarmed now by the vestiges of purist self-image so many poets retain, *art pour l'art* even among those with a tenuous grasp of art. On the other side of the ledger, what prospects actually exist for the committed critic? I was struck recently by Brian Reed's poignant reflection in the preface to *Phenomenal Reading*: "Why do I persist in writing such essays, when the poets whom I discuss might not highly esteem the results?" He should've written: "might not even notice." That made me reflect that the *creative* venture of writing has always been a priority for me even in critical essays and scholarly books. The response to *Wax* over the years suggests it was not only informative but *readable*. I relished the nugget-size stories in it, a propensity I picked up from Davenport and Kenner and Shattuck.

Bettridge: Given that you wrote *Wax* before you went to Georgia, I am interested to hear how your time there has affected your sense of how cultural institutions (like universities) police "American poetry." It is no doubt self-serving and a product of my own education, but I am interested in what institutions can offer poetry, or poets, given the more prevalent practice in our profession of critiquing institutions, universities in particular.

Rasula: The explosion of creative writing programs since the 1970s has spawned trends I expect will overtake English departments in the not-so-distant future. As state budgets shrink, and the service-learning model takes over, it will seem unsustainable for legislators to fund programs purporting to cover all the traditional historical periods of English literature. But legislators are quick to attach a cash value to *writing*, whether remedial or "creative." My guess is that the English department of 2030 will have a majority of writers, a large contingent of rhet-comp instructors, and a handful of literary specialists—whose specialty will no longer be period specific, they'll just be specialists in handling literary works as such.

What does this do for, against, or in spite of poetry? The most positive spin is that the ascendancy of poetry will dissolve the bitter pill of the rote scholarly essay. I think Charles Bernstein's "Artifice of Absorption" (and, later, Bob Perelman's "The Marginalization of Poetry") was an opening and salutary salvo. It demonstrated that intellectual rigor could be delivered in an unorthodox and playfully flexible form that didn't have to go through preapproved contortions to strobe-light its intellectual credentials. Karl Shapiro had preceded Charles by decades in his *Essay on Rime*, by the way, and a lot of Hugh MacDiarmid's poetry has a didactic mission. One of the exciting things about the first savor of French theory was the imaginative ingenuity behind it, in works like *S/Z* and *The Pleasure of the Text* by Roland Barthes, and *Dissemination* and *Glas* by Derrida. I remember the Canadian critic Stephen Scobie suggesting, in the mideighties, "the two greatest poets of the last twenty years have been Roland Barthes and Jacques Derrida." Hyperbolic, but to the point. Ashbery's *Three Poems* fit the bill, whereas James Dickey was in a brewery. With Charles Olson there was a continual graphism spanning lectures, notes, poetry, essays, blurring the difference between genres. Poetry now has a vast number of practitioners who have benefitted from those blurred boundaries. On the downside, the field as it's been "opened" risks an *anything goes* outlook, and what seems to *go* now is mannerism. Poetry has gulped down the social reflexes of standup comedy, bad TV and film, pop music and rap, internalizing the reflexes of *attitude* without really considering how and why all these influences crept into the text or got into the head.

Bettridge: Are you talking in some ways about the continued marginalization of poetics in the current poetry landscape? And/or the ambition of our poems? Or something else? I am thinking of the end of *Wax* in particular, which is one of my all-time favorite endings. You write, "In the entropic densities of our cultural centers, it makes perfect sense to think of poetry marginalized. Poetry can—and *should*—be our term for a language in crisis, driven to the outskirts to hear itself speak. . . . What seems in danger of being lost is the audacity of Whitman's attempt to make up a canon all by himself, sensing in the center cause for bereavement, because the sterilizing altitude of the 'universal' is in the end just a moribund stereotype—all that survives the eradication of the particular" (482–83). And then after citing Williams's amazing poem X from *Spring and All* you close: "The privilege of poetry is this drift, this insouciant disregard for the exemplary pose—and the tyrannous attitudes—of those figures in wax" (483). All of which is to say, how would you distinguish Whitman's and Williams's particulars from some poet's "anything goes" sifting through jokes, ironic pop culture references, and personal confessions of vulnerabilities and intimacies gone awry?

Rasula: This is an intriguing and probably unanswerable question. Or rather, it can't be answered by us, any more than the contemporaries of Whitman in 1860 or Williams in 1923 had any sense of what would be legible in their work a century later. This sort of issue has been commonly misconstrued as one of value—the "greats" being those who last—but I do think legibility is a key. And I don't mean *readability*. Rather, all writing happens inside a cultural force field, which is like a vast apparatus for making some things seem funny, others opaque, others impertinent, and so forth. It's like a preset series of options on a digital camera. Very few artists in any medium have the full measure of the device, so they tend to operate within the constraints that are programmed in their medium at a given moment. Of course, most writers refrain from making the kind of diagnostic declarations about their moment the way Kenny Goldsmith does in *Uncreative Writing*. Given the conceptual nature of his work, his whole approach would be pointless without taking a stance. But a stand is always being taken, whether explicitly or not—regardless of whether the poet knows it. There's a panoramic rainbow of discursive social gestures embedded in poems, ranging from "please like me" to "fuck you," "I'm a cool dude," or "let's get serious," and "don't you just love it when I . . ." These are noticeable contemporary gestures, anyway, that might usefully provide a template for looking at other periods to figure out what the equivalents might be. The raw, dry earnestness of thirties' political poetry is an obvious example of the ardently conscientious. But what, at a given moment, is genuinely *un*conscious, and therefore invisible even to a poet's contemporaries? That's why Whitman's contemporaries were unprepared to take him seriously as a poet, and why the first adulatory responses were from foreigners. They lacked the blinkers of American culture, and even though Whitman himself did everything he could to grab his fellow citizens by the lapels and get them to take notice, they didn't get it. Or wouldn't stand for it. He came across like a comedian who can't get a laugh. The apparatus of American perceptual norms couldn't bring *Leaves of Grass* into focus.

Bettridge: Concerning the practice and purpose of criticism written by poets, I want to ask about a passage from the beginning of *Wax*. You write: "To pretend to a 'tradition' not much more than a century old is premature. It's still under contention whether Pound and Stevens can belong to the same tradition. This is to admit, really, that we have no tradition. . . . To invoke 'tradition' as if it were an established consensus is hyperbolic at best, and at its worst is predatory philistinism. To insist prematurely on an established lineage is to foreclose on the very energies that seem unavoidably American: the ability (or need) to work in the open, to persist in (or despite, as in Keats's 'negative capability') a nagging uncertainty" (2). If a tradition is, at its most basic, a set of questions, practices, and commitments that one generation gives to the next so that they can in turn use them for their own lives and purposes, is not a critical tradition crucial to avoid participating in the wax museum, and to maintaining a measure of conscious, deliberate effort, a sense of our own criticism's context and function? I don't think it's that cheeky to suggest that the above writers help give life to a tradition of "persist[ing] in (or despite, as in Keats's 'negative capability') a nagging uncertainty." Writing in this tradition might not be good for one's career, but it does offer a path, or at least the possibility of criticism that is useful for one's own intellectual life, and maybe that of others.

Rasula: In this case I'd distinguish between a tradition and a genealogy. Your equilibrium and well-being as a critic thrive on the figures you list here, a sensible ensemble to me but maybe inscrutable to others. As a writer—of critical prose, poetry, whatever—you need to have a strong sense of genealogy, especially insofar as that can be distinguished from "influence" (concerning which I rather like Harold Bloom's baroque exegesis, as it places the poet in a psychodynamic force field that nobody could summon at will). I understand genealogy in Foucault's sense as that which disrupts the steady plod, and plot, encoded in the notion of tradition. It's the *imp* that attaches itself to propriety, inducing impropriety. Two quotes from Foucault: (a) genealogy "must record the singularity of events outside of any monotonous finality; it must seek them in the most unpromising places, in what we tend to feel is without history" (1980, 139); and (b) on the *archive* as what "deprives us of our continuities; it dissipates that temporal identity in which we are pleased to look at ourselves when we wish to exorcise the discontinuities of history . . . it establishes that we are difference, that our reason is the difference of discourses, our history the difference of times, our selves the difference of masks. That difference, far from being the forgotten and recovered origin, is the dispersion that we are and make" (1972, 131). Foucault's phrase "monotonous finality" is exactly what various dissident poets felt in the fifties about the united front I addressed in the *Wax Museum*. The misguided assumption among the Hall-Pack-Simpson crowd was that the steady fizz of awards and fellowships somehow amounted to a cross-section of "tradition," and that they and their cronies were therefore in the thick of it. But it was not an enabling arrangement, other than in the most crassly careerist terms (and, maybe, for personal rivalries like that between Lowell and Berryman). Donald Allen's clusters of poets, on the other hand, were allied strictly on the basis of what was enabled by their association, the sort of affinity I engaged in *This Compost*.

It's hard for me to imagine a venerable aspect to "tradition," a word I'm prone to associate with structurally generated behavior like institutional racism. *Tradition* is a way of saying "that's how we do it here." In a more positive sense, tradition can be observed in regional guitar-picking styles. But I balk when someone like Wynton Marsalis uses his institutional backing to plug a jazz heritage that leaves Cecil Taylor and Ornette Coleman out of the picture. Wynton, Cecil, and Ornette each engage the tradition, but Wynton has the gall to adopt a legislative attitude to it. This exposes the problem that accrues to a tradition, having to do with the coordinates of valuation that get surreptitiously applied. Because "tradition" is a valorizing term (we rarely get references to a *tradition* of dereliction or abuse: "pattern" is the word for *that*), it makes inclusion seem to be a matter of worth, so those not in it are implicitly those who didn't make the cut and aren't on the team roster. From the going models of tradition, I'd be hard pressed to make a case for including, say, John Thorpe. From Foucault's genealogical prospect, though, he could be just the man we're looking for. That's why Creeley used to speak of "the company," as in companionship, and Thorpe would presumably have been in Creeley's company as a fellow resident of Bolinas in the early seventies. I wouldn't be surprised if you've never heard of Thorpe, by the way, but his *Cargo Cult* is still one of my gold star books of that time.

Because tradition and conservation are linked concepts, it was easy in the era of the anthology wars to assume that conservatives had a lock on tradition; and where the New Critics are concerned, their seersucker suits and bowties personify the role of genteel gatekeeper. But tradition, as I suggested, conceals a dark side. So I hear Daniel Cottom's (1996) observation that "tradition is the housebroken past, the past made tractable and polite, like a domesticated animal. That is why tradition always tells a story of perverse conversion. The past is something else again."[1] Tradition is a way of covering over or disguising the past, in which something lurks like Kurtz's "horror," some unspeakable sacrificial legacy like René Girard probes in *Things Hidden since the Foundation of the World* and Roberto Calasso in *The Ruin of Kasch*. "Tradition and the Individual Talent" is still the most anarchic vision of tradition, because Eliot predicates tradition along multilateral lines. Accurately, I think, but who's ever taken him that seriously, especially among those for whom Eliot seems the paragon of orderly unilateral succession? But that's the beauty, for me, of any of our purported traditions in modern poetry, this snarl of contradiction even within a single avatar. Whitman's jovial "do I contradict myself" is like a slogan printed on currency issued from the Empyrean mint, where poetry is concerned.

Your question raises the issue of cross-purposes between poets and critics, where critics seem perennially banished to the side of decorum, tidying up the mess left behind by the poets. Well, *fuck that shit* is the perfect Americanism (in its pungency as well as its semantic oddity) that applies. In several of your questions I sense an undercurrent of curiosity concerning behavioral norms, engendered by institutional anxiety about intellectual comportment. The greater part of disciplinary behavior—by which I mean how people operate within a given discipline (but the very term "disciplinary" says it all, doesn't it!)—perpetuates what girls in junior high home-economics classes were taught in my generation: namely, how to walk without spilling the punch, the cocktails, whatever. And that's what *books* were for, to balance on the head while practicing that walk. Scholar/critics seem to have been consigned to that juvenile classroom, where it's all about "comportment." And I have to say, from years of being on the editorial boards of *PMLA* and *American Literature*, the submissions I read reveal greater concern about balancing a pile of books on the head than about taking thought, one step at a time. I agree with you that a "critical tradition"—allowing for my qualms about *tradition*—is vital for any lineage of poetic practice; but I doubt that literary criticism is the best medium. The problem has to do with discourse environments. In a broader sense, consider the table of contents of a standard textbook like Hazard Adams's *Critical Theory since Plato* (1992). From antiquity to modernism the theorists and the poets are often one and the same; then the final two dozen authors are critics (a floppy term, considering that they range from Kristeva to Showalter). It's as if the growth of academe post–World War II meant that authors like Robert Duncan were simply ineligible.

Bettridge: You are right that I never heard of John Thorpe, so I bought it after I received your response, and I've been reading *Cargo Cult* for the last week. I can see how Thorpe does not make the team if we take tradition to be about privileging particular forms of literary value, but that book is really great: the way it includes forms of oral history and documentation concerning Bolinas, and jarring third- and first-personal lyrics that interrupt all that documentation, almost attacking them as suitable context. The effect was quite compelling and wonderfully strange. Reading *Cargo Cult*—with its clear New American company, and what it foregrounds as particular human histories in this town (I'm thinking of all the dated letters and documents, use of personal memory, and the figure of "Blacksmith" that reoccurs throughout)—brought to mind another of my favorite passages from *Wax* in which you read Duncan's account of the violence of humanization (p. 129). I would be interested then to hear more about what you take your own epistemological foundations for *Wax* to be, and how they might have shifted or driven your criticism that followed. What is the animating, perhaps underlying, question or problem that led you to write *Wax*, and write it the way you did, and what were you trying to achieve, and where do you stand in relation to those questions and goals now?

Rasula: The origins of *Wax* bear directly on your interest in "epistemological foundations." In 1990 and '91 I gave several conference papers on related themes: "The Media of Memory" (American Historical Association), "Poetry's Voice-Over" (Modern Language Association), and "Anthologist's Ontologies" (American Comparative Literature Association). Each of these addressed malfeasances in the transmission of cultural objects in (and as) a tradition. "The Media of Memory" was about the impact of records on jazz history.[2] The other two were essentially absorbed into *Wax* a few years later. In each case, I found myself making claims I knew to be true but unverified. They were predicated on my supposition that the same poets and even many of the same poems got routinely passed along from one anthology to another. I started tracking the data, but the exigencies of preparing a conference talk forced me to make the claims first while I kept plugging away with the data mining afterwards. The result was that sheaf of appendices in *Wax*. At the time, I had to ask myself why bother accumulating evidence after the horse had left the stable, as it were. I had no thought of writing a book at that point (*Wax* came about because Steve North, who'd heard me talk about the issues, proposed I write a book for his NCTE series Refiguring English Studies). And I realized that ignoring the hard facts was exactly what irked me about the cultural custodians I was criticizing, so my response was to become obsessively scholastic.

That documentary impulse has persisted as a pleasurable foundation for everything I've done since then. I suppose it springs from the same source as baseball box-score stats for people who do that sort of thing, and I can tell you exactly where it comes from in my childhood: the Classics Illustrated comic books series. Growing up as an army brat, my access to anything of interest was compromised by moving so frequently. Whenever we moved, or took trips to visit relatives, roadside stops always had racks of comic books, and somehow I got hooked on Classics Illustrated. They were numbered, and their back covers listed the series, but the list was never complete, because when a given title (say, no. 20, *The Corsican Brothers* by Dumas) was out of print, they wouldn't list it, and some titles never were reprinted because of the House subcommittee investigation of juvenile delinquency.[3] So, from about the age of nine or ten I developed this pragmatic bibliographic urge, simply to know what was out there. What's often puzzled me during my professional career is how little this instinct is encouraged. The profession gives a lot more weight to fine-tuning what's called "argument." The curatorial aspect of literary studies is woefully neglected. By *curatorial* I mean really basic stuff, like paying attention to the actual books a poet published rather than passively accepting later renditions (like Marianne Moore's *Observations* as opposed to her *Complete Poems*). The text of David Antin's *Definitions* is unchanging, but what a difference it makes to see it printed on graph paper in a school primer spiral binder the way it was published in 1967. Anyway, to return to *Wax*, as I mentioned earlier this instinct eventually led me to *read* the New Critics instead of accepting the usual dismissal.

Given the polemical nature of that book, I now realize there may be a childhood basis for that too. Up until I was about twelve I imagined I'd grow up to be a Civil War historian. I loved going to the battlefields, and the subject provided another domain in which there were a lot of names and dates to absorb. In fourth grade I flunked a quiz on the subject, because instead of simply writing Grant (it was fill in the blank) I wrote Hiram Ulysses Simpson Grant, and so forth, all the way through. The teacher was having none of what she took to be insolence. And naturally

I was incensed. So my fastidiousness about facts has ever since then been coupled with rage against a supercilious and unrelenting propriety—given the opportunity, anyway, which *Wax* afforded.

By the time I wrote it I'd developed a profile as fearlessly outspoken. I remember being intrigued to hear from Marjorie Perloff that Jerry McGann thought me an iconoclast. From an academic point of view, I guess calling it as I saw it meant iconoclasm on the prowl, and hearing that usefully alerted me to issues of propriety I'd not considered. My naïveté about academia was exorbitant, I must say. First of all, my sole exposure to English departments consisted of one class in my freshman year, followed by a seminar on D. H. Lawrence I audited. I attended a few poetry readings, including one by Denise Levertov, and at the reception was astounded to find her all alone, amid a hefty contingent of faculty all jabbering amongst themselves, indifferent to their guest. That taught me a lot (and nothing has changed). By that point I dropped out of school, with no degree in hand, and spent the next dozen years raising children and doing a variety of odd jobs, during which I maintained my involvement in the poetry community, a zone devoid of any thought of "career development." Since I became a professor, whenever I've divulged anything about my background I've done it with reluctance because nothing in my experience is remotely paradigmatic or instructive. It was all a fluke.

I've often heard academics lament the exigency of having to rework their dissertations into a tenure and promotion book. Often they're just so sick of the material that malaise, indifference, or bitterness creeps into the final result. I was fortunate to bypass all that, because I wrote my dissertation strictly as a kind of intellectual charter for my own development: the 550 pages of "The Poetics of Embodiment, A Theory of Exceptions" summed up the world as I saw it at the age of thirty-seven. I didn't publish any of it. That left me free, when thinking what to do for tenure, to write on a subject I knew thoroughly, had been publishing on continuously since I was twenty, but which I'd set aside while writing my dissertation, so it felt fresh to return to it. Another crucial factor is that *Wax* was written in Canada, where resources were astonishingly slim, but where I also felt immunized from the American scene. I figured I might as well write with impunity since I didn't anticipate ever returning to the States. I'm sure it would've been a much harder thing to pull off if I'd been looking over my shoulder, calculating risks, covering my ass in all the ways familiar to anyone starting an academic career.

Bettridge: So far we've focused on criticism in terms of authorship, but I would be interested in your thoughts on the role the audience plays when working on a critical project. In rereading your answers so far, this question of whom we write for, or to, really stood out: you mentioned Brian Reed's question of audience in the *Phenomenal Reading* and the abandonment of the public sphere by literary critics. Even still, I think of your point in *Wax* that the invocation of the general reader is often used to advance a lyric, voice-centered aesthetic (as opposed to the kind of poetry we've been discussing so far), as well as your discussion of how even the New Critics bemoaned the loss of readers once they entered the academy, so this question of audience is hardly limited to a single aesthetic problem. So where does this leave criticism, putting aside poetry for the moment?

Rasula: My sense of an audience has been quite varied, because of the varieties of audience I've encountered. For instance, from 1979–81 I had a radio show on KPFK in L.A. (kind of a lecture series based on current books) with over a hundred thousand listeners. I covered topics suggested by titles like Said's *Orientalism*, Foucault's *History of Sexuality, Iron Cages* by Ronald Takaki, *Beyond Geography* by Frederick Turner. Not much literature, though I did one program on *"A"* and the first installment of Ronald Johnson's *Ark*. The switchboard would light up after a broadcast and I'd talk with listeners on the spot, plus get lots of mail. That was a truly "general" audience, and it was a worthwhile challenge to deal with complex issues in an accessible way. But it didn't have anything to do with criticism.

The first critical piece I ever wrote was on Jack Spicer, at the invitation of Bill Spanos for *Boundary 2*. And within months of its publication (1977) I got a personal visit from a reader, so that put a human face on an abstract process and made me aware I wasn't writing in a vacuum. It also revealed that the poetry community of which I was a part—by virtue of having edited the magazine *Wch Way*—had some overlap with the scholarly world. Spanos had purposefully forged those ties, and I remember *Boundary 2* published David Antin's instructive essay on modernism, "Approaching the Present." Because I was immersed in a thriving poetry world, it was easy for me to sustain a phantom image of prospective audience, consisting of people I knew and others I wanted to know. And through the years the responses would come, unprovoked. I got a wonderful six-page letter from Robert Duncan once, responding to a piece I'd published in *Spring*, the journal of archetypal psychology edited by James Hillman (who I later introduced to Duncan). Another time John Ashbery called me on the phone, out of the blue. Barbara Guest too. These weren't people I knew, but they confirmed my sense of potential readership. In 1978 I got a letter from Bruce Andrews inviting me to contribute to *L=A=N=G=U=A=G=E*, just days after my friend Barbara Einzig made some obscure reference to "so-called language writing." I was always getting invitations like that, and presumably they were all in response to my publications.

So, from the beginning to the present I've had confirmation of being in a productive engagement with poets and people committed to poetry. That was happily reinforced during the years I wrote for *Sulfur*, Eshleman's magazine (1981–2000) for which I served on the editorial board. Because of the nature of my doctoral studies (History of Consciousness, UC Santa Cruz), my entry into academia offered no overlap with this poetry world to which I belonged. And in any case I held the "academic" treatment of contemporary poetry in such low repute that I was indifferent to it. During the eighties, however, McGann and Perloff got interested in Language writing, and I got to know both of them in Los Angeles. Oddly, back in 1975 Marjorie had struck me as a paradigm of academic malfeasance because of an omnibus review in *Contemporary Literature* (which I saw because the same issue had my interview with Charles Tomlinson) in which she savaged Clayton. Ironically, she and I were both on the *Sulfur* board years later, but by then she'd become a responsible advocate. I asked Marjorie about that early review, and what she told me reveals a lot about the relations (or lack thereof) between poets and academics at the time. Because she wrote on Lowell and Yeats the review editor sent her a stack of current poetry titles to review, though at that point she knew nothing at all about contemporary poetry.

There's a familiar model of author advocacy in the scholarly world. Kenner was the scholar-champion of Pound and Beckett, Vendler of Lowell and Jorie Graham, Perloff of Charles Bernstein and Susan Howe. But here's where the paradigm shifts a bit, because Graham and Bernstein are younger than their advocates, the advocacy shifts a bit. That is, neither Vendler nor Perloff have written books about these poets they've supported in other ways (grants, accolades, academic positions). This is a zone of advocacy that's cloaked by the normative procedures of confidentiality in academia, so it's not always apparent why certain poets are getting plum gigs while others languish; there may not be a paper trail of published articles, just files full of recommendation letters. At this point, the poetry world starts blending with the corporate university, yet another instance of the colonization of the lifeworld by entrepreneurial means. In any case, the absorption of the poetry world by universities suggests that poets are more likely to be aware of critical activity in general, because it's intimately bound up with their immediate livelihood.

Bettridge: Can you discuss in more detail the role of the political in your criticism, or criticism more broadly as it is practiced currently? I can't

help but hear a desire for more socially engaged criticism in your observation that the norms of academic criticism tend to dictate what gets written and how. Moreover, in *Wax* you discuss George Oppen's and Clayton
Eshleman's sense that poets, as writers of poems and criticism, are politically powerless in the United States, and you don't seem to disagree (387).
Still, a few pages later in "Politics of the Referent" you discuss how complicated anything we might call Language-writing is in practice, and how productive its formulation of politics in poetry could be, even as you write that
the writers associated with Language writing adhered "to a separation of
theory and practice" and that the "cost has been a practice, in the poetry, of
isolation and apparent autonomy. Language poets have thereby courted the
specter of preciousness, art for art's sake, and esotericism—despite repeated
denunciations of these qualities throughout their theoretical pronouncements" (405). While reading through these politically centered sections,
I became very interested to know how you might extend or reformulate
these readings, or your larger sense of the political in poetry and criticism,
nearly twenty years later.

Rasula: My position in *Wax* was close to that of the Language poets, rendered in the chapter "Politics In, Politics Of," based on a piece Bob von
Hallberg invited me to write for *Politics and Poetic Value* in the mideighties.
Where most attention to politics in poetry focused on political statements
or evidence of political beliefs and commitments *expressed* in poetry, I
looked instead at how a field of operations concerning poetry in the public sphere actually functioned, the workings of which could be construed as
political. It's true that Eshleman and Oppen lamented the political inconsequence of poetry in America, but I think they knew it was a misapplied criterion. Oppen, after all, made a point of saying he stopped writing poetry
for decades because poetry is not efficacious, and if you want results you
don't choose an ineffectual means. Poetry has never lacked for grand claims
being made on its behalf, but political efficacy has rarely been among them
since Plato took poets to task in *The Republic*.

The skepticism you detect is not about politics per se, but about intellectual fashions. Amid the dissipation of "Theory" in the late eighties/early
nineties a politicizing jargon emerged in which it was fashionable (call it
career-advantageous) to speak of "oppositionality," "subversion," "sites of
resistance," and so forth. This was an extension of Foucault and Michel de
Certeau, whose subtleties were commonly missed by junior scholars and
aspiring grad students who took up the cudgels of what became known as
"political correctness," a term I reviled. It says a great deal about that moment that Cary Nelson's *Repression and Recovery* (1989)—which actually
was all about politics and poetry—had little impact in academia. That tells

us something about how far poetry had fallen in the hierarchy of academic subjects since the reign of the New Critics, who wrote almost exclusively about poetry. But it's been prose fiction for a long time now, a subject in which it's easy to trace the vicissitudes of whatever theory has prevailed at a given moment in the criticism. This observation reveals me to be a sociologist of criticism rather than a critic myself. At any rate, I've generally found that the main benefit of reading criticism is tracking crowd behavior, collective instincts being flexed unwittingly by individuals you'd think might know better.

I incline toward an ecological approach to critical writing, based on a principle of cultivation. I regard literature as something to nourish in return for the nourishment it gives me. To do that responsibly means maintaining a disciplined sympathy for authors of any stripe; to approach them as plausible individuals rather than types, exemplars, or scoundrels. Also, taken to a certain limit in *This Compost*, it means regarding individuals as transitory phenomena in the larger scheme of things, so I try to keep an eye on that larger scheme, though not at the expense of the individual. But most important is sheer dogged curiosity. That's what I always marvel at in Guy Davenport's essays: the constantly blossoming fruit of curiosity. Curiosity is the opposite of "argument." An argument predetermines perception to a considerable extent, while curiosity is a vehicle without any brakes. One thing leads to another until I'm confronted with the chastening thought, "Can I find my way back to where I began?" Curiosity leads me into the land of serendipity, that wonderful word coined by Horace Walpole, the upshot of which is I always end up with a lot more fruit in my basket than I can possibly use. But I do think it helps, in a way, to write on the basis of having more than you can possibly squeeze in. It lends the prose an air of buoyancy, for one thing, almost levitation at times. Hovering over what's yet to be tasted. Like fine carpentry, you shouldn't be able to *see* the labor in the results, but you sense that such a result could never happen without the labor. By the time I'm done with a manuscript it feels less like something I've written, more like something found and treated, like an animal pelt. The final aspect of what seems to be coming out here like a credo, is being committed to writing, not as a ready-made vehicle conveying some content that's distinct from it, but writing as the medium in which all expression swims, like a fish in water. I'm always guided by principles of Sanskrit poetics, which uses a language of embodiment, gusto, and flavor to describe the way texts can be felt and tasted. I'm happy to add some succulence to the drift and sway and drive of thoughtful sapience.

Bettridge: It's intriguing to put your critique of poetry criticism over the last few decades against your conversation with Mike Chasar about the rise of poetry writing in the United States. That dichotomy is fascinating—how something like poetry can remain hugely relevant in some ways while the critical engagement with it becomes marginal at best. In your answer, you suggest that the downgrading of poetry criticism has something to do with "intellectual fashions," so I would enjoy hearing you play this line of thought out more. In *Wax*, for example, you do an amazing job of showing how the New Critics used poetry for particular ends, but also why certain forms of poetry were well suited for their projects. With that in mind, what is it about poetry, or the forms of poetry being written now, that makes it less useful for recent intellectual fashions?

Rasula: Social media have enhanced a certain sense of community and connection, but at the expense of what used to be understood as discourse. It's like remaking all discursive situations on the model of the sound bite. It's supremely democratic, but it's a democracy in which everyone feels entitled to speak without much obligation to listen. Or listen at length. The attention span has shrunk; bumper sticker culture is the norm. The buildup has been long in coming, and it seems that each generational turnover has been so precisely aligned with its concomitant technological transformations that historical perspective gets trumped by the present. With cell phones people may be talking to others more than they used to, but I doubt it's improved communication at all. "What are you up to?" "Oh, nothing much": that seems to be the script. Is it impairing the ability to follow longer structural arcs? Possibly. In terms of poetry, I sense a shimmer of poetry predicated on attention deficit, which superficially resembles Language poetry, but with a kind of eager beaver undertone of wanting to be adored. Weird combination! Anyway, to get back to your question, I doubt that it's anything about critical writing that keeps poetry lovers at bay; rather, poetry lovers may lack the inclination (and possibly the means) to follow longer arcs of deliberation. George Steiner made observations along these lines forty years ago, sensing a looming attention deficit in the Boomer generation!

An issue I've periodically addressed has to do with demographics, and that comes to the fore with the internet. I remember the Buffalo poetics discussion group online in the midnineties as it rapidly grew from a fairly localized conversation to something that bore no resemblance to a conversation because so many people were weighing in, and the feed was such that when you read a meaty response, it was hard to locate the original provocation, so it all ended up sounding like different radio stations as you spun the dial. Unless of course you became obsessed with that chat room, and followed every little twist and turn. After about a year I unsubscribed because it was so aleatory as to be dysfunctional. I was on a number of other discussion groups at the time, all of them trending the same way. Looking back, I can see that people were learning how to use a new medium, but I'm more inclined to say that the medium was commandeering the users. Now everyone's been to that boot camp and that's reflected in the manners and mannerisms of online behavior.

Bettridge: Reading back over your answers (and thinking about your criticism more broadly), your desire to find intellectual worth in a wide range of work, from the New Critics to Paul Mann, stood out to me, even as you use what you critique to develop a line of thought. I think this stood out to me because it seems different than the standard academic rhetorical maneuver that goes "while so and so does x, he fails to do y; therefore z," which is the kind of familiar trope you try to avoid. Perhaps it is just that I now expect much of the criticism I read to only use their secondary sources to establish a framework, and you, often, stay with the text you are investigating much longer—your essays even on occasion become extended close readings in their own fashion. And my sense is that this has to do with your procedure of writing to understand what you are writing, and also being curious about your subject. Still, it seems to create a form of criticism that does not offer critique as combat—I mean, the move to expose, or invent, faults as a way to advance one's own argument; even still, as you wrote yourself, *Wax*, for example, is "openly partisan," although I tend to understand this taking sides as a way to strip away feigned objectivity. So my question is, how conscious are you of wanting to give even your subjects of inquiry their due? How important is this to the kind of criticism you hope to write? How important is it to your sense of yourself as a writer?

Rasula: Your question already answers itself, quite elegantly, in its description of how you see me working. Yes, I avoid the standard posture of critical obeisance—although it is an effective way of joining a conversation. It clearly derives from classroom discussions, formalizing the informal concessions ("you first," nods and twitches of the head, smiles and worried looks, etc.). It's only a problem when it's done strictly for procedural reasons with no thought given to any alternatives. It must be a warm cozy feeling to be so caught up in an ongoing critical exchange like that implied by the formula, but I've rarely experienced such a thing because I scamper all over the place like Isaiah Berlin's fox. I should add that this instinct didn't begin as a repudiation of or disinterest in such conversations and their formalities. Rather, when I started writing critical essays they were on people like Spicer and Duncan, about whose work few had then written. So that convenient tool—your x, y, z—simply wasn't applicable. You contrast my procedure with "criticism as combat," but actually I don't think of the x-y-z method as combative: it may be nitpicking, but it's still subservient. The meticulous exposure of supposed "faults" in someone else's argument is traditional rhetorical practice, of course; but where humanistic scholarship goes haywire is in trying to retain this *oral* device in the slow-motion enterprise of writing.

Writing should enable you to create a world rather than just step into a ready-made one. So, although I do indeed want to give my subjects their due, I want just as much to give the little world that emerges through the writing its own due. I suspect this may give readers the impression that I can't keep my mind on the job, inasmuch as an essay that seems to be about X spends most of its energy rustling around at the other end of the alphabet. I've always delighted in writers who are masters of distraction, peregrination, prevarication, their curiosity abounding in discovery and fresh waves of enthusiasm, but with only a halfhearted impulse to pursue an argument like hound on hare: Thoreau, Sacheverell Sitwell, Roberto Calasso, Guy Davenport, André Breton, Walter Benjamin, at times even Fred Jameson, whose sentences are swollen with dialectical calipers. There are also examples of unrelenting critical clarity that never deviate from the goal, ones I admire and doubt I could duplicate, like Franco Moretti's *Modern Epic* or Gerald Bruns's *Modern Poetry and the Idea of Language*. Such works cling tenaciously to a basic paradigm, often a binary (like the Orphic and Hermetic in Bruns), and binaries have great appeal to the imagination, from nature to culture. It's increasingly rare for literary critics to venture such paradigms, but they can be useful strategies for avoiding the x-y-z-cancan.

A more ambitious paradigm is the fourfold scheme, like Hayden White (my dissertation director) employed in *Metahistory*, in which he draws on a whole sheepfold of prior quadrants, including those from Stephen Pepper's *World Hypotheses* (formism, mechanism, contextualism, organicism), Kenneth Burke's master tropes (irony, metaphor, metonymy, synecdoche), and Northrop Frye's *Anatomy of Criticism* (comedy, romance, tragedy, irony). Frye's book is itself a clattering cavalcade of fours, from the "Four Essays" of its subtitle (Historical Criticism: Theory of Modes, Ethical Criticism: Theory of Symbols, Archetypal Criticism: Theory of Myths, Rhetorical Criticism: Theory of Genres) to its reiteration in fours within these groups. There are plenty of other schemes of four out there: the fourfold typology of scriptural exegesis attributed to Dante (anagogic, moral, allegorical, literal); Anthony Wilden's orders of complexity in *The Rules Are No Game* (inorganic nature, organic nature, society, culture),

David Dilworth's "Archic Matrix" (perspectives, realities, methods, principles) in *Philosophy in World Perspective*; Philip Wheelwright's *Burning Fountain* (in which the types of symbolism are expressive, literal, phatic, and ejaculative), Roger Caillois (games of chance, agon, mimicry, vertigo), Freud's typology of the dream-work (condensation, displacement, dramatization, symbolization), and the structuralist paradigm of Greimas's semiotic square, which Jameson turns to again and again (cf. *The Political Unconscious*, in which the huge chapter "On Interpretation" revisits much of the above). Lacan's most entrancing book is *The Four Fundamental Concepts of Psychoanalysis*; Levi-Straus's four-volume *Mythologiques* put all sorts of pairs and quadrants into play; there are the four forms of multiplicity outlined by Michel Serres in *Rome: A Book of Foundations*. Slightly deviating from this model are the paired dyads in Yeats's *A Vision*, who in a way was following Blake (Tharmas, Urthona, Luvah, Urizen). Along similar occult lines are English magus Aleister Crowley's tarot configurations (create, preserve, destroy, redeem). From antiquity we have the four humors and the four elements (to which Bachelard dedicated a series of books). In his influential essay "Two Aspects of Language," Roman Jakobson avoids the four by precipitating variants out of his two (metaphor and metonymy, or selection and combination, yielding the similarity disorder and the contiguity disorder). Jakobson followed Saussure's *langue/parole* binarism, as did Kristeva in *Revolution in Poetic Language* (the semiotic versus the symbolic), and in a wonkier application, Baudrillard in *Symbolic Exchange and Death*, in which he piles it on so thick it begins to resemble a Tinguely sculpture rattling its extremities. Barthes's *The Fashion System* is even thicker, but somehow seems more possessed of Gallic lucidity. Most helpful is Jean-Joseph Goux's assimilation of Marxist and Freudian precepts in *Symbolic Economies*, in which he gives various terminological templates their due without regard for whether they fit a particular numerical order. Because there were six of them, Harold Bloom's "revisionary tropes" in *The Anxiety of Influence* have a deliciously different impact. A rare case of someone thinking completely outside the two/four box is anthropologist Roy Wagner in *Symbols That Stand for Themselves*, one of the really energizing books of pure poetics that I know, derived from the African Dairibi people the way Marcel Griaule's *Conversations with Ogotemmeli* synthesized Dogon cosmology.

As you're bound to infer from all this, I'm enthralled by excursions into system building, while never attempting anything remotely like it. Instead, I find myself operating in an agglutinative manner. What appeals to me about tropes of numerical organization is that they're serviceable for buoyancy: pontoons of conceptualization—but then you plunge back into the water and swim to the next one. Usually when I'm conceiving a talk or an essay, I compose diagrams on graph paper, and sometimes I'll organize my thoughts by way of numerical configurations; but I never write them out that way, so they tend to get buried deep in the mix.

Bettridge: In a related question, the balancing act I described above also has a tremendous impact on the tone of your prose, and on its sound, and its grammar, the way you shape your sentences and link them together. Other than just wanting to write well-turned sentences, what is your own sense of the role that tone, sentence structure, and sound play in your criticism? Is there a specific sound, or tone, you are working toward?

Rasula: That's delightful to hear, because I really do compose for the ear, not the metronome as Pound puts it. When I revise I make word substitutions according to sound values and sentence cadence. I adhere to certain principles from René Daumal's *Rasa*, a little book that tackles the key concept of Sanskrit poetics translated as "savor" and enlivening our under-attended Western references to "taste": "neither an object, nor an emotion, nor a concept; it is an immediate experience, a gustation of life, a pure joy, which relishes its own essence as it communes with the 'other.'"[4] When I look back at my own writing, I want something I can savor, especially as it recedes into the distant domain of the *other* the author of a given text has become to me—or become *of* me. As a writer, one is always in the position of *enunciator*, which is both a legislative and a performative stance. Our experience of enunciation as estrangement is most immediate in conversation, either when someone refers to what you said (to which you might defensively think, "supposedly!") or when you read the transcript of a taped exchange. It takes a lot longer to experience this estrangement in writing, but I assure you it does happen. For several years now I've found I no longer experience *Wax* as enunciation. The author has been expunged by time. No disavowal either: if you feel chagrined or want to fiddle and adjust the text, that's still the author haunting you. But to experience one's own writing by way of *rasa* is to become wholly reader. I always want to be an engaged and unembarrassed reader, of my own work as well as others'.

Bettridge: That is a wonderful list of fourfold schemes—I love how books like those end up having, in some ways, the feeling of Oulipo constraints used to generate writing, which makes me intrigued to hear more about how you use diagrams and numerical configurations when you conceive a talk. I'm interested to know how exactly do you use these diagrams? What do they consist of? Quotes? Sketches of ideas? Phrases? Or are they more formal, like an outline? Or are you using a flow chart? I'm curious too why you use graph paper? And when you say that you never write the talks in a way that follows the diagrams do you mean that the ideas change as you write (as you've indicated), or are the diagrams more like a first draft?

Rasula: I love diagrams—and books of diagrams, like the old *Time Chart of World History*—first published as *The Histomap* in 1931—and *Graphic Diagrams: The Graphic Visualization of Abstract Data* (1979). *Cartographies of Time: A History of the Timeline* by David Rosenberg and Anthony Grafton (2010) is a wonderful survey and visual compendium. Jessica Helfand's *Reinventing the Wheel* showcases circular diagrams. Books like *Maps* by Akerman and Karrow, and Harvey's *History of Topographical Maps* are always stimulating. Katharine Harmon takes the impulse into fantasyland with *You Are Here: Personal Geographies and Other Maps of the Imagination*. Decades ago I got so absorbed in the stuff I embarked on a successor project to Derrida, calling it "Diagrammatology." It didn't get much farther than photocopying a few thousand diagrams from books. Although I was always fascinated by anything diagrammatic hung on classroom walls or in textbooks when I was growing up, probably the primal stimulus for my adult interest goes back to John Willett's flowcharts in *The New Sobriety: Art and Politics in the Weimar Period*, which I got as a review copy in 1978. He was riffing, in turn, on Alfred Barr's famous diagram for the 1936 MoMA exhibition *Cubism and Abstract Art*. A motherload for modernism is Astrit Schmidt-Burkhardt's *Stammbäume der Kunst: Zur Genealogie der Avantgarde* (2005), with hundreds of diagrams and flowcharts and even artworks derived from those templates, illustrating an exhaustive text of nearly five hundred pages.

I have a very visual imagination, and probably the only reason I didn't end up as an art historian is that I was so clueless when I went to college I didn't even know art history was a subject. But as personal forms of expression, drawing and painting and doodling and taking photographs have always existed in tandem with writing. My poetry book *Tabula Rasula* (1986, but actually set and ready to print in 1981) was carefully subtitled "a book of audible visual matters." bpNichol's voco-visual practices always made eminent sense to me. Curiously, I found when working with Steve McCaffery on *Imagining Language* that my cartographic sensibility was utterly alien to him. Early on I showed him a vast template summarizing (for me) the parameters of the project, at which he gaped and said he simply couldn't process it. I think that, for him, it was like looking at the rabbit/duck diagram in psychology books and being unable to see more than one image. That experience has made me reluctant to foist diagrams on students; but I use them with abandon for jump-starting my own thought processes.

I often produce a visual synopsis of a text I'm teaching as an aide-mémoire in the classroom (see figure 13.1). I don't like to fumble around with notes and such when I'm teaching, but a diagram or a chart works quite nicely, informing the quick glance with a keyword or a name, architectonically positioned for ease of access.

Diagrams have different uses at different moments. Sometimes I've produced associative diagrams of key words simply to work toward a conceptual focal plane, working out how terminological components from different disciplines might inform one another. A handful of such diagrams have ended up being a veritable X-ray of my mind as it unwittingly germinates a new project. My entire dissertation unspooled from a single diagram. I don't recall ever producing a diagram *as* a plan for a book, however. When I'm really embarked on a project, I'll make diagrammatic sketches along the way simply to clarify what I've covered and what might ensue from that. All this is tantamount to saying that, where my own writing is concerned, diagrams are *dirty* and never make it into the end product, at least not yet.

Bettridge: I'm struck by what seems to be an almost paradoxical view on writing in your practice of "accidental research." On the one hand, this intriguing procedure speaks in a very practical way to much of what you have discussed so far, from writing to figure out what you are thinking, to being curious about your subject, to moving against academic convention, to questions of audience. The application might go something like, "if you want to write anything of value for others to read later, then write in a way that follows these asides, that operates without a clear end as published words."

Rasula: I *do* consider writing to be a practice one should engage apart from any considerations of publishing—and I use the word "practice" to suggest something similar to music. I find it odd that in the case of music and art we readily acknowledge the need for practice, yet somehow imagine writing gets hatched fully formed like Aphrodite from Zeus's head. Writers think of drafts as messy preliminaries; whereas the artist producing a sketch or the pianist playing an etude regards it as necessary for maintaining the skill. Creative writing workshops commonly include exercises in this sense, but scholars get no encouragement whatsoever. The profession—by which I mean, those credentialed in the humanities—teeters over an abyss of the incompetence fostered by the presumption that writing is the one thing in the world you just *do* and don't have to learn or think about.

The advantage I had coming into academia is that I was already a professional writer with a long track record. Ever since that essay on Spicer

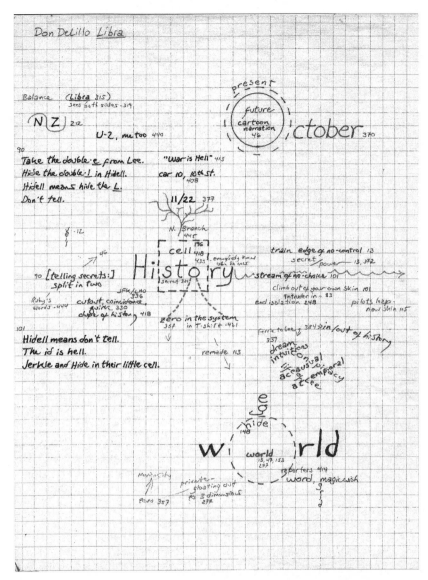

Figure 13.1. Jed Rasula, diagram of *Libra* by Don DeLillo (circa 1995)

written when I was twenty-three, I've had continuous invitations to publish. There's not been a day since 1976 that I haven't had a deadline pending. A deadline's useful; it creates a practical incentive. It also sets you up to confront the exigencies I've described above concerning detours and misfires. The *unproductive* approach is to be exclusively goal oriented, approaching each deadline ruthlessly, with anything that doesn't quite serve being balled up and tossed in the wastepaper basket with that timeworn gesture memorialized in movies, until finally the steady tap tap tap of the typewriter indicates the poor sap has found a groove and will make the deadline after all. The alternative is to recognize that writing is more like fishing: yes, you may want trout, but why toss the perch back in once you've hooked it?

I like deadlines because they make the challenge palpable. That old saw about the ticking of the tenure clock is a false premise, poisoning everything around it with the air of a countdown. A deadline should be an incentive to produce, like planning a meal. As things get hectic in the kitchen and the guests have already arrived you might pragmatically decide to omit an item from your menu, but you turn your attention to what's possible and serve it up. I love cooking, by the way, and gardening, two activities that replicate the studiousness needed for writing, but they're activities devoid of the kind of thinking I do the rest of the time. Empty mind, from Buddhism, suggests these are preconditions for filling it later (like a bellows). Writing is a respiratory engagement: it needs a determinate antithesis around it as balance.

Bettridge: I'd also be interested, given the above, to hear about the physical environment, or environments, in which you've worked, and how that affects, or has affected, the critical projects undertaken in them.

Rasula: For ages I was a manic scribbler, like Ron Silliman, except without a grand project like *The Alphabet*. I've got boxes full of notebooks of various sizes, filled with everything from billboard slogans and bits of conversations to book titles, names of artworks scribbled down in museums, musings during concerts, thoughts for essays, drafts of poems, and drawings. I don't do as much of that now, though I still have several notebooks underway; it just takes longer to fill them up. Graphomania has been siphoned off by the computer. The advantage of the notebooks was portability, and the computer era has compromised that. Of course, I've been typing continuously since 1966, and once the portable typewriter got replaced by an electric one the portability was lost. Time was, I could take a typewriter to a picnic table, but I've long been sucked into a world of power outlets—until, of course, the advent of the laptop. But I haven't felt comfortable with a laptop keyboard, so it's not the portable device for me it could be. Other portable devices like iPad and iPhone are great conveniences, but I can't *write* on them. There's a reason why the term "texting" means bite-size.

As for work environments, they've varied dramatically over the years. Variety is a vital stimulant. Each time I've lived temporarily in a new place it's been productive. I wrote a big chunk of my dissertation house-sitting

Nathaniel Tarn's place near Santa Fe for a couple months in 1988. The first draft of *This Compost* was written on a quaint indoors balcony of a rough-hewn stone cottage overlooking the Catskills across the Hudson River, in a year's penurious sojourn from Los Angeles. A couple years ago I had a wonderful fellowship at the American Academy in Berlin, with a lovely view out over the Wannsee. I have a strong sense of place, probably from growing up in the military and moving so often; so there's nothing I've written or read that doesn't coexist in memory with a specific environment, both geographic and architectural. *Wax* was written in a study/library that was a new addition to our house in Canada, and I still associate it with the crabapple tree out the window, the smoke tree blossoming beyond it, and a hedge of flowering weigela.

Bettridge: Given your commitment to cultural situations and historical particulars, were you aware at the time, or in retrospect, how those particular environments shaped or affected what you were working on? The landscape of Santa Fe is stark and beautifully arresting, and it must have been hard not to have Tarn's work in your head with all his books and objects of everyday life all around? And of course Wannsee is where the Nazis worked out the "final solution."

Rasula: The actual site of the "final solution" was almost visible across the lake from the American Academy, and I used to bike past there all the time. There's much made about the aura, positive or negative, of such world-historical sites, but the compelling enigma for me has always been the resounding silence, starting with battlefields I avidly visited as a youngster, like Gettysburg. You look at the photos and read the accounts and are ready for the place to let out a primal howl, but when you're there it's as if humans never existed. Some of my earliest memories are of the high desert plateau in Colorado, a milieu devoid of people but for that very reason never "vacant" for me. There's no explaining it, biographically, but it settled me pretty early into an abiding perception of planetary rhythms that supersede our species altogether. That may have prompted some tendency I have to be a sort of ecologist of cultural affairs. It's interesting that I didn't move into a scientific domain like ecology. I suppose that's because the itinerant life growing up in the military meant I never got on track where the sciences were concerned, where it was all about prerequisites I never managed to have. It wasn't until my senior year that I even had a course in geometry!

Bettridge: You've mentioned growing up in the military a number of times; would you mind talking about how that experience affects your work—your work's politics in particular?

Rasula: That's an intriguing and unsuspected question. For someone of my generation that upbringing was not uncommon. In all the military bases I lived on, I was immersed in a generational pack born after 1945, which tailed off precipitously after me (born 1952), so my personal orientation was always one of associating with older kids. Being an "army brat" means having a traumatic background to some degree. Tight-lipped fathers, radiating an oppressive paternal authority in a system designed to do just that, made models of masculinity compelling and distressing in equal measure. What made it work, and weirdly wonderful, is that our parents were all of the same generation and steeped in a shared world-historical experience, so it felt like a big clubhouse. I should add, though, that my father was an officer, so we lived a somewhat sequestered life (army post housing was segregated by rank, so I had minimal contact with the military equivalent of working-class kids except in school). It wasn't until I was in junior high that I ever had a friend from the enlisted ranks. We shared musical interests and on one memorable occasion I bought the Beatles' *Sgt Pepper* and he bought the Doors' first album, which we listened to in his bedroom. To be an officer's kid in that era meant being exposed to an intriguing mix of personalities, because the draft was like a purse seine that scooped up anybody and everybody, and many of the men who found themselves ranking officers after the war realized they were embarked on a career it would be pointless to abandon. So I had friends whose fathers had book-lined studies and were very professorial types. My own father was an artist, and had to give up a scholarship when the Korean War started because the army wouldn't allow him to resign. My perception of class was blunted by the military, where (for me anyway) "rank" didn't translate into "class." It was only much later that I realized most of the relatives on both sides of my family were working class. I'd grown up thinking of it in terms of character, personality, and region (rural Minnesota, rural Pennsylvania).

A military upbringing put a lot of us in that era on a collision course with politics. I was adamantly against the war in Vietnam, but my outlook was sharpened by my father, who was there in 1958–59, and from 1963–65 worked as a logistics advisor to the Joint Chiefs during the massive buildup. As a veteran of World War II as well as the Korean "conflict," he had a skeptical take on the way the situation in Vietnam was being run by the politicians rather than the military top brass. He did a final tour in Vietnam in 1971, and that soured him ("we've destroyed that country," he told me—and he had good reason to know, having seen it in its pristine prewar condition). Most of what I continue to know about the military is from my dad, but it's a very different thing today, decades after the end of the draft. He's always been very suspicious about what Eisenhower called the "military-industrial-conflict," witnessing an endless stream of men re-tiring from the service and taking up consultancy jobs in the arms indus-try, very lucrative—"double dipping" he derisively calls it. It's a national disease, for sure. Imagine being a professor and being able to retire at age forty or fifty as a consultant-advocate to the publishing trade, getting triple your old salary in order to pitch reprints of the things you used to teach!

An odd thing about the military is how much of a family tradition it can be. I was struck after high school by how many people I knew were going off to West Point, or joining the military without even being drafted. I think that tendency persists, but it may not be all that different from fami-lies that breed doctors or lawyers over successive generations. Possibly be-cause of my background, when I went to college I ended up hanging out with lots of vets. There were so many guys coming out of Vietnam who went to school on the G. I. Bill. I remember a philosophy class in which all the students but me and two or three others were fresh out of the combat zone. The level of existential engagement that vets brought to the class—and to anything outside the classroom—was phenomenal. Ever since I be-came a professor I've acutely felt their absence: teaching twenty-year-olds with no life experience often feels pointless. But it would be ludicrous to keep waging wars just to fill classrooms with committed learners.

For me, the great benefit of the itinerant military lifestyle in the Cold War was constant exposure to different geographies. I loved moving every two years and found the prolonged residences of adulthood challenging, actually. There were many others, of course (my brother, for one), who suf-fered with the moves; but I was always more attached to places than people, so it wasn't such a burden. I mentioned Colorado earlier, and going back to our old house there more than fifty years later was a revelation, not be-cause the house was so small, which I'd expected, but because the whole neighborhood was heavily forested. When we lived there it was a newly launched suburb on high chaparral, with no trees in sight except the little striplings recently planted. Fifty years later their maturity transformed the place.

Bettridge: I'm only just beginning to enjoy gardening, which I am adding to baseball as my determinate antithesis to writing. I have certainly found the physical need to have such things and ways of organizing time. If it is not too personal, I'd very much like to hear more about how you structure your daily, weekly, or yearly schedule to work these antitheses in, and more about what they are or have changed over the years.

Rasula: The personal is the most public, at least where these "antitheses" are concerned. I'm not an "outgoing" person in the glad-handing sense. I've never frequented cafés or hung out in bars. But when I'm away from my desk it tends to be way out. Circumstances dictate how. For about twenty-five years I was a runner, a serious runner at least five days a week. Not long distance, never more than about six or seven miles, usually three or four. Then I started playing soccer and did that for nearly twenty years, almost daily. If I could be born again I'd take a life as a top tier soccer player. Soccer added to the decades of my running regimen an unexpected sapience, like crossbreeding a greyhound with a vulture in an odd way. And speaking of greyhounds, we've had two retired racers who have provided the main source of my activity for many years (I finally had to give up soccer because I was playing with people decades younger: too much wear and tear). I've always had a knack for communicating with animals—and small children, though I prefer dealing with animals. I think I have an aversion, not to people as such, but to the cultural conditioning people helplessly radiate. I started being aware of this fairly young, when I perceived that most other kids would do whatever just because other people were doing it, and I instinctively recoiled. I didn't feel superior, just unwilling to partake. I remember an occasion when Archie Ammons told me in 1973, waving at a Jersey beach full of vacationers gleaming with sunblock, "I don't know who's right, them or me" (in terms of way of life, cultural orientation), and at the time I thought, *How could he be in doubt about that?* but I've been haunted by my peremptory judgment ever since. I still feel a deep disinclination to join hordes of people clumped into any scenario like that, from strand to stadium.

Bettridge: I'm interested to learn how memory works in your work, or how you imagine it as a motivating force; your interest in primary documents, for example, would seem to indicate a certain suspicion of memory, and yet much of your critical work is focused on recalling things to mind, for yourself and others, which suggests a desire to reshape our memories, so memory becomes foundational in that sense, personally and culturally.

Rasula: There's a profound difference between personal memory and what we call cultural memory. Cultural memory is a bird's nest constantly amended by new stuff; but it's a nest with a huge neon sign blinking over it, with changing messages. Cultural memory is often regarded as ideology, but ideology implies a program and there's nothing programmatic about cultural memory except when commandeered by those in power at sensitive thresholds, like after 9/11, or the bombing of Pearl Harbor. The slogan spouted by politicians (even Obama) about America being "the greatest country on earth" becomes a de facto sort of "memory," but it's really just a blanket thrown over the past to put it out of mind. That slogan is impervious to the legacy of slavery that touches everything in this country, for instance. So the slogans are certainly programmatic and ideologically saturated, and the neon sign blinking overhead conveys nothing but slogans, but in the bird's nest of cultural memory everything happens at a different level, a vagabond zone like that charted by Michel de Certeau in *The Practice of Everyday Life*. In the Reagan era, when Foucault's influence was paramount, there was a lot of leftist agonizing about whether all behavior was ideologically tainted. My sense is that the subsequent cultural fixation on vampires reflects the way cultural memory works. A fantasy domain with its own rituals and protocols is ceaselessly revisited in order to work through (in the Freudian sense) a trauma that can't be assimilated. The dominant fantasy domain when I was growing up was the western, and it's fascinating to look back and observe how suddenly that genre vanished, almost as if the appellation "Camelot" applied to the Kennedy White House disabled the cowpoke topos in a single stroke. Monument Valley and Sherwood Forest don't coexist.

The "suspicion of memory" you sense in my work has less to do with these vast ideological dominants and more to do with resource management in cultural ecology. The handling of the midcentury poetry canon, I might have argued (but didn't, simply because the analogy didn't occur to me), was similar to the behavior of the petrochemical industry, denying all the toxicity generated by its version of status quo. I was suspicious of the *selective* memory enshrined in anthologies and textbooks and literary history. The delicate part was figuring out what constituted deliberate omission, and what could be chalked up instead to laziness, indifference, or forgetfulness. Looking at the New Critics, I also came to appreciate the fact that advocacy has its limits: that is, one tends to advocate for a modest sample, whether you're canonizing poets or making an appeal to salvage a natural habitat. So I became a bit leery of presuming that a critic's advocacy of X entailed a surreptitious disavowal of Y and Z.

Tribal fixations may be unavoidable. When I was young, being attuned to Black Sparrow poetry meant being indifferent to whatever was going on with the Yale Younger Poets series. Today someone who's focused on the output of Omnidawn or Fence may be heedless of whatever Knopf or Norton are up to (much as they'd be missing out on poets like Kimiko Hahn or Cathy Park Hong—but their work probably gets noticed more by those whose charter is ethnicity). Is there "memory" involved in these predetermining lenses? If so, it's an anticipatory memory, open—maybe blank. When mushroom season comes along I keep returning to the same sites, which is a culinary equivalent to relying on certain presses and journals, following certain musicians, tuning in to particular radio programs, and so on. And some places previously swarming with chanterelles are vacant.

There's a judicious link between *memory* and *commemoration*, and it's the latter that has the most bearing on issues of literary or artistic history. The exigencies of personal memory can effectively blunt recollection; years go by and you do forget names and even people. So I can see how some people simply drop out of the history, unintentionally. But there are deeper structural issues at play that are transpersonal, and that's what I drew attention to in 1983 in the *Sulfur* article "A Renaissance of Women Writers," in which I raised the issue of what modernism would look like if canonized titles by men had gone out of print long ago—out of sight, out of mind— and suggested that that's exactly what had happened during the decades (half century, more like it) when Mina Loy, Mary Butts, Laura Riding, H. D., and even Gertrude Stein were more or less forgotten. That was a case in which the then-inevitable commemoration of male writers structurally obscured the "memory" that women had been major players in modernism. From a certain angle, in fact, *modernism* in Anglo-American letters might be defined as the eruption of women for whom the term "poetess" struck their contemporaries as so obsolete and degrading as to be unacceptable.

Bettridge: Do you think there is room for the sublime in criticism? Is an experience of the sublime possible, a worthwhile goal, for critical writing? Have you ever experienced the sublime in criticism?

Rasula: That's an unnerving and curious question. My impulse is to say that the sublime—with reference to its theoretical legacy—is inapplicable to all but the most extreme instances of human activity or production. In "Heeding the Heedless Sublime" (online *Omniverse* 33 in 2013) I have an image of the Central Arizona Project diversion canal that siphons off Colorado River water across three hundred miles of desert. The aerial photograph qualifies it as a sublime spectacle of the sort that Enlightenment philosophers would have recognized as such. But the question is, can more diminutive human creations qualify as sublime? Are there paintings, poems, musical works that impose an incalculable grandeur? Everything about our commitment to, and enthrallment with, works of art makes me think: *Why not?* Once you take that step, of course, you come dangerously close to buying into the whole vocabulary of monuments, and the canon as coercive weight comes crashing down. I suppose that was even the case with particular mountains in the old reckoning of the sublime—Mont Blanc rates higher than the adjacent peaks?! I don't want to venture into that sort of calculus, which is inapplicable anyway, because the sublime was never intended as a rating system. In Kant's understanding, the sublime is that which you can't get your head around. But to apply that to a book would misleadingly suggest that only the immature and untrained reader will sense the sublime; and to see a list of what *those* readers prize would not amount to a dossier of the sublime.

I think something closer to a meaningful sense of the literary sublime would be Emily Dickinson's reference to having the top of your head taken off. The range of possible experiences as a reader may be more extensive than the variety of things to be read, and Emerson's sense of the exalted mind getting high on a bare list of words suggests that the reader's sublime is existential, not exegetical. There's no sublime "content" deposited in the Pandora's box of the text, to be opened later by a suitably qualified recipient. The sublime is a meeting of mind with an openness that could plausibly be called mindless, if by that we mean not stupid or unthinking but upending the parameters of mind. In the Buddhist sense, at that point you're just left with *mindfulness.*

Your question deposits the sublime right in the bull's-eye of a supposedly debased, perfunctory, pro forma exercise that barely crosses any finish line of literary finality: "criticism." The whole genre, after all, is compromised by its obligatory protocols, its obeisance to institutional standards of "productivity." In many ways, literary criticism amounts to little more than interoffice memos taken to a bombastic extreme. In the old culture of belles lettres, an interplay was presumed between creative artists and a culture of generalized intelligence (I'm thinking of people like James Huneker and Paul Rosenfeld). But can the same be said about the relations between poets and scholars today? A tendentious question, obviously. The stylistic and procedural impediments of scholarly writing keep anybody at bay who isn't professionally invested, so I can't imagine why poets would check out the latest entries on "contemporary poetry" churned out by scholarly publishers. On the other hand, with more and more poets hanging onto the lifeline of academe for a living, they're closer to the fire, so they must feel some heat. But there seems to be more avid attention to internet chatter and the blogosphere, and stimulating as that may be, I assume that's not where your question is directed.

So, back to the sublime in criticism. Speaking personally, I'd admit the possibility insofar as a book may cohabit an imaginative space coextensive with poetry. We're lucky to have that in the figure of Whitman, whose prose and poetry are closely aligned and almost indistinguishable. Emerson and Thoreau both provide models, for me anyway, of a prose I prefer over most poetry. Without getting into fine points, these three Americans add up to a heady blast of the sublime, and between them the scale is tilted toward prose—albeit not really "criticism." Adding Dickinson to the mix trumps criticism altogether while plunging you into unmistakable blasts of the sublime. But these examples suggest why I resist the notion of criticism, which after all means *judgment*. I've avoided value assessments (better and best) in my writing, not because I prevaricate or doubt myself but because that's the side of criticism I find most discouraging. It's in cahoots with anthologists of the weakest and most derivative sort, the ones who compile canonical anthologies by poaching the names and often contents from previous anthologies, adding one or two tepid updates of their own. One of the things that mesmerized me in the 1970s about Harold Bloom was his unabashedly judgmental ranking system (Ashbery and Ammons: that was *it*) in a body of writing that seemed wholly absorbed in other matters; and his "revisionary ratios" remain for me an instance of critical writing hot in pursuit of the sublime. The closet drama of Bloom's own "readings" are almost unreadable, but that's beside the point in the end. *The Visionary Company* provides helpful and intelligible interpretations of the basic corpus of English Romantic poetry, but by the time he got a bead on contemporary American poets the theories outpaced exegesis. It marks a limit worth noting: literary criticism that operates on a plane of awareness about one centimeter above any possible text.

That's the incentive behind my flamboyantly "close" reading of Charles Bernstein's "Dysraphism" in *Syncopations*, first drafted around 1992 or '93. It was around that same time I wrote a comparably close-up essay on Joseph Conrad's *Nostromo*.[5] I was engaged then with a series of evocative theoretical investigations of hermeneutics, only one of which was ever published, "Syncope Cupola Pulse" at the end of *Syncopations*. That sort of writing is perched at a cusp between poem, notes, and exposition. I thought of it as critical writing pared down to a fine point. It provided a forum for my propensity for acute condensation most evident in *This Compost*—a book some reviewers clearly regarded as a poetic composition passim. I wouldn't disagree, and of all I've published it's unquestionably the closest model for attempting the sublime in critical prose, personally speaking (that is, I feel it that way, but am hesitant to suggest it as a model for others).

To cut to the chase, then, my sense of the sublime is obliged to German Romantic poetics, in which there's no fast distinction between theory and practice. They imagined a kind of open field in which each poetic object/event would also have to suffice as the theory of itself. Every poem inaugurates its own terra incognita, and would have to provide resources for the cognitive response. When I sense that equilibrium, I'm willing to call it sublime.

Bettridge: One thing I've found productive about the poetry communities I tend to engage is their status as, or participation in, secondary markets, or gift economies; of course, that is true only up to a certain point, and in very narrow ways, and I hardly mean to suggest that poets and critics need to go find a popular audience. But I wonder if it might be useful to push against my assumption a bit, rather than become too enamored by the lack of popular appeal of what I like, like some music aficionado who only likes bands that nobody else has heard of. And in this same line, how do you, as an essayist, write something that you believe even as you proceed with the understanding that it should still be worthwhile for somebody else to read?

Rasula: I'm intrigued by this complex array you've sketched out. The question of essay as/and theory is compelling. The term *theoria* in Greek originally means the testimonial provided by a pilgrim to a sacred site or event. So it's "witnessing," with a definite obligation to *behold*. The three wise men at the manger, in that respect, were primordial theorists. I certainly want to hold—and be beholden to—that sense whenever I think of the possibility of the essay, essay as probe, not just probative. It's a perspective that instantly discloses the liability of our inherited understanding of essay as argument. To behold is to find oneself transported beyond the realm of proofs. Ecce homo: I am the man, I was there, and as I was there I came to know. Now, this is not to countenance an unquestioned priority of personal testimony. Rather, it places a sanctioning burden on the existential experience.

So the *theoretical* account, in the original sense, would be close to Thoreau's gambit in *Walden*, as he makes himself out to be the measure of an experiment, an experiment transacted (so he presumes and suggests) on sacred ground. It's a "democratic" experiment in that he knows full well there are no such claims on Walden Pond; it's just a local pool, with a railway embankment nearby, and a few woodlots around it—a civic site more than anything that might qualify as wilderness. And yet his insistence on discerning the wildness it may accommodate is where his *theoria* or witnessing takes hold.

Where, then, or how, do we distinguish "between theorizing and writing an essay"? Actually, I'd like to hear you elaborate on literary criticism "under the spell of theorizing." I expect we have different perspectives on that, for generational reasons, as I lived through a genuine *spell* that extended from the midseventies into the nineties. I remain intrigued by the circuitous manner in which continental theory percolated into the North American environment. Histories have been written, confirming the role played by Yale faculty and the significance of the 1966 Johns Hopkins conference that brought Lacan, Derrida, Barthes, Todorov, and others over from France (published as *The Structuralist Controversy*). But historians don't know about the subaltern literary milieu in which, for instance, excerpts from Foucault's *Les mots et les choses* appeared in Richard Grossinger's *Io* before its commercial translation. I recall the first Ethnopoetics conference in early 1975 abuzz with references to continental theory, along with semiotics, cybernetics, information theory, and a lot more. In those quarters attentive to Olson's ramshackle but inspiring penchant for essay-cum-bibliography (especially the miscellany gathered in *Additional Prose*), "theory" was part of a grand eclectic adventure that ranged from the ruminations of Carl Sauer to the latest intellectual flares from Paris. At the time, my sense that the poets were first at the table was confirmed by the TRG (Toronto Research Group) exchanges in *Open Letter*, mostly involving Steve McCaffery and bpNichol. This preceded the convulsions that rippled through academia. *Boundary 2* was a kind of interface between the literary world (the title was a nod to Olson) and academia, publishing my interview with Nathaniel Tarn in 1974 (Tarn effortlessly straddled the two realms, and was editor of the series of small format Cape Goliard books, with titles ranging from Lévi-Strauss to Zukofsky's *"A" 22–23*). Around that time the *Georgia Review* took a deep plunge into theory when John Irwin became editor (author of a great book called *American Hieroglyphics*, and poet under the name Bricuth), but that only lasted about two years before it reverted to its belles lettres orientation. I must have been one of the few in its history who subscribed *only* during its dalliance with Derrida and company.

By the time I entered grad school in 1986—when History of Consciousness at UC Santa Cruz was its national apex—theory had become a kind of raging affliction everywhere. To *think* meant to strap on a theoretical thinking cap. But the proliferation of perspectives from different theorists increasingly forced people to limit themselves to one or two because it was just impractical otherwise. Consider what it meant to "do" continental theory: anything emanating from Paris presumed a thorough familiarity with the work of Marx, Hegel, Nietzsche, and Freud. Now, seriously, who had time to assimilate all that *plus* keep up with the torrent of translations (to say nothing of the originals) gushing forth the latest from Lacan, Barthes, Foucault, Derrida, Kristeva, and an ever-expanding tribe? Understandably, the result was an odd combination of grandstanding and faking it, at least in American universities. It's interesting now to thumb through the run of various journals: you can see wave after wave of current theory percolating through the contributions like a newly patented pharmaceutical. And then, a few years later, no trace, as if a purgative had washed it out of the system. The symptomatic model in literary studies was old school close reading spiced up with a dose of some Lacanian or Foucauldian additive. Mostly deadly, with occasional brilliance. My general impression, though, is that many people didn't know what they were talking about and were parroting current trends just to keep some skin in the game. And it was a high stakes game, for sure. From MLA job ads during that time it was clear that every English department in the country thought it necessary to have a resident theorist, and as the tsunami of theory grew, many departments tried to hedge their bets by getting a theorist for each trending current. The upshot, finally, was that faculty members thought it incumbent to declare a theoretical allegiance as a sort of intellectual armband. Somewhere along the way the vogue for postmodernism came into play, and that became a catch-all term for the whole spectrum of available theories; and then the bubble burst, early nineties. Suddenly "theory" and "postmodernism" simply stopped being viable references. But since you've raised the issue of theory, I assume there's an afterlife I'd be intrigued to hear about.

Bettridge: Until recently, our English major had a theory requirement, as did our MA, and even though we've revised that requirement they continue to read theory in many of their classes, and all our students write research papers, etc. More and more, however, I find myself wondering what we want our students to gain from their engagement with theory and I find myself encouraging students to turn in essays that are a mess—nonpolished prose, often short, almost occasional, close readings. I care less and less that they demonstrate theoretical and critical competency. And when it comes to research, I just want them to read as much as possible between their jobs, other classes, families, and not worry so much about incorporating secondary sources into a polished essay. I want them to write essays that are useful for their lives—and it happens, these are often essays that simply engage the text at hand, essays that attend to a poem's logic because what it seems many students want to do is practice thinking, and work on their prose, both of which are hard enough on their own.

Rasula: The term *theory* has been a gateway drug, of sorts, in that it beckons the innocent (Jamesian) American chastened by a leering European in the dungeon of experience (a.k.a. unimaginable thoughts, prancing around in a prose of "pleasure" induced by pain). This deliberately Sadean scenario literally has the Marquis standing behind it, chastening *thought* as such with its wardrobe of erotic tourniquets. I do wonder, at times, whether a proper understanding of Foucault is only available to those who survived, against all odds, the gay bathhouse culture of San Francisco. All the other "uses" (abuses) of his work are speculative, filled with supposition—and opportunism. Likewise Barthes, whose *Barthes on Barthes* I found the most compelling of his works, not just because the title seems to aim himself *at* himself (pain again!), but also because it reveals the deeply autobiographical roots of a compulsion to theorize: a close order drill, a reality check on what we ourselves witness, day after day.

I think the main reason theory continues to be associated with European examples has to do with the American educational system, which is disciplinarily *compulsive* in a manner that tends to inhibit any infusion of thinking with imagination. Despite the political leanings of most faculty, American universities are hotbeds of foreclosed conservatism. Not that everything is about tradition and precedent; rather, the system structurally impairs its operatives. "Keeping up with the scholarship," demographically speaking, is lifetime servitude, ball and chain. Who wants to be Houdini? Compared to the disciplinary self-policing of Americans, the venturesome promenades of European scholars (in translation) seems like an unchained melody. Think of Agamben, for instance, a "philosopher" whose work ranges from animal rights to medieval poetics and angelology. Not happening in an American philosophy department! The result: Agamben's a rock star, relatively speaking, while the last publicly visible American philosopher may have been Richard Rorty. But of course Agamben operates in a milieu in which the role of public intellectual still survives. Here, by contrast, the "anti-intellectualism of American life" (to quote the title of Hofstadter's classic book) comes with a smiley-face emoji.

So *theory* dangles at that impossible altitude where American academics are consigned to *commitment* as inconsequentiality. Maybe this overstates the situation, but by and large "intellect" in American life means speaking to the converted, a system bolstered by academic institutions. I wish I could come up with a viable alternative, but I really don't see it—despite, for instance, the salutary role played by Judith Butler as public intellectual. The environment is itself as *specialized* as academia. Popular culture is its own ivory tower, despite accommodating hundreds of millions. It's not like legions of skeptics tune in to Fox News (I just mistyped that: *Fix* News!) just to see what's going on over there. By the same token, I don't imagine Jameson and the other Verso authors are "winning hearts and minds" (to patch in the foreign policy slogan) to the cause. Marxism is a seminar room here, whereas in Europe it's a lingering ingredient in politics.

Mention of Jameson reminds me of your reference to "good prose," not because I think of him as a great stylist, but because he writes sentences like a cowboy handling a lasso, with a lot of circular sweeps before tossing it over the cow without getting it caught on the horns. There are places in *The Political Unconscious* where a single sentence exceeds a page. Jameson's prose keeps me interested even when I can see a mile off how he's building up to yet another recapitulation of the message he feels duty bound to impart. Reading *Fables of Aggression* on a bench in the Huntington Garden in Pasadena in 1979 remains one of the luminous reading experiences for me. A whole book on Wyndham Lewis—whose work I'd never even tried to read—kept me spellbound. This kind of reading experience always seems to integrate the environment with the text, like that great passage in *The Professor's House* when Cather's character Tom Outland recalls reading Vergil atop a southwest mesa: "When I look into the *Aeneid* now, I can always see two pictures: the one on the page, and another behind that: blue and purple rocks and yellow-green piñons." Reading theory in the hands of someone like Jameson, then, evokes a standard less contingent on the case ventured than on Barthes's pleasure of the text.

Much concerning theory has to do with the disciplinary milieu from which instances emerge and to which the authors refer. So the misleading reference to "French theory" obscures the pertinent backgrounds of particular writers: Lacan (psychoanalysis), Barthes, Kristeva (semiotics), Derrida (phenomenological philosophy), Serres (biology and cybernetics), for example. For the Anglo-American student, unintended intellectual confusion ensues—*especially* when the home base is in an English department, where the disciplinary orientation even in the heyday of high theory still retained the periodizing of literary history. So "theory" tended to operate within certain area studies, like Fish and Greenblatt in English Renaissance scholarship. When I was teaching in Canada in the nineties, theory was belatedly making its claim for a place in the curriculum, and these issues were quite transparently on display in disputes about its relevance and acceptability. Most of my colleagues were advocates of the particular theoretical approach that prevailed in their field: feminism and psychoanalysis for Victorian lit, Marxism for Romanticism, New Historicism for early modern. When those colleagues taught the required theory course for majors, the syllabus consisted largely of samples of theoretical "approaches" within these historical fields, with a smattering of Aristotle, Plato, Kant, and Hegel as a kind of vitamin supplement. That wasn't my approach, but I could see the disciplinary sense it made, intuitively confirming theory in service to interpretive possibilities.

In most cases, some theoretical paradigm emerged initially as a way of solving a local problem in a scholarly discipline. Foucault, for example, made possible a way of accessing and speaking about history apart from

the usual roster of names and dates and the attribution of historical efficacy to movers and shakers. Derrida recalculated the ratios of agency in
textual rhetoric, aiming at a target in philosophy that turned out to have
greater bearing on literary hermeneutics. But to generalize such solutions under the general heading of "theory" makes it misleadingly seem
like theory is a self-contained discipline. By now, of course, there's such a
huge corpus of writing that qualifies as theory it might as well be a discipline of its own. Pragmatically speaking, who has time to read all the ba-
sics? But if you're that immersed, you end up speaking in an echo chamber.
In fact the most antisocial public lectures I've witnessed in the past decade
have been cases in which scholars chose to delve with microscopic exactitude into theoretical issues so rarefied I doubt anybody in attendance knew
what they were talking about or what was at stake. That's the sort of thing
that gives theory a bad rap, though of course it's not all that different from
the normal period/author-specific talk, the difference being that the latter is
self-identifying—you'll at least know you're hearing a talk on a poet you've
not read—whereas "theory" however construed seems to portend something of general interest.

Bettridge: You mention reading *Fables of Aggression* as a "luminous reading
experience," and particularly intense reading experiences have been in the
background of much of our conversation; it would be great to hear about
other such reading experiences.

Rasula: "Luminous" is a word I used phenomenologically. I didn't mean it
in any aesthetic sense, or as a substitute for "a great read," say. It's a word
with an aura around it. One of my favorite titles is Gustaf Sobin's *Luminous
Debris* (made resonant for me in part because he showed me some of the
artifacts he'd found in the watershed near his house in the Luberon, and
took me to the very site where he found one perfectly preserved Roman
jug). That's why I quoted the passage from Cather, because it evokes the
aura. The Emily Dickinson quip about having the top of your head clipped
off by a poem is maybe a reference to what I mean, though her image
is masochistically supercharged in her unique way. For me, the lumi-
nosity always entails an environment, as if the text somehow leaches into
the surrounding atmosphere and gives off a kind of sonar ping, but almost
visually.

   I deliberately read *Moby-Dick* for the first time on a camping trip up the
northern California coast, knowing that every time I looked up from the
page I'd see the Pacific, the heaving surf, the boulders, and sometimes seals
and sea lions, all the while hoping for a whale. That was choreographed,
admittedly, but Melville's book may have had the same impact if I'd read it

in a bank vault. Calvino's *The Baron in the Trees* is another novel I experimented with by reading it on a platform about fifteen feet off the ground in a pecan tree in my backyard (it's a novel about a guy who, in a snit, flees the family dinner table and climbs up a holm oak, never to descend). The glow I associate with certain books doesn't necessarily reflect my estimation of them, or appreciation for them. I have slippery memories of reading and rereading Wallace Stevens's poems in the sauna in my parents' house in Helsinki ("she sang beyond the genius of the sea"); oddly, I recall rereading Rilke's *Duino Elegies* in the Dallas airport. The first chapter of *Ulysses* is seared into my skull, it feels, along with the dormitory room I lived in during the eleventh grade at Frankfurt American High School, where I'd bought the black-covered Penguin edition when it first came out in 1968 (the English language bookstore in Frankfurt was a Penguin outlet, and *Ulysses* was the only title that didn't have art work on the cover). That first chapter was so delectable I just kept reading it over and over, and didn't get into the rest of the book until several years later. I read *The Unconsoled* during a trip to Ghent, unexpectedly the perfect site for that novel—not least because I kept getting lost late at night, a seamless match for Ishiguro's oneiric mood.

Sometimes a book can feel like a lozenge, textual Alka Seltzer, but instead of dissolving in water it dissolves the sphere around it into the text itself. There's a poem by Louis MacNeice that gives off that vibe for me, called "Snow," reading the first line of which I can see as clear as day the window looking out on a balcony in my parents' house in Helsinki, with snow outside. Here's the first stanza (I probably haven't reread this in forty years!):

> The room was suddenly rich and the great bay-window was
> Spawning snow and pink roses against it
> Soundlessly collateral and incompatible:
> World is suddener than we fancy it.

I know why I associate Auden with the German railway system: not only because I read a lot of his poems on trains, but because he invited me to visit him down in Austria, though that trip never happened (my father forbade it because of an ill-timed *NYT* article disclosing Auden's homosexuality). I associate Prince Andrei's death in *War and Peace* with the upper berth of a sleeper car which I think of as being in Denmark, but was I ever on a train in Denmark? It must have been a hotel room. In the autumn and winter of 1975–76, while my wife was growing big with our first daughter, I spent a lot of time in the New Hampshire woods, reading in interludes; so Beckett's *Mercier and Camier* is suffused with autumn leaves, and Zukofsky's *"A"* 22–23 (in that conveniently diminutive Cape Goliard paperback) is refracted with the snow I cross-country skied on.

Bettridge: As I read *Shadow Mouth*, and how you introduced the very idea of the "shadow mouth" as "a repeating machine, a waterwheel, a mill of particulars," I become more and more interested in how you use citation and this wide range of reference as argument, not just as argument making elements (Rasula 2009, 12). Could you speak to this formal characteristic in more detail?

Rasula: I love Benjamin's aspiration to produce a simulacrum of critical argument using nothing but quotations. Ben Friedlander accomplished that in *Simulcast: Four Experiments in Criticism* (2004), in which most of the material is sourced from Edgar Allan Poe, including a chapter called "Mr. Rasula's History," mapping a Poe text onto my book with name changes passim. It works, oddly—and it works *oddly*. A few years ago Jonathan Lethem published his manifesto for open-source poetics in *Harper's*, at the end of which he chronicled the sources of every sentence in his own seemingly original text. And the increasing ease of cut and patch audio sampling has made the technique ubiquitous, culturally speaking. You're clearly right to feel its proximity to the practices I've evolved, the most explicit of which was inducing a big chunk of an essay on *Don Quixote* by cannibalized citations from the scholarship.[6]

A long time ago I remember talking about "ventriloquial poetics," and probably published thoughts along those lines somewhere. This gradually merged with the attention to the legacy of the muse in *The Shadow Mouth* (that was my title, but the press insisted on demoting it to subtitle). It's a natural progression, it seems to me, that if you're writing exegetical criticism you get the text in bits and pieces in your head, so they subtly infiltrate and start taking over in moments of ventriloquized rapture. It happens more surreptitiously when a critic starts tilting the argument to the moment of quotation, when you feel that the quotation itself has summoned the argument rather than the other way around. There's an antiphonal dynamic, and explicit interplay, between text and countertext. I'm obviously describing what's happened to me—by which I also mean it's not a strategy, more like an existential buzz. So when I write it often feels like I'm prowling around in a Paleolithic cave full of inscriptions on the walls, as I burrow my way forward. The liability is a kind of regression to infantile play, losing sight of the "argument" altogether, just delighting in the shapes and sounds of the material. In any of my books you can probably find moments when you (as reader) sense something going on but can't parse it. Well, me too! I try to remove those patches, or refocus them, during revision. But sometimes it happens that my personal proximity to the crawl or trawl is still too close for me to recognize that the sense it *feels like* isn't likely to mean anything outside that sensory space Dadaist Raoul Hausmann called "the chaotic oral cavity."

To return to the question of citations, it's something I approach in a somewhat pictorial way, like collage. That is, I work with a cultivated batch, maybe 70 percent of which I'll end up using. The terms of use feel like careful placements of three-dimensional matter on a surface. This description will itself reveal that I rarely approach writing in terms of an "argument" (which may explain why I've had little success with grant proposals). The larger part of whatever gets worked into the fabric will arise as needed in composition. I don't have the kind of memory like Harold Bloom apparently had, quoting without even consulting the original, but I do have a pretty thick repertoire of afterimages, trace elements that can send me to a bookshelf and find the relevant passage in a heartbeat. Sometimes the heart beats more slowly, of course, and the more languid consultation yields rewards of its own. Horace Walpole's neologism "serendipity" names that circumstance. Geographically, I spend a lot of time on the exotic isles of Serendip.

Bettridge: Another form/style question: your attention to the muse leads you to employ a lush, often lyric prose style that often includes a religiously inspired vocabulary. Here is an example: "As the prophetic sensibility attunes itself to the vaporous moaning of chasms, the groan of trees in wind and the bubbling of springs, vocalization extends throughout a sacred landscape. The world speaks, while at the same time obliging *us* to be ventriloquists if we would hear nature's voice in our own language" (2009, 116–17). In the introduction you also write nonironically about the "sacred mission" of poetry. What role does this style and vocabulary play in how you want readers to respond to your text?

Rasula: Any devotional aspect of my writing acknowledges the transaction undertaken in any medium as sacred, above and beyond the profane. Pro-fanum = "before the temple," but once you cross the threshold you're inside, where a devotional care must be observed. It's a procedure of attention, which is to say a ritual. I feel close to a writer like Roberto Calasso, who in *The Ruin of Kasch* can be dealing with international diplomacy in the Enlightenment, while elucidating how all politesse can be traced back to the most remote rituals and forms of supplication. Without that broad anthropological reach, it's easy to get sucked into some freeze-dried sociological package disbursed in the jargon of the moment. One reason so many poets and novelists pay no attention to literary criticism is that they can sniff the chloroform a mile away; the prose reeks of "procedure," not passion.

It's interesting to consider how goal-oriented activities infiltrate our subliminal sense of behavior in general. There's a big difference between "I'm going to take a walk" and "I'm going to the market." Taking a walk is the more applicable model for most activity, though our current blizzard of techno-hyperactivity obscures that fact even more. I think the humanities are often at the mercy of unhelpful initiatives not carefully thought out, especially in an academic environment where the going standard of efficacy is "results." How would we begin to describe the *result*—or "outcome" (the European term)—of an article in a scholarly literary journal or book? Our system is slipping closer and closer to a kind of Nielsen's rating system, in which results are what can be concretely tabulated (number of citations, for instance). That says nothing about *efficacy*, though. Anyone can have a poorly written, rote argument, published in a prominent journal; it will tabulate "results" because of the venue; but these results will not disclose how many readers recognize the ineffectuality of the piece and simply put it aside.

This is a roundabout way of pleading the value of being "nonironic" about the "sacred mission of poetry." How can that be done in the jargon of administrative efficiency, evolved by ad hoc if strictly regulated means in an academic environment (in which secularism is the standard value)? From *that* perspective, I've always figured I'd have to play my hand straight and not try to convince anybody I'm playing another game. The risk is being taken as incompetent, clumsy, too serious or not serious enough, insufficiently informed, and so on. I've always erred on the side of *The Truth and Life of Myth*. I should also add—because the terminology you've asked about can be misleading, or assumptions can be made—that I don't mean "sacred" strictly in a religious sense, more in the sense of *dedication*, devotion, care, something that would as readily apply to John Cage as to H. D.

Bettridge: The direction of this answer seems crucial to me, so if you don't mind, could you extend it a bit? I want to ask how you might qualify the words, "dedication, devotion, care"? I mean "dedication to…"? "Care for…"? How? Why?

Rasula: There's nothing grandiose behind these terms. Anybody with children can intuit what's at stake, simple as that. Well, maybe not *anybody*, judging by the spectrum of malignancies that afflict children, ranging from addicted parents to those angling to assure their toddler gets in a queue for Harvard. With children, you want to protect them and at the same time encourage them to take risks. I was fascinated recently by an *Atlantic* article on the risk aversion of parenting now. The article quoted numerous parents of my generation whose childhoods were completely unsupervised. We were like free-range poultry. My daughters are grateful to have had the same upbringing in Echo Park (L.A.), but are acutely aware how rare that was for their generation, born mid to late seventies. And it's only gotten more antiseptic since. But to bring this back to my reference, John Cage embodies artistic risk, not by blindly striking out in aggressive or antagonistic ways but by exploring ambient domains without regard to routinized perceptions of propriety. Art as sensory exploration, at risk of becoming unrecognizable from the safety zones. Such behavior has always been depicted in middlebrow venues as zany, kooky, or in more ominous tones as unprincipled, even dangerous. That rhetoric refuses to recognize the care, devotion (dedication to the unpredictable) that goes into it.

Bettridge: Given your title, I was very interested in how little *Modernism and Poetic Inspiration: The Shadow Mouth* discusses Modernism as a movement, historical period, cultural force, aesthetic activity, etc.—in the more familiar academic book use of the word, if that makes sense. Can you say more about why you chose to write the book that way, and would you mind talking a bit more about how "Modernism" in that old-fashioned historical and aesthetic use of the term functions in your own thinking and writing?

Rasula: A simple answer, really. I didn't "write" the book so much as gather it. Rachel Blau DuPlessis launched the series at Palgrave and asked me if I had a book. Her query sparked the realization that maybe I did, combining previous publications with ongoing drafts. Of the six chapters, four drew substantially from publications. So "modernism" entered into it as a broad sweep of the hand over the bubbling cauldron, a gesture of ritual supplication.

Modernism is an unavoidable enchantment, in which a tale of disenchantment lurks, captivating some and distressing many. Part of the allure comes from the diversity and slackness of uses. In 1922 André Breton tried to assemble a "Congress of Paris" to investigate the spirit of modernism, an abortive effort that proved too controversial at the time when the famous *isms* (Futurism, Cubism, Expressionism, Dada) were still ongoing. Tristan Tzara refused to participate, saying he didn't believe in modernism—an intriguing response, suggesting it could be a derogatory term for those we unhesitatingly call modernists—but not surprisingly, because the more common use of the term "modernism" from the late nineteenth century onward was journalistic, and carried an innuendo of suspicion. It could mean *faddish* as well as *advanced*. It was only gradually, during the twenties and thirties, that it took on more positive implications, derived largely from industrial design, having to do with the modernist stylings of Norman Bel Geddes, Raymond Loewy, sans serif type fonts, and the architecture of Le Corbusier and others.

I've found it important to resist confining the term modernism to the English department version of "high modernism." It's such a blinkered view, with Eliot on the throne, Joyce in a palace outhouse, and the ambient buzz of intrigue. But even the expanded model of modernism is misleading—the one that adds Picasso and Kandinsky, Stravinsky and Schoenberg, Isadora Duncan and Martha Graham. "Not that there's anything wrong with that," to quote a fabled line from Jerry Seinfeld (on homosexuality). So my approach has thrived on attending to overlooked figures, like Mary Butts or Frederick Kiesler, who are worth the attention anyway but who reveal with unencumbered clarity the stakes of the game, because their reputations haven't been varnished over with layer upon layer of curatorial embellishment.

Bettridge: There is in *Shadow Mouth* a good deal of theoretical paradoxes, retractions, and negations. In chapter 1, for example you write about: Foucault, Blanchot, and negation (pages 13–14, among other places); "reading in order to unlearn reading, looking so as not to see, listening so as not to hear" (42) (and of course I love the revision of Jesus's words here); and "The artistic challenge is, how to accomplish the opposite of accomplishment? How to disclose and revoke at once. How displace intention by serendipity? How does one become precisely lucky?" (39); or the "murmur" as "the cosmic vibration that brings things into being and tears them apart in a single pattern of convulsive energy"; "Literature is the exhaustion of the salutary instance" (21). These examples are doing very different things critically, in terms of your argument, but can you discus what this explicitly philosophical or theoretical approach makes possible, critically and intellectually? Especially given the skepticism with which you've discussed the use of theory (in our profession specifically) in other parts of our exchange? How do you see what you are doing here with this mode and with these authors?

Rasula: *Shadow Mouth* is largely predicated on the aporia you note. Hopefully, I provided enough documentation to make it clear this is hardly original with me. Blanchot was a personal provocation from back in 1980–81 when I was typesetting the translation of his essays by Lydia Davis (*The Gaze of Orpheus & Other Essays*). Blanchot's vertiginous prose is unique, but his themes are part of the broader genealogy I drew upon for *Shadow Mouth*, going back to Mallarmé and extending its perturbations through

Foucault and Derrida and Kristeva. Blanchot himself was indebted to André Breton for transmitting Hugo's vision of language as murmur. This model of language harboring an extrasemantic dimension—inadequately evoked by the term "nonsense"—has been crucial to many artists and cults over time. Hugo Ball reveled in his discovery of long, multisyllabic entities in Gnosticism, justification he sensed for the magical advent of sound poems at Cabaret Voltaire. To cite Dada is to invite consideration of the role of chance in artistic expression, and that's a significant force behind *murmur*. Murmur suggests something you can't properly hear, so you compensate, making up what *might* be said.

Procedures of mis-attention and auditory obstacle have been germane to my own experience for a long time. When I was an undergraduate I had a friend read passages of Kant to me as fast as possible while I tried to transcribe what I heard. It was a procedural inducement to nonsense, deliberately extracted from the most fastidious kind of sense. Another time I plucked out all the italicized words in a text by Husserl, disclosing a laborious parade of emphases. A few years later, when Bruce Andrews contacted me and I was drawn into the fringes of the Language poetry scene, it was a relief to realize such procedures were acceptable. Shortly before, I'd been living in the Midwest, where the prevailing outlook on poetry did not just admire but was *mired* in James Wright, Robert Bly, Richard Hugo.

Your question makes reference to literature as "the exhaustion of the salutary instance," but it's important to quote the whole sentence. "Literature is the exhaustion of the salutary instance; and from this exhaustion a singularity is exhaled, disclosing the domain of one-of-a-kind"—a proposition instructively following a reference to *Moby-Dick* (which I generally offer up when people ask me what's my favorite book). In some biopic of Jack Kerouac, probably mid-1980s, Kerouac ruefully reflects (as lesson learned from becoming a celebrity) something like "don't make an example of yourself." And I found that resistance to exemplarity—well, exemplary. It was a goad to my investigations of canon, canonicity, masterpiece in the *Wax Museum*. This resistance relates to the murmur, and the whole Muse legacy, in that the creator/author knows, deep down, that such transmission is beyond legislation, if not blatantly out of control, and that any accruing personal glory is misplaced. It's a primal story with infinite variations. Why is Ahab Ahab?—because he lost his leg to a whale: the moment of chance that gives rise to his hubris, his moment of construing himself as an extra-human force. Isn't that the model of an artist?

Bettridge: In *Shadow Mouth* you seem to make a distinction between literature as a phenomena and particular literary works (page 21 in chapter 1, for example). Am I reading that at all right, or is that not quite it? If the latter, can you discuss why this distinction is important? How it allows particular critical approaches to a text, or the idea of one? This question might also draw in what you discuss about the relationship between language and discourse, and how literature attends to what the murmur emits, not what the subject reports, and the discussion of Foucault/Blanchot on 13–14.

Rasula: This continues from the previous (and you even cite the same page again). What I'm after here derives from the peculiarity of "literature" as a category. In practice, it summons a legion of exemplary works, a roster of masterpieces. Yet these works are singled out for their typicality. If you rotate the lens just slightly, finding a focal point in Hollywood, you get the same conundrum. Each "star" is one of a(n in)finite series—casting calls are notorious for assembling a room full of dead ringers—but plucked out of the lineup each seems singular, star-worthy. Leaving the star system behind and returning to the more pedestrian enclave of literature, the issue of singularity (and exemplarity) is enhanced because of the claims we tend to make concerning the typical. Every pedagogic approach in the classroom is destined to underplay the demonstrable weirdness of the text at hand. Nobody teaches *Moby-Dick* as the ultimate freak-book, but isn't it precisely that? How many of its readers, for starters, are Quakers?!—a category further reduced by the unlikelihood of their being whalers. And then, for head whaler, a peg-legged monomaniac. It goes on, and on, into a delirium of unapproachable specificity in the Land of Unlikeness. It makes for a wonderful counterweight to *Leaves of Grass*, in which the (originally anonymous) author does cartwheels to make his singularity seem normal, affably unexceptional.

So "literature" bears a peculiar sociological burden. It aspires to engage and depict the "human condition" with a cast of misfits and outcasts. Even if we take away the exalted category of "literature" and settle on genre fiction, like Harlequin romance, the same pattern recurs. The Harlequin plot makes necessary accommodations to the plight of the heroine, who can be anyone hankering for the unexpected, but the narratological savior is another oddity. He may not be called Ahab, but he's a thirtysomething widower with a charming five-year-old in need of a mom. How convenient. Sociologically improbable, but imaginatively powerful (this could serve as a definition of literature).

For my initial exposure to this anomaly I have to credit Lukács, whose rancor against modernism was based on his claim that it foisted atypical types on a guileless public. Leopold Bloom hardly qualified as Everyman, he thought, despite Joyce's expert ministrations. The work of literature,

Lukács insisted, was to render the "typical" in the most accurate fashion. A simple claim, it seems, but for me it opened onto an abyss. Like most readers of "serious" literature, I was always in search of something out of the ordinary, and even literary depictions of the ordinary were extraordinary in their own way, like those of Chekhov. So Lukács's seemingly innocuous reference to the typical struck me (and still does) as a misapplication of the term. The *typical* doesn't exist in literature, because "literature" is the categorical proclamation of the atypical. It nurtures the category of the exception.

My doctoral dissertation was titled "A Theory of Exceptions," by the way, though very little of it concerned literature. But it built the platform for subsequent investigations. I suppose it arose from longstanding experience of myself as an anomaly, something I surmised gradually as a child in visits to relatives. At a fairly early age I detected a certain insularity in their view of the world, and later came to see it was a natural byproduct of being grounded in a particular place, whereas I was moving every two years as a military brat. An advantage, but with liabilities. I saw the same pattern repeated in aesthetics, with its models, its calibrated dimensions of the beautiful, and its prejudicial consignment of deviation to the realm of the grotesque. In a truly ecumenical world everything would be understood (and celebrated) as an exception rather than a deviation.

Bettridge: Based on your previous answer and reference to Hugo Ball, I think I see where poetry might come in here, but, if you would not mind staying with it a bit longer, how does discussing this distinction you are making in relation to poetry (and avant-garde poetry in particular) redirect or expand on it, given that your main example above is a novel? Or another way to ask it: what is the poetry equivalent of *Mòby-Dick*?

Rasula: There's a sense in which poetry, being generally diminutive, can cast off bizarre specimens almost effortlessly. I suspect that Gerard Manley Hopkins played a huge role in making me expect this Moby-like characteristic even in lyrical moments. In large prose works the weirdness factor isn't always immediately apparent—unlike, say, a glance at the poetry of Jack Spicer or Emily Dickinson. Of course, poetry can also make my mind glaze over, especially when it seems to derive from an indiscriminately aggregate identity, when the "voice-over" one detects is not the humbling trauma of the Muse but a layer of contemporary sensibility averaged out into generic accessibility like an emoticon. I'm reluctant to make this sound judgmental, though. Although there's a prodigious amount of poetry that's of no interest whatsoever, for me it just recedes into vacancy like tabloid fodder. The fact that legions of other people are avid about something has never triggered much curiosity on my part, but I have to acknowledge that even poetry emits its own equivalents of bestsellers—by which I don't mean "popular" poetry, but poetry that aligns with a certain spectrum of tastes I don't share.

So what's the equivalent in poetry of *Moby-Dick*? A host of long poems, obviously, like *The Cantos* and *"A"* and *The Maximus Poems*, along with lesser known but comparably gnarly specimens like *The Anathemata* by David Jones, or *A "Mölna" Elegy* by Gunnar Ekelöf. But I'd return to the model of the diminutive I mentioned above: the great withdrawing roar of poetry's rubble-freaks.

Bettridge: I've been working on a book about our own moment's relationship to Modernism, and I find your discussion of periodization as a poetic vision very helpful.[7] Two questions, then:

> How do you read your own "urge to narrate beginnings and ends, to distinguish one sort of time from another"?

and

> What kind of knowledge do you think writing in such a vein produces? How can or should we use it, as readers, poets, critics, students?

Rasula: Historical writing, on any topic, necessarily feeds on the tropological possibilities of storytelling. This statement is a nod to Hayden White (my dissertation director), and it's as pertinent to how we talk about literature as about Hayden's domain of historiography. In the stories we tell, beginnings and endings tend to be provisional: that is, they reflect the occasion of their telling and are not strictly truth statements. But they do carry the force of key words, terms of temporal placement, like *before* and *after*.

As for any "urge" to narrate: I operate with an acute sense of periodicity, one that's been enhanced over time simply because I've lived more than sixty years now and have experienced some rather dramatic mutations in collective sensibility. Apart from merchandising equations like "the Sixties" and "the Baby boomers," there really are discernible shifts and rifts that have often been conveniently arrayed along nameable decades. When Janis Joplin, Jim Morrison, and Jimi Hendrix died in 1970, the same year the Beatles broke up—the year I graduated from high school—it became all too easy to pronounce the sixties dead, even though nearly everything associated with that decade persisted well into the seventies.

To address poetry or other cultural activities, periodization can be a precarious gesture. Artists in any medium often thrive on their historical fixations, so in some sense they can't be said to be strictly of their time. When

Ezra Pound confided to a correspondent in 1938 that he could still get sentimental about the Vagabondia books of verse by Bliss Carman and Richard Hovey, he was revealing a debt to a bygone era (his own youth, in that instance). So (playing off Kenner's conceit of a Pound "era") when exactly was Pound's *moment*? In the guise of Mauberley, he diagnosed himself as "out of step" with his time. When others were avidly exclaiming the advent of a new age filled with motorcars and airplanes, Pound was steeped in the world of troubadours. So I think we need to retain a sense of polytemporality when dealing with the creative imagination, which rarely consigns itself entirely to the present moment.

* * *

Bettridge: Since our last exchange, a number of events occurred—namely the larger controversy that emerged around conceptual writing and race in spring 2015 and the presidential election of 2016—and I wonder how they might have affected your thinking about the terms that have centered our conversation, notably the avant-garde, poetics, and the place of the academy in our present cultural landscape. Or perhaps a better question is, how do these two events help clarify, or add to your sense of what you take the work of poetics, poetry, teaching to be? Have any of your previous definitions of these key points of focus, or investments in them, shifted or changed?

Rasula: It sure does seem like the world has tilted off some axis, doesn't it? With Trump's election I couldn't help but be reminded of the Reagan era, which delivered a visceral punch at the time that seemed unprecedented, and I continue to be perplexed at the way the rightward turn of American politics, combined with the usual nostalgia for bygone days, has made Reagan out to be a jolly good bloke. The big difference now is social media, so the endless handwringing and bellyaching postinauguration on Facebook certainly registered the disorientation. There's no question that Trump is a clown, a psychopath, and completely unfit to hold any public office, let alone the presidency. But I think perhaps the tipping point came when it leaked out that Hillary Clinton called his supporters "the deplorables."

Now, I have an instinctual aversion to mobocracy, or even crowds—the most resonant thing I experienced in high school was Sartre's line in *No Exit*: "l'enfer, c'est les autres" (hell is other people)—and democracy means being in brutal proximity to those *others*. After some particularly unwholesome events in my department this year I jotted down this observation: "A university is a meritocracy mired in democracy." But politics replaces meritocracy with money, and not long before he died I heard Ted Kennedy say that "Congress is the best money can buy"—which he meant as a description, not an assessment.

But to get back to the "deplorables": they're far from being an ideologically uniform bloc. They do, however, reflect the economic ravages of globalization and the technological reduction of labor (e.g., factories across the country that used to employ hundreds are now staffed by less than a dozen). We are devolving society into an elite class and an underclass, with a terribly confused, afflicted, and dwindling middle. Combine that with longstanding disinvestment in infrastructure and education, and you get a sizeable populace bewildered by job flight, bad roads, meth labs, and opioids. Add the spin on all that by Fox, Breitbart, talk radio, and you get Trump in the White House. His base consists of the 24 percent who give him high-fives regardless of what he does or doesn't do, but that percentage wasn't enough to get him elected, so others voted for him as an act of desperation, like throwing pancake batter at the ceiling to see if it might stick. What his election revealed is that we're now treading the same waters as Germany in the Weimar era, where intuitively felt values about nationhood ran smack up against "imported" or "alien" institutions (like liberal democracy), while struggling with the global phenomenon of modernity. By modernity I mean all those beliefs and practices that promise and often deliver improvements to everyday life, however construed, but can't help doing so without unintended consequences. Twitter and Facebook are perfect examples of unintended consequences: envisioned as convenient interpersonal messaging platforms, they turned out to be perfect hosts of hate speech and predatory misinformation.

But the drift of America to a fundamentalist state can hardly be blamed on Trump, who's merely the most recent beneficiary of magical thinking. It may be more evident to those of us living in the south, but a recent article in the *Atlantic* ("How America Went Haywire" by Kurt Anderson, September 2017) reports startling statistics that may be imprecise or unprovable, but strike me as plausible: namely, that two-thirds of Americans believe the Biblical story of Genesis, believe in ghosts, telepathy, and the intervention of angels and demons in human affairs; and fully a third are convinced that climate change is a hoax, along with evolution (It's hard not to be unsettled by such figures, but it's even more shocking to think that the great majority of those who believe these things are stockpiling weapons and openly brandishing their firearms. In the USA more people are killed annually by firearms than all those who died in the Vietnam war (and this is about the same number as annual opioid deaths, and traffic deaths—a weird numerical synchrony).

Toxicity is the prevailing tone now, leached up out of the emotional sewage system facilitated by the internet. Anonymity clearly gives license to people's worst instincts, and since there's no end of things to tick them off, their instincts swell. What happened around Kenny Goldsmith's talk at Brown seems to have solicited the whole spectrum of possible responses, but most of what I saw combined a plausible retort (he bungled the issue of race) with a barely concealed glee that resentment over his meteoric career finally had an outlet. In the poetry world there's general consensus on issues of social justice, but social media has also facilitated a vigilante attitude toward perceived missteps. "Political correctness"—that chilling Stalinist slogan—is now out and about again, footloose and fancy free, juiced on the toxic abandon of American political havoc.

Bettridge: A last question, then: given what you said about the biological component of your writing and modernism, and the swarms it draws us to, how do you end writing projects like *Acrobatic Modernism*, or any of your other long studies? Given that they (like this exchange of ours) spread out and still feel incomplete, and given that the personal connection to them can feel more rewarding and urgent than the professional obligation to finish and publish, how do you, personally, stop? I ask in part because much of this exchange has focused on the role and form of criticism; in part because we recently realized we should try to finalize this exchange, which has proven hard to do over the years; and in part because with our shared interest in poetics that privilege openness, ongoing investigation, and fragments (which seem more easily sustained in poetry) we still can find ourselves at odds with the genre conventions of criticism, which move toward summary, definitiveness, and narrative closure—we are, in a way, using a genre to attend to a set of ideas and practices somewhat at odds with it, and nowhere does that become more apparent than at the ending.

Rasula: Wonderfully engaging thoughts and questions, Joel. By raising the issue of finishing a book, you've moved me to reconsider what a book is— not for the reader, for whom it's clearly a delimited object, but for me as author. That word also summons *authority*, which makes me realize the difference I've felt all along, book by book, in that I haven't felt myself to be authoritative, like a judge weighing evidence in a dispute. That *is* the role of a critic, properly understood (*krites* = *judge*). Yet the kind of adjudication so buoyantly exercised by Harold Bloom and Helen Vendler always dismayed me, especially given their notable discernment as readers. I felt that if you could produce such insightful readings it would be best to refrain from passing judgment. That may be fine for a review, in which it's sensible to exhort readers to consider a given item as exemplary, but it comes off like a squeaky wheel in a book. So what is a book?

Like most readers, I can only speak from experience, but for me a book (speaking *as* a reader) is a cabinet of marvels through which one wanders in amazement. Without the amazement it's lacking that special frisson that makes it a book. *Eccentric Spaces* by Robert Harbison, purchased in the Nepenthe bookstore in Big Sur on my first trip up the California coast in February 1977, could serve as Exhibit A. Not that I hadn't been thunderstruck by books before, but that one made me heedful of the marvel, and somehow predisposed to aim at such a prospect as a writer. Leafing through it now, I see that what got to me was Harbison's way of shuttling instantaneously between the most incongruous things, from Horace Walpole to *Finnegans Wake* inside a sentence; so although at the time I could claim familiarity with few of his subjects and references, I was somehow (stylistically, phenomenologically) already *included* as a companion or familiar of the journey. I'd already benefitted from this same sense of invitation from Olson, Duncan, and others, so you might say I immersed myself in *Eccentric Spaces* as if it were a long poem.

So how do I stop, finish a book (this percipient exudation of my curiosity), you ask. Maybe I've avoided that prospect by juggling so many of them at once, easing each departure. Whenever one's done, others are waiting. But the actual business of completion is more subtle, and protracted, the practical (and impractical) model of which is in the page proofs of Joyce's books, which clearly register composition as on-going right up to the moment of publication. My interventions haven't been that obstreperous, but I've availed myself of temporal possibilities, to be sure. In the end, *ending* or completing is different from *concluding*, and I've resisted the deliberative assessment of a *conclusion*. Last word? No thanks, or: I'll think it over. Get back to me!

An Ocean—a Notion—of Poetry

An Interview with Ming-Qian Ma

MING-QIAN MA IS the author of *Poetry as Re-Reading: American Avant-Garde Poetry and the Poetics of Counter-Method* and an associate professor of English at SUNY-Buffalo. His research interest is modernist and postmodernist poetry and poetics in relation to philosophy, science, and the arts.

Ma: As far as I know, you are the first, and probably the only, literary scholar and poetry critic who, in your recent work, has explicitly called attention to "a paradigm-changing state of affairs" evidenced in the contemporary poetry scene, in the current "condition of poetry." This "condition of poetry" pivots on a phenomenon of what you have referred to squarely as "glut," a surfeit of publishing poets and poetry publications resulting from the fact that now "everybody is a poet." While I certainly agree with you on your assessment that such a paradigm change "[has] to do with demographics," I do have a question regarding your position on "demographics," which seems to have been assumed as given, historical or otherwise. For as much as "demographics" can be, and has been, a viable "register" of the issue in question here, as your reference to Arthur Davison Ficke's 1911 observation clearly shows, the contemporary population explosion of publishing poets is, without any doubt, unprecedented.

Hence the following questions: Why is there such an explosion in the recent years, and from where or what does such an explosion result? Other factors granted (advent of digital technology, easy access to online publications, small presses, etc.), could it also be, and more pertinently, the direct consequence of the wholesale embrace, by the crowds, and hence swift popularization of the types of poetry and poetics that currently dominate the contemporary poetry scene? If such questions can be reasonably entertained at all, a follow-up question would be this: What is it, in these poetry and poetics, which appeals so irresistibly, if not unconsciously, to the populace, virtually guaranteeing that anybody who wants to be a poet can become a poet, even overnight? More specifically, your "indelible mug shot" of "conceptual poetry," the "post-literary micro-poetries," and "populist poetry" taken together, with which you begin your paper on "The Condition of Poetry When Everybody Is a Poet," and which remain the major examples therein, seems already to have implicated these three types of poetries, but especially their respective poetics, in their contributing to, if not determining, the "glut" phenomenon of contemporary poetry. In other words, could it be that the "demographics" in question is, to a great extent, as much a historical or technological phenomenon as it is a poetics one?

Rasula: Actually, the glut is far from recent. You only have to look at anthologies from the nineteenth and even the eighteenth century to encounter a surfeit of what anyone might actually absorb. Demographics are a defining feature of modernity—modernity being a plausible term for every social instance in which sheer numbers prevail. Poetry was immunized from demographic consequences for a long time, consigned to coterie culture, bound to a patronage system from troubadours through royal courts and aristocratic beneficence. But with print culture, increased literacy, and various forms of social democratization, poetry escaped that inherited genie and fled the bottle. So for generations of Americans, now, "poetry" seems a birthright, a sanctioned avocation, even as it retains its role in a market economy in which it can seem gratuitous, and possibly pointless.

No matter how widely disseminated, poetry is a minority affair. In American public and private life, for instance, "The Man With the Hoe" by Edwin Markham is as close to having served as *The* Poem as Poe's Raven; yet who's ever heard of it now? One person is Mike Chasar, whose fastidious plunge into the popular reception of poetry in the most unlikely places reveals that poetry is far more pervasive than anyone realized. But most people who self-identify as poets would probably find little of interest in Chasar's honey pot. So we should distinguish, when speaking of demographics, popular poetry and literary poetry. The two rarely coincide. To use a mass media analogy, literary poetry is more like the Amazon TV series *Transparent*, or an HBO show like *The Wire*, while popular poetry is closer to the bestseller fiction list, a network TV show, or talk radio. I'm speaking strictly of demographics here.

Bearing all this in mind, the glut I've written about weighs more heavily on the literary side, because by definition anything that's truly popular or pervasive is already in glut mode. What I mean by the poetry glut is the impediment to any attempt at coherent overview or assessment of the sort that has traditionally enabled cultural gatekeepers to make solemn pronouncements about the best and the brightest. Charles Bernstein has long campaigned against the gatekeeper model, celebrating the proliferation of poets and poetry as a demographic challenge to the implementation of authority. But the oddity of his position is that he's been speaking from a position of authority for thirty years, becoming by default another gatekeeper, which of course he knows and wrestles with (the rhetorical jiu-jitsu of his pronouncements is a marvel to behold).

It's curious for me to witness the eminence of old friends like Charles, Will Alexander, and Nate Mackey, poets whose work I valued but never imagined could win the sort of acclaim it now has. Their ascendancy reflects a gravitational shift of Official Verse Culture, the most conspicuous aspect of which I identified in the first chapter of Syncopations, "Women, Innovation, and 'Improbable Evidence.'" The point, very simply, was that you could eliminate the men and still have a surfeit of superb poets. That's not necessarily a recent phenomenon. In recent years I've been trawling through American poetry from 1910 to 1950, and unearthed dozens of interesting women I'd not heard of before. Many stand out from the prevailing idiom of their time, the "voice-over" as I've called it. The point here is that the gatekeepers of that era, like F. O. Matthiessen and John Ciardi, categorically left women out of the equation. By 1950 the poetry scene consisted of white male G. I. Bill Ivy Leaguers with special access to the gravy train of Guggenheims and other perks. The winnowing out of untold hordes by midcentury was a dream come true for the gatekeeper mentality, which thrives on a reduced sample of contenders. The question now facing us with our demographically enhanced glut is how anyone could pretend to speak authoritatively about "contemporary poetry" at large, or promote a modest number of "leading" poets. I've noticed that Dan Chiasson refrains from such pontifications in his periodic New Yorker reviews, which sensibly focus on the works of individual poets without venturing comparisons.

Another factor is the rise of the internet and its hapless promotion of special interests of every kind. As political commentators lament, it's now possible for anyone to exist in a bubble of pluralized narcissism, and the same applies to the poetry scene. Academically driven forms of entitlement and curricular readjustment—race, gender, disability, ecopoetics, etc.— are now full-fledged constituencies online and offline, each with its thriving poetry scene. It's a diasporic phenomenon, one that's reflected in the old-style (fitfully canonical) anthologies with their principled inclusion of poets based on the demographic categories they represent. Because the gatekeeper role is relinquished in favor of these preappointed templates, we end up with the awkward case that assessments are being processed only at the microlevel (which two or three Native American poets get the call, and how that gets parsed with respect to gender, etc.). I don't want to be misconstrued as saying that this way of bundling poets for anthologies is derelict; it's certainly no worse than the "we know who we are" model of Ciardi and his midcentury clan. But I do think that the current configurations so closely adhere to prevailing trends in academia that they risk obsolescence as those trends shift, which they tend to do.

Consider, for instance, the parallel rise of continental theory in the academy and language writing in the avant-garde. Theory prevailed just long enough for language poetry to get an academic hearing, but by the late nineties both were subsiding, the buzz of the previous decades tapering off. There are demonstrable ways in which their impact lingers, but my point here is to suggest that academia works with a built-in model of obsolescence similar to that of commercial products. So I can (dimly) foresee a time when future readers perusing an anthology circa 2010 will genuinely scratch their heads and wonder how *these* particular poets seemed to merit inclusion at the time.

You raise the issue of technology as a factor of the glut, and that's relevant. But I wouldn't overlook the preponderant role of the educational system, as creative writing programs (along with rhetoric and composition) are the biggest growth factor in recent decades as tracked by the Modern Language Association. In the past forty years the number of creative writing programs has swollen from a dozen to nearly five hundred. Applications to our doctoral program in creative writing have risen in recent years while those on the scholarly side have plunged. I can envision a future in which English will more closely approximate art schools, with a majority of practitioners and a small contingent of art historians or, in English, period-specialist scholars. What this suggests about the future of poetry is an ever-widening sprawl of interconnected constituencies; so poets homing in on a certain ethos and poetics will have about the same level of interest as, say, a scholar of the eighteenth-century English novel. Will there be "stars" as this new system emerges? Undoubtedly, but it may have less to do with any consensus on the merits of the work and more to do with the volatility factors endemic to the internet, as mediated by the stakeholders in the writing programs.

Ma: I am intrigued by your strict demarcation between "inside-university" and "outside-university," a demarcation that parallels rather neatly the distinction between the "literary" and the "popular": Poetry of the "inside-university" is literary, but may engage popular culture, whereas poetry of the "outside-university" is, and remains, populist. I am wondering, however, about the extent to which such a demarcation is still tenable. After all, some of the "literary" poetry is not produced inside the university, such as that of Ron Silliman and Vanessa Place (even Kenneth Goldsmith's work cannot be considered, strictly speaking, as the product of the university). The issue, then, seems to be how the "inside-university," or the literary, absorbs the "outside-university," or the popular, and I will come back to this topic later.

My question now is about the very understanding of poetry. It seems that you hold a "reflectionist" view of the contemporary poetry. As you put it, poetry today "reflects a wholesale transformation of American culture in the past thirty or forty years," which "have opened up the referential scope of poetry." This view not only situates poetry vis-à-vis culture but also assumes poetry to be passive, functioning merely to mirror the change of culture. My question is this: What is the relationship between poetry and culture *nowadays*? If "American culture" has gone through "a wholesale transformation," has American contemporary poetry also gone through such a wholesale transformation? If it has, what are the specific impacts of the wholesale transformation of culture on poetry and vice versa? And consequently, what has become of poetry, and what is poetry *now*?

The answers to these questions are, to some extent, relatively clear in the context of the radical cultural changes in the 1970s, 1980s, and 1990s, which have given birth to an equally radical understanding, radical concept, and radical practice of poetry, evidenced powerfully in Language poetry that articulates, reciprocally, a "cultural poetics." In the context of the cultural changes since the 2000s, however, the understanding of the so-called post-Language poetry of various sorts, but especially the conceptual poetry, remains nevertheless ambiguous, and there has been strong resistance from different quarters of the contemporary poetry scene to any effort to probe this issue. As rhetorical as it is largely coterie-based, such an ambiguity and resistance have already led to serious sociopolitical consequences. Therefore, it is imperative, I think, that we tackle the question of what poetry is in the contemporary period, not for reaching a consensus of any kind but for a historical understanding of our current poetic thinking and practice.

Rasula: These are fascinating questions, and I suspect you may have more to say on the subject than I do! But I do have a few thoughts, so here goes. Your second paragraph makes me realize that the "wholesale transformation" I had in mind is one that absorbs poetry as such into a broader wash of sociocultural phenomena. It's unlikely that there are any poets now who are immune to the internet, for instance. Whereas in the older domain of literary culture, when Robert Lowell held sway, it seems to have been possible to act as if the whole media world of the time simply didn't exist. Movies, television, even sports, were simply not on the horizon of poets.[1] Such phenomena didn't appear in the poetry, and weren't even a rudimentary integer of everyday awareness or interest in literary circles. Serious poets of an earlier era operated as if they lived not in the twentieth century but in a space apart, somehow—at least until Frank O'Hara and Ted Berrigan, whose naming rituals would now be construed as product placements.

In Lowell's day, the stakes were proprietary. Poetry was part of Literature, and literary matters were adjudicated in the university and disseminated commercially by New York trade presses. Literary prizes were administered by the joint trustees of these domains. There are few vestiges remaining of that system. Prizes have proliferated nearly as dramatically as creative writing programs, transforming the publishing apparatus into a giant lottery, albeit with fewer aspirants than the megabucks state lotteries. And the number of publishing venues has mushroomed as well. There are proprietary gestures here and there, but they don't appear to be taken very seriously. The anthologies make dutiful homage to the prevailing criteria of academia, so diversity in the sanctioned categories comes into play, but it's so transparently at the behest of market forces that the question of poetry is compliant with identity politics. I'm not disputing the social justice of such tactics, but suggesting that it has succeeded by releasing poetry from the helium balloon of Lowell-era aesthetics. Those aesthetics were predicated on criticism, which still had strong roots in the Greek origins of the word, meaning *judgment*. My sense is that there's little will to judgment in the contemporary arena, in part because the sheer mass of poetry renders it unmanageable; and the decorum of millennials' behavior frowns on agonistic rituals.

To be earnestly dedicated to reading and assessing the bulk of published poetry now would require far more than the regulatory eight-hour day. It could only be accomplished by a committee, and the committee would need to be the size of a military unit. I recently had the dispiriting experience of looking over the poetry section in a used bookstore in Philadelphia: I estimated there were about a thousand titles there, 90 percent "contemporary" (published in the past thirty years). I recognized many of the authors, but realized with a shock that I had read no more than two dozen titles. And I have been a committed, at times even voracious, reader of contemporary poetry for fifty years. Now I can't even keep up with the poetry published by my friends!

So the challenge of addressing contemporary poetry risks subsiding into scantily informed generalities, opportunistic advocacy, or concentrating on a handful of supposedly symptomatic figures, at the expense of any broader purview. Another, and more traditional approach, is to trace particular historical traditions and their trajectories up to the present, the way you can follow Robert Duncan through Nate Mackey and Michael Palmer today. While historically informed, that approach risks the synecdochic fallacy, taking a particular poetic vein for "poetry" in general—which, obviously, many are content to do.

You used the term "radical" repeatedly in your final paragraph, and it makes me wonder how the radical might be computed or even identified now. With the shock tactics of the historical avant-garde being commemorated in centenaries (and as an historian of Dada, I've been giving a lot of talks this centenary year), there's been a multigenerational legacy of radical interventions in all the arts, though poetry may be more conservative than most. So even today there are many who wouldn't regard the publications of Kenny Goldsmith as poetry, though they might recognize the conceptual pertinence of his procedures—unlike the way that, say, the late David Antin passed almost without notice in the poetry world of forty years ago. So if "radical" in 1970 meant *not poetry*, at least now it's regarded as a kind of poetry *over there*, in some acknowledged cul de sac.

The situation of poetry is simply part of the larger situation of literature generally, the most concise summary of which is this, from Amy Hungerford's book *Making Literature Now*:

> If the lopsided demand for creative writing courses over literature courses in universities and the weakness of trade literature sales have anything to tell us, it is that there are plenty of aspiring writers who seem not to read, or whose reading is culturally invisible. What if literary culture is thriving but is simply not shared, or shared only within tiny social networks, or shared between so few people spread so far apart socially or geographically that its tangible presence *as* a shared culture is impossible to sense? What if literary culture is a culture of making rather than a culture of reading? What if such reading is, first and last, a private act—untraceable, undocumented, and unspoken— and not the foundation of a public culture at whatever scale? (2016, 9)

There are several points of interest in this passage. First, on the issue of what aspiring (or even successful) writers read: Hungerford's supposition that they "seem not to read" is drastic, but it points to a plausible scenario. I'd estimate that what aspiring writers read now is commensurate with that of previous generations. The difference is that to have read that

way in 1920 meant being more comprehensively informed than reading
that way now, simply because the sheer mass of available texts is exponentially larger. Second, Hungerford's concluding question provokes serious
concern about "public culture," rightly so if shared reading is microscopic
relative to the dominant blockbuster mentality. And it's certainly something
I've witnessed, inasmuch as "literature" is generally registered by way of
novels, and Hungerford's attention to the success of Jonathan Saffran Foer
and David Foster Wallace reminds me of how many people I know (scholars, and others) have read those and other prominent novelists to "keep
up," but don't bother with poetry.

But even within the poetry world, I think it would be difficult to identify trendy figures whose new books everyone reads. Is there really a national wave of compelling interest in each new book by Ashbery, or Jorie
Graham? At the MLA last January I attended a panel on the state of poetry
now, in which Stephen [now Stephanie] Burt proposed that Claudia Rankine's *Citizen* was that rare book dividing now from formerly. It's plausible,
but if so it's not because it's a book of poetry but because it's a book that
makes compelling claims about race, and in that respect its success reflects the even greater prominence of Ta-Nehisi Coates's *Between the World
and Me*. Coates's book is now listed at #116 on Amazon's sales list, whereas
Citizen—with comparable awards and accolades—is #3,117 (yet by 2017 it
had reportedly sold some two hundred thousand copies). Pretty good, but
three thousand slots below Coates.

Finally, as to your hope that we might discern "what poetry is" at this
historical juncture: my own hope is that it may have developed a healthy
diversity in practices, outlook, and provocations to experience—enough so
that its inherited snobbism and the mystification surrounding it can seem
simply laughable.

Ma: Your observation that the "wholesale transformation" of American culture is "one that *absorbs* poetry as such into a broader wash of sociocultural
phenomena," which "*collapses* the distinction between inside/outside the
university," is, I think, not only historically discerning but also intellectually
helpful in understanding what poetry has become in the present. Indeed,
the "absorption" and the "collapse" in question are not only thorough but
also reciprocal, so much so that, in both aesthetics and formal tactics, for
example, the similarities between Hollywood and conceptual writing are so
striking as to be totally uncanny. From this perspective, Amy Hungerford's
"what if" question, such as "What if literary culture is a culture of making
rather than a culture of reading," turns out to be both intellectually hesitant
and conceptually belated, still positioned vis-à-vis culture at large. Just the
other day, for instance, there was a TV commercial on comedy, and the guy

said, to the effect, "Talking about whether a comedy is funny or interesting is absurd; doing comedy is another thing."

One question I have, in this context, is the issue of "Official Verse Culture." When you mentioned the "eminence of old friends like Charles, Will Alexander and Nate Mackey," more specifically, you attributed "their ascendancy" to "a gravitational shift of Official Verse Culture." Such a view seems to endow these poets and their work with a degree of innocence and passivity, as if they were waiting patiently for the Official Verse Culture to finally turn its eye on them and recognize them as such. Would it be more accurate to say that history repeats itself here, and that these poets and their works *have*, themselves, *become* the Official Verse Culture?

As you surely know, Language poetry launched itself as a reaction against and a critique of the Official Verse Culture, and it was Charles Bernstein who coined the term and he defined it very specifically in an essay titled "The Academy in Peril: William Carlos Williams Meets the MLA." In addition to other constitutive features, such as literary or academic publication venues, university poetry writing workshops, poetry prizes, and awards, "What makes official verse culture official," Bernstein contends, "is that it denies the ideological nature of its practice while maintaining hegemony in terms of major media exposure and academic legitimation and funding."

It seems that, nowadays, Language poetry and the post-Language poetry of various sorts have taken over all the domains that Charles Bernstein previously referred to as the manifestations of the Official Verse Culture: their poetries published in both commercial and academic presses (Chicago University Press, Norton, etc.) and reviewed in mainstream journals and magazines (*New Yorker, Boston Review*, etc.), their works winning major prizes and awards (Pulitzer, Ruth Lilly Poetry Prize, National Book Award for Poetry, etc.), their poetics and practices taught in university creative writing workshops (UB, Temple, Iowa, etc.), their poets elected into the Academy of Arts and Letters (Bernstein, Howe, etc.), their major representative invited to read poems in the White House (Goldsmith), and their accesses granted to media exposure, academic legitimation, and funding, all characterized, to various degrees and with some exceptions (such as those on race, gender, etc.) by an oblivion to, if not denial of, the ideological nature of their practice.

If all these are legitimate and acceptable observations, would you please assess, from this perspective, the condition of poetry at the present?

Rasula: Thanks for this provocative reading of my previous response. I realize that it's probably no longer useful to refer to Official Verse Culture, a term best consigned to what Bernstein originally intended. *That* OVC was clearly an old boy's club, by any measure. But your concern is whether the assimilation of Language-oriented poetry into major media outlets and institutions compromises the ideology critique from which it arose. Ideology critique back in the sixties and seventies was practically unheard of in poetry circles and in academic discussions of poetry, so the Language initiative brought that to the table. But the table, so to speak, has persisted as an ideology-free zone to the present, hence the irony of Language poetry being quasi-canonized with faint notice of its political claims. However, numerous books on contemporary poetry pointedly address this issue with reference to Language poetry and other provocations and practices, so there's been a shift in scholarship. The venues you cite (from the *New Yorker* to the Pulitzer) have rarely been regarded as hothouses of ideology critique. They're disposed to assimilate Rae Armantrout as handily as Mona Van Duyn, implicitly consigning *all* poetry to a low-level recreational curiosity.

Is there "passivity" involved in the elevation of poetic innovators to figureheads of Official Verse Culture? It's the wrong term, I think, implying acquiescence to a set of presumably alien norms. But I haven't noticed that Nate Mackey or Susan Howe write or behave any differently now than when they were obscure poets publishing exclusively in little magazines and small presses. Their careers, in fact, suggest that the official venues of poetry thirty years ago were so oblivious to the range of poetry, and so self-assured, that an entire replacement brigade rose up from the margins and eventually filled the vacancy—the vacancy being intellectual, not available seats. A revealing document in this respect is the *Morrow Anthology of Younger American Poets* (1985). When I wrote about it in *The American Poetry Wax Museum* a decade later, those "younger" poets were tenured figures in universities and prominent in the AWP circuit, but their days were numbered. *They* were the presumed heirs to the royal vestibules occupied by the likes of Mark Strand and Anthony Hecht and Donald Hall, but that system evaporated. There was no palace revolt, just a gradual shift in sensibility and a greater awareness of poetic diversity. I imagine the ascendancy of Ashbery had much to do with it, since his work clearly tilted the sensibilities of readers toward the cognitive dissonance of Language writing. Then Michael Palmer and Lyn Hejinian began to be noticed and even acclaimed by readers likely to be repulsed by Bruce Andrews.

In retrospect, a signal event may have been the early death of Robert Lowell in 1977 (he was only sixty when he had the fatal heart attack in a taxi). His dominance meant that a whole flotilla of his cronies was deemed worthy. (Writing *Wax* and parsing all those anthologies, I gradually discovered that they were amply stocked with Lowell's allies.) It wasn't instantaneous, but it gradually created a space in which, for instance, someone like

Robert Duncan could be noticed *as a poet* and not as a caricature of "raw" poetics.

Now, concerning the assessment you ask for concerning poetry today: it bears no comparison to these historical events. Lowell died forty years ago, and while we've had numerous poets momentarily lionized by one claimant or another (Jorie Graham, Anne Carson, Louise Glück, C. D. Wright— hard not to notice they're all women), nobody has replicated the leonine imprimatur of a Lowell (or, across the aisle, an Olson or a Ginsberg). Instead, diversity rules. I don't just mean diversity in the actuarial (PC) sense, but in forms of poetic reckoning. The key factor is demographic, the issue with which we began this exchange. It's a consideration that applies as readily to music, movies, television, *any* cultural activity in fact. If Lowell Inc. was the name brand of poetry during the postwar decades, *I Love Lucy* was the television equivalent. As long as there were only three broadcasting networks (NBC, ABC, CBS), TV shows always had the potential to acquire hegemonic status, and this lasted as long as *All in the Family* and *M.A.S.H.* And then came cable. My daughter Hilda spent three seasons working as a film editor on Jill Soloway's Emmy-winning show *Transparent* on Amazon, during which time I was constantly coming across articles about it, radio interviews, buzz, and yet nobody I knew had ever seen it. In the literary world, it's as if *Howl* could be published and would only be known to a small circle of initiates.

Something similar happened with poetry, and it was not attributable to ideology critique but to transfigurations of infrastructure. A revealing history of American poetry since the seventies could be written by documenting the impact of printing protocols established by companies like McNaughton and Gunn, founded in 1975: it was their pricing model that made it possible for me to launch *Wch Way* that year as a perfect bound 150-page poetry magazine, the size of which became an industry norm, still prevalent today in most poetry publications. I make a point of showing students (and colleagues) the contrast between standard format now and the diversity of print formats up until the midseventies. So what we now have is an abundance of poetry, nearly all of which looks interchangeable.

The ubiquity of the 6½ x 9-inch perfect bound poetry book is a handy symbol of the current predicament, which readily translates into the platitude "so many books, so little time." To be interested in "poetry" as such may be a winsome kink of character, but an implausible vocation. And it did used to be a vocation. Poetry is now an ocean, but there is no corresponding science of oceanography. All the expert witnesses operate as free-standing aesthetic tasters rather than members of an investigative unit. So awareness of poetry replicates the Robert Parker syndrome in the wine industry, with a ratings system as shorthand point of engagement. As Amazon handily demonstrates, poetry books get ratings, mostly perfect fives, and this sociological factor shovels poetry into the clan-specific bubble system that has, among other things, enabled the ascendancy of the alt-right in public discourse in the United States. I was about to write "But that's another story" before realizing it isn't. It's a continuum. It points to the great danger facing poetry today, that it's simply another product line in Amazonia. Walking down the warehouse aisles, you might look up and see a big banner identifying the poetry section, bearing the exasperating Auden declaration: "Poetry makes nothing happen."

Ma: You have highlighted some very revealing phenomena in the contemporary poetry scene and offered useful concepts and terminologies that help us understand, articulate, and put into perspective the current condition of poetry. I would like to hear more of your elaborations on them, but particularly in terms of some concomitant perplexities. Let me start with one of your epitomes. "Poetry is now an ocean," as you have aptly summarized it, "but there is no corresponding science of oceanography." This absence of a science of oceanography entails, naturally, a number of closely related issues, both conceptual and practical. What comes to mind immediately and most urgently is the question of the role of the critic and criticism. You touched upon this issue already in your exchange with Mike Chasar when you asked him whether or not his attempt at "critical validation of vernacular uses of art" based on his "faith in the Situationist *dérive*, or what [he called] re-purposing" also "[risked] abandoning the critical role altogether."

If, as you made it clear in that exchange, "the role of the critic, as the word in Greek means, is to judge," how does, or more accurately put, how can a critic or criticism go about judging a poetic work when "there is no corresponding science of oceanography"?

It is clear that the conceptual ambiguity and the pragmatic confusion regarding the role of the critic or criticism have been a vexed polemic for some time now, however implicit; but the urgency of this question has become so palpable lately as to be finally voiced out in Nathan Heller's review essay of A. O. Scott's book *Better Living through Criticism*. Titled "Says You" and published in the *New Yorker*, nothing in Heller's essay raises the concern more succinctly and pointedly than its subtitle: "How to Be a Critic in an Age of Opinion," which pursues the line of inquiry that you already started in your exchange with Mike Chasar.

While Heller's answer to his own question is not without interest, what is your response to this question? More specifically, what is poetry criticism without a science of poetic oceanography? How to be a poetry critic when, as Heller puts it, "a peacock spread of hermeneutic attention has become our basic greeting for creative work"? In other words, does a critic function nowadays no more than just a "freestanding aesthetic taster"? Finally, and what amounts to asking the same questions, are "critic" and "criticism" still viable conceptual-functional terms in the present condition of poetry in which "diversity rules"?

Rasula: Once again I have to thank you for coming up with such probing questions. The haunting reference to a science of oceanography reminds me how rapidly the looming planetary peril has descended, for there's a genuine science of oceanography behind that, one that should have had a more consequential impact on public policy.

As for the ocean of poetry, any critical "science" flounders for several reasons. One is a lack of consensus about what poetry is, what it can and should do. Instead we have workshop training that, being institutionally administered, is not really consensual, so any putative consensus is induced—like an administered sedative. Another reason (to sound that old horn again) is the "glut." Any critical strategy is tacitly propped up by a general understanding of a suitable domain, and such a domain was readily at hand in the raw-versus-cooked debates, when critics might choose not to read the opposing side, but at least they recognized the names and the attributes of the opposition. Now, with no sides to speak of (except whatever splinter issues rebound online like a pinball), we have an indiscriminate mass. In *Syncopations* I offered some page count (in the thousands) a reader would confront just reading canonical living poets whose last name started with the letter M. One could go further and propose that an intelligible map of the current scene could be obtained by a comparable numerical solution: just read all poets whose last names begin with the letter of your choice.

This Dada solution suggests divergent paths for criticism, I think. One would be rigorously Dada, or maybe it would be better to say pointedly anarchist (and I think here of the consistency with which Charles Bernstein has laced his critical perceptions with his own brand of Betty Boop impishness). This approach tacitly concedes that public discourse is at such a pitch of dereliction that to take it on face value—to maintain the interpersonal stance of critical authority—is pointless: better to point it out with a calculated discursive flatulence, as it were. But the alternative approach (accessible reasonableness) perilously aligns with careerism, especially given the ever-expanding empire of the writing programs and its support industry. To proceed that way is to don the mask of the most up-to-date common sense, perfumed with a *fin-de-millennium* spritz of political correctness.

This is not to say there aren't strategies of betweenness, mixing reason with sedition. But whatever you're searching for in the way of "criticism" has little chance of prevailing in a milieu poisoned by the retort of "Says You," where slander is the coin of the media realm. I say this with some regret, of course, since I spent much of my youth as an advocate for poets I felt undeservedly neglected. There were so many of them that I was never lacking for an opportunity. At the same time, I couldn't help feeling like I was letting down the other side, which had (and has) many poets I admire and would have liked to weigh in on. But in the schismatic world of that time (1970s–'90s) I was being conscientious. I suppose, then, by the same token, that conscientiousness might guide someone now. What would such conscientiousness look like?

First of all, it could not be arbitrary or casually applied. It's far too easy now to drift off on whims and solitary pleasures. So the conscientious critic would now have to figure out how to indicate the coordinates of an un-mappable plane (and I distrust anyone who pretends an overview is within reach). Then she or he would have to elucidate what their values are in poetry, from the libidinal to the cognitive. But then—and this may be the most important part—the aspiring critic would need to be truly ecumenical, exposed to an ungovernable diversity, and this is the tricky part, because it's a bit like an undercover operation by DEA agents. To what degree must you sample the drugs and partake of the lifestyle to truly get what it's all about (before you take it down)?

But I'm dissatisfied with these options insofar as they sound like the normative protocols of critical behavior in the past. Maybe a map of terra incognita is beyond individual reach. What, then, if instead of prescribing a critical posture at the scale of an individual we imagine a critical collective? How about teams of investigators, along the lines of a scientific research initiative, working together to pool their diverse backgrounds and sensibilities into a working model of poetic experience—and take it out from there? Again, as soon as I put it that way I hesitate, because it evokes the widespread scholarly practice of convening a bunch of articles on a given topic, a "Cambridge Companion" approach. And, as I've written about in "A Potential Intelligence," the derelictions of that approach are considerable.

To answer your final question as to whether there's a place for criticism in or amid the tide of "diversity rules": absolutely, but it won't get any traction by being merely the latest incarnation of *same old same old*. Poetry has been so busy reinventing itself for such a long time that maybe criticism needs a good look in the mirror as well. But the dogmas of behavioral compliance in academia will continue to put a check on that impulse, to some extent. And the internet trolls will sweep up the rest, I expect. So any critical stance now finds itself (for better, and not for worse) in the midst of the fray, challenged to invent its own modus operandi and conjure its authority from the eclectic stew of perceptions it convenes in the act of reading.

Ma: Your point on the "floundering" of "any critical 'science'" is well taken; but, to the extent "any critical science" always "flounders" for various reasons, I think that the difference between the time of the domain-based "raw-versus-cooked debates" and the present condition of "an indiscriminate mass" is a difference not so much in nature as in degree.

What you said about criticism and the critic, negatively ("anarchist," "careerist") as well as positively ("the conscientious critic" and what he or she should do), implies an important issue, and leads to my next question: The "ethics" of criticism and the critic.

If I understand you correctly, you find "ethics" in "conscientiousness," of which you have offered a definition in your answer to the question "What would such conscientiousness look like." "Conscientiousness" is then specified as 1) "not be arbitrary or casually applied," 2) "to figure out how to indicate the coordinates of an unmappable plane," 3) "to elucidate what their [critics'] values are in poetry," and 4) "to be truly ecumenical, exposed to an ungovernable diversity."

Regardless of your own self-reflexive "dissatisfaction" with such a characterization, this is, I must say with great appreciation, the much-needed language in the critical rethinking of the nature and function of criticism and the critic in the present condition of poetry.

It is clear that, in your quadruple definition of "conscientiousness," the fourth criterion is the ethical focal point, upon which is predicated the viability of the previous three. But the "tricky part" of the fourth criterion, which is your concern, does not seem tricky at all, for the question of "to what degree" simply does not exist. More specifically put, in the present condition of "glut," most criticisms and critics become sort of "hack criticisms and hack critics." They turn into what Nathan Heller calls, rather aptly, "first responders," who "called the genius of Patti Smith before she was Patti Smith." But "first responders" are not investigators or examiners. Although they are the first to arrive on the scene, their job is to deal with what is immediately present or superficially obvious, and they do not have the time, nor are they in the position, to "call," i.e., to discover, understand, and point out the "genius" of anyone or any work.

The examples of criticisms and critics as "first responders" are readily

available, as evidenced, perhaps most illustratively, in Stephen Burt and
his work. So far as I know, there are quite a few poetry critics who, as either anarchists or careerists, would write on anything and everything that
happens to come along their way, with neither any personal interest in the
work engaged nor even any concern about the merits of the work.

In light of your definition of "conscientiousness" in general, and the
fourth criterion in particular, would you please elaborate further on the following questions: Is there such a thing as the "ethics" of criticism and the
critic in the present condition of poetry? If there is, what is this "ethics"?
And if not, what then should "guide" criticism and the critic, as you have
put it?

Rasula: I would situate such an ethics in the space between poetics and
scholarship. By poetics I mean that expansive repertoire of testimony
from poets themselves, along with ventures into that domain by scholars
and others who are willing to dispense with the strict protocols of the discipline. As for scholarship, that's a potentially compromised stance—
compromised, that is, by disciplinary "norms" and (more compromising
still) "trends."

One of the disciplinary norms that has prevailed since the origins of
serious scholarship on contemporary poetry is the single author "reading,"
usually done in monographs where a couple of poets each get a chapter.
Such readings can be informative, but I find the whole format uninterest-
ing. It's too much like window shopping, gazing at deftly organized vitrines.
A comparable approach is the close reading, which can be revelatory but
only insofar as it bears some resemblance to *midrash*, Jewish devotional an-
notation and exegesis. Also off-putting to me in scholarly discourse is the
kind of locution in which "we see," with the first-person plural legislating
all manner of polite coercion. This gets parleyed into a comparable anonymity when critics refer to "the poet" rather than naming the author, as
if authorship were suspended midway between someone with a driver's
license and a phantom visitor from Porlock. (This is equally a problem
with poets, who seem all too ready to pontificate on "the poem" and "the
poet": an annoying feature of the cascade of poets' manifestos solicited by
Rebecca Hazelton and Alan Michael Parker for *The Manifesto Project* in
2017.) These sorts of things are tics of the profession that produce a kind
of rictus supposed to pass as seriousness. My main complaint here is that
"criticism" as widely practiced, both inside and outside academia, is rarely
practiced *as writing*. It's artless, expending considerable energy scrutinizing
other writing while bereft of attention to its own characteristics.

About forty years ago I coined the term *wreading* as a reminder that any form of writing that professes to "read" another text is itself *writing*: that is, the reading or scrutiny advances by means of the silently parenthetical (w). For me personally it was a way of committing to being as scrupulous in my critical prose as I was in my poetry (and over time I discovered that much of what I wrote as poetry was not written with the same discernment as my prose: this realization led to a helpful reduction of indulgence). Pound's dictum about poetry needing to be as well written as prose has long resonated with me, mainly in its tacit demystification of poetry. Pound was thinking of Henry James—who certainly does epitomize such a consistency of mentation in his syntax that just reading his sentences is to submit to an exacting hallucination—but when I first read that quip of Pound's I was already disposed to get his point by way of Joyce and Beckett, and not long afterward *Gravity's Rainbow* came along, and I still regard extended passages in Pynchon's novel as more compelling than most contemporary poetry.

While I do appreciate your questions, in this instance I'm stumped for an answer. I think in previous answers I was basically pleading for decency in a world of indecencies unleashed by the internet. I'm beginning to feel like Newland Archer in *The Age of Innocence*: "Just say I'm old-fashioned"! By the same token, *ethics* is an old-fashioned word, an old-fashioned sentiment. There's a lot of moral snobbishness afoot, and much indignation that both accompanies and greets the claims of identity politics, and these elements filter into discourse on poetry and even become talking points by poets themselves. But it all too easily sounds moralistic, which is why I prefer to speak of ethics: there is no *ethicalistic* because I think of ethics as behavioral, while morals are both deterministic and judgmental. And that brings us back to the role of judgment as critical obligation, but with a crucial difference. From my perspective, the critic is not there to *judge* in the juridical sense—this one goes to Parnassus, while that one gets the chair—but to make informed assessments of conditions on the ground. An ethical criticism will refrain from asserting what's good and bad, opting instead to clarify the stakes of reading what's there, and particularly helping orient the reader to what's involved in (w)reading it, because it's truer than ever that one can't assume any "common human interest" to which to appeal. Reading bears the risk of seamless understanding as well as misunderstanding, and neither pitfall is evident up front.

Ma: This is very helpful, and I would appreciate it very much if you would clarify and elaborate on two issues you have raised. First, I am particularly interested in your notion of criticism itself as *writing*, as *silently parenthetical (w)*, as *wreading*, with *its own characteristics*. Moreover, your references to Pound's dictum on good writing, to your own experience with the prose work by Joyce, Beckett, and Pynchon, and your complaint against criticism "widely practiced both inside and outside academia" as "artless" all seem to indicate that criticism, as such, is itself an art.

If I understand you correctly, your notion of criticism resonates with a question that A. O. Scott also ponders over, albeit from a different perspective, in *Better Living through Criticism*; and that question is whether or not "criticism is an art in its own right."

Would you please say something more about your idea of criticism that you have outlined so far? What, for example, are criticism's "own characteristics"? If criticism, in the present condition, needs to "invent its own modus operandi" instead of "being merely the latest incarnation of *same old same old*," what would that newly invented modus operandi look like? Is "*wreading*" the reinvented modus operandi of criticism? If it is, how does criticism, as reading and scrutiny of another text, "advance by means of silently parenthetical (w)"? Otherwise put, in what sense is criticism itself a form of art?

Rasula: The inspirations for me as I set out writing critical work in the 1970s were things like Roland Barthes's *S/Z* and *The Pleasure of the Text*; Foucault's *Language, Counter-Memory, Practice*; Adorno's *Minima Moralia*; Heidegger's *Poetry, Language, Thought* and *Early Greek Thinking*; Derrida's *Dissemination* and *Glas*; Marshall McLuhan's *Verbi-Voco-Visual Explorations*; the concept of ta'wil in Henry Corbin's work; and two juicy anthologies, *The Structuralist Controversy* (based on the legendary Johns Hopkins conference that brought Barthes, Foucault, Derrida, Lacan, and others to America in 1966) and *Textual Strategies* edited by Josué Harari. There were other inspirations, of course, in more or less conventional form, like Kenner's *The Pound Era*, but I was quite taken with the prospect of critical work as "écriture," working through the issues while working through itself, as it were. We've since seen the rise of the "lyrical essay" and other hybrids, and I've just finished teaching David Shields's *Reality Hunger: A Manifesto*, a latecomer to the assortment listed above (to which I'd add, obviously, Walter Benjamin's *Arcades Project*, but also Jan Zwicky's *Lyric Philosophy* and Norman O. Brown's *Love's Body*). These works suggest that criticism should be as ingeniously exploratory as the work it addresses.

That's too tall an order to *demand*, I suppose, but it certainly guides my own reading and writing. For the most part, reading "criticism" is a nonstarter for me. I'm sure there's much to learn from recent critical commentary on poets I like, but at this point in my life my relation to long-familiar

poets is *personal*, possibly past the point of interpretive tweaks. This doubt-
less reflects my weariness at witnessing decades of a parade of critical
tweaks, a processional of clever/hopeful/aspiring additives to prepackaged
critical formulas, so now we add a soupçon of class, a digestif of race, a
dose of gender, and voilá. Having said that, it's certainly the case that these
and other perspectives have been instructive, often consequential, but I've
just seen so much of it in rote form at this point that critical essays feel
more like State Department memos than anything else (I say this as a recovering veteran of terms on the editorial boards of *PMLA* and *American
Literature*).

Reflecting on what I've just said, I believe it all comes down to self-
awareness on the level of form, or creative imagination applied to the medium itself. I remember the impact of Anne Carson's book *Eros the Bitter-
sweet* when I was writing my dissertation back in the eighties. Innocuously
presented as another entry in classical mythology studies by a qualified
scholar (in a field I then routinely perused), I realized this was a Trojan
Horse if ever there was one—published by Princeton University Press, no
less. Carson had ingeniously straddled the line between scholastic responsibility and creative abandon. Because this was long before she published
poetry, I took it as critical precedent, and provocation.

Now, as to "wreading." The term infused the writing of *This Compost*
(first drafted 1980–81). Early in the book (footnote on page 11) I give
this explanation: "'Wreading' is my neologism for the collaborative momentum initiated by certain texts, like *The Maximus Poems*, in which the
reader is enlisted *as* an agent of the writing. Reciprocally, the writer discloses his or her own readerly orientation (albeit in ways that vary from
work to work)." It was prompted, as the reference indicates, by Olson's blurring of the reader/writer distinction in *Maximus*, with the poems absorbing a notational procedure, but rather than citations as in a scholarly work
he ventriloquizes, occupying the place of Hesiod or Winthrop or whoever's
words he's puffing onto the page as though onto a windowpane. The reader,
in turn, reads Olson reading Hesiod and in the process writes or projects
an overlay, continuing the creative initiative. With composition by field, it's
almost as if he's left ample space on the page for the reader to start filling it
up. Anyway, *wreading* can be easily found in *This Compost* because I put it
in the index.

Because *This Compost* wasn't published until 2002, an earlier appearance in print of the term wreading was in *Sulfur* in 1989: "Literacy Effects:
Handling the Fiction, Nursing the Wounds." I'd delivered it as a talk at
the Sulfur symposium in Michigan in 1988. It was reprinted in *Syncopa-*

tions in 2004. There you'll find a particularly raucous paragraph on wreading on page 163. I won't quote it here, but this may be useful: *"wreading, or how poetics exceeds its poetry."* That turned out to be an unwitting portent of the book I had not yet begun, *Modernism and Poetic Inspiration: The Shadow Mouth* (2009), although chapters had appeared earlier, which explored the porosity between a mythopoetic imagination going back to antiquity equally abundant in prose and poetry, with my own writing firmly wedged between the two practices. Much of it reads to me now like a kind of critical prose poetry. Crucial to my approach there was to find the most succulent quotations, and sort of suck on them, imaginatively. This turned the normative critical ethos upside down, as I revealed myself as quite uninterested in value judgments, assessments, and placements of writers and their works. Instead, I undertook a passage through a welter of texts, accumulating chunks and streaks and stains as it were and smearing them along the way into the final text.

This review of "wreading" as it threaded its way through my publications omits its earlier vestiges in conversation, notebook writing, and so forth going back to around 1976. I remember Steve McCaffery visiting us in Echo Park in February 1977 when we both snapped up copies of Derrida's *Of Grammatology* just as the translation came out; and Steve provocatively pronounced the author's name with "reader" audible inside it, as in *Duh-Reedah*. So, by the time Bruce Andrews invited me to contribute to *L=A=N=G=U=A=G=E* in 1978, I'd spent a couple years working up the concept of wreading. It's possible I even used the word somewhere, maybe even in my poetry magazine *Wch Way*. My short manifesto on the reader as creative agent, "Statement on Reading in Writing," appeared in *L=A=N=G=U=A=G=E* #5 (October 1978) but oddly didn't use the term, though it was clearly the distillation of how I understood it at the time, but with a somewhat different emphasis than in *This Compost*, anticipating instead something more along the lines of *The American Poetry Wax Museum* in its objection to the mystification of the writer at the expense of the reader—"writing as a selfish indulgence in the notion of originality." I also ventured the claim that "there exists *enough writing* already," a position more familiar now from Kenny Goldsmith's *Uncreative Writing*.

To answer your question more explicitly, I'd say that the w in wreading is a placeholder or reminder that the "readings" a critic undertakes are inaccessible without being written (unless, of course, disseminated orally), and the writing can be either serviceable—commensurate with bulletins, directives, instructional guides, etc.—or it can be inspirational. What I look for is best expressed by the consummate wreader-poet Marianne Moore, from "Picking and Choosing" (2017, 48):

only the most rudimentary sort of behavior is necessary
to put us on the scent; "a right good
    salvo of barks," a few "strong wrinkles" puckering the
skin between the ears, are all we ask.

—to which I'd add, from another of her poems ("When I Buy Pictures"):
it must be "lit with piercing glances into the life of things" (51).

Ma: Thank you for the review of your neologism "wreading" and its evolution over the years through your own writing, which is, I think, productively suggestive. In many ways, you seem to have delineated, through this
term, the contour of what could be a different theory of criticism, one that
might indeed be described, to borrow a phrase from Bruno Latour, as "Enlightenment without the Critique." To continue this line of thinking, would
you please now say something about the second and related issue that has
implicitly connected all your ideas? That is, if the contemporary poetry
scene is "an ocean" without the "science of an oceanography," if the condition of contemporary poetry is one in which "diversity rules" without
"a common human interest," but with "clouds" of poetic groups and cote-
ries each conveying "pragmatic valencies specific to its kind," as Lyotard
has thusly put it, and if ethical criticism "is not there to *judge* in the juridical sense . . . but to make informed assessments of conditions on the
ground . . . to clarify the stakes of reading what's there, and particularly
helping orient the reader to what's involved in (w)reading it," has not criticism become, in both its nature and its function, rhetoric? In the current
condition of poetry as such, isn't it appropriate and necessary, if not imperative, to replace this dated concept of "criticism" with other terms or
concepts such as "rhetoric" or "hermeneutics"?

Rasula: Bringing up rhetoric is a rhetorical move on your part, and one
that I certainly welcome, not least because it gives me the opportunity to
pay homage to the late Hayden White, my dissertation director at Santa
Cruz. His scrupulous attention to the modes of rhetorical figuration latent
in the seemingly fact-based idiom of history writing was a revelation to
me back in the seventies, and his graduate seminars have remained models for me of pedagogy as both boxing ring and three-ring circus. When I
first read Hayden's work I was already familiar with Harold Bloom's recruitment of certain tropes in his theory of "misprision," or poetic influence. So
between Bloom and White my understanding of rhetoric was anchored in
the ancient arsenal of tropes—tropes as incipient poetics—and this added
historical and conceptual substance to the background I already had in
structuralism and semiotics (conveniently aligned in Anthony Wilden's *The*

Rules Are No Game). So you're quite right to suggest that "criticism" comes up short if not grounded in the art of language.

Observing the way in which literary studies keep chasing new topics in a kind of disciplinary fashion cycle reveals how far rhetoric has been left behind, as the magic trinkets of "trauma," "disability," "globalism," and other strobe-lit slogans seem to hold out the promise of a game change. I don't mean to dismiss such trends, since they can induce meaningful enlargements of perspective, but from this vantage looking back to the influx of continental theory fifty years ago it seems that literary criticism has been in flight from anything construed as "formalism" ever since. But rhetoric (and semiotics) are formalist in the way that a living organism is a formalist template, a program for life to sustain itself. What comes to mind in this respect is from that consummate rhetorician, Kenneth Burke: "The symbolic act is the *dancing of an attitude*" (1941, 9). By symbolic act he means anything that signifies as a mode of action and not just the passive imprint of materiality. The symbolic act is postural. Burke grounds signifying in the body, and in this respect affirms something the artist Kandinsky maintained: an artwork signifies primarily *Here I am*. It's like a handprint—and handprints, remember, are the most copious indications of human presence in all the Paleolithic caves, which are otherwise crowded with depictions of animals.

This may seem to have drifted from the topic of criticism, but that drift is my own rhetorical nudge, a way of acknowledging my disdain for normative critical modes. Another reason I welcome your introduction of rhetoric into the discussion is that it reveals something crucial about criticism and professionalism. That is, donning the mantle of authority snuffs out curiosity, which I take to be the animal root of interest in anything at all. And criticism, I believe, begins at the basic level of animal sapience. A reader is simply curious about and quickened by the poems of Hopkins or Dickinson, Sappho or Tu Fu. But there's something about professionalism that marginalizes curiosity, or that has been unconcerned with giving curiosity a voice. Maybe it's due to the prevailing use of third person in academic writing. It's pretty hard to suggest anything like *collective* curiosity, whereas the sound of authority settles quite comfortably into the plural form.

Returning to your question, the prospect of "diversity" without "a human interest" is genuinely haunting, if we take those two particles as left versus right affiliations in a political sense. Diversity is clearly a value for the Left, and while human interest doesn't factor into public discourse, my sense living here in the American south is that it thrives as a tool of political recruitment—"human" being a code word for white male. Why aren't they talking about (idolizing) us any longer? Hence (pardon the formulaic proposition): Donald Trump. Rhetoric works in mysterious ways, and I bring up our imperial grifter as the paragon of everything rhetoric is not, at least in the ways I'd valorize it. His tweets and twitches are so routinely venomous as to shed all the nuance germane to rhetoric. The *art* of rhetoric was never concerned with blunt assaults, name-calling, and muddying the waters (though Quintillian's bounty of rhetorical tropes probably has names for them). The old Latin category *panem et circenses*—bread and circuses— is what applies to Trump. And his prancing and preening voids (I use the verb in the alimentary sense) tropological nuance. What this has done to the public sphere is equivalent to the baring of canine teeth. It's all snarl and growl, followed by grammatically intelligible snippets of humanoid barking.

What does this have to do with poetry? For me, it brings Bruce Andrews's strategies back into the equation, as he was preternaturally alert to the sound of menace in the patter of American patois back in the Reagan era, when a certain kind of menacing vigilance was the law of the land. He entered into, and drew upon, the jargon of the day with the clear understanding that "oppositionality" as it came to be called was a witless and toothless alternative—*protest* was *so* sixties. If that sounds cynical now, I'd only add that the cynicism in his case was hard won, and well earned.

So the prospects of criticism are now suspended between several poles. There's the political righteousness of the Left, which encompasses a ma- jority of poets and critics. There's a broader nonaffiliated craving for hu- man values (not always humane: viz. the border wall, which purports to preserve the human rights of citizens while dehumanizing noncitizens). And there's the disciplinary matrix in which criticism is little more than a line item on an annual performance review. These positions or inclinations have no place for curiosity and its consequences, but they reveal an acute anxiety about authority, and authorization.

Ma: What you have said brings two issues to my mind immediately. First, your elaboration of criticism as the "art of rhetoric" seems to gesture to- ward a form of criticism that could be subsumed under the rubric of "rhe- torical criticism." Secondly, your White-Bloom-Burke-oriented concep- tion of rhetoric in terms of "formalism" and "art of language" resonates, rather uncannily, with Henry Louis Gates Jr.'s theory of signification, which he defines as, among many other features of course, formal, tropological, and postural. If my understanding of your position is not too far off base, my question to you then is this: Between the three "poles" you have iden- tified where the "prospects of criticism are now suspended," do you find any possible space left for a formalist criticism? In other words, in the current condition of criticism, have you detected a return to, or a renewed interest in, formal-rhetorical approach? And would you consider your own concept and practice of "wreading" as a model of the criticism you have so envisioned?

Rasula: Rhetoric is the art of persuasion (I'd emphasize the *art*). And insofar as we're accustomed to strategies of persuasion in professional life, we tacitly adopt them as models, devices to be redeployed. The devices of critical rhetoric can be vices, and foremost among them is the third person plural. It has the virtue of a seeming inclusiveness, and at its best it can solicit a reader's attention as if two people together were engaged in a laboratory experiment, peering closely at some experiment in progress. But as I mentioned earlier, it's tacitly coercive in its inclusivity: not me and you, but *us*. Another academic de/vice is "argument," a term so pervasive as to be transparent as glass. Writing, it's assumed, always has an argument. But an argument carries an implicit threat, as arguments can escalate. What I'm describing here is what Hayden White called "the content of the form," and the form of an argument carries with it the Trojan Horse of ulterior contents, albeit not often recognized as such. Readers avid for messages and eager to be persuaded look through the glass of the form as pure transparency, and swallow the bait of argumentative form.

A formalist criticism in the rhetorical sense we're talking about is not criticism that's concerned with formal issues (there's an abundance of it in studies of "the novel," for instance), but criticism that adapts itself formally to its subject. When Continental Theory washed over academia in the seventies it was a revelation to many to find that one could arrange critical prose in unorthodox configurations, like the numbered paragraphs in Barthes's *S/Z*, or the parallel columns in Derrida's *Glas*. But literary critics generally didn't take that as permission, because they were busy trying to absorb and verify some putative doctrine purveyed from abroad. It turned out to be poets who availed themselves of the formalist opportunity, like Charles Bernstein's verse essay *The Artifice of Absorption*, Bob Perelman's lineated MLA talk "The Marginalization of Poetry," or Wittgenstein scholar/Canadian poet Jan Zwicky's parallel pages in *Lyric Philosophy*. And going back a bit, there are those extraordinary books by Norman O. Brown—*Love's Body* and *Closing Time*—when he shed the pretense of scholarly discourse and pledged allegiance to poetry.

As for my own practice, you're right to point to my neologism "wreading" as the incentive and model. It was certainly behind the procedural gambits of essays like "Seeing Double: The Grapes of Dysraphism" in

Syncopations, which deliberately took the charter of "close reading" to the brink. And *Syncopations* ends with "Syncope, Cupola, Pulse," which dangles provocatively between poetry, prose, and assembly (a reader for the press objected strenuously to its inclusion, as I recall). But even in apparently straightforward critical works I've been mindful of formal strategies. *The American Poetry Wax Museum*, for instance, has five chapters, one of which is over two hundred pages long. I was tickled to find that not a single reviewer noticed this exorbitant design, essentially a book inside a book.

Way back when I came up with the term wreading, there was a phrase I wrote in a notebook (and may have ended up in print somewhere) in the form of a question: *What does this do with you reading?* I felt very distinctly that the differential in the equation of reading is the particular reader. After all, the text is relatively stable, even though its seemingly inherent stability gets dislodged over time as new social norms emerge (it takes a particular kind of attention to read, say, an eighteenth-century essay now because the mannerisms of discourse are so different). Regardless, any text consists of a rudimentary equation: *text + reader*, and the reader is always *this* reader, *here and now*. It's ludicrous to speak of "the reader" as if they (we) were interchangeable. So my question had a tacit point of emphasis: What does this do with *you* reading?

We should also add place and time to the reader, to make an occasion of it. For instance, for many years (probably decades) I read Wallace Stevens mainly outdoors, thanks to that portable Vintage paperback edition of *The Palm at the End of the Mind* (pulp fiction format, roughly 4" x 7"). After all, he makes such constant reference to weather, why not be exposed? Along the same lines, my first reading of *Finnegans Wake* was (appropriately, for Joyce's "book of the dark") in a dim flicker because I only read it on camping trips by firelight. Such occasions are not neutral, yet how often do you find a critic mentioning such circumstances? I've certainly been guilty of much omission in that respect, so I'm glad I can now correct an egregious omission I've long sought to address: I neglected to mention in the foreword to *This Compost* that the first draft was written almost exclusively to the music of jazz musician Eric Dolphy. The elliptical nature of my prose in that book definitely registers the impact of his inside/outside playing (to use the argot of jazz).

I don't want to suggest that wreading is just criticism with a personal note. There's already a considerable market for what's called the personal essay, and it's not a cult of personality I'm interested in. Wreading is in some sense the measure of what exceeds personality, like a fingerprint. It's just there, the inescapable residue of the body, but a body whose actions leave traces in the world and on the objects of its attention. I suppose in conventional terms we might call it style, but only if style suggests something as singular as the way Eric Dolphy plays the alto saxophone, the flute, the bass clarinet. There's no mistaking it, just as there's no mistaking the "late style" of Henry James. But style is too readily construed as mannerism, a surreptitious way of being pushy, or getting noticed. I think, rather, in the more honorific sense, style is making do with the hand you've been dealt. It's lighting a spark to a deficit in order to awaken unrealized potential in whatever's at hand. A term that spoke to me around the time I coined "wreader" was *bricoleur*, from Claude Lévi-Strauss's book *The Savage Mind* (1966). The bricoleur is the nonspecialist who makes do with whatever material is at hand in order to get the job done. The English equivalent is handyman, a noun, so I guess the corollary to the action, *bricolage*, would be *handymanner*.

To return to your question, then, I'd reiterate my point about authority with reference to the bricoleur, a figure lacking authority, operating without license, yet capable of addressing any situation with ingenuity, imagination, and what used to be called mother wit. Levi-Strauss contrasts the bricoleur with the engineer, suggesting that "the engineer works by means of concepts and the 'bricoleur' by means of signs" (20)—his book, remember, was a primary document of structuralist semiotics. A concept is symptomatic of authority, as it readily shades over into rules and laws. A sign, on the other hand, always remains embedded in a material dynamic. For Levi-Strauss, the consummate medium for handling signs is mythopoesis; and "the elements of mythical thought," he suggests, "lie half-way between percepts and concepts," making it "impossible to separate percepts from the concrete situations in which they appeared" (18). By this means the concept is wrenched away from authority. It's a scenario that Hollywood loves to depict (cf. the Die Hard cycle, the Bourne cycle), when a lone operator with no authority but possessing the skills of a bricoleur goes up against the amassed force of the law or some hierarchy that avails itself of force. In more localized terms—terms more adaptable to critical practice—it's the distinction Isaiah Berlin made between the hedgehog and the fox. The hedgehog knows One Big Thing, the fox many little things. The hedgehog commands and surveys a particular domain (think of single-author scholarship) while the fox traverses many domains (a prototype of the Situationist dérive, drifting and straying as a way of eluding prescription and authority).

Ma: So far, we have talked about contemporary conditions of poetry and criticism, and I think you would agree that we cannot understand them properly without talking into consideration another issue, which is the internet. In our conversation up to this point, you have already mentioned internet in passing, or in parenthesis, a number of times, and would you please now say something about your view of the internet—its functions, effects, and consequences, etc.—in relation to and in the context of contemporary conditions of poetry and criticism?

Rasula: I am probably less qualified to comment on the internet than almost anyone you know. It's a wonderland of resources, for sure, but I have not adapted to it the way so many of my peers have. I remember long ago seeing a course syllabus by Charles Bernstein and marveling at how much online material he integrated, whereas I don't think I've ever provided website links on a syllabus. I remain regressively bookish, I'm afraid. Even with a high-quality pdf at hand, for instance, I still hunt out copies of a book for sale (online!).

As for its impact on contemporary poetry, it's obviously been game changing. Access to intelligent commentary, interesting writing, and archival materials makes it an unprecedented resource—and all at the click of a mouse. The clickability is what I find worrisome, not because of what it affords access to, but because of the way it infiltrates behavioral outlook and instinct. Despite his pop-guru reputation, Marshall McLuhan remains for me a go-to source for thinking about the way modern technologies rewire the human sensorium. As he puts it somewhere, the real avant-garde is the technosphere. The early poetic adaptations to the tidal wave of modern technologies—rapid transit, airplanes, radio, cinema—is what Tim Conley and I put into play in our anthology *Burning City: Poems of Metropolitan Modernity* (2012). A comparable project could be done concerning the internet environment. Chris Funkhouser might be just the person to do it, given his extraordinary research in *Prehistoric Digital Poetry*. But behaviorally speaking, internet use contributes to a dwindling attention span, even as it sparks a keener sense of interactive connectivity. For a number of years (around 2006–2012) I contributed reading notes to Steve Evans's online "Attention Span" on the Third Rail website, and I thought the sound-bite format was perfectly suited to his title. It might take fifteen seconds to read a review or "notice" of a particular publication—about the length of a blurb, actually. And that seems about right for web browsing. Where it gets tricky is the blending of hard print formats into that environment, which has suggested to younger people that *everything* alphabetic can and should be available on the internet. As a consequence, I now find many of my students read assigned novels online—and worse, for their eventual ocular health, they read the books on their phones.

Another factor of the internet that has been made more conspicuous in the age of Trump is trolling and various kinds of online predation, along with the poison that gets leached out into the cultural atmosphere. It's put very well by Adam Gopnik in this week's *New Yorker* (January 6, 2020, "Talk of the Town"): "No one has ever improved on Yeats's expression of indignation after the Great War: the best lack all conviction, while the worst are full of passionate intensity; though in our time the best often share the passionate intensity but can't be heard, because the worst have a smartphone with a Twitter app."

As for the "functions, effects, and consequences" of the internet for poetry, I cede the floor to Mike Chasar, whose book *Poetry Unbound: Poems and New Media from the Magic Lantern to Instagram* is due out this spring. Judging from his previous book *Everyday Reading: Poetry and Popular Culture in Modern America* (2012), *Poetry Unbound* is likely to provide the most informative and thoughtful assessment of the brave new digital world we inhabit.

Ma: Thank you for the heads up, and I am sure we are all looking forward to reading such studies. The contemporary condition of poetry is, without any doubt, a multifaceted, fast changing, and fascinating phenomenon of culture that demands our careful studies and understanding, and I am grateful to you for your pioneering contribution to this area of study. Any further thought on the condition of poetry and its related issues?

Rasula: Thank you for understanding my shortcomings, which I don't hesitate to acknowledge, bearing in mind a sage observation made by Samuel Taylor Coleridge in one of the issues of his periodical *The Friend*: "To attempt to make a man wiser is of necessity to remind him of his ignorance, and in the majority of instances, the pain actually felt is so much greater than the pleasure anticipated, that it is natural that men should attempt to shelter themselves from it by contempt or neglect. For a living writer is yet *sub judice*: and if we cannot follow his conceptions or enter into his feelings, it is more consoling to our pride, as well as more agreeable to our indolence, to consider him as lost beneath, than as soaring out of our sight above us" (Coburn 1951, 194–95). Coleridge's diagnosis of this all too familiar human frailty reminds me of the outlook that I started out fighting against more than forty years ago, when living writers could be dismissed with a peremptory wave of the hand (the hand then likely to brandish a cigarette). During my undergraduate years at Indiana University I witnessed two instances of this, each of which ignited in me a determination to make my own way rather than capitulate to authority. One was a lecture in which the esteemed critic René Wellek ridiculed and dismissed the critical writings of Ezra Pound, on the grounds that he was simply unqualified to comment on matters of poetics. The second was the poet Robert Penn Warren, who in a meeting with a small bunch of us undergrads was asked which younger poets he might recommend (at that time he was in his late sixties). He said there were none, and that he knew because people sent him books all the time and they weren't worth reading. This pronouncement was made before I had even heard of Olson or Zukofsky or Duncan, let alone anyone younger, but I somehow knew it couldn't be true.

As I've traversed the decades and am now the age Warren was then, I still agree with my younger self but also see that the world has drastically changed. I've commented on this in our exchange, the key point being that the vast demographic bulge we occupy—combined with the ubiquity of current opinion, whim, and awareness facilitated by the internet—threatens to abolish the past altogether. "A Potential Intelligence" addresses the holocaust of cultural memory of American poetry before midcentury. In short, the present has trumped the past, but the present is a precarious place to be if the present takes on the character of a lively party or a special event like a sports playoff—precarious because the excitement subsides, the bubble bursts, the hangover begins.

Everything in the cultural legacy is predicated on memory and commemoration, and these are values I hold; although, *because* they are values, I have consistently objected to the abuses that can accrue to them in the procedures of canon-formation across the arts. I think my model of a canon would be: for every canonical figure you can think of, imagine there's another one just as compelling that you can't bring to mind because they've been forgotten, misplaced, or were barely legible in the first place. I now see that the situation never changes, even if the names change. Now with so much buzz around Mina Loy the question might be: who's gone missing as a consequence?

Finally, since you've graciously invited a last word on the subject of contemporary poetry: I'm about to teach what's likely to be my last undergraduate course before I retire. The rubric is Contemporary American Literature, and we'll be reading books of poetry published since 2000, all by women. The choices of both authors and titles was excruciating because the field is so rich. That says much about current and future prospects, of course, and reflects my conviction that the gravest peril in the world is the continuing dominance by men in positions of power, or (gender specific) "man" as default figure of authority in human communities and in cultural affairs.

Standing Bare to the Blast

An Exchange with Nathan Brown on Modernism

NATHAN BROWN IS an associate professor of English and Canada Research Chair in poetics at Concordia University, Montreal, where he directs the Centre for Expanded Poetics. He is the author of *Rationalist Empiricism: A Theory of Speculative Critique* and *The Limits of Fabrication: Materials Science and Materialist Poetics*. With Petar Milat, he is coeditor of the volume *Poiesis*.

Brown: In the midst of *History of a Shiver* (2016) there's a passage quoted from Rilke's *The Book of Images* with which I'd like to begin:

> And again my inmost life rushes louder,
> as if moved now between steeper banks.
> Objects become ever more related to me,
> and all pictures ever more perused.
> I feel myself more trusting in the nameless . . .

These are the opening lines of a poem titled "Fortschritt," which could be translated as "Progress" or "Advance."

In the poem the focus is personal, but it seems to me that much of what we name "modernism" is bound up with the possible tension in the sense of its title, between progress and advance. *Progress* implies a familiar narrative of social, technological improvement, of history moving in the right direction—the kind of historical narrative loathed by Baudelaire or heralded by Le Corbusier, or the kind of illusion said to have been "shattered by the Great War" in off-the-shelf stories about the relation between modernism and modernity. "Advance," on the other hand, suggests a more tenuous relationship between moving forward and moving in the right direction—it implies a sense of risk, of stemming into the unknown, that we might associate with the avant-garde. Perhaps something like the *problem* of modernism, and its pathos, consists in the rift between moving forward and making progress, such that the latter can be both denounced and affirmed, reviled and championed, while the former seems to have been pervasively acclaimed under the banner of the new, the sine qua non of modernism.

But it's Rilke's invocation of "trusting in the nameless" that I want to get to, in connection with this tension between progress and advance. Terms like "modernism" or "romanticism"—or even symbolism, surrealism, constructivism, etc.—perform a classificatory function enabling us to forget or at least contain much of the ambiguity and ambivalence at stake in the actual *production* or *making* of artworks we might consider under these names. In *History of a Shiver* (2016) and *Acrobatic Modernism* (2020) you take up the challenge of paying attention to artistic production across mediums and across genres from the 1890s to the 1950s. Of course one can't pay attention to *everything*, but considered together these two books seem to approach a limit case of that kind of critical effort. In the Introduction to *History of a Shiver* you refer to "Oblique Modernism," and the subtitle of the book is *The Sublime Impudence of Modernism*. It's far too late to have done with modernism as a designation at this point, but what I appreciate about these two books is that together they nevertheless testify to a capacity for "trusting in the nameless," or what Keats described as negative capability. Beneath or behind or alongside or perhaps even out in front of our cultural terminology, there is a namelessness of the encounter with what has been made, and with making, that seems to accrue, paradoxically, the more one knows about what is glossed by the name—the more objects become related to me, or the more closely pictures are perused.

In *Acrobatic Modernism* you cite a closely related passage by Rilke, this one a description of Rodin's sculptures:

> parts of different bodies, brought together by inner necessity, become for him a single organism. A hand laid on the shoulder or limb of another body is no longer part of the body to which it properly belongs: something new had been formed from it and the object it touches or holds, something which was not there before, which is nameless and belongs to no one. (Rasula 2020, 124–25)

Here it's the relational structure of *composition* that brings into being a new form "which is nameless and belongs to no one." There's a compelling gentleness of the new in this passage, which perhaps contributes to its anonymity and dispossession, the way it floats free of property and is released into the strange intimacy and familiarity of the unknown and the unnamable.

Moving from Jena romanticism to abstract expressionism, between music, literature, dance, painting, and cinema, and even ranging *From the Avant-Garde to Prehistory*, the books close with a meditation on the hand-print as a symbol—as if only so *generic* an index could gather together so much specificity. What strikes me about your method is that it assembles something like a company of the nameless from a vast concatenation of names, sometimes a cacophony, drawing them together from "romanticism" to "modernism" as if to displace the self-evidence of those categories by taking seriously the profusion of what they include. Perhaps one might consider it a methodology of the nameless . . .

Rasula: It's a discerning reading to notice Rilke's references to the nameless in both of my books, and I'm intrigued by the programmatic aura you lend to the notion, with "a company of the nameless" emerging from the riot of names amassed especially in *Acrobatic Modernism*. Its chapter on heteronyms and pseudonyms toys with the prospect that names are fictive ingredients of a creative venture, but I didn't move in the direction implied by the nameless there. So Shakespeare's question, "What's in a name?" has a different ring when amended to "What's in the nameless?"—a question enhanced by Rilke's pledge to *trust* in the nameless.

It's easy to think of "the nameless" as special pleading, a mark of Rilke's characteristic other-worldliness—we pass from name to nameless going from life to death—and there's a bit of that in the poem from *Buch der Bilder*; so it's important to add the other "nameless" as applied to Rodin's grouping of bodies in *Gate of Hell* (Rilke doesn't cite it in the passage you quote, but he moves on to it right after). Here the context is more chilling, Dante's inferno and Rodin's sculpture resonate through the century with images of mass slaughter, bodies stacked like cordwood at Buchenwald, the Gulag, Pol Pot's Cambodia, and more. In those scenarios the nameless resounds with horrible specificity. I want to add this resonance not as a corrective to or adjustment of what you make of the nameless, but to bring out the double image that guides everything I'm doing in these books, rendered in the title of the journal *Modernism/Modernity*. Never one without the other. The phenomenon of Wagnerism in *History of a Shiver* is the medium through which I render the two terms porous to each other: a social epiphenomenon that in turn breeds or feeds other kinds of art.

The context in *Acrobatic Modernism* in which I cite Rilke on Rodin is in the midst of a parade of citations and references having to do with bodily dislocation, and traumatic reallocation of corporeality—sandwiched between Djuna Barnes's *Nightwood*, Woolf's *The Waves*, and Hans Bellmer's doll. It's literally the origin of both books, as that section ("Pathic Receptacles," concluding the long chapter with a title from Mina Loy, "Luminous Sores") was initially a talk at a conference at Université François Rabelais in Tours, 1997, not long after a sabbatical year living in the south of France in the Luberon. That talk was a deliberate return to materials in my dissertation, "The Poetics of Embodiment: A Theory of Exceptions" (1989), and one of the claims I made there is that "modernism is the diagnostic term for a certain affliction." Without going into detail (the dissertation was 550 pages), the basic issue was the deformative imprint of all those social and technological transfigurations of modernity, reflected in the "affliction" I saw registered in the arts of modernism.

Does it amount to a "methodology of the nameless," as you put it? Interesting to consider, because I keep a wide berth from the sort of artist-centered approach prevalent in modernist studies from *The Pound Era* to the present. I've been much too absorbed in and enchanted by the multitude. Even though as a teenager I started out with Pound and Eliot—and, importantly, never left them behind or got disenchanted—I've been equally drawn to relatively obscure figures. I hearken to them all as individual lives. My essay "A Potential Intelligence"—a quizzical look at the way current scholarship has abandoned a vast number of American poets of the first half of the twentieth century—ends with the exhortation to just be apprised of *the names*, an appeal I now realize shares something with the way New York streets were festooned with names of the missing in the wake of 9/11. So, yes, I'll go along with *methodology*, which I've been practicing without a name for it. But I should stress that it's a post facto methodology, arising from a practice, the practice reflecting a temperament.

Brown: "The Poetics of Embodiment" was a formative text for me: its incisive review of theories of deixis; attention to phenomenological accounts of body-image and body-schema; the section on ideological detritus orbiting as "satellite concepts;" the theory of canontology you pursue as well in *The American Poetry Wax Museum*; the philosophical/historical engagement with prosthesis, "phantom objectivity," and "eccentric predicates" (drawing also on Helmuth Plessner's theory of "eccentric positionality," little known at the time in anglophone circles); the treatment of Stelarc's body suspensions; its thinking of "the language homunculus;" the extended meditation upon the figure of the cyborg—proximate to, yet so different in tonality from, Haraway's manifesto; and, overall, the striking fusion of modes of thought drawn from figures like Olson and Duncan, Lacan, James Hillman, Susan Howe, Thomas Pynchon, Ralph Ellison, Elaine Scarry, Octavio Paz,

Clifford Geertz, Gabriele Schwab . . . the list could go on and on in its singular heterogeneity. I think it's one of the most astonishing and important theoretical works of the past fifty years; it really should be published!

So I noticed the relay of certain strains of the dissertation into the account of artworks as "pathic receptables" in *Acrobatic Modernism*. Since this is also a theme that runs through *History of a Shiver*, it's worth taking up in detail. There it's Carl Dahlhaus's concept of "the pathos of emancipation" that you take up in the first chapter, where you write:

> The elevation of music to an absolute standard did not come without cost. It's too great a burden for any art to epitomize freedom as such, for that is to envision a creative adventure that can't help but destroy the ground it stands on. . . . In the development of a given art, the pathos of emancipation—with its procedures of purification—reveals that the senses are insufficient to their assumed task. While the organism perceives by means of a sensory manifold, the arts have traditionally been theorized in terms of their unique sensory inputs, as if painters were deaf and composers blind. Synesthetic reveries reflect a yearning to surmount the input/output ratio of sense-specific arts, rousing visual artists with the awareness that their art need not be strictly optical and haunting composers with the realization that music could enchant, disarm, and provoke but could neither prove nor openly declare. In the fin de siècle, however, the passion for synesthesia ameliorated the burden of pathos by shifting suppositions of freedom from one art to the *potential* liberation in another art. (Rasula 2016, 23–24)

As I understand it, the pathos at issue bears upon what we might call the necessary *economy* of medium-specificity. It's "too great a burden for any art to epitomize freedom as such" because such *absolute* freedom is in contradiction with the constraints of the medium—of *any* medium, and even of a synthesis of media. Yet the prospect and promise of working between the arts, or of "shifting suppositions of freedom" from one art to another, alleviates the burden through what you call "a game of aesthetic hot potato." What's interesting is that the prospect and promise is "ideological," yet it has enormously productive results for what we understand as modernism. And what I find important about the concept of artworks as "pathic receptacles" is that it registers the *pathology* at issue here without thereby dismissing it as illusory, as ideological material to be cleared away by critique. Rather, what is necessary is to *understand*, or at least encounter, the specificity of the affective and historical problem that is lodged in the very materiality of modernist artworks.

You cite Adorno's *Aesthetic Theory* in this vein at one point in *Acrobatic*

Modernism, and certainly that book offers tremendous resources for thinking through the pathic dimension of artworks as intrinsic to their formal constitution (productively displacing the antinomy of formalist and expressive understandings of artistic production). What strikes me specifically about your approach is evident in the passage I quoted above: there is a *cybernetic* attunement to what you call "the input-output ratio of sense-specific arts." This is an attunement drawn from Charles Olson or Thomas Pynchon or Donna Haraway as much as from Norbert Wiener himself, and it results in attention throughout *Acrobatic Modernism* to what you call "sensory ratios," the manner in which these came into crisis and required adjustment—both painful and exhilarating—under the conditions of modernity particular to the late nineteenth and early twentieth century.

You note that "one of the great lessons of modernism concerns the pathic dimension of aesthetic bereavement: namely, that art's receptacles hurt when they undergo transformation. The hurt is commensurate with the body because subjectivity is spread out across a grid of cultural transmitters, free-standing registers of sentience" (Rasula 2020, 114). The latter is the kind of sentence one doesn't come across every day. Implicit in it is the whole "poetics of embodiment" and "theory of exceptions" you develop in your dissertation. But it also registers a simple recognition: the body is extended in social space, and it is suffused with technological and cultural determinations. As Freud noted, "Psyche is extended, knows nothing about it"—the body *is* the unconscious, which is not only a private psyche but a social psyche, extended. If it "knows nothing about it," nevertheless that *absence* of conscious knowledge is indexed by artworks.

One thing I appreciate about *Acrobatic Modernism* is its explication of tensions, contradictions, and regions of common ground between surrealism and constructivism, and perhaps we could understand the relation of those apparently opposing *isms* through this thinking of pathic receptacles. Even if the unconscious is disavowed, it permeates the construction in the artwork; and even if it takes center stage, it is nevertheless social, technological, and political determinations that are at issue. These displacements, extensions, and inclusions (like flaws in the crystalline structure of a gem) saturate the pathic dimension of artworks as a kind of personal/historical/technical complex—Pound's figure of the image, as you note—which is given a "receptacle" insofar as something is *made* out of it.

Rasula: You've touched on something central to these projects, having to do with the *fragility*, the inescapable precariousness of artifacts. Human culture is a vast concatenation of objects, creative augmentations of the given world (species of what Heidegger calls *zuhanden*: put "there," not just naturally given). We've always been interested in ruins, because they harbor this special dose of intentionality that goes into the enterprise of *making*. They're not accidental remnants. But it's been too easy to emphasize the intentionality, with the result that we keep on asking of artworks what they mean. And the distinction that persisted like a neurological woodpecker while writing these books was the need to distinguish *saying* from *making*, because artworks are first and foremost *made*, while any communicative signal thought to emanate from them has as much to do with historical and cultural context as it does with artistic "expression." I think this is behind Frank Kermode's thesis that masterpieces are naïve: they're readily available platforms for projection and supposition. You can add Bakhtin and say they partake of heteroglossia, so they say many things. My distinction between the made and the said is manifested in modernist art, like the sculptures of Arp or Brancusi—so purely deposited in a material medium it's impossible to imagine them as utterances. They're *deposits*.

Now, the great thorn in the side of the "general reader" (which applies as well to the viewer and the listener) is the supposition that because these aesthetic objects appear meaningful they must harbor meaning(s) that can be extracted from materiality. This issue permeates my treatment of Wagner, who more than anyone else conjured a vast domain of meaningfulness in which people were willing to submerge themselves without (à la Keats) "irritable grasping" after meaning. As the case of Wagner also reveals, basking in the rosy glow of meaningfulness can be a way of abdicating responsibility (cf. Olson's "ability to respond"). The rosy glow throws open a huge back door for opportunistic infiltration, so Bayreuth became political theater for the Third Reich. And this brings me back to pathic receptacles, which are depositories of sentience, and sentience is never far from the fragile and the precarious. The artwork begins by harboring accretions of sentience deposited by the artist, but *as* a receptacle it remains open to further infusions. That's what's behind my neologism, *wreading*. Borrowing the "w" from w̲riting is a way of indicating that the writing never ceases but is continued in the act of reading. Nor is reading a simple executive maneuver like mounting a bicycle. Rereading has been one of the most instructive experiences of my life, because it reveals how far it is, as a cognitive act, from comprehension ("How could I have overlooked that before?"), while also disclosing that our own changing natures provide us as individuals with a multitude of readers. I often have the experience of seeing marginalia in my hand in books I don't recall reading; or, in books I love, finding completely insensible responses to particular passages.

Your mention of "sensory ratios" raises a corollary concerning pathic receptacles. It's phrase from McLuhan, who started out as a scholar of modernism before becoming a media theorist. By sensory ratios he meant there's no strictly organic human sensorium; our lifeworld solicits attentiveness from the senses, and this solicitation is differential. The ears hear differently after attending to Beethoven's late piano sonatas. The eyes have a different relation to color thanks to the Fauves. What turned McLuhan's interest to media was his realization that the technological bonanza of the late nineteenth and early twentieth centuries perpetrated an even more abundant and consequent reallocations of sensory ratios than in the arts. Ears listening through telephones and eyes seeing movies were changed by doing so. And it goes on at an even quicker pace now: just think of the behavioral change the cell phone has brought to a global population (displacing, in the process, the former ubiquity of cigarettes). How does this pertain to pathic receptacles? Considering that this term signals the broader domain in which artworks are housed, it means that any shift in the ratios of the senses have a potentially transformative impact on art. *History of a Shiver* is basically a documentary study in what happened across the arts when music attained a previously unthinkable eminence in Western cultures. *Acrobatic Modernism* addresses activities across the arts at a point of creative and conceptual parity, when music, dance, theatre, art, photography, and literature were all equally heady with emerging possibilities, and by "modernism" I mean the mutual fertilization of each art by some or all the other arts, a kind of cultural psychedelia. As numerous episodes in the book convey, at the root of it all was an intense focus on sensory ratios, their volatility and malleability—and, for artists testing new prospects in a given medium, their potentiality.

I realize that this scenario could be registered more palpably with reference to adolescence, that biological threshold when omnipotentiality surges through the organism. And in these books I've tried to retain some measure of that, like with the Eccentric group in the USSR, whose members were actually teenagers. But it's characteristic of modernism that this corporeal sensation of fresh openings was sustained through many individuals' life cycle, not as libidinal perpetuum mobile but as an ongoing receptivity. From this perspective, it's intriguing to note the self-willed blinders accompanying volatile political circumstances, from Eliot's Anglican turn to the quiescent adaptation to Soviet norms by Rodchenko, Stepanova, Tatlin, and others. I look at them now as cradling a cherished juvenilia of creative momentum, like a fragile egg. I'm more disposed than ever to register this sensation of age as a preservative of youth from my own vantage approaching seventy, when aging is insistent but hasn't wiped out the truly aspirational and spirited enthusiasm youth provides. And I say this as someone besotted by modernism since age fifteen, while also burdened by being of the boomer generation—by which I mean, helplessly whirled into a cultural blender of indignation and nostalgia rolled into one. Apart from the normal media prognostications, there are only two generations of the twentieth century singled out as avatars of a Zeitgeist, the Roaring Twenties crowd and the boomers. Unfortunately, both apply in equal measure, but for different reasons. The "lost generation" were hapless survivors of the Great War, catapulted into boom times, economically, while my generation had the benefits of a comparable economic boom while being sufficiently educated to realize that the fix was in, with respect to race, gender, and the suffocating imperative of normative values. "What are you against?" asks a citizen in *The Wild Ones*, to which Marlon Brando responds, "Whaddya got?" We got it, and are still getting it, though the fraying strands of *getting it* reveal how diverse the constituencies are.

Somewhere in the Combray episode of the *Recherche*, Proust says that adolescence is the only time when we're capable of learning anything. While that's obviously not true, the point is that the educative receptivity of that threshold is unparalleled. But it needn't expire at eighteen or twenty-one or whatever juridical designation. The point is that there's a biological embryonic capacity for recognizing change in its natal state that gets snuffed out by social norms and behavioral adjustments. For me, pathic receptacles—quite apart from the question of art—are ways of registering and retaining this capacity. The precariousness of this prospect is succinctly put in *Acrobatic Modernism*: "Innocence could be the new omniscience" (321).

Brown: If adolescence is "that biological threshold when omnipotentiality surges through the organism," is romanticism the adolescence of modernity? The question isn't entirely serious—or maybe not entirely *literal*—but I pose it because it's with the Jena Romantics that your account of modernism begins. Thus I would add to your earlier insistence, no modernism without modernity, the importance of the same stipulation for what we normally *distinguish* from modernism: no romanticism without modernity. "Omnipotentiality" is to the point here, because your interest in linking early German romanticism with modernism, through the crucible of Wagnerism, is the investment of the circle around the *Athenaeum* in the omnipoteniality of "literature," the sense that it can and should be and do everything. You begin your chapter on "Synaesthesia and Music from Romanticism to Modernism" as follows: "Long before Friedrich Nietzsche thought up the Übermensch, there was an Über-genre, variously called *Poesie*, *Mischgedicht*, or *Roman*." Later, quoting Friedrich Schlegel's recognition that "the romantic imperative demands the mixture of all genres," you note:

> The *Mischgedicht*—or blended poetic composition—fanned the flames of an ambitiously synesthetic compulsion revisited with increasing urgency throughout the nineteenth century. In its most familiar (some would say debased) realization, it was the dream of the *Gesamtkunstwerk* epitomized by Wagner's music dramas. (Rasula 2016, 61)

And then, of course, we see this programmatic incitement toward inter-arts collaboration, and indeed potential unity of the arts in something like an Über-genre, pursued in contexts like the Vkhutemas, Bauhaus, or Black Mountain College ("design" would come to name this aspiration, for better or for worse).

Can something like a historical adolescence last 150 years? Might it be coextensive with modernity? The periodizing implications of terms like "romanticism" and "modernism" are stretched by your account in a way I find extremely productive and also difficult to square with most approaches to the relation between modernism and modernity. If we can specify the romantic imperative of the mixture of all genres as the crux of the problem, as an imperative that will be relayed through the nineteenth century and taken up with explosive consequences by early twentieth-century avant-garde movements, how does this position us with respect to other possible accounts of the relation between modernism and modernity? I think of T. J. Clark, for example, who also begins his elegiac meditation on the history of modernism, *Farewell to an Idea*, in the late eighteenth century, but for him it is the eruption of political contingency in the form of the French Revolution that is at issue. And his focus is entirely on painting.

My own way of approaching these questions is by thinking through the parameters of what I call "expanded poetics," by which I mean to designate the "interdisciplinary" scope of poetry and poetics. That term, "interdisciplinary," is an ideological keyword of the contemporary university, but it also indexes the *problem* of disciplinarity that has its roots in the formalized division of academic disciplines in the university around the late eighteenth century—and also the differentiation of social systems theorized by Niklas Luhmann. *Poesie* or the *Mischegedicht* would then be something like an attempted antidote to such differentiation, which goes through all kinds of modulations and contortions in concert with the development of media systems across the past two hundred years. As Thierry de Duve argues in *Pictorial Nominalism*, institutions like the nineteenth-century Parisian Salon do the work of policing generic criteria ("that is not a painting"), but this itself leads through dialectical indirections to negations of generic criteria like Duchamp's readymade, progenitor of what de Duve calls "art in general."

From a Marxist perspective, I tend to think of the synesthetic ambitions of Jena romanticism as emerging in the context of the industrial revolution: the division of labor and of the process of production in pursuit of efficiency gains, along with all the "separations" of social life and material production (what Marx calls a *Scheidungsprozess*) that accompany that historical phase of capitalism with increasing intensity into the mid-twentieth century. At least this is one way in which I try to understand a certain *unity* of artistic production from the late eighteenth to the mid-twentieth centuries: its synthetic dynamic responds (at a structural level always mediated in different forms) to that process of separation. The virtue of your work's attention to *so many* and so discrepant a range of practices and contexts is that it forces close empirical attention to how particular those mediations are—but you are also offering a sweeping picture of the relation between modernism (*including* romanticism) and modernity. How do you conceptualize these periodizing questions?

Rasula: I've generally refrained from using the term romanticism, addressing instead a particular group of people in a certain place and time, Jena in eastern Germany at the end of the eighteenth century. They're conventionally cited as Romantics, not least because they fashioned that moniker for themselves in a dual gesture: *romantisch* referring to the medieval romances, plus *der Roman* meaning the novel, which they felt was a nascent genre with more potentiality than legacy. Their icons were literary: Dante, Shakespeare, Cervantes, authors in three different genres but, importantly, they did not regard them as models. Dante was not, for them, a poetic exemplum, nor were Shakespeare's motley plays to be taken as rivals to Racine. And the appeal of *Don Quixote* was as a distinctly modern genre, the novel, a gesture of defiance against genre as such (I've written at length about this in my next Oxford book, *Genre and Extravagance in the Novel: Lower Frequencies*). By according the Jena group an initiatory role, I resist Romanticism as historical period, not to disavow it but to concentrate instead on the broader phenomenon of modernity.

Regardless of how modernity is defined or its historical parameters determined, modernity involves change, transformation, and at its symptomatic limit, revolution. So if we push the temporal parameters back five hundred years, the revelation of the New World defines the countenance of modernity. Add to that the Gutenberg press and the religious strife within

Christianity, presaging the eventual democratic revolutions in politics, followed by the industrial revolution, and you've got century upon century of momentous changes registered both gradually and convulsively, depending on the locale. So, from that perspective, romanticism is not an era, but the arousal of a certain sensibility that stretches from Herder and Rousseau well into the twentieth century. One way I absorbed it into my account of modernism was by way of Irving Babbitt, for whom romanticism was a derogatory specification covering exactly the time span I've just indicated: meaning a pervasive sensibility, not a temporal domain. As I put it in *Shiver*: "the first *modernism* was Romanticism," and then quoted Baudelaire: "To say the word Romanticism is to say modern art" (2016, 73).

So how is modernism distinct from romanticism? Isn't it possible that modernism, like romanticism, is not temporal but refers instead to some propensity in human striving that might erupt at any time? I was motivated to think about this during the years when postmodernism was ubiquitous. The prefix rendered it unambiguously temporal, and I just kept thinking: How could that be? How could modernism be peremptorily cancelled? Because modernism, as I understood it, is part and parcel of modernity, and as long as this five-hundred-year convulsion continues to periodically recalibrate the sensory ratios of humans and the social codes of human aggregates, there's no getting over or beyond modernism, which is the adaptive mechanism cultures have devised to engage the onslaught of constant change. And that's why romanticism is a preliminary seismograph of modernism.

Here's the extreme registration of romanticism in Babbitt: "For over a century the world has been fed on a steady diet of revolt. Everybody is becoming tinged with eleutheromania, taken up with his rights rather than with his duties, more and more unwilling to accept limitations" (Rasula 2016, 74). Reading this now, I can't help but think of the American response to the coronavirus pandemic: spot on! Babbitt thought he detected some disabling component of democratic institutions, though for him they weren't uniquely American, but components of Western civilization. The brunt of his critique presses close to claims of artistic efficacy, especially in the twentieth century, when creative "eleutheromania" was in abundance, thanks to which we have the fruits of Futurism, Surrealism, Poetism, and all the rest. Your "expanded poetics" is obviously a more nuanced term than "eleutheromania," suggesting as it does a natural (not a manic) propensity for development. And it was under the sway of Jena theory that the very notion of artistic development could gain credence. But just as compelling was the *Spieltrieb* theorized by Friedrich Schiller, which inspired the Jena folks. It was predicated on his perception, before the Industrial

Revolution, that modern life was remaking people into specialists, so the restorative factor would draw from the artistic spirit of the play-drive. The Spieltrieb is a direct nudge to the "universal progressive poetry" envisioned by Friedrich Schlegel, fortified in totalizing directions in Wagner's Gesamtkunstwerk, and achieving something like multilateral lift-off in modernism as the attempt to unite or unify the arts was transformed into maximal exposure *between* arts, restoring developmental prospects to specific art practices (most influentially accounted for in Clement Greenberg's thesis of medium specificity) while inviting such developments to be mindful of parallel activities in other arts.

On the issue of periodization, I bear in mind Edmund Wilson's reminder from *Axel's Castle*: "What really happens, of course, is that one set of methods and ideas is not completely superseded by another; but that, on the contrary, it thrives in its teeth" (Rasula 2020, 44). So you can still find people writing poetry in a romantic idiom; the best seller lists regularly include realist novels; and in the concert hall you can hear music without a trace of dissonance composed by someone under forty. It's not that you could mistake these things for actual products of 1820 instead of 2020; rather, the identifying traits of historical phenomena like romanticism and modernism get misleadingly applied to period characteristics. In the twentieth century such phenomena are assigned to brief temporal spans like decades. Mention a decade and associations tumble out: the twenties = speakeasies, raccoon coats, mah Jong, and flagpole sitting; the fifties come with pompadours and saddle shoes; the sixties with bell bottoms and long hair, etc. One of the benefits of old novels is that they helplessly identify what's passé, bringing it into differential focus as something that had been unquestionable just yesterday. So the danger of rendering romanticism and modernism as periods is that they're eligible for unthinking dismissal, consigned to the past.

On the subject of modernist periodization, I can't help but think of instances like Rilke, whose association with Rodin attuned him to a vanguard of sculptural possibilities, remaking himself as poet of dedicated austerity in the *Neue Gedichte* and author of one of the most resonant portraits of urban despondency in *The Notebooks of Malte Laurids Brigge*. But *Duino Elegies* and *Sonnets to Orpheus*, clearly summits of twentieth-century poetry, are tentative instances of modernism. Maybe the same applies to *Las Alturas de Macchu Picchu* by Neruda, a masterpiece unencumbered by period specification. Another factor arises, however, in the case of Huidobro's *Altazor*, in that his wizardly absorption of phono-poetics invites comparison with the Lautgedichte of the German Dadaists, and similar initiatives in France. The way in which I've just turned to examples suggests a necessary disclaimer: I don't work with overarching concepts, adhering instead to an immediate response to particular instances. This approach clearly signals liabilities to those who proceed otherwise, who have prefabricated notions of modernism and are on the lookout for verifications. By contrast, I'm willing to be proven wrong every step of the way, the challenge in my books being: you have to walk the walk with me. In an odd way I feel like a census taker, going door to door, tabulating the results. I hope a reader feels that sense of contact (William Carlos Williams's *Contact* being the exemplary modernist title for a journal), that my resources are *encounters*. And it's not like I've gone looking for obscurities. It's just that the normal course of investigation turns up names, and I respond like a sleuth: Who's this? And so it goes.

One of the reasons an unhelpful period-based model of modernism persisted for so long was the "men of 1914" congregation, with its male Anglo-American focus. So in Lawrence Rainey's *Modernism: An Anthology* (2005), seventy-five pages are given to W. B. Yeats, a thoroughly romantic poet who as late as 1929 qualified his friendship with Ezra Pound by noting that his "art is the opposite of mine" and "whose criticism commends what I most condemn" (Rainey 370). So it's only by virtue of temporal special pleading that Yeats gets a seat at the table. But it's useful to have him in the mix, visibly in the case of the photograph I included in *History of a Shiver* (163) where generations assemble, from Yeats and Wilfrid Scawen Blunt (married to Byron's granddaughter) to Pound and Aldington. Yeats is a figure, like Rilke and others—Sibelius in music, Hopper in painting, etc.—who bear the imprint of romanticism amid the otherwise fervent modernizing tendencies of the twentieth century, plausibly seen as "moderns," but not "modernists."

The difference between moderns and modernists has to do with mimesis. Mimesis takes a turn in modernism. From antiquity, mimesis had meant imitation of some perceptible source, and while that understanding never receded, modernists began to think of mimesis as imposing certain perceptual and conceptual reckonings. Mimesis was not a straightforward replication of reality, but a stylized treatment subject to approval. And as I say somewhere in *Acrobatic Modernism*, one way of understanding modernism is that certain artists simply decided to forego middle-class peer review. Of course, interesting artists find ways to write, paint, compose in a way that bears the mark of their distinction, and I think of that as *performative*. The spirit I identify with the Jena theorists, which culminates with modernism, is not performative because it regards its mission as the creation of a new genre or presentational mode: to "start from scratch," as Barnett Newman put it (Rasula 2020, 368), taking up a pledge or prospect of Symbolism, outlined in *History of a Shiver*'s chapter "Drawing a Blank."

I tossed a considerable number of such thematic lines over the trajectory of the two books, hoping not so much that readers might notice them, but to reinforce a subterranean sense of recognition. Again and again I'd come to the point of realizing that the normative scholarly way of handling this stuff was to line it up and make a prosecutorial case: a + b + c = x, where x equals some variant of modernism. My approach differs in that I adhere to some recognition of particular human agents as informants in an anthropological sense. I'm an anthropologist of modernism. The fact that these people were alive means a great deal to me, and I try to encounter them in the spirit of their vivacity, their aspirations, and at times their dismay. They're never simply sources of quotations (and I can't tell you how much time I've spent tracking down details about the lives of obscure figures I've quoted, acutely aware that they may not have been mentioned in print for quite a while). So there's a lot that doesn't end up in the books, kind of like background research an actor might do for a part but never makes it on screen since it's not in the script.

Brown: "Some propensity in human striving that might erupt at any time"—let me take that up. On the one hand, I like the formulation "anthropologist of modernism" as a description on your attunement to individual human agents in the throes of *poiesis*. On the other hand, those throes traverse individuals in a manner irreducible to their subjective particularity, and also to their historical circumstances. That may be the crux of the matter. *There are* historical circumstances, and *there are* individual human agents who respond to more or less "the same" circumstances in radically different ways. But there *is also* that striving which subtends, seizes, transfigures, and is expressed through particular individuals and circumstances at any given time. That shift from the plural (there are) to the singular (there is) registers a tension and perhaps even a contradiction that is constitutive of the dialectical relation between making and unmaking: whatever is made unmakes the one (or the several) who makes it, even as it indexes the peculiarity of their existence in its concreteness as pathic receptacle: registration of the damage that is done to historical individuals and the transmutation of that damage by an activity (*poiesis*), which is not only its inscription but also its transfiguration, if never quite its overcoming.

The power of these two books—which I appreciate as the gift of a whole life, of a life's work—is that up close, in the act of reading, one is immersed in a thicket of qualitatively dense information quantitatively different from what one encounters in proximate accounts of the same phenomena. Yet at even the merest distance, stepping back from the books for a day or two while reflecting on their effects, one begins to feel the huge and unassimilable *restlessness* that echoes through their composition. Their composition is an instance of that restlessness, and that suffices to distinguish them from most criticism. And perhaps this is where (w)reading comes in as a reader of your own work—as it comes in right now, in this act of composition. The books we need are not just those that break the frozen sea within us but those which, in doing so, force us to *become adequate* to the rupture of the encounter they become. To *encounter* what is called "modernism"—isn't that the problem and the task? We all do it; it happens all the time: at thirty-five I finally read *Ulysses*, somehow never having done so until then, and found myself devouring the last two hundred pages in a frenzy of reading in the middle of the night in a cabin in the woods and it was as though I knew for sure, amid the Nighttown episode, *this is the most subversive text I have ever read*, turning the pages as if my life depended on it, because it did and it still does. We have to be that *hungry* for the art we are given, or that we make—in my affirmation of that principle I am willing to be guilty of the most absurd naiveté.

So, when we write books on these productions, on vast constellations of these productions, and, beyond the constellations they form, of the great disorder, the formless yearning they make manifest, I view it as an ethical demand that we should become adequate to the occasion. But what does that mean? No one can *become equal* to "modernism." But that *no one*, and that negation, that sense of *insufficiency* should become the measure of sufficiency: of what has to be done. Or at least we can say: once in a while, certain books should come along that shake something loose, that break free, in their extremity, a certain *passion* that had been otherwise contained. It is paradoxical that, in the midst of your chapter on the slogan "Make It New" in *Acrobatic Modernism*, a certain tedium sets in. Why not open up some space *to write*, I asked myself? *To think*? Why this torrent of information, of the name, of quotation, of the example, of *all* the examples? "Enough of this" you write at one point, yet the chapter continues in the same vein, as if it were unable to obey its own imperative. And yet, at a slight distance from the act of reading that chapter, and considering the books in tandem (in which ample space is accorded to *writing*, to *thinking*), one recognizes that there are good answers to these questions. There has to be a space, as well, for the mere fulguration of what was said, for the profligacy of saying the same thing with minor differences, for the whole futility—and yet within that the odd accomplishment of that futility—of saying "new" over and over and over again with slight or sometimes massively consequential variations. How strange, that "the new" should accomplish itself with such undeniable self-evidence amid the reign of tautology its imperative bespeaks. . . .

Now there is a method in that strangeness, that limit point of "defamiliarization" so oddly inscribed by saying the same thing. We see it in your luminous chapter in *History of a Shiver*, "Symbolist Retraction," where reduction to the zero is recognized as the prius of significance at its apogee, the symbol. We recognize it also in your chapter on "Jazzbandism" in *Acrobatic Modernism* where—peerless historical contingency—the *sound* of jubilee, the transmission of its contradictions in the break, should amount to what you call "the inaugural global convulsion of modernity in the early twentieth century, nothing less than 'the electric jolt of the universe'" (quoting Antonio Ferro in that last phrase). "Periodizing rubrics tend to downplay transitions," you write in the chapter on symbolism. And we see in Jolas's journal, so important to your relation to modernism (and to *Finnegans Wake*), that *transition* itself can be made the very principle of modernism: something like that "dark principle" Schelling touches upon— that "indivisible remainder" which "remains eternally in the ground"— which gives rise to *something new*, that "essence of yearning" which reveals without ever itself becoming accessible to revelation. "Transition" is the name of that *ontological ground* disclosed in the title of a journal or evident within any historically specific "movement." But movement is precisely that which is irreducible to the name of any avant-garde, to any journal, insofar as it traverses all their discrepant instantiations. It portends, on the one hand, the zero, and on the other, the untotalizable becoming of differential infinities. Modernism takes place in *that* break, *is* the site of that rupture.

We want a *critical* relation to modernism that could register all that, without being swept away by it into a stutter—but one would have to register, inscribe, indeed *become* the stutter in order to make clear the enormity of the difficulty. *History of a Stutter*? That would also be a good book. The methodological task imposes real risks one would have to run in order not to avoid them. I take it that's the point of your enterprise. What's interesting is that the whole problem of what making anything at all entails becomes evident in the pursuit. There is this *superfluity*—which I know you insist on, and rightly so—to *poiesis* that is one of the strangest and most essential things about human existence. Why should it be that there are artworks at all? The last two chapters of *Acrobatic Modernism* return us to this question. Which implies: *modernism* poses this question, with especial force. And I think that is true. I think that "modernism" bespeaks an attunement toward what you call "human striving," what we could even describe ontologically as "the essence of yearning," which is in some sense unprecedented. Indeed, I consider it something like a criterion of hope: *could there ever be something like modernism again?* It goes on, we are not after its tendency, but could there be something like that impetus again? How awful, and how horribly necessary, that capitalist modernity (the ideological crux of "futurism" and "primitivism") should be the cradle of such astonishing developments. But so it is. Adorno's integrity is his registration of this horror while registering the fullness of its truth.

My point is: I do think *History of a Shiver* and *Acrobatic Modernism* install us in this problem, in the way they make manifest the restlessness of spirit at the core of the artwork as pathic receptacle and historical icon (a black square, etc.—where everything depends on the "etc."). Let me ask the question point blank (along with and hopefully not canceling all the other incitements of this response): what is the *ontological* dimension of your relation to modernism, its luminous sores and its multiplied subjects? I ask because I do think modernism itself is a registration like no other of the rift between, and the unsurpassable problem of the relation between, *history* and *being*, through those "individual human agents" whose aliveness means so much to you. We know—in some sense we know—that *poiesis* inhabits this rift between being and history. These books bring this knowledge to light, in the context of modernism, with an intensity I have not otherwise encountered.

Rasula: All that you raise here strikes me as emanating from your analysis of "The Seven Old Men" in your book manuscript on Baudelaire, especially this: "The experience of the poem's existence demands attention to *poiesis* as processual determination, not merely by authorial construction but by the way in which the poem *takes place* as the construction that it is, through the extension of its temporalization." The gist of your questions is an unspoken query as to how my engagement with modernism is reflected in, or impinged upon, by the subject itself. Or, in more mundane terms: do I write differently about modernism than I would about Shakespeare or Homer? I tend to write my way *into* my writing, as it were, before consciousness has set an agenda. So there's a relation of immanence between the *what* and the *how*. There are lots of other voices in *Acrobatic Modernism* especially, and I hear them as speakers jostling for space, not as quotations. A quotation is normally subsumed in the verification of a case, a link in a prosecutorial chain. But I rarely deploy quotations that way. They're part of a hubbub that I have some hand in convening, but it precedes me by far and I can detect signs of it disappearing into the future without me. I think of the amazing line from "Mother of Muses" in Bob Dylan's *Rough and Rowdy Ways*: "I've already outlived my life by far."

I'm curious about your sense of a "huge and unassimilable *restlessness*" in the composition of *History of a Shiver* and *Acrobatic Modernism*. The act of writing them felt more like a prolonged and welcome repose, with the understanding that for me "repose" means basking in the sleuthing side of research, exulting in serendipitous discoveries in unexpected places or by unexpected means. But I can infer from what you say that the multitudes of individuals assembled and cited in those books probably give off a vibe of metropolitan activity, the ferment of artistic associations, alliances, friendships, and rivalries. And the sheer plethora of details is what you rightly sense as tedious in the "Make It New" chapter, which I cast that way deliberately. I mean, Pound's slogan was already overhyped, so when I started to realize there was a full-throated chorus behind it, I decided that a slow pan over the faces (quotes) would provide that jack-hammer sense of ceaseless irritating pounding. The chapters in both books are very deliberately strategized as to tone, length, modes of elaboration, level of detail, and pace. The chapter on H. D. and Warburg is the opposite of "Make It New," in that it proceeds with analytical and conceptual precision, whereas the parade of the New imposes the numbing sense of inevitability in the Pasadena Rose Parade: one float after another, so the intrigue is all in the details until the details wear you out. I was concerned about the "Multiplied Man" chapter on pseudonyms because it started, like "Make It New," as little more than a list, and two in one book seemed a stretch. So it took me longer to write, as I had to devise ways of irrigating the theme, as it were, and patiently watching the seeds grow.

On the subject of multiplicity, I want to quote this passage from Novalis: "In a *genuine discourse* one plays all roles—goes through all characters— all conditions—just to surprise—to regard the object *from a new angle*, to suddenly astonish the hearer."[1] This is a fairly accurate reflection of what I meant by expressing my appreciation for lives *lived*. I've always found it easy to get into the particularities of different artists, inhabiting their perspectives in a thespian way. I'm the opposite of a skeptical reader. Not that I'm gullible, it's just that before I got into literature I was heavily involved in theatre—acting, directing—so I tend to approach creators in any medium as if they were "parts" to be played. And it's often the case with lesser-known figures that I can exhaustively trawl through a lot of sources only to find few or no biographical details, which is a bit like having to play a role not robustly written by the playwright. In any case, this informs my research but not to any great extent the exposition in these books, though I suppose I do drop in a bit more character portraiture and narrate a few more incidents than you find in thesis driven scholarship. The only chance I've had to develop a full-scale thespian approach was in the Dada history,

Destruction Was My Beatrice (2015), which I drafted very much as if I were writing a novel, digging into the characters' perspectives as much as possible. Then, in rewriting, testing every supposition for plausibility and, most of all, for documentable accuracy. I've never had any aspiration to write a novel, so this was an interesting experience.

To your question, Why should there be artworks at all? From a thespian perspective: Why are there other people? That's an ontological concern, but in the practical business of examining modernism it takes another form: Why *these* people? And I don't mean that in the canonical sense, as in Why pay attention to X and Y, but not Q and Z? I mean rather the compulsive curiosity I've always felt about modernism, something that was readily hatched for me at age sixteen when I read the first biography of Pound by Charles Norman (published in 1958). All the people he knew were like a checklist: Who's George Antheil? Who's Jane Heap? Who's Jean Cocteau? Who's Francis Picabia?—on and on and on. Fifty years later I'm still tracking some of them down! This is, in a way, edging around to your question about the "*ontological* dimension of [my] relation to modernism." And it's right to apply it to the question of *poiesis* as you do, which "inhabits this rift between being and history." I think the habitation is where ontology comes into play (this is a distinctly Heideggerian response). It has to do with *Dasein*, "being there," where both the *being* and the *place* (spatiotemporal modernism) are worked out simultaneously. It has to do with what I call "endless modernism," which is a way of deposing periodization, because periodization implies a known zone—the past, over yonder—and you just step into it like going into a building. But part of what's transfixing about modernism pertains to what Picasso said about Cubism being "like a perfume, in front of you, behind you, to the sides, the scent is everywhere but you don't quite know where it comes from" (Rasula 2020, 61). Modernism is not a place but an aroma, so researching it is more like following a culinary possibility.

Picasso's analogy epitomizes the *imposition* legislated by modernism, the demand for an encounter as you put it. It's not a conceptual matrix to be parsed, a puzzle to be solved, though many have approached it that way—the most thoroughgoing instance being *Preface to Modernism* by Art Berman (1994), so fastidious in its analytic rigor that hardly a proper name appears (even the index, normally a roll call of names, only occasionally registers a human presence). The more common approach was germinated by those who lived it even if, like Malcolm Cowley, they disavowed the term modernism. Cowley's *Exile's Return* (1951), Matthew Josephson's *Life among the Surrealists* (1962), Robert McAlmon's *Being Geniuses Together*, revised by Kay Boyle (1968), and most famously *A Moveable Feast* by Ernest Hemingway (1964): these and scores of similar titles made modernism eligible for the awestruck homage in Woody Allen's film *Midnight in Paris*. This is the postcard modernism of legendary lives and high times, which translated equally well into fiction, like *Nightwood, Women in Love* and the *Berlin Stories* of Isherwood, which invite mapping onto actual people and incidents. But reading Hemingway and Cowley and the rest has become a form of literary tourism in which generations of people learned to genuflect before the Big Names. To respond to modernism on that level is to utterly evade the aromatic allure of the encounter, which is above all the enticement to go bushwhacking, to break away from the guided tour (or in the analogy I used in *The American Poetry Wax Museum*, the headset voiceover), the easily informative companionability of modernist institutions like MoMA and the Tate Modern. And so, in heeding that call, I feel like someone from the nineteenth century returning from the Amazon, wondering whether anyone would credit the report of what I witnessed. *History of a Shiver* and *Acrobatic Modernism*—to stay with the anthropological claim—are my *Argonauts of the Western Pacific*, or (not that I include transcriptions of my dreams) my *Phantom Africa*.

This is what "being adequate to the occasion" entailed for me, though it's not a matter of being "equal" to modernism, as you surmise. It's not a prizefight in a ring. It's not even another person, but I like the way *perfume* and *person* share an initial phoneme. A more recognizable term for perfume/person is T. S. Eliot's "historical sense," which I've always found compelling in his specification that it's something you feel deep in your bones. It's corporeal. To heed it that way is to realize it's not strictly retrospective, it's not "just history," it's also premonitory. That's something we're feeling right now in the midst of the coronavirus pandemic. It looms large—uncomfortable and discomforting—in the future, and as such has scarcely cast a shadow on the past. Modernism is a sort of cultural pandemic, in that it is readily transmissible and can even spread through asymptomatic carriers; it's global, it straddles political divides with impunity, but it's more contagious in urban environments. By characterizing modernism through the traits of a virus reveals how it is that many are spooked, dismissive, or just wish it would go away. A constant refrain from colleagues over the years working in pre-twentieth-century literature is the confession that their worst literary encounter (as grad school obligation) was with Joyce's *Ulysses*. There's a world of difference, of course, between reading an assignment and reading as exploration, which is how I construe adequacy to the occasion. The exploratory mode is of no use as long as you disable your own resources by genuflecting in front of a "masterpiece," which is what so many modernist works have been dubbed. "Recover the ugliness" was Gertrude Stein's recommendation, though I think *grotesque* is a more helpful term than ugly.

I would hope that anyone reading my books would come away with a long list of things to look into, and not a single work in any medium having been declared a masterpiece.

Brown: Let's come back to the relation between "those feisty antagonists, Surrealism and Constructivism" (Rasula 2020, 350), which runs through much of the book in different forms. The concept of artworks as pathic receptacles offers an approach to their common ground since, as you note, "it brings to the notion of the artwork a biomorphic insistence, a biologically exigent extension of corporeality; a way of suggesting that the composer, poet, or painter is not trying to 'say' something but to *make* something, and this generative impulse is profoundly embedded in a somatic manifold" (62). One thinks of that Lissitzky self-portrait, *The Constructor*, which you cite in the last chapter of *Acrobatic Modernism*: even the hand adjoined to the compass, such that one has to wonder, within the formal parameters of the composition, *which is the prosthesis*? Surrealism realizes that "biologically exigent extension of corporeality" via the unconscious, so often and so erroneously understood as the province of the private subject—whereas the unconscious is the unbounded extension of the psyche into and throughout history, technics, and indeed all those *images*, all those *impressions*, that traverse the production and reception of artworks over millennia. One can thematize the extension of the unconscious, in the mode of what gets called Surrealism, but it also pervades those manifestations of formal rigor we might associate with Constructivism.

Hans Arp plays an important role in the penultimate chapter of *Acrobatic Modernism*, titled "The New Mythology"—especially via the commentaries of Carola Giedion-Welcker, who emerges as a crucial figure toward the end of the book. I hadn't encountered her work before, but the passages you cite from her essays are striking: "if 'subject' tends to disappear, content does not;" or on Arp's sculptures, "something growing, welling, gliding which admits neither of formal nor mental frontiers and fixations." Content does not disappear; there is *something* growing, welling, gliding. If subject disappears by submitting to the rule of the protractor, the latter is somehow also invested, by way of the relation of the circle it traces to other elements of the composition, with psychic content (whether it be the face of Lissitzky or even just the decision to place one geometrical form beside another). You reproduce the beautiful and illuminating juxtaposition in Giedion-Welcker's book, *Modern Plastic Art*, of melting blobs of snow constellating a river with a sculpture by Arp, its smooth white contours akin to those of the snow—but which would have seemed "abstract" without the mimetic reference. There is *something* growing, swelling, gliding—but what is it that grows, and swells, and glides in those mounds of snow? The image bespeaks the spirit of matter, through the apprehension of its forms and their rendering as artwork, pathic receptacle of a sense of the world. For we are also that matter that becomes of a great thaw, as well as that configuration of matter which could be erased by rising temperatures.

Anything that we construct is an inscription of the unconscious; the unconscious is inscribed by every construction we encounter. Artworks, as pathic receptacles, would seem to be registrations of this chiasmus: the difference and indistinction of Constructivism and Surrealism located right at the crux, like the crossing of the Symbolic and the Imaginary on Lacan's L Schema. It strikes me that modernism, through "abstraction" and the radically different paths it may take, makes this crux inescapable by pushing certain contradictions to their limits. The *isms* of art, in their conflict and through their claims, inscribe a great reckoning with liminal possibilities in the history of artworks and their relation to the psyche. So again the challenge is to traverse the *differences* among those possibilities sufficiently to bring them together. One might think of conflicting "versions" of modernism forwarded by Greenberg (medium specificity, Malevich) or de Duve (art in general, Duchamp), but the incisive writing of a figure like Giedion-Welcker gets us closer to the heart of the matter as it unfolded, wherein retrospective "versions" of modernism (claims upon cultural capital) will have to wait until later, as one tries to figure out what's going on while it is taking place.

In the 1980s and '90s you were a correspondent for *Sulfur* magazine, "A Literary Tri-Quarterly of the Whole Art." *Sulfur* is a great example of a publication, an orientation toward "the whole art," that traversed the distinction between Constructivism and Surrealism. Your reviews for *Sulfur* are exemplary instances of trying to figure out what's going on while it is taking place, and also of *delimiting* what really matters, of taking seriously the contestation of claims upon art. The problem is how to take up "the whole art" without giving way to a dull eclecticism for which anything goes. And there again, in that context much closer to our own moment, everything depended on orientations toward what Olson called "the going live present." I take it such a designation bears upon the *responsibility* toward the function of artworks as pathic receptacles: given that they do function as such, they had better not be saccharine or purely opportunistic, since the genuine pain of history as it goes on is encoded in their contours.

Rasula: I first came across Carola Giedion-Welcker in *Transition* back in the mid-'90s when I was writing an essay on *Finnegans Wake* (which was absorbed into "The New Mythology" chapter in *Acrobatic Modernism*). When I tracked down the posthumous collection of her essays, *Schriften*

1926–1971, it was inspiring to see the people she wrote about (Joyce, Brancusi, Ernst, Arp, Moholy-Nagy, Kandinsky, Klee, Schwitters, Giacometti, and others) and most were her friends. It became even more intriguing when I realized her husband was Siegfried Giedion, whose magisterial book on Paleolithic cave art I had long been familiar with, *The Eternal Present* in the Bollingen Series. Carola was a stalwart supporter and friend of James Joyce, and one of the few people who celebrated both *Ulysses* and *Finnegans Wake*, recognizing them as models of artistic plasticity. She mostly wrote about the visual arts, not literature, and I think that enabled her to recognize in Joyce a propensity for managing, deforming, and forming raw material. He worked with words, she saw, the way Schwitters combed the streets for reusable rubbish or Giacometti whittled his figures down to the edge of erasure. She closely followed the avant-gardes while remaining distant from the polemics, and that enabled her to focus on the creative trajectories of artists as individuals rather than types or exponents of a program.

Figuring out what's going on while it's taking place is a matter of instinct, I think. I did a mountain of book reviews during my twenties, in print and on the radio, and that's the kind of work that can send you in two directions. The more common one is appraisal, judgement: good or bad, plus or minus, and the actual content of the books is almost beside the point. For me it was the other way around. I read and reviewed for the content, and content is invariably broader than a given book, so content leads to context, and context eventually opens out on the panorama of *History of a Shiver* and *Acrobatic Modernism*, works I can't conceive of having written if I had not gotten a review copy of John Willett's *Art and Politics in the Weimar Period* in 1979, with its compelling diagrams and profusion of photographs. It revealed to me a breadth of avant-garde activity I knew from isolated individuals like Brecht, Mayakovsky, Kandinsky, but Willett brought them vividly together into a vast assemblage of moving parts. At the same time I was absorbed in Willett I was involved in a network of American poetry, in a decidedly preinternet era when people would phone, letters arrive in the mail, and personal visits (often out of the blue) were the order of the day. It's probably important that none of this involved universities, or barely. Nate Mackey was the first professor I ever met, socially. And at the time (1977) that was of no more interest than if he'd been a chef or a lifeguard.

The spell of modernism, for me, is the sheer heterogeneous welter of activity and interaction, that sense of so much going on all the time. So biographies of people like Mina Loy are of interest not only because of her but the cast of characters and the enhanced sense of simultaneity. People then had to be quick on the uptake, ready to respond to instant flashes of creative abandon. In some respect the sectarianism of the Surrealists or the various groups of abstract or nonobjective art reflects not so much their theoretical platforms but the pressure of constant contact. Hans (or Jean) Arp was a rare figure who could meet up with Breton's crowd at a café in the morning and then get together at a different café in the afternoon with the geometric purists. I assume Arp just responded to interesting people, regardless of where they were on some aesthetic or political spectrum, and my interest in modernism is similar. The antagonism between the Surrealists and the abstract/Constructivist proponents was ferocious, and yet coexistence proved possible in the end, largely as a result of historical cataclysm. The trauma of exile and displacement puts everyone in contact with primal instinct, paranoia, anxiety neurosis, basic manifestations of the unconscious. Those key Freudian features of the dreamwork, condensation and displacement, move closer to the surface.

But what about supposedly normal circumstances? I was intrigued by your insistence that the unconscious was as formative for Constructivism as for Surrealism, not that they would agree. But where it makes sense is in the utopian charter they bought into in the Soviet Union. When Rodchenko, Stepanova, and others who followed "art into production," it was a leap of faith for them to abandon easel painting and other fine art practices, so their pledge to the future was no less invested in the unconscious than the Surrealist games of Exquisite Corpse. In any case, one of the more striking things I discovered along the way was the longevity of modernists across the board, as if their creative adventures kept rejuvenating them over the decades. Few of them ever got into the rut of self-parody or mechanical churning of the wheels. They kept reinventing themselves, and their art, time and again. Moholy-Nagy is a perfect example—the big retrospective I saw at LACMA a few years ago was a revelation of just this point—although, killed by leukemia at fifty-one, he's an exception to the longevity rule. If we speak of an unconscious playing a role in geometric abstraction, I think it has more to do with the potential response rather than the artistic orientation. It's revealing that abstract art could be so vilified during the thirties, as much so as Surrealism was. But with Surrealism people saw intentional transgression, whereas abstraction just seemed inhuman, a kind of microbial threat. We've been so long accustomed to such work—the dissemination of Mondrian's grids in popular culture is handsomely documented in *The Afterlife of Piet Mondrian* by Nancy Troy—it's hard to imagine why anyone would object. Yet the *sensation* of encountering modernism across the board is best registered by Roger Fry in 1920 (though here was talking about the discovery of the Paleolithic): "Knowledge and perception have poured upon us so fast that the whole well-ordered system has been blown away, and we stand bare to the blast, scarcely able to snatch a hasty generalization or two to cover our nakedness for a moment" (Rasula 2020, 360). Standing bare to the blast captures what I tried to do, writing about modernism.

Brown: Snapshots:

(1) "Gertrude Stein recognized in jazz an anxiety comparable to that felt in the theatre in the gap between the anticipatory restlessness of the audience and the performance itself" (Rasula 2020, 254).

(2) "Brigman's naked dryads in the high Sierras, like Imogen Cunningham's Edenic nudes of her husband on Mount Rainier, emphatically place the figure in a dynamic landscape, as if the body were the key that opens the lock of the sublime, like [Isadora] Duncan dancing as a child on a beach in California. For thousands of years, the dancing figure had been traced, sculpted, drawn, painted, summoned in song and verse, and set in motion on the stage. Mallarmé had conceived of such a figure as writing directly on space. But now space had a new ally, a new medium, in the photographed image. The Arcadian dream was ready at last for its close-up" (Rasula 2016, 198).

(3) "Endless melody is posited in the nineteenth century, alongside (but without reference to) the dream of the perpetual-motion machine. At the same time, the second law of thermodynamics is being formulated, which stipulates that no new source of energy is available in the universe, so perpetual motion is a phantasm. Melody, of course, bore its adjective *endless* as euphemism, hope, enticement. No melody could be endless, so *endless* here meant something like exceeding the parameters, going out of bounds" (Rasula 2016, 228).

I cite the first and third of these passages to draw music more directly into the conversation, since Wagnerism and jazz, in particular, are central to these books. But to set these in an even more complex relation, I've cited as well a passage from your chapter on "Pictorialism, Dance, and the American Arcady" in *History of a Shiver*, wherein the intersection of embodied movement with both the freeze frame of the flicker of the cinematic apparatus instantiates a specifically modernist form of pastoralism.

Stein registers the *Erwartung* of swing and syncopation, as if the "different tempo" of jazz produced a motion capture image of an emotional state *just before* the onset of endless melody, while the photographic framing of Arcadian gesture on the cliffs of Big Sur captures a kind of planetary resonance of the body in motion, torn out of willed anachronism by the historical specificity of a medium. Somehow these three elements of the books seem to me joined by an elaborate tracery, though they draw together very different cultural contexts. Melody *would* be endless, as one *would* make a new Greece of California, and disjunction of the conditional in these and so many other examples requires a "new" rhythm, adequate to the scission between the past and the future, the historical torque of new media encountering ancient desires.

"Wagnerism" and "Jazzbandism" capture the synesthetic impulses of artists and the international rapture of infectious tonalities of the soul in their respective centuries—how do you think about their relationship across those centuries? And how might an evidently more "local" and peculiar phenomenon like West Coast pageantry and pagan dance settle in between these instances of synesthetic fervor? I'll close with this invitation to address image, movement, melody, and rhythm as they conjoin with technology and desire across the sweep of these two books.

Rasula: In some ways, synesthetic fantasies and aspirations were a byproduct of melomania, or excessive devotion to music, outsized expectations of music as a transformative spiritual and/or social agent. Wagnerism drew on the cult of musical genius that started with Beethoven and expanded with Liszt (Wagner's father-in-law). But Wagnerism was not limited to adulation of the composer, being instead the enfranchisement of the audience. A cult, in other words, with the potential to become a social movement. Jazzbandism was something else altogether because it was the first global phenomenon in the age of mass media, circulating as much by recordings and radio as by live performance. By the time jazz appeared, synesthesia was long gone, having faded away before the Great War. The *spectacle* of jazz inspired an occasional reference to the Gesamtkunstwerk, which for some might carry a faint suggestion of mingled sensory receptivity. For fans, especially the French, jazz was all about realism, not fantasy, revitalizing the body politic after the calamity of industrial warfare. It's because they're so different that I focused on Wagnerism in one book and Jazzbandism in the other, since each could be understood as an *ism* and thus congruent with the panoply of other isms, while their sociohistorical roles diverge. Jazz was not a later eruption of something familiar in Wagnerism. What they share and shed light on is the durability of melomania, and if I were to extend the chronology from midcentury on, rock would be the unavoidable next phase of this historical trajectory. I have no such plans, but recently read a number of books on Bob Dylan (anticipating his new CD, *Rough and Rowdy Ways*, yet another glorious entry in the "style of old age"), and have been reminded all over again how persistently melomania translates into complete fantasy (*Like a Rolling Stone* by Greil Marcus) and indulgent esoterica (*Bob Dylan in America* by Sean Wilentz). Elijah Wald, by contrast, is grounded in documentation and dispassionate reflection on the events he narrates in *Dylan Goes Electric*. Rock reintroduced the synesthetic prospect with light shows at the Fillmore in San Francisco, aided by hallucinogens.

Your fetching phrase, "international rapture of infectious tonalities," is accurate without needing to bring in synesthesia, which was a fairly localized if inspiring fantasy, especially among those for whom the Jena Romantics' dream of the Mischgedicht or mixed-genre composition was an incentive. The more compelling trend was to take inspiration from another art in the creative explorations of one's own art, so a painting could not just be "like" music but, by some rhetorical jiu-jitsu, *be* music. In the end, this somewhat delusional aspiration had exorbitant formal consequences in the recalibration of artistic resources, although the often-utopian expectations of social consequence foundered. As you sense, in laying out the terms image, movement, melody, and rhythm, there is a polytemporal interlocking of resources that spurred the organization of materials in *History of a Shiver* and *Acrobatic Modernism*. Your reference to the historical specificity of a medium is a crucial aspect. The formalist approach to modernism regarded medium-specificity as an internal development with little regard for the historical positioning of the medium itself. Because Clement Greenberg's formalism centered on easel painting, it could be assumed to have somehow overcome the vicissitudes of temporality, establishing a "pure" and seemingly timeless resource for artistic composition. I tried to push back against this, not by confronting it directly but by positioning film as a periodic focal point in both books, neither of which has a chapter on film per se. So it's kept a bit undercover. Also, there are few references to actual films, so my attention is mostly on the theoretical fantasies incited by early cinema before the talkies came in. But this theoretical agitation provides a through-line to German Romantic theory, which in some respects was protocinematic. Film theory by Canudo, Epstein, Eisenstein, Vertov, and others I cite is often addressed to the "emotional state *just before*" in your expression, because they were near the beginning of the medium, figuring out its potential in words as well as on screen.

One of the things that cinema brought into focus—conceptually, I mean, not visually—was the rhythm of accentual interruption, musically known as syncopation. A disruption, a hiccup. And because this was an increasingly normative experience in urban life, as a new art film seemed to be preternaturally astride this nascent perceptual horse. So much modernist art registers perceptual disjunctions that were encountered every day, while films worked in a medium that was literally disjunctive, composed of moving image sequences spliced together, and the practical challenge was how to splice for continuity and comprehensibility. The other arts were in some sense overburdened by these features, so the advent of cinema emboldened some to reverse the process, to abandon continuity and comprehensibility and invent strategies of disruption. *Ulysses* is a great example. In 1909 Joyce interested some venture capitalists in Trieste in bankrolling the first cinema in Dublin. Later, dubious about the prospect of translations of *Ulysses*, he thought it might be better "translated" into film. So the great shift is not one art borrowing from another, but arts using other arts to catapult over themselves.

Here's where rhythm comes into play, as such acrobatic aspirations require precise rhythms of attention. As a longtime soccer player I could understand how artists came to value the examples of acrobatics, circus, and competitive games. Every sport imposes its own rhythms of attention. How long can the batter stand in the box and sustain focus while the pitcher fidgets on the mound? How does a quarterback gauge the collapse of the pocket before either throwing the pass, making a run for it, or crumpling under the onslaught? The soccer pitch escalates that to a geometric dizziness, and the European avant-gardes are surely indebted to the uninterrupted flow of soccer. American sports, by contrast, have periodic stoppages (innings, time-outs, etc.). Soccer only pauses at a penalty, or an injury. It would be going too far to suggest that I patterned the chapters in my books on the rhythms of particular sports, but it would be accurate to say that the sense of rhythm I brought to composing and sequencing them reflects the lessons I've learned as participant and spectator. I'd expect that someone with a musical background would bring a comparable kinetic instinct. Whatever one's personal orientation may be concerning modernism, the fulcrum of attention—or maybe *attentiveness* would be the better word—is "the category of 'almost,'" as Schlegel puts it (1971, 152).

What I was saying earlier about disjunction really comes to the fore with respect to rhythm, because the kind of acrobatic rhythm in team sports is predicated on interruption. By contrast, the Olympics highlight "individual achievement" in a way also enshrined in the arts. But the collectivist sensibility of modernism creates a kind of detour, a workaround. Hans Arp's insistence on producing sculptures that blend into nature is also a way of saying he's fine with his works complying with the group effort of Surrealism as well as abstraction. It's rare to find Dada and even Surrealist poetry in anthologies, tainted it seems by doctrinaire implications. But read it in the context of the journals—and especially the collaborative books with artists—they occupy the space precisely. The ensembles engineered by jour-

nal editing in the heyday of the avant-gardes created the optimal environment for artworks, writings, blueprints, photographs, and other material; so
it can be disconcerting to see these things redistributed in art history books
and exhibition catalogues, denuded of context. Many of the local contexts
of modernism were fleeting, but I've focused on these ephemeral alliances
in preference to institutions, fascinating as the latter can be (I think of
Herwarth Walden's "Sturm" enterprise with its magazine, gallery, theatre,
and publications).

A curious example I resisted incorporating was the Abbaye de Créteil,
a cooperative guild and residence from 1906–1908 where Unanisme arose.
Participants included the poet Jules Romains and future cubist Albert Gleizes.
It's an unfamiliar instance of a familiar phenomenon in modernism: site
of a momentary fertilization of artistic possibilities. Similar congregations
like Imagism, Vorticism, Poetism, and Surrealism dominate the histories,
overshadowing the Abbaye. Where it gets interesting is in the life-long attempt by one of its participants—Henri Martin Barzun—to rewrite history
and place it at the very center of "the modern movement." After the Abbaye
closed down, Barzun was active in the Parisian arts scene, editor of *Poème
& Drame* and author of *L'Ere du drame* (1912). You can look in vain in
the scholarship for anything about Barzun, exceptions being Pär Bergman's
chapter on him in *"Modernolatria" et "Simultaneità"* (1962) and Cyrena
Pondrom's *The Road from Paris* (1974), which consists mostly of reprints
by F. S. Flint and other English commentators on the French scene before
1914. Barzun's erasure is likely due to his repudiation by Apollinaire and
Cendrars after he tried to claim paternity of Simultanéisme, on the grounds
that the choral poetry he pioneered was a "simultaneous" mobilization of
voices. Of course, this is like saying that abstract art originated with Christianity because of the pure geometry of the holy cross. Barzun moved to
America during the First World War and spent the rest of his very long
life giving historically revisionary lectures on his primordial role in the an-
nus mirabilis 1913 as cradle of modernism. He self-published a number of
books that give a reasonable account of modernism compounded by unreasonable claims for his own centrality (cf. Barzun 1956). In one of his
histories of modernism, Serge Fauchereau mentions the English poet Skip-
with Cannell as typifying the minor figure, "avec beaucoup d'ambition et
peu de talent littéraire, tout comme H. M. Barzun qu'il connait" (2005,
205). Barzun's most egregious presumption, thanks to his friendship with
Gleizes, was to present his choral hypothesis as equivalent to the revolution
of Cubism: "The *Cube* and the *Chorus* of the new century were *not* theories but *technical forms* cast from life," he wrote in 1956 (17). Similarly, the
choral group activities in America I chronicled in *History of a Shiver* largely

preceded his arrival and potential influence, but in his retrospective accounts that distinction is not made. Barzun is like a John Smith resentful of the fact that America is named after an Italian predecessor.

Panning back (in the cinematic sense) from the Abbaye, a multitude of other locales and concentrations of artistic enterprise appear. Imagine a sweeping aerial view over a landscape in which these sites begin to light up as at dusk, until a panoramic twinkling is pervasive. This is the scenario that defines modernism for me, something far vaster and still filled with unknowns than the Anglo-American "men of 1914." The single most pertinent adjective is *teeming*. It was in order to facilitate this sense that I played fairly loosely around definitions of modernism. I offer plenty of characterizations, but usually in the thick or thicket of concrete instances. This is also why things appear that might baffle the credulity of readers, like the civic pageants in the American Arcady chapter of *Shiver*. There's nothing remotely "modernist" about those pageants, but they help flesh out a milieu that encompasses Isadora Duncan and *Camera Work*, among other things, and the whole chapter could be characterized as an investigation of the transit of Dudley Murphy from the bucolic *Soul of the Cypress* filmed at Point Lobos to the hypermodernist *Ballet mécanique* in just a few years. Given that the book begins around 1800 with the German Romantics and is considerably absorbed in the nineteenth century, this chapter—along with the one on symbolism—is crucial to getting into the twentieth century. And where much is usually made of the sudden eruption of the "absolutely modern" in the avant-garde, circa 1910, that's a retrospective account. Prospective eruptions continually arose. The "absolute" happened every day, whether anyone realized it or not. I don't think artists are uniquely cognizant in this regard, but the fixation on artistic pursuits tend to register more acutely the daily wager. The drama of handling a period, a comma, a verb tense, was for Mallarmé equivalent to calculating the truss of a bridge span over a crevasse. If it's all in the details, how do you make the details glow (or, as the case may be, glower)?

So I tried to adhere to the kind of historicism advocated by Hugh Trevor-Roper, who offered this admonition:

> We exist in and for our own time: why should we judge our predecessors as if they were less self-sufficient: as if they existed for us and should be judged by us? Every age has its own social context, its own intellectual climate, and takes it for granted, as we take ours. Because it was taken for granted, it is not explicitly expressed in the documents of the time: it has to be deduced and reconstructed. It also deserves respect. (in Blanning, 125)

What I appreciate in this is his precise calibration of intent—whether explicit or not—in historical research. Do the dead compliantly await the benediction of a resurrectionist trade? Or might they, rather, be seen as active agents of their own lives? If the latter, it's incumbent on us to attune ourselves to the rhythmic perspicacity of their attentions, preoccupations, exaltations, the charge of which is handsomely spelled out in the first sentence of Jackson Lears's *Rebirth of a Nation*: "All history is the history of longing" (2009, 1). So modernism continues, unrestrained, self-perpetuating, forever *almost*.

Notes

A Potential Intelligence

1. Kreymborg's list is rich with titles undeservedly forgotten, including *Letters to Women* by Joseph Auslander, *Deep South* by Carl Carmer, *Blue Juniata* by Malcolm Cowley, *Astrolabe* by S. Foster Damon, *The Tall Men* by Donald Davidson, *Sonnets from the Patagonian* by Donald Evans, *Notations for a Chimaera* by Herbert Gorman, *Aphrodite* by Wallace Gould, *Chelsea Rooming House* by Horace Gregory, *Curtains* by Hazel Hall, *Carolina Chansons* by DuBose Heyward and Hervey Allen, *Europa* by Rolfe Humphries, *The Devil Is a Woman* by Alice Mary Kimball, *Intellectual Things* by Stanley Kunitz, *O City, Cities* by Raymond Larsson, *Nursery Rhymes for Children of Darkness* by Gladys Oaks, *God-Beguiled* by George O'Neil, *Trinc* by Phelps Putnam, *The Box of God* by Lew Sarett, *The Temptation of Anthony* by Isidor Schneider, *A Marriage with Space* by Mark Turbyfill, *Bands and Rebels* by Keene Wallis, *The Hesitant Heart* by Winifred Welles, and *Poets, Farewell* by Edmund Wilson—to cite only from the 1930 edition.

2. The notable exception to prevailing trends is the Library of America's two-volume anthology, *American Poetry: The Twentieth Century*, with 182 poets, all of whom made their debut before 1950, and a great number of whom have not appeared in any other anthologies since midcentury.

3. Kinnahan's compilation offers a case in point. Its topical arrangement has the virtue of avoiding the canonical highlighting of particular poets, even as it squanders the opportunity to restore to visibility—or even *name names* of—a considerable number of women poets from the prewar (some extending into postwar) years. Omitted, for instance, are Léonie Adams, Helen Bevington, Kay Boyle, Nancy Bruff, Josephine Young Case, Katherine Garrison Chapin, Adelaide Crapsey, Joy Davidman, Babette Deutsch, Abbie Huston Evans, Hildegarde Flanner, Hortense Flexner, Elizabeth Hollister Frost, Leone Rice Grelle, Gwendolen Haste, Barbara Howes, Jeremy Ingalls, Florence Burrill Jacobs, Josephine Jacobsen, Josephine W. Johnson, Bernice Kenyon, Alice Mary Kimball, Dilys Bennett Laing, Ruth Lechlitner, Helen Magaret, Charlotte Marletto, Marjorie Meeker, Eve Merriam, Josephine Miles, Mary Owings Miller,

Rosalie Moore, Virginia Moore, Helene Mullins, Gladys Oaks, Bonaro Overstreet, May Sarton, Evelyn Scott, Leonora Speyer, Roberta Teale Swartz, Eve Triem, Marie de L. Welch, Margaret Widdemer, Charlotte Wilder, Audrey Wurdemann, and Marya Zaturenska. (This is an abbreviated list, omitting for instance devotional authors, poets mired in Victorian diction, and writers of humorous verse like Margaret Fishback.) These women were all published by major commercial presses, often authoring multiple titles over many years. And they're all worth reading.

4. Girard follows the precedent of well-intentioned studies like *The First Wave: Women Poets in America 1915–1945* by William Drake (1987) and *Sentimental Modernism: Women Writers and the Revolution of the Word* by Suzanne Clark (1991) that have reinforced a coterie model of feminine sensibility inapplicable to many female authors. Thus, the estimable Frances Frost, for instance, has disappeared altogether, despite six ambitiously varied volumes, from her Yale Younger Poets entry, *Hemlock Wall*, in 1929 to *Mid-Century* in 1946. Most telling is the brief Wikipedia entry that identifies her as the mother of poet Paul Blackburn.

5. Edmund Wilson made a similar point in *Axel's Castle*: "What really happens, of course, is that one set of methods and ideas is not completely superseded by another; but that, on the contrary, it thrives in its teeth" (1931, 14).

6. The cultural nationalism promoted by *The Seven Arts* was even more insistently propagated by the individual careers of its editors, who included Waldo Frank, Paul Rosenfeld, Randolph Bourne, and Van Wyck Brooks, honorifically profiled in *Beloved Community* (1990) by Casey Nelson Blake.

7. As Untermeyer writes in his autobiography, Alfred Harcourt observed "there were at least twenty years between the acceptance of an idea and its adoption in the academic schools. First the experiment; a decade later its prevailing use; a score of years had to ensue before it was incorporated into the textbooks. It was Alfred who urged me to shorten the gap" (Untermeyer 1939, 327). Having published Untermeyer's *New Era in American Poetry*, he solicited an accompanying anthology. In 1919 the textbook market in literary studies was nearly nonexistent, so any such recommendation was aimed at a general audience as well.

8. Among those who began publishing prewar and whose work was reprised postwar in substantial commercial editions, but whose profiles have since waned (often unjustifiably): John Beecher, Ben Belitt, R. P. Blackmur, John Malcolm Brinnin, Witter Bynner, Donald Davidson, Abbie Huston Evans, James Feibleman, Thomas Hornsby Ferril, Robert Fitzgerald, Hildegarde Flanner, Hortense Flexner, Robert Francis, Brewster Ghiselin, Horace Gregory, Ramon Guthrie, Hazel Hall, Robert Hillyer, Lindley Williams Hubbell, Rolfe Humphries, Raymond Larsson, Janet Lewis, Josephine Miles, John Frederick Nims, Hyam Plutzik, H. Phelps Putnam, Norman Rosten, May Sarton, Winfield Townley Scott, Wilbert Snow, A. M. Sullivan, Mark Van Doren, and John Wheelwright. Conrad Aiken and Archibald MacLeish might plausibly be added to this list, but at least a modicum of name recognition continues to play in their favor.

9. In the critique of Hans Robert Jauss, "when literary history adopted the paradigm of positivistic history, reducing the experience of literature to causal links be-

tween work and work and author and author, the historical communication between author, work, and reader disappeared behind an hypostatized succession of monographs that remained history only in name" (1982, 52). Jauss's characterization of this approach captures the normative practices of literary history, in which "the sequential link between one work and the next is lost in a historical vacuum, which would be obvious simply from the chronological order if it were not concealed by the vague generalization of 'currents' or 'schools,' or bridged by an external nexus, borrowed from pragmatic history—first and foremost, that of nationhood" (47).

10. In a pastiche on the poetry scene in 1936, Genevieve Taggard wrote: "At the corner of Auslander and Wurdeman they say business is brisk. / But observe: the stucco fronts are flimsy; the paint peels. / I like Fearing Sq., myself. It is so central" (19). Wurdeman won the Pulitzer in 1935, and Auslander had enough clout that Harper published two collections that year, *Green World* (113 pages) being a reprint of sections five and six of the larger *No Traveler Returns* (233 pages).

11. Tate applied the same criteria to his friend Hart Crane: "His chief defect is the lack of a system of disciplined values which would clarify and control the most prodigal poetic gift in America" (1983, 85).

12. The poets receiving the largest share of Wells's chapters on the twentieth century are Robinson ("The New England Conscience"), Frost ("Nearer and Farther Ranges"), Lindsay ("Romanticism and the Frontier"), Sandburg ("New America"), Jeffers ("Grander Canyons"), Ransom ("Dynastic Wound"), Stephen Vincent Benét ("Democratic Vista"), Crane ("American Rhapsody"), and Merrill Moore ("The Pragmatic Temper").

13. Yeats is the most commanding presence in *This Modern Poetry*, and the chapter on politics is about Auden. Americans conspicuously distributed through the other chapters are Frost, Lindsay, Masters, Pound, H.D., Williams, Robinson, Eliot, Crane, Ransom, Wylie, Jeffers, Cummings, MacLeish, Gregory, and Fearing—all, however, subordinate to Deutsch's themes.

14. In addition to the profile I've offered above, Kreymborg's list cited at the outset offers a substantial bibliography, although there's a wealth of excellent books not included, such as *Arid* by Phillips Kloss, *Proud Riders* by H. L. Davis, *Poems 1923–1943* by James Daly, and any of numerous titles by Frederick Mortimer Clapp or Walter Lowenfels. Kreymborg's list is also a reminder of the relative gender balance that prevailed before the midcentury return to male dominance (80 of his 270 titles were by women). Another point of entry might focus on the decade of the 1940s, which has largely been regarded as backdrop to the rise of Lowell, Berryman, Jarrell, and Roethke, and inflected by Auden's move to America. In fact, the decade was a torrent of divergent possibilities, accommodating surrealism and wartime patriotism along with the testimony of combat veterans—all in all, a diverse younger generation testing the waters amid a myriad of elders, themselves ranging from the modernist upstarts of thirty years earlier to the careerists and fashionable poets who'd always played it safe.

15. The goal of "thick description"—a term Geertz took from philosopher Gilbert Ryle—is to facilitate the "three characteristics of ethnographic description: it is interpretive; what it is interpretive of is the flow of social discourse; and the interpret-

ing involved consists in trying to rescue the 'said' of such discourse from its perishing occasions and fix it in perusable terms" (1973, 20).

From Corset to Podcast: Or, the Condition of Poetry When Everybody Is a Poet

1. The inadequacy of the traditional terminology of criticism is a matter of concern for many of the contributors to *New Media Poetics: Contexts, Technotexts, and Theories* edited by Adalaide Morris and Thomas Swiss (2006). The single term that the authors most frequently avail themselves of is *materiality*, which may reflect a certain level of anxiety about the dematerializing capacity of digital media as such.

2. "This Mere Guy," *Guernica*, October 27, 2006, https://www.guernicamag.com /this_mere_guy/.

3. Figures from Amazon.com are aggregates, culled from weekly samples of selected titles over a two-month period, August–September 2011.

4. Robert Haven Schauffler went on to compile *The Poetry Cure: A Medicine Chest of Verse, Music and Pictures* (1927). In his prefatory "Directions (Read Well Before Using!)," he outlines a therapeutic approach with tongue modestly in cheek while insisting on the curative virtues of verse. "A large, ordinary anthology of verse is like a drug store. It contains just the thing for your complaint—that is, if you know where to look for it" (xxvii). Schauffler provides pharmaceutical guidance in the "Ten Minute Cures" preceding the table of contents, offered in the confidence that "in almost every compartment of the chest you will find poems both of escape, defense, and compensation" (xxviii). The poems are organized as follows: Stimulants for a Faint Heart (Poems of Courage), Mental Cocktails and Spiritual Pick-Me-Ups (Poems of Laughter), Massage for a Muscle-Bound Spirit (Poems of Emancipation), Poppy Juice for Insomnia (Soothers and Soporifics), To Deflate the Ego (Ingredients for a Humble Pie), Tonics for an Anemic Soul (Tissue Builders and Vision Strengtheners), Hasheesh for a Torpid Imagination (Magic Carpet Poems), For Hardening of the Heart (Poems of Sympathy), Accelerators for Sluggish Blood (Poems of High Voltage), Sedatives for Impatience (Poems of Reassurance), Beauty's Wine (A Specific for Ugliness), For Times When "The World is Too Much With Us" (Antidotes for the Strenuous Life), "Pilles to Purge Melancholy" (Poems of Cheer), Anodynes for Sorrow (To be Taken in the Hour of Great Need).

5. The "revolutionists" were not alone in resisting the palliative care approach to poetry. Regional poet Roy Helton, for instance, who wrote many poems in dialect, adopted a Whitmanian persona in "My Land, Your Lover," concluding with a reproach to the school of gentility: "The trees are sane, the rocks, the placid dew, / All things that grow seek peace with sun and rain / Save I, your man and lover, come at last / With hands not tender nor considerate / To clutch you to the star hot kiss of song" (1930, 99).

6. Cf. *Poems of Pep and Point for Public Speakers* edited by Will H. Brown (Cincinnati: Standard Publishing, 1918). As the title suggests, there was a widespread link in the early twentieth century between poetry, public speech, and elocutionary training. The phenomenon of "language eurhythmics" was a holdover from the nineteenth-

century success of Delsarte body posture exercises, gaining renewed strength after Marjorie Gullan organized a Verse Speaking Choir in Glasgow in 1922. John Masefield was so impressed by witnessing this choir in performance ("I had heard no speech so beautiful: I could not sleep for three nights" [1952, 145]) that he went on to organize the Oxford Festival and then the London Speech Festival, which ran until 1935. T. S. Eliot's *Murder in the Cathedral* is a byproduct of these choral recitations. See also Marjorie Gullan, *The Speech Choir* (New York: Harper, 1937), Elizabeth E. Keppie, *The Teaching of Choric Speech* (Boston: Expression, 1932), and for the Delsarte legacy, Carrie J. Preston, *Modernism's Mythic Pose: Gender, Genre, Solo Performance* (New York: Oxford University Press, 2011). A useful compendium of primary sources—the supply chain of vocalism—is *Parlour Poetry: A Casquet of Gems* edited by Michael R. Turner (New York: Viking, 1969).

7. This figure is estimated from average annual publications of presses represented by Small Press Distribution (albeit only those specializing in poetry), along with those trade and university presses with regular poetry lists, but two thousand is a conservative estimate. In *American Hybrid*, Cole Swensen observes that the old tiered system of trade publishers and university presses with a modest number of small presses rounding out the profile has been supplanted in recent years. "The most recent shift has been the explosion of the bottom tier until, in terms of sheer numbers, the bottom is now the top" (2009, xxiv).

8. The combatant anthologies were *The New Poets of England and America* edited by Donald Hall, Robert Pack, and Louis Simpson (1957), and *The New American Poetry* edited by Donald M. Allen (1960). As one measure of the demographics involved: in 2008 there were seven million bands posting their music on the internet site My Space, according to Eliot Van Buskirk (2008). The implications for poetry are harrowing, to say the least: now anybody who wants to get their work out there can, and probably will.

9. The situation was wryly noted by David Orr: "As of 2011, it remains very much the case that publishing a book is essential to being considered a poet, and that getting attention for that book is essential to being considered an Important Poet. If you want an academic job, you can't wait until you're forty, as Robert Frost did, before getting your work between covers. So today we're getting more poems more quickly from more people, many of whom are hoping for the same type of employment, and almost all of whom have no audience outside the art form itself" (2011, 153).

Flesh Dream Books

1. Mike Erwin and I subsequently embarked on a series of interviews with contemporary poets. The interviews that were published were with Kelly, Nathaniel Tarn, A. R. Ammons, Roy Fisher, Charles Tomlinson, and Peter Redgrove. Unpublished are interviews with George Barker, Edwin Morgan, Peter Porter, Jon Silkin, Adrian Mitchell, David Wevill, George MacBeth, and Theodore Enslin. We began with Americans on the East Coast, spent November 1973 in England, and were unable to continue as planned with more Americans because of Mike's untimely death in March 1974. As this list of interviewees suggests, we were aiming to talk to poets

one or more generations beyond ours (we'd scheduled an interview with Auden, who died before we made it to England; and Bunting, misconstruing us as academics, denounced us roundly in a letter of refusal). It says much about the orientation of aspiring young male poets at that moment that we never considered interviewing women, nor apart from Levertov and Rich were we aware of any living women poets.

2. Kelly addresses the heritage of this emancipation from the left margin in his 1974 conversation with Quasha and Charles Stein, "Ta'wil or How to Read," 118–19.

3. *America a Prophecy* had a blurb by Hugh Kenner, but the anthology was dealt a lethal blow by Helen Vendler's front page review in the *New York Times Book Review*. See Rasula, *The American Poetry Wax Museum*, 334–38.

4. I was sufficiently enthralled by the tide of long poems that I tried to fasten a theoretical bandana around the phenomenon in "The State Meant" in my magazine *Wch Way* 2 (Fall 1975).

5. "Ongoing obscurity" extends beyond that moment. Blaser, Johnson, and Irby are nowhere to be found in the seven hundred pages of *The Oxford Handbook of Modern and Contemporary American Poetry* edited by Cary Nelson (2012). Kelly is only mentioned in a footnote, as is Rosmarie Waldrop; and Alice Notley stands in for all too many buried in the etcetera of a list. It's ironic, given Nelson's exemplary advocacy for the erased legacy of activist poetry, that this insightful array of articles would themselves collectively legislate a comparable act of erasure on a (I would say *the*) vital strand of late twentieth-century American poetry. Among all too many others overlooked here are David Antin, Jackson Mac Low, Jack Spicer, Nathaniel Tarn, Clayton Eshleman, Gustaf Sobin, Clark Coolidge, Edward Sanders, Anne Waldman, and Nathaniel Mackey. Even Laura Riding has vanished from this account. In fairness, this sort of topic-driven omnibus is not intended as a comprehensive guide, but such conspicuous indifference to or unawareness of the field opened by Olson and Duncan is symptomatic of an unpleasantly evasive collective mindset. Like similar compilations and histories, the *Oxford Handbook* leaves even farther behind a rich tapestry of small press poetry that's highly instructive about the historical milieu; what's more, much could be gleaned about the practical coordination of poetry with an expansive outlook from a perusal of such titles as *Dawn Visions* by Daniel Moore (City Lights 1964), *Ghost Tantras* by Michael McClure (Four Seasons 1964), *The Tapestry and the Web* by Joanne Kyger (Four Seasons 1965), *Provisional Measures* by Charles Stein (Gnomon 1966), *Not a Word* by d. alexander (Oyez 1966), *Transmutations* by Stephen Jonas (Ferry 1966), *The Heavenly Tree Grows Downward* by Gerrit Lansing (Matter 1966), *The Ladder* by David Schiff (Dariel 1967), *Word Alchemy* by Lenore Kandel (Grove Press 1967), *Tombstone as a Lonely Charm* by d.a. levy (Runcible Spoon 1967), *The Dainty Monsters* by Michael Ondaatje (Coach House 1967), *Peace Eye* by Edward Sanders (Frontier 1967), *Roads to Dawn Lake* by John Oliver Simon (Oyez 1968), *The Ends of the Earth* by David Bromige (Black Sparrow 1968), *Fertilized Brains* by Brown Miller (Open Skull 1968), *A History of America* by Bill Hutton (Coach House 1968), *Ing* by Clark Coolidge (Angel Hair 1968), *Homestead* by Keith Wilson (Kayak 1969), *Leaf Leaf/s* by Daphne Marlatt (Black Sparrow 1969), *Shining Leaves* by Bill Berkson (Angel Hair 1969), *Yesod* by David Meltzer (Trigram 1969), *Skull Juices* by Douglas

Blazek (Twowindows 1970), *Babalon 156* by Harvey Bialy (Sand Dollar 1970), *Geode/ Rock Body* by Gretel Ehrlich (Capricorn 1970), *California Poems* by James Koller (Black Sparrow 1971), *Desde Alla* by John Brandi (Tree/Christopher's 1971), *Maps* by Howard McCord (Kayak 1971), *Nobody Owns th Earth* by Bill Bissett (Anansi 1971), *Early Selected y Mas* by Paul Blackburn (Black Sparrow 1972), *America* by Victor Coleman (Coach House 1972), *The Cargo Cult* by John Thorpe (Big Sky 1972), *The Spirit by the Deep Well Tank* by Drummond Hadley (Goliard 1972), *Somapoetics* by George Quasha (Sumac 1973), and *A Palaeozoic Geology of London, Ontario* by Christopher Dewdney (1973)—to give a symptomatic profile of books easily spotted on shelves next to now more familiar titles like *The Sorrow Dance* by Denise Levertov, *The North Atlantic Turbine* by Ed Dorn, *The Back Country* by Gary Snyder, *Rivers and Mountains* by John Ashbery, *Power Politics* by Margaret Atwood, *The Will to Change* by Adrienne Rich (this was a time, I might add, when Gilbert Sorrentino and Jim Harrison were primarily known as poets). I can't resist quoting Dennis Lee's recollection of a milieu in which "everyone was scruffy and apocalyptic, making up our lives as we went along": exactly (Coach House Books website).

Panorama, Sentence by Sentence

1. Debord writes: "Detournement, the reuse of preexisting artistic elements in a new ensemble, has been a constantly present tendency of the contemporary avant-garde both before and since the establishment of the SI [Situationist International]. The two fundamental laws of detournement are the loss of importance of each detourned autonomous element—which may go so far as to lose its original sense completely—and at the same time the organization of another meaningful ensemble that confers on each element its new scope and effect" (1981, 55). Needless to say, examples of detournement abound in language writing practices, as well as in works like Ronald Johnson's *RADI OS*, a complete detournement of the first four books of *Paradise Lost*. American practitioners would surely agree with Debord that it "leads to the discovery of new aspects of talent," a neutral formulation; but how many would concur with his insistence on detournement as "a real means of proletarian artistic education, the first step toward a *literary communism*"? ("Methods" 11).

2. At the symposium "Joyce and the Arts" at the University of California, Santa Cruz, in 1988, Silliman gave an impassioned talk on *Ulysses* as exemplary for contemporary writing in all genres—a handy contrast on that occasion to my own advocacy of *Finnegans Wake* (later published: Rasula 1997).

3. I was intrigued to find this reference to panorama months after coming up with my title. Perelman doesn't elaborate on his use of the term, which seems to be a way of evoking the range of references *Ketjak* accommodates. My sense of panorama, on the other hand, is specific to the sentence, the individual compositional unit. These "sentences" range from individual words to multiclause propositions, although none have the bewildering protraction of those found in Proust, Henry James, or Derrida. So how do you get a panorama into a sentence? Panorama is specific to the nineteenth century, ranging from 360° history paintings to the popular nature canvases of Frederick Edwin Church, like *Niagara Falls* or *The Heart of the Andes*, a proto-

cinematic spectacle in which the audience sat on raked benches with opera glasses, while black curtains parted to reveal the painting lit by gas jet, surrounded by tropical vegetation. *The Heart of the Andes* netted Church three thousand dollars in a month. Imagine a grid superimposed on this painting and you'll find that every square is subordinate to the big picture of the whole. Its scale is compromised, in fact, to the extent that its delivery of a single image could be as readily offered in a miniature. It doesn't have to be this big, other than to mimic by its own scale the bravura dimensions of the geological phenomenon it depicts. By contrast, imagine a page of *The Alphabet*: the grid is integrated into the compositional procedure so that, unlike Church's *Niagara* where every part is exclusively dedicated to the whole, every sentence here is the recipient of an investment *by* the whole.

From Verse Narratives to Documentary Poetry

1. *Roan Stallion, Tamar and Other Poems* (1925) had a much larger share of shorter poems than any subsequent title by Jeffers. It was followed up by *The Women at Point Sur* (1927), the only one given over exclusively to a narrative poem, followed by others in 1928, 1929, 1932, 1933, 1935, 1937, 1941, and 1948. The twelve long poems in these books amount to about 1,100 pages, with the shorter poems taking up 570 pages. Comparable distribution is evident in the *Selected Poetry* of 1938, with four hundred of the 615 pages given over to the narratives. The sole exception to this pattern is *Descent to the Dead* (1931), a signed limited edition of lyrics chronicling a trip to Ireland.

2. Here, as in all subsequent citations of reviews from the *New York Times*, I provide only author and date to reflect online access through the TimesMachine search engine.

3. Lampson wrote of his book, "This story is not necessarily to be thought of as a long poem, but as a novel to be read with emphasized cadence, preferably aloud . . . written in what I call *free hexameters*—lines having six wave-tops each and making use of the natural cadences of English speech rather than of such classical devices as iambics, rhyme, and stanzas" (Langdon 1936, ix).

4. A poetic precedent for Rukeyser's attention to a mining disaster is *Blue Juniata* by Malcolm Cowley (1929), the title sequence being on the "ulcerated hill" country of his boyhood in Western Pennsylvania. Cowley retained the title for two later issues of his poetry, but he meddled with the texts, and I recommend the first edition.

5. I quote from the reprint of the series—which lacks the title "Jews"—in Reznikoff's 1927 collection *Five Groups of Verse*.

An Interview with Tony Tost

1. "Oblique Modernism" eventually split into the two books, *History of a Shiver: The Sublime Impudence of Modernism* (2016) and *Acrobatic Modernism from the Avant-Garde to Prehistory* (2020).

An Interview with Joel Bettridge

1. Daniel Cottom, *Ravishing Tradition* (1996), 31.

2. "The Media of Memory: The Seductive Menace of Records in Jazz History," published in *Jazz Among the Discourses* edited by Krin Gabbard (Duke University Press, 1995), is the most frequently cited of all my publications.

3. *Classics Illustrated* led to my becoming interested in literature—exactly what the critics said comics would never do! It also led to my first peer-reviewed article: "Nietzsche in the Nursery: Naïve Classics and Surrogate Parents in Postwar Cultural Debates," *Representations* 27 (Winter 1990). An eminent scholar advised me not to write about comic books because it would ruin my career prospects, but I couldn't help myself and, needless to say, it helped in the end. I should also acknowledge Barrett Watten's role in getting the editorial board at *Representations* to consider the essay in the first place.

4. Daumal 1982, 41. When it comes to taxonomy, ancient Sanskrit poetics is far more diversified than anything in the West. Check out the *Dhvanyāloka* of Ānanadavardhana and the *Locana* of Abhinavagupta, heady stuff.

5. "*Nostromo* as Fairy Tale Epic," *Genre* 33, no. 1 (Spring 2000): 93–113; now a chapter in my book *Genre and Extravagance in the Novel: Lower Frequencies* (Oxford University Press).

6. "When the Exception Is the Rule: *Don Quixote* as Incitement to Literature," *Comparative Literature* 51, no. 2 (Spring 1999), 123–51—now a chapter in *Genre and Extravagance*.

7. Rasula 2018.

An Interview with Ming-Qian Ma

1. This statement applies mainly to Official Verse Culture. The poets gathered by Donald Allen for *The New American Poetry* (1960) were not so prim. The poetry of Jack Spicer and Frank O'Hara, by contrast, is awash in the whole sprawl of cultural ephemera, to say nothing of the gender politics of their references.

An Exchange with Nathan Brown

1. "In einer *wahren Rede* spielt man alle Rollen—geht durch alle Charaktere durch—durch alle Zustände—nur um zu überraschen—um den Gegenstand *von einer neuen Seite* zu betrachten, um den Zuhörer plötzlich zu illudieren" (Safranski 291, note 62).

Works Cited

Adams, Hazard. 1992. *Critical Theory since Plato*. Rev. ed. Orlando: Harcourt Brace Jovanovich.

Ades, Dawn, ed. 2006. *The Dada Reader: A Critical Anthology*. London: Tate.

Adorno, Theodor W. 1970. *Ästhetische Theorie*. Frankfurt am Main: Suhrkamp.

———. 1974. *Minima Moralia: Reflections from a Damaged Life*. Translated by E. F. N. Jephcott. London: Verso.

———. 1981. *Prisms*. Translated by Samuel and Shierry Weber. Cambridge, MA: MIT Press.

———. 1997. *Aesthetic Theory*. Translated by Robert Hullot-Kentor. Minneapolis: University of Minnesota Press.

Allen, Donald, ed. 1999. *The New American Poetry, 1945–1960*. Berkeley: University of California Press.

Alpert, Barry. 1974a. "Robert Kelly—An Interview." *Vort* 2 (2): 5–43.

———. 1974b. "Robert Kelly's Reputation." *Vort* 2 (2): 166.

———. 1975a. "David Antin—An Interview." *Vort* 3 (1): 3–33.

———. 1975b. "Jerome Rothenberg—An Interview." *Vort* 3 (3): 93–117.

Altieri, Charles. 1979. *Enlarging the Temple: New Directions in American Poetry during the 1960s*. Lewisburg, PA: Bucknell University Press.

Altrocchi, Julia. 1936. *Snow Covered Wagons*. New York: Macmillan.

Anderson, John William. 1936. *Prelude to "Icaros."* New York: Farrar and Rinehart.

Andrews, Bruce. 1996. *Paradise and Method: Poetics and Praxis*. Evanston, IL: Northwestern University Press.

Anonymous. 1921. "In a Style of Steel." *Nation* 112:596.

Antin, David. 1965. "Silence/Noise." *Some/thing*, no. 1, 60–63.

———. 1972. "Modernism and Postmodernism: Approaching the Present in American Poetry." *Boundary 2* 1 (1): 9–133.

———. 1991. *Selected Poems: 1963–1973*. Los Angeles: Sun and Moon.

Arp, Jean. 1971. "Dadaland." Translated by Ralph Manheim. In Lippard, *Dadas on Art*, 23–31.

———. 1972. *Arp on Arp: Poems, Essays, Memories*. Edited by Marcel Jean. Translated by Joachim Neugroschel. New York: Viking.

Ashbery, John. 1970. *The Double Dream of Spring*. New York: Dutton.

Auden, W. H., and John Garrett, eds. 1935. *The Poet's Tongue: An Anthology*. London: G. Bell.

Austin, Mary. 1932. "The Story of the Conquest." *Southwest Review* 17 (3): xiv–xvi.

Bachelard, Gaston. 1988. *Air and Dreams: An Essay on the Imagination of Movement*. Translated by Edith R. Farrell and C. Frederick Farrell. Dallas: Dallas Institute of Humanities and Culture.

Bacon, Leonard. 1927. *Guinea-Fowl and Other Poultry*. New York: Harper and Brothers.

———. 1936. *Rhyme and Punishment*. New York: Farrar and Rinehart.

Ball, Hugo. 1974. *Flight Out of Time: A Dada Diary*. Edited by John Elderfield. Translated by Ann Raimes. New York: Viking.

Barnes, Djuna. 1961. *Nightwood*. New York: New Directions.

Barthes, Roland. 1972. *Critical Essays*. Translated by Richard Howard. Evanston, IL: Northwestern University Press.

———. 1974. *S/Z*. Translated by Richard Miller. New York: Hill and Wang.

Barzun, Henri Martin. 1956. *Orpheus: Modern Culture and the 1913 Renaissance, a Panoramic Survey 1900–1956*. New York: Henri Martin Barzun.

Bean, Heidi R., and Mike Chasar. 2011. *Poetry after Cultural Studies*. Iowa City: University of Iowa Press.

Beckett, Samuel. 2006. *Samuel Beckett, The Grove Centenary Edition*. Vol. 4, *Poems, Short Fiction, Criticism*, edited by Paul Auster. New York: Grove Press.

Beckett, Samuel, and Georges Duthuit. 1965. *Proust: Three Dialogues*. London: Calder and Boyars.

Beecher, John. 1940. *"And I Will Be Heard."* New York: Twice a Year Press.

Bely, Andrey. 1985. *Selected Essays*. Translated and edited by Steven Cassedy. Berkeley: University of California Press.

Bendixen, Alfred, and Stephen Burt, eds. 2015. *The Cambridge History of American Poetry*. New York: Cambridge University Press.

Benét, William Rose. 1942. *The Dust Which Is God*. New York: Dodd, Mead.

Benjamin, Walter. 1969. *Illuminations*. Edited by Hannah Arendt. Translated by Harry Zohn. New York: Schocken.

———. 1999. *The Arcades Project*. Edited by Rolf Tiedemann. Translated by Howard Eiland and Kevin McLaughlin. Cambridge, MA: Harvard University Press.

Bernstein, Charles. 2011. *Attack of the Difficult Poems: Essays and Inventions*. Chicago: University of Chicago Press.

Bersani, Leo. 1990. *The Culture of Redemption*. Cambridge, MA: Harvard University Press.

Bishop, John Peale, and Edmund Wilson. 1922. *The Undertaker's Garland*. New York: Knopf.

Blake, Casey Nelson. 1990. *Beloved Community: The Cultural Criticism of Randolph Bourne, Van Wyck Brooks, Waldo Frank, and Lewis Mumford*. Chapel Hill: University of North Carolina Press.

Blanding, Don. 1933. *Let Us Dream*. New York: Dodd, Mead.

Blanning, Tim. 2011. *The Romantic Revolution: A History*. New York: Modern Library.

Blanton, Smiley. 1960. *The Healing Power of Poetry*. New York: Crowell.

Blaser, Robin. 1975. "The Practice of Outside." In Spicer, *Collected Books of Jack Spicer*, 271–329.

———. 1993. *The Holy Forest*. Toronto: Coach House Press.

Bly, Robert. 1959a. "On English and American Poetry." *Fifties*, no. 2, 45–47.

———. 1959b. "Some Thoughts on Lorca and René Char." *Fifties*, no. 3, 7–9.

———. 1959c. [as "Crunk"]. "The Work of Robert Creeley." *Fifties*, no. 2, 10–21.

———. 1962. *Silence in the Snowy Fields*. Middletown, CT: Wesleyan University Press, 1962.

———. 1963. "A Wrong Turning in American Poetry." *Choice*, no. 3, 33–47.

———. 1990. *American Poetry: Wildness and Domesticity*. New York: Harper and Row.

Bodenheim, Maxwell. 1920. "Modern Poetry." *Dial* 68 (January–June): 95–98.

Bohrer, Karl Heinz. 1994. *Suddenness: On the Moment of Aesthetic Appearance*. Translated by Ruth Crowley. New York: Columbia University Press.

Bök, Christian. 2005. "A Silly Key: Some Notes on *Soliloquy* by Kenneth Goldsmith." *Open Letter* 12, no. 7 (Fall): 62–68.

Bowman, Peter. 1945. *Beach Red*. New York: Random House.

Bragdon, Claude. 1928. *The New Image*. New York: Knopf.

Breton, André. 1969. *Manifestoes of Surrealism*. Translated by Richard Seaver and Helen R. Lane. Ann Arbor: University of Michigan Press.

———. 1993. *Conversations: The Autobiography of Surrealism*. Translated by Mark Polizzotti. New York: Marlowe.

———. 1996. *The Lost Steps*. Translated by Mark Polizzotti. Lincoln: University of Nebraska Press, 1996.

Brown, Norman O. 1966. *Love's Body*. New York: Random House.

———. 1971. "From Politics to Metapolitics." In *A Caterpillar Anthology: A Selection of Poetry and Prose from Caterpillar Magazine*, edited by Clayton Eshleman, 7–20. Garden City, NY: Anchor Books.

———. 1973. *Closing Time*. New York: Random House.

———. 1991. *Apocalypse and/or Metamorphosis*. Berkeley: University of California Press.

———. 2005. "John Cage." *Aufgabe* 5 (Fall): 73–94.

Brown, Will H. 1918. *Poems of Pep and Point for Public Speakers*. Cincinnati: Standard Publishing.

Buck-Morss, Susan. 1989. *The Dialectics of Seeing: Walter Benjamin and the Arcades Project*. Cambridge, MA: MIT Press.

Burke, Kenneth. 1941. *The Philosophy of Literary Form: Studies in Symbolic Action*. Baton Rouge: Louisiana State University Press.

———. 1989. *On Symbols and Society*. Edited by Joseph R. Gusfield. Chicago: University of Chicago Press.

Byrd, Don. 1994. *The Poetics of the Common Knowledge*. Albany: State University of New York Press.

Caillois, Roger. 2003. *The Edge of Surrealism: A Roger Caillois Reader*. Edited by Claudine Frank. Translated by Claudine Frank and Camille Naish. Durham: Duke University Press.

Calas, Nicolas. 1942. *Confound the Wise*. New York: Arrow Editions.

Calasso, Roberto. 1993. *The Marriage of Cadmus and Harmony*. Translated by Tim Parks. New York: Knopf.

Carlyle, Thomas. 1984. *A Carlyle Reader*. Edited by G. B. Tennyson. Cambridge, UK: Cambridge University Press.

Carmer, Carl. 1930. *Deep South*. New York: Farrar and Rinehart.

Carr, Julie. 2018. *Real Life: An Installation*. Oakland: Omnidawn.

Carruth, Hayden, ed. 1970. *The Voice That Is Great Within Us: American Poetry of the Twentieth Century*. New York: Bantam.

Carson, Anne. 1999. *Economy of the Unlost: Reading Simonides of Keos with Paul Celan*. Princeton: Princeton University Press.

Cendrars, Blaise. 1992. *Modernities and Other Writings*. Edited by Monique Chefdor. Translated by Esther Allen in collaboration with Monique Chefdor. Lincoln: University of Nebraska Press.

Central Office of Dadaism. 2006. "Put Your Money in Dada!" Translated by Kathryn Woodham. In Ades, *The Dada Reader*, 86.

Certeau, Michel de. 1984. *The Practice of Everyday Life*. Translated by Seven Rendall. Berkeley: University of California Press.

Chasar, Mike. 2012. *Everyday Reading: Poetry and Popular Culture in Modern America*. New York: Columbia University Press.

Chiasson, Dan. 2010. "Southern Discomfort." *New Yorker*, December 27, 2010.

Chinitz, David E., and Gail McDonald, eds. 2014. *A Companion to Modernist Poetry*. Malden, MA: Wiley Blackwell.

Chirico, Giorgio de. 1938. "Mystery and Creation." *London Bulletin* 6 (October): 14.

Clapp, Frederick Mortimer. 1943. *Against a Background on Fire: 1938–1943*. New York: Harper.

Clover, Joshua. 2007. "Poetics Statement." In Rankine and Sewell, *American Poets in the 21st Century*, 163.

Coburn, Kathleen, ed. 1951. *Inquiring Spirit: A New Presentation of Coleridge from His Published and Unpublished Prose Writings*. London: Routledge.

Cockerell, T. D. A. 1940. "Death Loses a Pair of Wings." *Bios* 11 (1): 56.

Coleridge, Samuel Taylor. 1951. *Selected Poetry and Prose*. Edited by Donald A. Stauffer. New York: Modern Library.

Collins, Billy. 2003. *Poetry 180: A Turning Back to Poetry*. New York: Random House.

Converse, Florence. 1934. *Efficiency Expert*. New York: John Day.

Cookson, William. 2001. *A Guide to the Cantos of Ezra Pound*. Rev. ed. New York: Persea.

Cottom, Daniel. 1996. *Ravishing Tradition: Cultural Forces and Literary History*. Ithaca: Cornell University Press.

Cowley, Malcolm. 1929. *Blue Juniata*. New York: Jonathan Cape & Harrison Smith.

Crane, Hart. 1926. *White Buildings*. New York: Liveright.

Creeley, Robert. 1962. *For Love: Poems 1950–1960*. New York: Scribner's.

Creeley, Robert, and Jerome Rothenberg. 1962. "An Exchange: Deep Image and Mode." *Kulchur* 2 (6): 25–42.

Cullen, Countee. 1929. *The Black Christ*. New York: Harper.

Cummings, E. E. 1931. *ViVa*. New York: Liveright.

Damon, Maria. 2011. *Postliterary America: From Bagel Shop Jazz to Micropoetries*. Iowa City: University of Iowa Press.

Daumal, René. 1982. *Rasa, or Knowledge of the Self: Essays on Indian Aesthetics and Selected Sanskrit Studies*. Translated by Louise Landes Levi. New York: New Directions.

Davenport, Guy. 1974. "Kelly in Time." *Vort* 2 (2): 163–65.

———. 1981. *The Geography of the Imagination*. San Francisco: North Point.

Davidson, Donald. 1931. "Expectancy of Doom." *Virginia Quarterly Review* 7, no. 3 (July): 432–40.

Davis, Alex, and Lee M. Jenkins, eds. 2015. *A History of Modernist Poetry*. New York: Cambridge University Press.

Davis, William V. 1992. *Critical Essays on Robert Bly*. New York: G. K. Hall.

Debord, Guy. 1981. "Detournement as Negation and Prelude." Translated by Ken Knabb. In *Situationist International Anthology*, edited by Ken Knabb, 55–56. Berkeley, CA: Bureau of Public Secrets.

———. 1994. *The Society of the Spectacle*. Translated by Donald Nicholson-Smith. New York: Zone Books.

Debray, Régis. 2000. *Transmitting Culture*. Translated by Eric Rauth. New York: Columbia University Press.

Derrida, Jacques. 1981. *Dissemination*. Translated by Barbara Johnson. Chicago: University of Chicago Press.

———. 1986. *Glas*. Translated by John P. Leavey Jr., and Richard Rand. Lincoln: University of Nebraska Press.

Deutsch, Babette. 1935. *This Modern Poetry*. New York: W. W. Norton.

Donaldson, Scott. 2007. *Edwin Arlington Robinson: A Poet's Life*. New York: Columbia University Press.

Dorn, Edward. 1975a. *Collected Poems, 1956 – 1974*. Bolinas, CA: Four Seasons Foundation.

———. 1975b. *Slinger*. Berkeley: Wingbow.

Duncan, Robert. 1968. *Bending the Bow*. New York: New Directions.

———. 2014. *Collected Later Poems*. Edited by Peter Quartermain. Berkeley: University of California Press.

Dworkin, Craig, and Kenneth Goldsmith, eds. 2011. *Against Expression: An Anthology of Conceptual Writing*. Evanston, IL: Northwestern University Press.

Eisenstein, S. M. 1988. *Selected Works*. Vol. 1, *Writings, 1922–34*, edited and translated by Richard Taylor. Bloomington: Indiana University Press.

Eliot, T. S. 1954. *Selected Essays*. London: Faber and Faber.

Emerson, Ralph Waldo. 1983. *Essays and Lectures*. New York: Library of America.

Epstein, Jean. 1988. "Magnification." In *French Film Theory and Criticism: A His-*

tory/Anthology 1907–1939. Vol. 1, 1907–1929, edited by Richard Abel, 235–41. Princeton, NJ: Princeton University Press.

Ernest, P. Edward, ed. 1959. *The Family Album of Favorite Poems.* New York: Grosset and Dunlap.

"Erutarettil." *Littérature,* nos. 11–12, October 1923.

Erwin, Mike, and Jed Rasula. 1974. "Excerpts from an Interview with Robert Kelly." *Vort* 2 (2): 135–44.

Evans, Frederick H. 2014. "What Is a 'Straight Print'?" In *Photographic Theory: An Historical Anthology,* edited by Andrew E. Hershberger, 118–20. Oxford: Wiley Blackwell.

Fauchereau, Serge. 2005. *Hommes et mouvements esthétiques du XXe siècle, I: Les premiers ismes, l'occultisme, la naissance de l'abstraction.* Paris: Éditions Cercle d'Art.

Ficke, Arthur Davison. 1911. "The Present State of Poetry." *North American Review* 194 (September): 429–41.

Fisher, Philip. 1998. *Wonder, the Rainbow, and the Aesthetics of Rare Experiences.* Cambridge, MA: Harvard University Press.

Ford, Karen Jackson. 2012. "The Fight and the Fiddle in Twentieth-Century African American Poetry." In Nelson, *Oxford Handbook,* 369–404.

Foucault, Michel. 1972. *The Archaeology of Knowledge, and The Discourse on Language.* Translated by A. M. Sheridan. New York: Pantheon Books.

———. 1980. *Language, Counter-Memory, Practice: Selected Essays and Interviews.* Edited by Donald F. Bouchard. Ithaca: Cornell University Press.

Fox, Josef. 1946. "The Ennobled Warrior." *Poetry* 68, no. 1 (April): 51–54.

Frost, Robert. 1923a. *New Hampshire: A Poem with Notes and Grace Notes.* New York: Henry Holt.

———. 1923b. *Selected Poems.* New York: Henry Holt.

———. 1928. *West-Running Brook.* New York: Henry Holt.

———. 1936. *A Further Range.* New York: Henry Holt.

———. 1947. *Steeple Bush.* New York: Henry Holt.

———. 2006. *The Notebooks of Robert Frost.* Edited by Robert Faggen. Cambridge, MA: Belknap.

Funaroff, Sol. 1938. "Armored Car Robbery." *Poetry* 52, no. 4 (July): 230–33.

Funkhouser, Christopher. 2007. *Prehistoric Digital Poetry: An Archaeology of Forms, 1959–1995.* University of Alabama Press.

Gay, Peter. 2008. *Modernism, the Lure of Heresy: From Baudelaire to Beckett and Beyond.* New York: Norton.

Geertz, Clifford. 1973. *The Interpretation of Cultures: Selected Essays.* New York: Basic Books.

Gelpi, Albert. 1987. *A Coherent Splendor: The American Poetic Renaissance, 1910–1950.* New York: Cambridge University Press.

Gessner, Robert. 1933. *Upsurge.* New York: Farrar and Rinehart.

Giedion-Welcker, Carola. 1930. "Work in Progress: A Linguistic Experiment by James Joyce." Translated by Eugene Jolas. *Transition* 19–20 (June): 174–83.

———. 1935. "New Roads in Modern Sculpture." Translated by Eugene Jolas. *Transition* 23 (July): 198–201.

———. 1937. *Modern Plastic Art: Elements of Reality; Volume and Disintegration.* Translated by Morton Shand. Zurich: Girsberger.

———. 1938. "Prehistoric Stones." Translated by Eugene Jolas. *Transition* 27 (April–May): 335–43.

———. 1973. *Schriften 1926–1971: Stationen zu einem Zeitbild.* Edited by Reinhold Hohl. Schauberg: DuMont.

———. 1979. "Meetings with Joyce." In *Portraits of the Artist in Exile: Recollections of James Joyce by Europeans.* Translated by Willard Potts, 256–80. Seattle: University of Washington Press.

Ginzburg, Carlo. 1980. "Morelli, Freud and Sherlock Holmes: Clues and Scientific Method." Translated by Anna Davin. *History Workshop* 9 (Spring): 5–36.

Girard, Melissa. 2012. "'Jeweled Bindings': Modernist Women's Poetry and the Limits of Sentimentality." In Nelson, *Oxford Handbook,* 96–119.

Goldsmith, Kenneth. 2005. "Paragraphs on Conceptual Writing." *Open Letter* 12, no. 7 (Fall): 98–101.

———. 2011. *Uncreative Writing: Managing Language in the Digital Age.* New York: Columbia University Press.

Gombrich, E. H. 1986. *Aby Warburg, an Intellectual Biography.* 2nd ed. Oxford: Phaidon.

Gregory, Horace, and Maria Zaturenska. 1946. *A History of American Poetry 1900–1940.* New York: Harcourt, Brace.

Guillory, John. 1993. *Cultural Capital: The Problem of Literary Canon Formation.* Chicago: University of Chicago Press.

Harrington, Joseph. 2002. *Poetry and the Public: The Social Form of Modern U.S. Poetics.* Middletown: Wesleyan University Press.

———. 2016. "The Politics of Docupoetry." In *The News from Poems: Essays on the 21st-Century American Poetry of Engagement,* edited by Jeffrey Gray and Ann Keniston, 67–83. Ann Arbor: University of Michigan Press.

Hausmann, Raoul. 2006a. "Dada in Europe." Translated by Jean Boas-Beier. In Ades, *The Dada Reader,* 92–95.

———. 2006b. "The German Petit Bourgeois Is Cross." Translated by Rebecca Beard. In Ades, *The Dada Reader,* 88–89.

Heidegger, Martin. 1949. *Existence and Being.* Chicago:·Regnery.

———. 1971. *On the Way to Language.* Translated by Peter D. Hertz. New York: Harper and Row.

Hejinian, Lyn. 2000. *The Language of Inquiry.* Berkeley: University of California Press.

Helton, Roy. 1930. *Lonesome Water.* New York: Harper and Brothers.

Hill, Frank Ernest. 1934. *The Westward Star.* New York: John Day.

Hill, Jason E. 2018. *Artist as Reporter: Weegee, Ad Reinhardt, and the* PM *News Picture.* Berkeley: University of California Press.

Hillyer, Robert. 1973. *A Letter to Robert Frost and Others.* New York: Alfred A. Knopf.

Hirsch, Edward. 2002. *The Demon and the Angel: Searching for the Source of Artistic Inspiration.* New York: Harcourt.

Hix, H. L. 2016. *American Anger: An Evidentiary.* Wilkes-Barre, PA: Etruscan Press.

Höch, Hannah. 1971. "Interview with Hannah Höch by Edouard Roditi." In Lippard, *Dadas on Art*, 68–77.

Hofer, Matthew. 2014. "Contemporary Critical Trends." In Chinitz and McDonald, *Companion to Modernist Poetry*, 565–77.

Honig, Edwin. 1940. "History, Document, and Archibald MacLeish." *Sewanee Review* 48, no. 3 (July–September): 385–96.

Howe, Susan. 2005. "Hermes." *Aufgabe* 5 (Fall): 158–59.

Huelsenbeck, Richard. 1951a. "Dada Lives!" Translated by Eugene Jolas. In Motherwell, *Dada Painters and Poets*, 277–81.

——. 1951b. "What Is Dadaism and What Does It Want in Germany?" Translated by Ralph Manheim. In Motherwell, *Dada Painters and Poets*, 41–42.

Huelsenbeck, Richard, ed. 1993. *Dada Almanac*. Edited by Malcolm Green. London: Atlas.

Humphries, Rolfe. 1928. *Europa*. New York: Gaige.

Hungerford, Amy. 2016. *Making Literature Now*. New Haven: Yale University Press.

Iijima, Brenda, ed. 2010. *Eco-Language Reader*. Brooklyn: Portable Press at Yo Yo Labs.

Ingalls, Jeremy. 1945. *Tahl*. New York: A. A. Knopf.

Jack, Zachary Michael, ed. 2008. *The Plowman Sings: The Essential Fiction, Poetry, and Drama of America's Forgotten Regionalist Jay G. Sigmund*. Lanham, MD: University Press of America.

Jakobson, Roman. 1960. "Closing Statements: Linguistics and Poetics." In *Style in Language*, edited by Thomas A. Sebeok, 350–77. Cambridge, MA: MIT Press.

——. 1987. *Language in Literature*. Edited by Krystyna Pomorska and Stephen Rudy. Cambridge, MA: Belknap.

Janco, Marcel. 1971. "Dada at Two Speeds." Translated by Margaret I. Lippard. In Lippard, *Dadas on Art*, 36–38.

Jauss, Hans Robert. 1982. *Toward an Aesthetic of Reception*. Translated by Timothy Bahti. Minneapolis: University of Minnesota Press.

Jeffers, Robinson. 1925. *Roan Stallion, Tamar and Other Poems*. New York: Boni and Liveright.

——. 1927. *The Women at Point Sur*. New York: Random House.

——. 1931. *Descent to the Dead, Poems Written in Ireland and Great Britain*. New York: Random House.

——. 1938. *Selected Poetry*. New York: Random House.

Joyce, James. 1968. *Finnegans Wake*. New York: Viking.

Kalaidjian, Walter, 1992. "From Silence to Subversion: Robert Bly's Political Surrealism." In Davis, *Critical Essays on Robert Bly*, 194–211.

Kalaidjian, Walter, ed. 2015. *The Cambridge Companion to Modern American Poetry*. New York: Cambridge University Press.

Kane, Daniel. 2003. *All Poets Welcome: The Lower East Side Poetry Scene in the 1960s*. Berkeley: University of California Press.

Kant, Immanuel. 1992. "From *Critique of Judgment*." Translated by J. H. Bernard. In Adams, *Critical Theory since Plato*, 376–93.

Keillor, Garrison, ed. 2002. *Good Poems*. New York: Viking.

———. 2005. *Good Poems for Hard Times*. New York: Viking.

———. 2011. *Good Poems, American Places*. New York: Viking.

Keller, Lynn. 2017. *Recomposing Ecopoetics: North American Poetry of the Self-Conscious Anthropocene*. Charlottesville: University of Virginia Press.

Kelly, Robert. 1961a. *Armed Descent*. New York: Hawk's Well Press.

———. 1961b. "Notes on the Poetry of the Deep Image." *Trobar*, no. 2, 14–16.

———. 1962. "Statement." *Nomad* 10–11 (Autumn): 58.

———. 1963. "Letter to Kenneth Irby," *Sum*, no. 1 (December), 24–25.

———. 1965. "Letter to the Editor," *Eleventh Finger* 2 (Autumn): 25–26.

———. 1968. *Statement*. Los Angeles: Black Sparrow Press.

———. 1971a. *Flesh Dream Book*. Los Angeles: Black Sparrow Press.

———. 1971b. *In Time*. West Newbury, MA: Frontier Press.

———. 1973. *The Mill of Particulars*. Los Angeles: Black Sparrow Press.

———. 1975. *The Loom*. Los Angeles: Black Sparrow Press.

———. 1980. *Sentence*. Barrytown, NY: Station Hill Press.

———. 1981. *The Alchemist to Mercury*. Edited by Jed Rasula. Richmond, CA: North Atlantic Press.

———. 1995. *Red Actions: Selected Poems 1960–1993*. Santa Rosa: Black Sparrow Press.

———. 2011. *Uncertainties*. Barrytown, NY: Station Hill Press.

———. 2018. *Calls*. Catskill, NY: Lunar Chandelier Collective.

Kenner, Hugh. 1987. *The Mechanic Muse*. New York: Oxford University Press.

Kinnahan, Linda M., ed. 2016. *A History of Twentieth-Century American Women's Poetry*. New York: Cambridge University Press.

Kinnell, Galway. 1972. *The Book of Nightmares*. Boston: Houghton Mifflin.

Kittler, Friedrich. 1990. *Discourse Networks 1800/1900*. Translated by Michael Metteer, with Chris Cullens. Stanford, CA: Stanford University Press.

Kramer, Lawrence. 1992. "A Sensible Emptiness: Robert Bly and the Poetics of Immanence." In Davis, *Critical Essays on Robert Bly*, 212–23.

Kreymborg, Alfred. 1933. "American Poetry after the War, II." *English Journal* 22, no. 4 (April): 263–73.

Kreymborg, Alfred, ed. 1929. *Our Singing Strength: An Outline of American Poetry (1620–1930)*. New York: Coward-McCann.

———, ed. 1930. *An Anthology of American Poetry*. New York: Tudor.

———, ed. 1941. *An Anthology of American Poetry*. New York: Tudor.

Kruchenykh, Alexei. 1988. "New Ways of the Word." In *Russian Futurism through Its Manifestoes, 1912–1928*, edited by Anna Lawton and translated by Anna Lawton and Herbert Eagle, 69–77. Ithaca: Cornell University Press.

LaFarge, Christopher. 1934. *Hoxsie Sells His Acres*. New York: Coward-McCann.

Langdon, Mabel. 1936. "*Laughter Out of the Ground* by Robin Lampson." *Prairie Schooner* 10, no. 4 (Winter): 319–20.

Lears, Jackson. 2009. *Rebirth of a Nation: The Making of Modern America, 1877–1920*. New York: HarperCollins.

Lévi-Strauss, Claude. 1966. *The Savage Mind*. Chicago: University of Chicago Press.

Levine, Philip. 1972. *They Feed They Lion*. New York: Atheneum.

Lewis, Wyndham. 1954. *The Demon of Progress in the Arts*. London: Methuen.

Libby, Anthony. 1984. "Robert Bly: Alive in Darkness." In *Robert Bly: When Sleepers Awake*, edited by Joyce Peseroff, 37–53. Ann Arbor: University of Michigan Press.

Lindsay, Vachel. 1929. *Every Soul Is a Circus*. New York: Macmillan.

Lippard, Lucy R., ed. 1971. *Dadas on Art*. Englewood Cliffs, NJ: Prentice-Hall.

Lowell, Robert. 1946. "Current Poetry." *Sewanee Review* 54, no. 1 (January–March): 145–53.

Luster, Deborah, and C. D. Wright. 2003. *One Big Self: Prisoners of Louisiana*. Santa Fe: Twin Palms.

Lyotard, Jean-François. 1991. *The Inhuman: Reflections on Time*. Translated by Geoffrey Bennington. Stanford: Stanford University Press.

MacLeish, Archibald. 1932. *Conquistador*. Boston: Houghton Mifflin.

———. 1938. *Land of the Free*. New York: Harcourt, Brace.

Magaret, Helene. 1934. *Trumpeting Crane*. New York: Farrar and Reinhart.

Mallarmé, Stéphane. 1988. *Selected Letters*. Edited and translated by Rosemary Lloyd. Chicago: University of Chicago Press.

March, Joseph Moncure. 1928a. *The Set-Up*. New York: Covici-Friede.

———. 1928b. *The Wild Party*. Privately printed.

Masefield, John. 1952. *So Long to Learn*. New York: Macmillan.

Masters, Edgar Lee. 1915. *Spoon River Anthology*. New York: Macmillan.

Matthiessen, F. O., ed. 1950. *The Oxford Book of American Verse*. New York: Oxford University Press.

Memmott, Talan. 2006. "Beyond Taxonomy: Digital Poetics and the Problem of Reading." In *New Media Poetics: Contexts, Technotexts, and Theories*, edited by Adalaide Morris and Thomas Swiss, 293–306. Cambridge, MA: MIT Press.

Merwin, W. S. 1967. *The Lice*. New York: Atheneum.

Michaud, Philippe-Alain. 2004. *Aby Warburg and the Image in Motion*. Translated by Sophie Hawkes. New York: Zone Books.

Monroe, Harriet. 1926. "Power and Pomp." *Poetry* 28, no. 3 (June): 160–64.

———. 1932. "Robinson's Matthias." *Poetry* 39, no. 4 (January): 212–17.

Monroe, Harriet, and Alice Corbin Henderson, eds. 1932. *The New Poetry*. Rev. ed. New York: Macmillan.

Moore, Marianne. 2017. *New Collected Poems*. Edited by Heather Cass White. New York: Farrar, Straus and Giroux.

Moore, Merrill. 1938. *M: One Thousand Autobiographical Sonnets*. New York: Harcourt, Brace.

Morris, Adalaide, and Thomas Swiss, eds. 2006. *New Media Poetics: Contexts, Technotexts, and Theories*. Cambridge, MA: MIT Press.

Morris, Joseph, and St. Clair Adams, eds. 1927. *Silver Linings: Poems for Hope and Cheer*. New York: G. Scully.

Motherwell, Robert, ed. 1951. *The Dada Painters and Poets*. New York: Wittenborn, Schultz.

Murphy, Patrick D. 1987. "Reclaiming the Power: Robinson Jeffers's Verse Novels." *Western American Literature* 22 (2): 125–48.

————. 1989. "The Verse Novel: A Modern American Poetic Genre." *College English* 51, no. 1 (January): 57–72.

Naumann, Francis M. 2009. "Marius de Zayas and Alfred Stieglitz Part Ways: The Publication of 291 and the Formation of the Modern Gallery." *Francis Naumann*, http://www.francisnaumann.com/PUBLICATIONS/291%20entry.pdf.

Nelson, Cary, ed. 2012. *The Oxford Handbook of Modern and Contemporary American Poetry*. New York: Oxford University Press.

Newcomb, John Timberman. 2012. "Out with the Crowd: Modern American Poets Speaking to Mass Culture." In Nelson, *Oxford Handbook*, 248–67.

Norris, Margot. 1985. *Beasts of the Modern Imagination: Darwin, Nietzsche, Kafka, Ernst, and Lawrence*. Baltimore: Johns Hopkins University Press.

Nowak, Mark. 2009. *Coal Mountain Elementary*. Minneapolis: Coffee House Press.

O'Brien, Geoffrey. 1988. *Dream Time: Chapters from the Sixties*. New York: Viking.

Olson, Charles. 1967. *Human Universe and Other Essays*. New York: Grove Press.

————. 1974. *Additional Prose: A Bibliography on America, Proprioception and Other Notes and Essays*. Edited by George F. Butterick. Bolinas, CA.: Four Seasons Foundation.

————. 1983. *The Maximus Poems*. Berkeley: University of California Press.

Orr, David. 2011. *Beautiful and Pointless (A Guide to Modern Poetry)*. New York: HarperCollins.

Ossman, David. 1963. *The Sullen Art: Interviews with Modern American Poets*. New York: Corinth Books.

Ozenfant, Amédée. 1916. "Psychotypie & Typométrique." *Le Elan* 9 (February 12): 2.

Palmer, Michael. 1988. *Sun*. San Francisco: North Point.

Parini, Jay, ed. 1995. *The Columbia Anthology of American Poetry*. New York: Columbia University Press.

Paz, Octavio. 1973. *The Bow and the Lyre*. Translated by Ruth L. C. Simms. Austin: University of Texas Press.

Pearce, Roy Harvey. 1961. *The Continuity of American Poetry*. Princeton: Princeton University Press.

Perelman, Bob. 1987. "*Ketjak* by Ron Silliman." *San Francisco Review of Books* 4, no. 4 (October): 22–23.

Perkins, David. 1976. *A History of Modern Poetry: From the 1890s to the High Modernist Mode*. Cambridge, MA: Harvard University Press.

————. 1989. *A History of Modern Poetry: Modernism and After*. Cambridge, MA: Harvard University Press.

————. 1992. *Is Literary History Possible?* Baltimore: Johns Hopkins University Press.

Piccione, Anthony. 1992. "Bly: Man, Voice and Poem." In Davis, *Critical Essays on Robert Bly*, 53–56.

Poirier, Richard. 1992. *Poetry and Pragmatism*. Cambridge, MA: Harvard University Press.

Pound, Ezra. 1925. *XVI Cantos*. Paris: Three Mountains Press.

————. 1935. *Make It New*: Essays. New Haven, Yale University Press.

————. 1938. *Guide to Kulchur*. New York: New Directions.

———. 1947. *The Unwobbling Pivot*. New York: New Directions.

———. 1948. *Pisan Cantos*. New York: New Directions.

———. 1972. *The Cantos*. New York: New Directions.

Power, Kevin. 1975a. "Conversation with Jerome Rothenberg." *Vort* 3 (1): 140–53.

———. 1975b. "An Image Is an Image Is an Image." *Vort* 3 (1): 153–63.

Proust, Marcel. 2003. *In Search of Lost Time*. Vol. 2, *Within a Budding Grove*, translated by C. K. Scott Moncrieff and Terence Kilmarton. Revised by D. J. Enright. New York: Modern Library.

Putnam, H. Phelps. 1927. *Trinc*. New York: Doran.

Pynchon, Thomas. 1973. *Gravity's Rainbow*. New York: Viking.

Quasha, George, and Jerome Rothenberg, eds. 1973. *America, A Prophecy: A New Reading of American Poetry from Pre-Columbian Times to the Present*. New York: Vintage.

———, and Charles Stein. 1974. "Ta'wil or How to Read: A Five-Way Interactive View of Robert Kelly." *Vort* 2 (2): 108–34.

Rainey, Lawrence, ed. 2005. *Modernism: An Anthology*. Oxford: Blackwell.

Rankine, Claudia, and Lisa Sewell, eds. 2007. *American Poets in the 21st Century: The New Poetics*. Middletown, CT: Wesleyan University Press

Ransom, John Crowe. 2001. "Waste Lands." In T. S. Eliot, *The Waste Land*, edited by Michael North, 167–70. New York: W. W. Norton.

Rasula, Jed. 1977. "Spicer's Orpheus and the Emancipation of Pronouns." *Boundary 2* 6, no. 1: 51–102.

———. 1996. *The American Poetry Wax Museum: Reality Effects, 1940–1990*. Urbana, IL: National Council of Teachers of English.

———. 1997. "*Finnegans Wake* and the Character of the Letter." *James Joyce Quarterly* 34, no. 4 (Summer): 517–30.

———. 2002. *This Compost: Ecological Imperatives in American Poetry*. Athens: University of Georgia Press.

———. 2004. *Syncopations: The Stress of Innovation in Contemporary American Poetry*. Tuscaloosa: University of Alabama Press.

———. 2009. *Modernism and Poetic Inspiration: The Shadow Mouth*. New York: Palgrave Macmillan.

———. 2013. "Heeding the Heedless Sublime." *OmniVerse* 33: unpaginated online journal.

———. 2015. *Destruction Was My Beatrice: Dada and the Unmaking of the Twentieth Century*. New York: Basic Books.

———. 2016. *History of a Shiver: The Sublime Impudence of Modernism*. New York: Oxford University Press.

———. 2018. *Avant-Garde Pieties: Aesthetics, Race, and the Renewal of Innovative Poetics*. New York: Routledge.

———. 2020. *Acrobatic Modernism from the Avant-Garde to Prehistory*. Oxford: Oxford University Press.

———. 2021. *Genre and Extravagance in the Novel: Lower Frequencies*. Oxford: Oxford University Press, 2021.

Rasula, Jed, and Steve McCaffery, eds. 1998. *Imagining Language: An Anthology*. Cambridge, MA: MIT Press.

Rasula, Jed, and Tim Conley, eds. 2012. *Burning City: Poems of Metropolitan Modernity*. Notre Dame: Action Books.

Reilly, Evelyn. 2009. *Styrofoam*. New York: Roof Books.

Reverdy, Pierre. 1918. "L'Image." *Nord-Sud* 13 (March): 3–5.

Reznikoff, Charles. 1927. *Five Groups of Verse*. New York: Charles Reznikoff.

———. 1965. *Testimony, The United States 1885–1890: Recitative*. New York: New Directions.

———. 1976. *Complete Poems of Charles Reznikoff*. Vol. 1, *Poems 1918–1936*, edited by Seamus Cooney. Santa Barbara: Black Sparrow Press.

Rich, Adrienne. 2001. *Arts of the Possible: Essays and Conversations*. New York: Norton.

Richardson, Mark, ed. 2015. *The Cambridge Companion to American Poets*. New York: Cambridge University Press.

Robertson, Lisa. 2002. "How Pastoral: A Manifesto." In *Telling It Slant: Avant-Garde Poetics of the 1990s*, edited by Mark Wallace and Steven Marks, 21–26. Tuscaloosa: University of Alabama Press.

Robinson, Edwin Arlington. 1921. *Avon's Harvest*. New York: MacMillan.

———. 1937. *Collected Poems*. New York: Macmillan.

Rodman, Selden, ed. 1938. *A New Anthology of Modern Poetry*. New York: Random House.

Rosten, Selden. 1946. *The Big Road*. New York: Rinehart.

Rothenberg, Jerome. 1960. *White Sun Black Sun*. New York: Hawk's Well Press.

———. 1961. "Why *Deep* Image." *Trobar*, no. 3, 31–32.

———. 1962. "Deep Image: Footnote." *Nomad* 10–11 (1962), 52–53.

———. 1965. [Letter to the Editor]. *Eleventh Finger*, no. 2, 27–28.

———. 1989. *Khurbn and Other Poems*. New York: New Directions.

Rothenberg, Jerome, and Robert Creeley. 1962. "An Exchange: Deep Image and Mode." *Kulchur* 2 (6): 25–42.

Rubin, Joan Shelley. 2000. "Modernism in Practice: Public Readings of the New Poetry." In *A Modern Mosaic: Art and Modernism in the United States*, edited by Townsend Ludington, 127–52. Chapel Hill: University of North Carolina Press.

———. 2007. *Songs of Ourselves: The Uses of Poetry in America*. Cambridge, MA: Belknap.

Rukeyser, Muriel. 1938. *U. S. 1*. New York: Covici, Friede.

———. 2018. *The Book of the Dead*. Morgantown: West Virginia University Press.

Said, Edward. 1976. "Roads Taken and Not Taken in Contemporary Criticism." *Contemporary Literature* 17, no. 3 (Summer): 327–48.

Sanders, Edward. 1976. *Investigative Poetry*. San Francisco: City Lights.

———. 1981. *The Z–D Generation*. Barrytown, NY: Station Hill Press.

———. 1997. *1968, A History in Verse*. Santa Rosa: Black Sparrow Press.

———. 2000. *America, A History in Verse*. Vol. 1, *1900–1939*. Santa Rosa: Black Sparrow Press.

Sarett, Lew. 1920. *Many Moons: A Book of Wilderness Poems.* New York: Henry Holt.

Sartre, Jean-Paul. "Why Write?" In Adams, *Critical Theory since Plato*, 984–92.

Schauffler, Robert Haven. 1927. *The Poetry Cure: A Medicine Chest of Verse, Music and Pictures.* New York: Dodd, Mead.

Schauffler, Robert Haven, ed. 1925. "The Poetry Cure: A Novel Remedy for Weary Hearts." *Good Housekeeping* 81 (October): 37ff.

Schlegel, Friedrich. *Lucinde and the Fragments.* 1971. Translated by Peter Firchow. Minneapolis: University of Minnesota Press.

Schwitters, Kurt. "Dadaism in Holland." Translated by Michael Kane. In Ades, *The Dada Reader*, 289–96.

Shipley, Joseph T. 1984. *The Origins of English Words: A Discursive Dictionary of Indo-European Roots.* Baltimore: Johns Hopkins University Press.

Shklovsky, Victor. 1965. "Art as Technique." In *Russian Formalist Criticism: Four Essays.* Translated by Lee T. Lemon and Marion J. Reis, 3–24. Lincoln: University of Nebraska Press.

Shostac, Percy. 1930. *14th Street.* New York: Simon and Schuster.

Silliman, Ron. 1978. *Ketjak.* San Francisco: This.

——. 2008. *The Alphabet.* Tuscaloosa: University of Alabama Press.

Siskin, Clifford. 1988. *The Historicity of Romantic Discourse.* New York: Oxford University Press.

Sloterdijk, Peter. 2013. *You Must Change Your Life: On Anthropotechnics.* Translated by Wieland Hoban. Malden, MA: Polity Press.

Smith, Chard Powers. 1936. *Prelude to Man.* New York: Peter Pauper Press.

Sollers, Philippe. 1983. *Writing and the Experience of Limits.* Edited by David Hayman. Translated by Philip Barnard with David Hayman. New York: Columbia University Press.

Soupault, Philippe. 2006. "Literature and the Rest." In Ades, *The Dada Reader*, 185–86.

Spicer, Jack. 1957. *After Lorca.* San Francisco: White Rabbit.

——. 1975. *The Collected Books of Jack Spicer.* Edited by Robin Blaser. Los Angeles: Black Sparrow Press.

Stauffer, Donald. 1974. *A Short History of American Poetry.* New York: Dutton.

Stein, Gertrude. 1970. *What Are Masterpieces?* New York: Pitman, 1970.

Stein, Maurice, and Larry Miller. (1970) 2016. *Blueprint for Counter Education: Curriculum, Handbook, Wall Decoration, Shooting Script.* New York: Inventory Press.

Stepanchev, Stephen. 1965. *American Poetry since 1945, a Critical Survey.* New York: Harper and Row.

Stevens, Thomas Wood. 1938. *Westward under Vega: A Novel in Verse.* New York: Covici-Friede.

Stevens, Wallace. 1955. *Collected Poems.* London: Faber and Faber.

——. 1990. *The Palm at the End of the Mind: Selected Poems and a Play.* Edited by Holly Stevens. New York: Vintage.

Stratton-Porter, Gene. "Let Us Go Back to Poetry." *Good Housekeeping* 80 (April 1925): 35, 194–96, 199–200.

Surani, Moez. 2016. عمليّة *Operación Opération Operation* 行动 *Операция*. Toronto: Book Thug.

Swensen, Cole. 2011. *Noise That Stays Noise: Essays*. Ann Arbor: University of Michigan Press.

———. 2012. *Gravesend*. Berkeley: University of California Press, 2012.

Swensen, Cole, and David St. John, eds. 2009. "Introduction." In *American Hybrid*. New York: Norton.

Taggard, Genevieve. 1936. *Calling Western Union*. New York: Harper.

Tate, Allen. 1983. *The Poetry Reviews of Allen Tate 1924–1944*. Edited by Ashley Brown. Baton Rouge: Louisiana State University Press.

Thompson, Dunstan. 2015. *Here at Last Is Love: Selected Poems*. Edited by Gregory Wolfe. Salem, OR: Slant.

Thompson, Michael. 1979. *Rubbish Theory: The Creation and Destruction of Value*. New York: Oxford University Press.

Thoreau, Henry David. 1992. *Walden and Resistance to Civil Government*, 2nd ed. Edited by William Rossi. New York: Norton.

Thorpe, John. 1972. *The Cargo Cult*. Bolinas, CA: Big Sky.

Tzara, Tristan. 1951a. "Dada Manifesto 1918." Translated by Ralph Manheim. In Motherwell, *Dada Painters and Poets*, 76–82.

———. 1951b. "Manifesto on Feeble Love and Bitter Love." Translated by Ralph Manheim. In Motherwell, *Dada Painters and Poets*, 86–98.

Untermeyer, Louis. 1919. *The New Era in American Poetry*. New York: Henry Holt, 1919.

———. 1923. *American Poetry since 1900*. New York: Henry Holt.

———. 1939. *From Another World: The Autobiography of Louis Untermeyer*. New York: Harcourt, Brace.

Untermeyer, Louis, ed. 1919. *Modern American Poetry*. New York: Harcourt, Brace.

———. 1921. *Modern American Poetry*. New York: Harcourt, Brace.

———. 1930. *Modern American Poetry: A Critical Anthology*. New York: Harcourt, Brace.

———. 1950. *Modern American Poetry: Mid-Century*. New York: Harcourt, Brace.

Van Buskirk, Eliot. 2008. Interviewed by Terry Gross. *Fresh Air*, National Public Radio, March 13.

Van Doren, Mark. 1928. "This Decade." *English Journal* 17, no. 2 (February): 101–8.

Waggoner, Hyatt H. 1968. *American Poets, from the Puritans to the Present*. Boston: Houghton Mifflin.

———. 1984. *American Poets, from the Puritans to the Present*. Rev. ed. Baton Rouge: Louisiana State University Press.

Waldman, Anne. 2011. *The Iovis Trilogy: Colors in the Mechanism of Concealment*. Minneapolis: Coffee House Press.

Walker, Margaret. 1940. "Proving the Rule." *Poetry* 56, no. 5 (August): 281–82.

Wellburn, Ronald G. 1983. "American Jazz Criticism, 1914–1940." PhD diss., New York University.

Wells, Henry W. 1942. "Complexity under Simplicity." *Sewanee Review* 50, no. 3 (July–September): 430–32.

———. 1943. *The American Way of Poetry*. New York: Columbia University Press.

Westerfield, Hargis. 1949. *Words of Steel*. New York: Dutton.

Whitman, Walt. 1933. *Leaves of Grass, Selected and Illustrated by Charles Cullen*. New York: Thomas Y. Crowell.

———. 1982. *Complete Poetry and Collected Prose*. New York: Library of America.

Williams, William Carlos. 1934. *Collected Poems 1921–1931*. New York: Objectivist Press.

———. 1938. *The Complete Collected Poems of William Carlos Williams 1906–1938*. Norfolk, CT: New Directions.

———. 1944. *The Wedge*. Cummington, MA: Cummington Press.

———. 1976. *Interviews with William Carlos Williams: "Speaking Straight Ahead."* Edited by Linda Welshimer Wagner. New York: New Directions, 1976.

———. 1992. *Paterson*. Edited by Christopher MacGowan. New York: New Directions.

———. 2011. *Spring and All*. New York: New Directions.

Wilson, Edmund. 1931. *Axel's Castle: A Study in the Imaginative Literature of 1870–1930*. New York: Scribner's.

Winner, Thomas G. 2015. *The Czech Avant-Garde Literary Movement between the World Wars*. Edited by Ondřej Sládek and Michael Heim. New York: Peter Lang.

Wittgenstein, Ludwig. 2001. *Philosophical Investigations*. 3rd ed. Translated by G. E. M. Anscombe. Oxford: Blackwell.

Wolfert, Helen. 1946. *Nothing Is a Wonderful Thing: A Story Poem*. New York: Simon and Schuster.

Wright, C. D. 2007. *One Big Self: An Investigation*. Port Townsend, WA: Copper Canyon Press.

———. 2010. *One with Others*. Port Townsend, WA: Copper Canyon Press.

Wright, James. 1963. *The Branch Will Not Break*. Middletown, CT.: Wesleyan University Press.

Wylie, Elinor. 1923. "Jewelled Bindings." *New Republic* 37 (December): 14.

Yeats, William Butler. 1962. *Explorations*. New York: Macmillan.

Yeats, William Butler, ed. 1936. *The Oxford Book of Modern Verse, 1892–1935*. Oxford: Oxford University Press.

Young, Kevin. 2007. "Poetics Statement." In Rankine and Sewell, *American Poets in the 21st Century*, 190–92.

Zaturenska, Marya. 2002. *The Diaries of Marya Zaturenska 1938–1944*. Edited by Mary Beth Hinton. Syracuse, NY: Syracuse University Press.

Zola, Émile. 1998. "Dedication to Cézanne" and "The Moment in Art." Translated by Kate Tunstall. In *Art in Theory 1815–1900: An Anthology of Changing Ideas*, edited by Charles Harrison and Paul Wood with Jason Gaiger, 550–65. Oxford: Blackwell.

Zukofsky, Louis. 1973. *"A" 22–23*. New York: Grossman.

———. 1978. *"A."* Berkeley: University of California Press.

Index

Page numbers in italics refer to figures